HENRY OSSAWA TANNER

THIS EXHIBITION AND
CATALOGUE WERE MADE POSSIBLE
BY FORD MOTOR COMPANY.

ADDITIONAL SUPPORT WAS PROVIDED
BY THE PEW CHARITABLE TRUSTS AND THE
NATIONAL ENDOWMENT FOR THE ARTS. FUNDING
FOR INITIAL RESEARCH WAS ALSO PROVIDED BY THE
SAMUEL S. FELS FUND AND THE COMMONWEALTH
OF PENNSYLVANIA COUNCIL ON THE ARTS.

HENRY OSSAWA TANNER

INTRODUCTORY ESSAY
AND CATALOGUE CHAPTERS BY

DEWEY F. MOSBY

CATALOGUE ENTRIES BY

DEWEY F. MOSBY AND DARREL SEWELL

BIOGRAPHICAL ESSAY BY

RAE ALEXANDER-MINTER

PHILADELPHIA MUSEUM OF ART

RIZZOLI
NEW YORK

SPONSOR'S STATEMENT

Ford Motor Company is proud of its partnership with four great American museums in the Henry Ossawa Tanner exhibition. Corporate resources, both human and financial, have helped make possible a wide array of related educational and community programs, in addition to the exhibition itself.

We believe that the arts and humanities form a record of human life that should be accessible to all. Ford and its dealers are pleased to assist in bringing the spirit and artistry of Henry Ossawa Tanner to people across the United States.

HAROLD A. POLING

CHAIRMAN AND CHIEF EXECUTIVE OFFICER
FORD MOTOR COMPANY

LENDERS TO THE EXHIBITION

ESTATE OF SADIE T. M. ALEXANDER

DR. RAE ALEXANDER-MINTER, NEW YORK

ALLENTOWN ART MUSEUM, PENNSYLVANIA

AMERICAN RED CROSS, WASHINGTON, D.C.

ARCHIVES OF AMERICAN ART,
SMITHSONIAN INSTITUTION, WASHINGTON, D.C.

THE ART INSTITUTE OF CHICAGO

BEREA COLLEGE ART DEPARTMENT, KENTUCKY

CARL VAN VECHTEN GALLERY OF FINE ARTS,
FISK UNIVERSITY, NASHVILLE

THE CARNEGIE MUSEUM OF ART, PITTSBURGH

CEDAR RAPIDS ART GALLERY, IOWA

CLARK ATLANTA UNIVERSITY, ATLANTA

WILLIAM H. AND CAMILLE O. COSBY

DALLAS MUSEUM OF ART

DES MOINES ART CENTER

THE DETROIT INSTITUTE OF ARTS

WILLIAM RANDOLF DORSEY,
SILVER SPRING, MARYLAND

RICHARD C. EDGEWORTH, CHICAGO

WALTER O. EVANS, M.D., DETROIT

PETER MICHAEL FRANK, ALEXANDRIA, VIRGINIA

THE FREE LIBRARY OF PHILADELPHIA

GREATER LAFAYETTE MUSEUM OF ART,
INDIANA

HAMPTON UNIVERSITY MUSEUM, VIRGINIA

HERBERT F. JOHNSON MUSEUM OF ART,
CORNELL UNIVERSITY, ITHACA, NEW YORK

HIGH MUSEUM OF ART, ATLANTA

HOWARD UNIVERSITY GALLERY OF ART,
WASHINGTON, D.C.

JANE VOORHEES ZIMMERLI ART MUSEUM, RUTGERS,
THE STATE UNIVERSITY OF NEW JERSEY,
NEW BRUNSWICK

BENJAMIN T. JOHNSON, JR., BERKELEY,
CALIFORNIA

JOHN QUINCY JOHNSON, SHARON, MASSACHUSETTS

LASALLE UNIVERSITY ART MUSEUM, PHILADELPHIA

LOS ANGELES COUNTY MUSEUM OF ART

THE MENIL COLLECTION, HOUSTON

THE METROPOLITAN MUSEUM OF ART, NEW YORK

MILWAUKEE ART MUSEUM

THE MORRIS MUSEUM OF ART, AUGUSTA, GEORGIA

MUSÉE D'ORSAY, PARIS

MUSKEGON MUSEUM OF ART, MICHIGAN

MUSEUM OF ART, RHODE ISLAND
SCHOOL OF DESIGN, PROVIDENCE

NATIONAL ACADEMY OF DESIGN, NEW YORK

NATIONAL GALLERY OF ART, WASHINGTON, D.C.

NATIONAL MUSEUM OF AMERICAN ART,
SMITHSONIAN INSTITUTION, WASHINGTON, D.C.

THE NEWARK MUSEUM, NEW JERSEY

NEW ORLEANS MUSEUM OF ART

PENNSYLVANIA ACADEMY OF
THE FINE ARTS, PHILADELPHIA

ARTHUR PHELAN, CHEVY CHASE, MARYLAND

PHILADELPHIA MUSEUM OF ART

GRACE SCULL SAWYER, PHILADELPHIA

N. N. SERPER, NEW YORK

MERTON SIMPSON, NEW YORK

SCHOMBURG CENTER FOR RESEARCH IN
BLACK CULTURE, THE NEW YORK PUBLIC LIBRARY

SHELDON ROSS GALLERY, BIRMINGHAM, MICHIGAN

SPELMAN COLLEGE, ATLANTA

STATE HISTORICAL SOCIETY OF IOWA,
MUSEUM BUREAU, DES MOINES

JACQUES TANNER, LE DOUHET, FRANCE

TERRA MUSEUM OF AMERICAN ART, CHICAGO

VASSAR COLLEGE ART GALLERY,
POUGHKEEPSIE, NEW YORK

WADSWORTH ATHENEUM, HARTFORD

MR. AND MRS. E. T. WILLIAMS, JR., NEW YORK

SIX ANONYMOUS LENDERS

EXHIBITION ITINERARY

PHILADELPHIA MUSEUM OF ART
JANUARY 20–APRIL 14, 1991

DETROIT INSTITUTE OF ARTS
MAY 12–AUGUST 4, 1991

HIGH MUSEUM OF ART, ATLANTA
SEPTEMBER 17–NOVEMBER 24, 1991

THE FINE ARTS MUSEUMS OF SAN FRANCISCO,
M. H. DE YOUNG MEMORIAL MUSEUM
DECEMBER 14, 1991–MARCH 1, 1992

CONTENTS

FOREWORD

A century has passed since the chilly day in January of 1891 when Henry Ossawa Tanner, a young African-American artist from Philadelphia, arrived in Paris to pursue his dream of becoming a successful painter. This exhibition and catalogue celebrate his career, from the compelling naturalism of his early efforts as a student at the Pennsylvania Academy of the Fine Arts and the Académie Julian to the almost visionary religious paintings of his last years. The exhibition is the product of the enthusiasm and research of three scholars—Dr. Dewey F. Mosby, Director of the Picker Art Gallery at Colgate University, Dr. Rae Alexander-Minter, Director of Public Programs at the New-York Historical Society and Tanner's grandniece, and Darrel Sewell, the Robert L. McNeil, Jr., Curator of American Art at the Philadelphia Museum of Art—and it has benefited from their diverse and lively points of view and from their collective aim of presenting the art and life of Henry Tanner with clarity and freshness.

Tanner's life spanned some of the most turbulent decades of modern times. Born two years before the outbreak of the Civil War, he lived through the devastating years of the First World War and the Great Depression. The visual arts underwent upheavals almost as radical, as modernist movements emerged within powerful, conservative traditions, first in Europe and later in America. Just as Tanner found his own individual mode within a welter of stylistic alternatives, so he confronted the profound injustice of prejudice against his race with dignity and self-esteem, determined that it would not stand in his way as a painter.

Thanks to the great generosity of the lenders to the exhibition, it is possible to present the full sweep of Tanner's achievement and to show and publish here a number of works for the first time. The assistance of so many members of the artist's family, who have preserved many of his lesser known paintings, studies, and sketches, has been invaluable. Heartfelt thanks are also due to the National Museum of American Art, Smithsonian Institution, and to Hampton University, each of which possesses an extensive and highly important group of Tanner's work, for their collaboration and their generosity with both works of art and information. Dr. Elizabeth Broun, Director of the NMAA, Dr. William R. Harvey, President of Hampton University, and Jeanne Zeidler, Director of the Hampton University Museum have our warmest gratitude.

It has been a pleasure to work with colleagues at the Detroit Institute of Arts, the High Museum of Art, Atlanta, and the Fine Arts Museums of San Francisco to ensure that the exhibition reaches a wide audience across the United States. Samuel H. Sachs, Gudmund Vigtel, Harry S. Parker, directors of the respective museums, and their staffs have been most sympathetic partners.

Elsewhere in this catalogue, the three authors express their thanks, here most warmly seconded, to a multitude of individuals and institutions for advice, assistance, and access to information on Tanner, without which this project would not have been possible.

This handsome book was skillfully produced under a tight schedule by Marquand Books of Seattle, Washington, and we are especially grateful to Scott Hudson for his ingenious design and to Suzanne Kotz for her patient, thoughtful, and professional editing.

At the Philadelphia Museum of Art, the public presentation of the exhibition, together with its attendant programs, was the combined effort of a large number of dedicated staff. Darrel Sewell, whose idea it was over six years ago to take a new look at Tanner's achievement, has brought intelligence and flair to its realization. Suzanne F. Wells, Coordinator of Special Exhibitions, and Sandra Horrocks, Manager of Public Relations, have each coped with myriad details of arrangements for the exhibition in Philadelphia and on its tour. Danielle Rice, Curator of Education, and Marla Shoemaker, Associate Curator, have worked with the staff of the Division of Education to convey a wealth of information through diverse mediums, both in the museum and in the classroom. Cheryl McClenney-Brooker, Vice-President for External Affairs, played a crucial role in coordinating the activities of a large and distinguished Tanner Committee co-chaired by Dr. Constance E. Clayton, Hiliary H. Holloway, Esq., and Dr. Bernard C. Watson, under whose able and energetic leadership the staff received invaluable guidance concerning the widest public exposure and community support for the exhibition.

In its enthusiastic and most generous sponsorship of this exhibition from its earliest stages, Ford Motor Company has again demonstrated its remarkable commitment to significant cultural projects that strive to broaden and deepen our understanding of the art of the past, bringing fresh insight to bear on an artist and his context while exposing his work to a new audience. We are deeply grateful to Ford and its Chairman and Chief Executive Officer Harold A. Poling, and to James E. N. Huntley, Program Officer, Ford Motor Company Fund; Mabel H. Brandon, Director, Corporate Programs; and Helen Love, Manager, Urban Programs for their thoughtful assistance. The National Endowment for the Arts and the Pew Charitable Trusts have also made substantial grants to this project, which is the result of a public/private partnership as important for its collective spirit as for its financial support.

ANNE D'HARNONCOURT

THE GEORGE D. WIDENER DIRECTOR
PHILADELPHIA MUSEUM OF ART

Henry Ossawa Tanner, c. 1935.

REFLECTIONS ON RACE,

PUBLIC RECEPTION, AND CRITICAL

RESPONSE IN TANNER'S CAREER

Henry Ossawa Tanner (1859–1937) emerged as one of the best known and most highly esteemed artists of his time in both the United States and France. One contemporary critic stated in 1911: "He makes his home continuously in Paris, where many claim that he is the greatest artist that America has produced."[1] Tanner was the first black artist to acquire an international reputation in this century,[2] and he remains well known today in museum and academic circles, although his name is not familiar to a more general audience. It is the aim of this exhibition and catalogue to present his life's work in a fuller context; this essay seeks to give a historical overview of certain paradoxes that arise in any assessment of Tanner. For example, as an artist he has been discussed concurrently by French critics as a history painter and by their American counterparts as a religious painter, while other writers disregarded his subjects altogether in order to concentrate on his style or technique.[3] These diverse responses have their roots in the evolution of his work; Tanner pursued traditional modes with an often striking individualism.

Primary among the questions to be addressed at the outset is Tanner's race and his attitude toward it in relation to his career, because this issue is at the core of much of what has been said about him. His parents gave him the middle name Ossawa in tribute to the abolitionist John Brown of Osawatomie, and Tanner was fortified with a solid grounding in racial issues from his father, Benjamin Tucker Tanner, who tackled the subject as early as 1869 in the small book with the startling title *The Negro's Origins and Is the Negro Cursed*. The Reverend Tanner wrote: "No people now exists who can trace more clearly their paternity than the Negro. The genealogical table of the Negro, written in his own flesh, remains. Ages of scouring have not sufficed to erase it. Written by the finger of God, it is more enduring than the stones of Sinai. It remains, and will remain the badge of our suffering, the triumph."[4] Benjamin Tanner's lifelong and forthright pursuit of social justice and his defiance of prejudice must have been powerfully stimulating for his children.

An excellent introduction to the link between Tanner's development as an artist and his race, and the plight of many creative black people in general, is articulated by a biographer of the talented poet Paul Laurence Dunbar (1872–1906): "The black writer must not merely live in two worlds; he inevitably writes for two worlds. Whatever he writes is affected by what Ralph Ellison has called 'the complex relationship between the Negro-American subculture and North American culture as a whole.' "[5] Tanner can be said to have painted for three worlds—for Paris, for America, and for African-Americans—and surely he was conscious of the responses of each.

Tanner was celebrated as an artist by African-American intellectuals from the outset of his career. After only a short period as a professional painter, he was included, together with artist Edward Mitchell Bannister (1828–1901), in William J. Simmons's biographical study of black leaders entitled *Men of Mark: Eminent, Progressive and Rising*, published in 1887.[6] By 1898 Tanner's name was linked with Dunbar's and with the great educator Booker T. Washington (1856–1915) in a letter to Washington from an admirer: "God has undoubtedly exalted you to be our Moses. We read about you in the greatest papers and magazines published in our great country—Washington, Tanner, and Dunbar. We stand before them with uncovered heads. We follow them without questioning their right to lead."[7]

Washington himself knew the Tanner family and was deeply impressed by Henry's achievement as an artist. In *Up from Slavery* he wrote about seeing Tanner's work on view at the Musée du Luxembourg in Paris: "Few people ever stopped, I found, when looking at his pictures, to inquire whether Mr. Tanner was a Negro painter, a French painter, a German painter. They simply knew that he was able to produce something which the world wanted—a great painting—and the matter of his color did not enter into their minds."[8] W. E. B. Du Bois (1868–1963), the distinguished black scholar who demanded full and immediate equality for African-Americans, in contrast to Washington's emphasis on first achieving economic parity, also knew Tanner and cited him in a 1901 article in the *Dial* as one of a vital group of black leaders who "seek . . . that self development and self realization in all lines of human endeavor which they believe will eventually place the Negro beside the other races."[9]

In 1908, an essay by an anonymous American writer drew together a number of themes, exemplifying the complex problem of discussing Tanner as both an American artist and a black artist:

> For several years part of the art world of Paris has shown a steadily increasing interest in the work of Henry O. Tanner, a young American painter who has done much towards strengthening that higher position in contemporary art which was won for us by [John Singer] Sargent and [James A. M.] Whistler. In America, public recognition of Tanner's greatness has been somewhat retarded by the fact that he is a Negro and our publications have persistently spoken of him as the greatest Negro painter. It has pleased them to slight his art in the exploration of his race.[10]

The writer's own rather confused, if well-meaning tone—characteristic of its date—is illustrated by a further passage:

> Booker T. Washington wrote of him: "Tanner is proud of his race. He feels deeply that as the representative of his people he is on trial to establish their right to be taken seriously in the world of art." But this classification of Tanner's work, while literally true, gives an erroneous impression. Although his paintings exhibit that full-blooded sense of rhythm and color which give a peculiar charm to the art productions of his race, Tanner's work is above all racial distinctions. He should no longer be classified as

the foremost negro painter, but rather as one of the greatest artists whom America has produced.[11]

The notion of a "full-blooded sense of rhythm," in spite of the good intentions of this writer, can be interpreted as subtle racism.[12] Throughout his career, Tanner's art continued to be associated with his race, by black and white writers alike. The headline for a 1924 article in the *New York Times*, to cite one of many instances, read: "Tanner Exhibits Paintings: Negro Artist Shows Pictures at Grand Central Art Galleries."[13]

The complicated nature of Tanner's own thinking about race is partly conveyed in a long letter discovered by his biographer, Marcia M. Mathews. On May 25, 1914, Tanner wrote to a woman who planned to publish a long article on his work in *International Studio*:

> Your good note and very appreciative article to hand. I have read it and, except [being] more than I deserve, it is exceptionally good. What you say is what I am trying to do and in a smaller way am doing (I hope). The only thing I take exception to is the inference in your last paragraph — and while I know it is the dictum in the States, it is not any more true for that reason. You say "In his personal life, Mr. T. has had many things to contend with. Ill-health, poverty, and race prejudice, always strong against a Negro." Now am I a Negro. Does not the 3/4 of English blood in my veins, which when it flowed in "pure" Anglo-Saxon men and which has done in the past effective and distinguished work in the U.S. — does this not count for anything? Does the 1/4 or 1/8 of "pure" Negro blood in my veins count for all? I believe it, the Negro blood counts and counts to my advantage — though it has caused me at times a life of great humiliation and sorrow but that it is the source of all my talents (if I have any) I do not believe, any more than I believe it all comes from my English ancestors. I suppose according to the distorted way things are seen in the States my blond curly-headed little boy would be "Negro." — True, this condition has driven me out of the country, but still my best friends I have are "white" Americans and while I cannot sing our National Hymn, "Land of Liberty," etc., still deep down in my heart I love it and am sometimes sad that I cannot live where my heart is.[14]

This letter was written when Tanner was deeply absorbed in painting scenes of North Africa and its people, whom his father had characterized as descended from Ham, the biblical progenitor of the black race, and we can take Tanner's emphatic statement, "I believe it, the Negro blood counts and counts to my advantage," as clear confirmation of his pride in his own roots.

Even during difficult later years Tanner continued to contribute to the NAACP, which valued the support sent from Paris. The famous author James Weldon Johnson (1871–1938), then secretary of the Legal Defense Fund, wrote to Tanner on New Year's Eve, 1925: "It was especially gratifying to us to receive your contribution of twenty-five dollars to the Legal Defense Fund which we are establishing. I think that the published report of your contribution stimulated others to give."[15]

During the last decade of his life, when he was more than seventy years old, Tanner began to be characterized as aloof from other African-American artists living in Paris. This idea was expressed, probably for the first time, by the black printmaker Albert Smith (1896–1940), who wrote about Tanner in 1936 to the distinguished bibliophile Arthur Schomburg (1874–1938): "Personally I remember seeing him but once since I have been in France. I understand through the chatty American secretary of the organization that he has a farm somewhere down the line and that with the communion that the earth gives you he finds the solitude that gives birth to his paintings. I must say that the American White artists hold him in deep respect."[16]

This personal view of Tanner seems to have evolved into such notions as those expressed by Cedric Dover in 1960 in *American Negro Art*:

> American appreciation kept the "dean of American painters" comfortably aloof in Paris for forty-six years. He liked the role of an expatriate phenomenon in search of artistic truth; and coloured artists who sought his help were accordingly reminded that they could have it as artists, not as Negroes. So, above nationality and group loyalty, he spent the last twenty years of his life in increasing isolation and decline.[17]

The above contention is rendered off the mark by Tanner's unpublished letters among the Alexander papers at the University of Pennsylvania Archives, which show that the sense of racial identity and pride he had demonstrated over previous decades continued during his final years. He wrote to his niece, Sadie Tanner Mossell Alexander, on March 23, 1936:

> Yes, I met Marian Anderson not in Paris, but if I am not mistaken, in the person in your house. . . . However whether I have met her or not I am very glad she has a so beautiful voice and it is being recognized. However, "we are coming." Have you met Zora N. Hurston who has written a book that "they say" is fine — *Mules and Men* — I suppose you know of it — I am only judging by what I see in print and I very hope it is so.[18]

The artist himself provided an eloquent summation of the issue of race and his artistic career shortly before his death, when he wrote to his niece about an African-American he had encountered: "[He] has very probably never heard of me, as have not many hundreds and thousands of our people whom you might expect would know of my work, but it was not all for myself that I have tried in the measure of my ability to make a success of my life."[19]

In addition to the attention his work received from distinguished African-American writers, Tanner garnered ample recognition in the international art literature of his time from critics for such periodicals as *Revue de l'Art*, *Gazette des Beaux-Arts*, *International Studio*, *Fine Arts Journal*, and *Brush and Pencil* as well as in the pages of general magazines of wide circulation such as *Harper's Weekly*, *Ladies Home Journal*, and *Cosmopolitan*. Daily newspapers including the *Philadelphia Inquirer*, *Atlanta Constitution*, *Chicago Daily Tribune*, *Detroit Free Press*, *New York Times*, and *Boston Evening Transcript* gave Tanner his due, and his career was the focus of articles in the *Negro History Bulletin* and W. E. B. Du Bois's *Crisis*.

A brief sampling demonstrates the esteem in which Tanner was held by critics. A writer in 1899 reviewed the Pennsylvania Academy of the Fine Arts annual: "Mr. Tanner continues to paint biblical scenes. . . . These paintings are naive, and yet they have strong sentiment, and a deal of honest fervor which leaves no place in one's judgment of them for anything but respect. Compared with these two paintings, Mr. Henri's two appear trivial."[20] The following year in *Cosmopolitan*, Vance Thompson discussed Tanner in an article on American artists in Paris: "A strange personage, this young mulatto — the product of Philadelphia and the Latin Quarter and Bethlehem — who is destined I like to think, to give the world a new conception . . . of the Bible."[21]

Not all the reviews were favorable, and Tanner took his share of criticism for being (depending upon the critic) too advanced or too conservative. Arthur Hoeber decried his work shown in the Pennsylvania Academy of the Fine Arts annual of 1901:

> The exhibition contains, too, much of an experimental nature of the latest developments in the art way, the extremists increasingly finding favor with the jury. Most of these, it must be confessed, are interesting rather for describing modern tendencies than for serious accomplishments, while a number are so freakish and so mannered as to count for little . . . for example, Henry O. Tanner . . . [22]

Biographical accounts of Tanner began with Simmons's *Men of Mark*, and in 1909 the artist was invited to tell his own story in two issues of a periodical published by Doubleday, *World's Work*. By 1911, "Henry O. Tanner" appeared as an entry in the eleventh edition of the *Encyclopaedia Britannica*. Later, brief biographies appeared in J. W. Cromwell's 1914 *The Negro in American History*[23] and Rilla Evelyn Jackman's *American Arts of 1928*.[24] After Tanner's death in 1937, biographical sketches continued to appear in such important studies as *The Negro in Art* by Alain L. Locke in 1940[25] and James A. Porter's *Modern Negro Art* of 1943.[26]

Professor Locke's subsequent writing[27] on Tanner set the stage for future negative criticism of the artist.[28] Locke was disappointed because the artist did not use his international prestige to take the lead in the development of a specifically African-American school of art, which Locke hoped would be centered around genre scenes of people of color, in spite of the fact that Tanner's reputation was based on his treatment of biblical subjects. Milton M. James came to the artist's defense in an article of 1957 in the *Negro History Bulletin*:

> Much can be said in support of Dr. Locke's point of view, however, it is the firm opinion of the writer that it is not the provenance of critics to say what a painter should paint. Painters, like other artists, must say what they have to say in their own way and through the mediums and motifs of their choice. The work of a painter must not be prescribed, for if it is, it will not be art but simply a slavish allegiance to the whims of theorists.[29]

The first book-length scholarly study of Tanner appeared in 1960, an informative doctoral dissertation by Walter Augustus Simon.[30] His unpublished work places Tanner's life in the ethnographic and sociological context of his time, but discussion of Tanner's art is limited. In 1987, Naurice Frank Woods, Jr., also wrote a dissertation on the artist[31] which considered recent literature and a cache of new letters and other documents. The standard biography of the artist, *Henry Ossawa Tanner, American Artist*, published by Marcia M. Mathews in 1969, drew upon letters and other documentation among the Tanner papers, which entered the Archives of American Art, Smithsonian Institution, in 1968 and 1971; contemporary articles and reviews; and the reminiscences of the artist's son, Jesse Ossawa Tanner (1903–1985). Mathews's text remains a major source of information on Tanner's life.[32]

Tanner's career was heralded both in his native America and in his adopted France, yet paradoxically, in the United States he tended to be seen as an expatriate absorbed into French culture, and in France he was always "citoyen américain." As a result, Tanner and other artists working abroad have tended to fall between the cracks in several books that deal with the art of his period. For example, Barbara Novak's 1969 seminal study, *American Painting of the Nineteenth Century*,[33] did not include the Francophile Tanner, it being beyond the author's scope to "find the native qualities and their transformation under the veneer of European modes" of Tanner and many of his colleagues.[34] As recent scholarship focuses on the more conservative Salon tradition of many American artists around the turn of the century, Tanner is increasingly recognized as an important figure in such books as Lois Marie Fink's *American Art at the Nineteenth-Century Paris Salons*, published in 1990.[35]

The exhibition history of Tanner's work is closely related to his critical reception. The chronology in this volume reveals how widely his works were shown during his lifetime in cities ranging from San Francisco to St. Louis, Chicago to Philadelphia and New York, and Paris to Rome. After his death in 1937, there was a long hiatus until a memorial exhibition was held at the Philadelphia Art Alliance in 1945.[36] From this time until the late 1960s, euphemistically called an era of "racial unrest," Tanner and his art were largely forgotten by organizers of exhibitions. Then a flurry of shows devoted exclusively to Tanner appeared between 1967 and 1972. These projects ranged from a modest but interesting exhibition of 1969 held at Spelman College in Atlanta[37] to the regional show organized by the Hyde Collection of Glens Falls, New York, in 1972.[38] The major undertaking of this period was a nationally touring exhibition organized for 1969–70 by the Frederick Douglass Institute/ Museum of African Art in collaboration with the National Collection of Fine Arts.[39] Following this new surge of interest, Tanner was included in a number of scholarly and often revisionist exhibitions such as *Turn of the Century America*, organized by Patricia Hills for the Whitney Museum of American Art in 1977;[40] *Themes in American Painting*, curated by J. Gray Sweeney for the Grand Rapids Art Museum in 1977;[41] and *American Imagination and Symbolist Painting*, organized by Charles C. Eldridge in 1979 for New York University and the University of Kansas.[42] The black artist was also included in ethnocentric exhibitions such as *Three Nineteenth Century Afro-American Artists*, 1980,[43] and *Americans in Brittany and Normandy 1860–1910* in 1982.[44] Nor was Tanner ignored in France, as is evidenced by the show held at Blérancourt in 1984, *La peinture Américaine dans les Collections du Louvre*.[45] The most recent exhibition in the "centric" vein to include Tanner, *Sharing Traditions: Five Black Artists in Nineteenth-Century America*, was organized by Lynda Roscoe Hartigan and toured the country from 1985 to 1988.[46] Yet a number of recent large survey exhibitions of nineteenth-century American art omitted Tanner. He was not seen in the major United States showing at Boston of *A New World: Masterpieces of American Painting 1760–1910*,[47] although his *Annunciation* (cat. no. 45) was added to the exhibition at Paris. Even though Tanner was heralded in print in 1913 as "the poet-painter of Palestine,"[48] he did not fit the mold carved by the organizers of *The Orientalists*, shown at the National Gallery of Art and the Royal Academy of Art in 1984.[49] There is no clear evidence that Tanner was deliberately excluded from large exhibitions in the mid 1970s and 1980s, but some omissions are surprising. *The Quest for Unity*,[50] which surveyed the arts in America between the World's Fairs of 1876 and 1893, included neither Tanner nor Edward Mitchell Bannister. Tanner was just emerging as an artist during these years, but at the Centennial Exposition of 1876, Bannister's *Under the Oaks* won a first-place bronze medal and certificate of award, and was considered "the best that an American artist could do."[51]

Representation in museum collections is as important to an artist's reputation as inclusion in major exhibitions. Almost from the outset of his career, Tanner's works were sought by public institutions as well as collectors. The French government bought two paintings—*The Resurrection of Lazarus* (cat. no. 38) in 1897 and *The Disciples at Emmaus* (see fig. 71) in 1906—for the Musée du Luxembourg, the official French repository for masterpieces of contemporary art, selected by a highly competitive acquisition process.[52] The support of American museums from coast to coast was demonstrated by such early purchases as *The Annunciation* (cat. no. 45) by the Wilstach Collection for the Pennsylvania Museum and School of Art in 1899, *Nicodemus Visiting Jesus* (cat. no. 47) by the Pennsylvania Academy of the Fine Arts in 1900, *Christ at the Home of Mary and Martha* (cat. no. 58) by the Carnegie Institute in 1905, and *Two Disciples at the Tomb* (cat. no. 59) by the Art Institute of Chicago in 1906. Major African-American colleges and universities also collected works by Tanner during his lifetime, beginning with the Hampton Institute, which received two paintings, including *The Banjo Lesson* (cat. no. 27), as a gift from Robert C. Ogden in 1894, and concluding with Howard University, which acquired an important picture by public subscription in 1937, shortly before the artist's death.

The largest group of Tanner's work now in the public domain—fifty paintings, watercolors, drawings, and etchings—was acquired by the Frederick Douglass Institute/Museum of African Art, Washington, D.C., through the energetic efforts of the museum's founder and director, Warren N. Robbins. This collection was transferred to the National Museum of American Art, Smithsonian Institution, in 1983. Tanner's works are now on view in many museums, from Los Angeles to Paris, but more are ensconced in the storage racks and offices of others. The latter situation, coupled with the fact that many of the works reproduced and discussed in this catalogue have been lost to view for nearly eight decades, has impeded a thorough assessment of the artist's career.

Because of this state of affairs, Tanner is frequently recognized purely as a painter of religious themes based on the fame of such uncontested masterpieces as *The Resurrection of Lazarus* and *The Annunciation*. The recent wide distribution of a poster of *The Banjo Lesson* and the attention paid to *The Thankful Poor* (cat. no. 28), owing to its dramatic rediscovery and the celebrity of its subsequent owners, William H. and Camille O. Cosby, have created another, different image of the artist as a painter of African-American genre. Tanner's full range, including Oriental subjects based on life in North Africa and the Near East, has been more accurately indicated in recent exhibitions such as *Sharing Traditions*. Critics, art historians, and curators do well to avoid pigeonholing Tanner according to the stylistic "isms" used to describe art of the late nineteenth and early twentieth centuries. It will become apparent from this catalogue that, without becoming eclectic, the artist put to work several modes for his own creative goals.

Almost from the beginning, Tanner found an impressive number of private patrons and collectors who purchased his work and promoted his career. Museum collections were enriched by paintings presented as gifts by many of these benefactors. The earliest example is Robert C. Ogden's gift of the famous *Banjo Lesson* to the Hampton Institute in 1894. In 1922 the California collectors Mr. and Mrs. William Preston Harrison pledged Tanner's late version of *Daniel in the Lions' Den* (cat. no. 87) to the Los Angeles County Museum of Art. Atherton Curtis, the Francophile American print collector and author of several books on prints,[53] presented a version of *Sodom and Gomorrah* (see cat. no. 98) to the Metropolitan Museum of Art in New York in 1924. J. J. Haverty of Atlanta acquired several works from Tanner in the late 1920s, paving the way for important gifts to the High Museum of Art, Atlanta.

But this widespread patronage also had a paradoxical aspect. As early as 1899, Tanner's supporters were concerned that his paintings were not reaching the black community, an audience of great importance to him. Booker T. Washington wrote in the *Washington Colored American*:

> An earnest effort was made in Philadelphia and elsewhere sometime ago to get our people to contribute sufficient money to purchase *The Bagpipe Lesson*, an early work of the artist, but with little or no practical success. . . .This first work of Mr. Tanner's was finally, I believe, purchased by some Philadelphia white people. Few of the race are able individually to purchase Mr. Tanner's original paintings, but hundreds are able to secure the photographs of these productions. . . .This is the practical test in a large measure of our gratitude to and admiration for Mr. Tanner. . . . Will we help to do this or shall we leave it all to others to do?[54]

Some twenty-five years after Washington's plea, W. E. B. Du Bois returned to the same subject in the *Crisis*: "Once in Paris, years ago, Henry Tanner, the great artist, voiced a complaint—a little complaint, hesitatingly and diffidently expressed. 'Do you know, I never have been able to sell one of my pictures to a colored man.' "[55] Du Bois's response to Tanner's understated but moving remark is still relevant: "I mumbled vague apologies: We are poor ('We own 100,000 automobiles,' said my soul); We have not yet come to appreciate art ('We are the only American artists,' murmured my mind); We are not yet sufficiently familiar with your work ('Tanner is a perennial essay subject,' remarked my sinking heart): In fact it was our muddling carelessness. Who of us buys even books, much less pictures?"[56]

By 1924 several African-American institutions had commissioned work from Tanner, and Du Bois did have good news to report about private black patronage of his art:

> But the ice is broken. At the last New York exhibit of Tanner's marvelous canvasses [held at Grand Central Art Galleries in 1923] . . . John E. Nail of New York City paid a price that ran into four figures for two paintings worth a journey of a thousand miles to see. And another young colored man, Dr. Godfrey Nurse, bought a third; and we learn that two or three Negroes are actually considering similar purchases. These are sure signs of civilization.[57]

The mention of "prices paid" raises the question of what level of income the sale of pictures provided Tanner during his lifetime. In 1897 the French government paid him 1800 francs, or roughly $346, for *The Resurrection of Lazarus* while a work of comparable size, *Paysage d'Automne* by the French artist Eugène Tanguy (1830–99), fetched 600 francs the same year.[58] Rodman Wanamaker paid $1750 for *The Annunciation* in 1899, and the Pennsylvania Academy bought *Nicodemus Visiting Jesus* for $1500 in 1900. Between 1901 and 1902, the *Ladies Home Journal* commissioned four paintings to illustrate a series on the mothers of the Bible (cat. nos. 51–53). Customs declarations valued these works at 7500 francs each, and their frames at an additional 10 francs,[59] a total of just under $6000.[60] Several years later, in 1909,

Tanner set the price of his enormous picture *The Wise and Foolish Virgins* (see fig. 50) at $15,000 because it was "the result of three years work."[61] Dr. I. M. Cline of New Orleans paid $600 for *The Good Shepherd* (cat. no. 88) in 1918,[62] and during the economic boom of the middle 1920s, a version of the Nicodemus theme was commissioned by the Richard Humphreys Foundation through the Cheyney Training School for Teachers for the substantial sum of $3000.[63] Not suprisingly, in the years of the Great Depression, prices for Tanner's pictures plummeted. He wrote in 1935 to a cousin, Maudelle Bousfield, in Chicago:

> To buy a picture you come in a very good time. I have two small pictures, a *Hiding of Moses* and *The Flight into Egypt*, size about 24 × 28 inches, for which in ordinary times I would receive from $350 to $400 and which I believe are very good examples of my work. I would take two hundred. . . . I am making it especially easy not only on account of the times but because I should like some of my family to have some of my work. On account of the hard times all over the world even some of the most successful artists have temporarily reduced their prices. This is my case.[64]

The vast majority of Tanner's sales occurred in America, and his prices can be compared to those asked by his teacher Thomas Eakins. Early in 1897 the Pennsylvania Academy of the Fine Arts bought *The Cello Player* for Eakins's asking price of $500.[65] Tanner asked $1750 for *Nicodemus* and received $1500; he paid a commission of about 10 percent to his art dealers and others who aided his sales.[66] Eakins's biographer Lloyd Goodrich has pointed out that Eakins by 1914 was pricing his works anywhere from $2000 to $10,000,[67] but "none of these works shown at these increased prices found buyers," and Eakins returned to more modest rates ranging from $500 to $2500.[68] Tanner's prices were consistent with and even exceeded those paid to his erstwhile teacher. Nevertheless, he often complained about a lack of sales.[69]

Tanner appears to have made a decent living from his artistic production. During the first years at Paris in 1891 to 1893, he "kept a strict account of all money spent, and it amounted to $365, including tuition and every expense."[70] A decade later, his earnings allowed for the purchase of a long, one-story peasant house called Les Charmes at Trépied, near Etaples, in the Pas-de-Calais region of northwest France. Tanner spent summers there while maintaining an apartment in Paris and a studio at 51 boulevard Saint-Jacques near the Latin Quarter.[71] However, assistance from patrons and admirers, including Rodman Wanamaker, who subsidized two trips to the Near East, and Tanner's good friend Atherton Curtis, who helped with educational expenses for his son, Jesse, must have been most welcome. Tanner was also able to afford frequent travel during most of his life. In 1921 he sold Les Charmes and built a new house at Trépied,[72] but in the last decade of his life, the African-American artist found that his straitened circumstances were not so different from that of so many others during the Great Depression.

The attention paid to Henry Ossawa Tanner by the art world during his lifetime also included many awards. Beginning with an honorable mention in 1896 from the Paris Salon, he received some form of important official recognition every decade of his life. Among the awards of the first ten years of this century was the Art Institute of Chicago's Harris Prize for "the most impressive and distinguished work of art of the season,"[73] awarded to *Two Disciples at the Tomb* (cat. no. 59) in 1906. Even more important that year was the second-class medal awarded at the Paris Salon to *The Disciples at Emmaus*, the highest recognition Tanner could receive from the jury since the first-class gold medal was reserved for French artists. With the 1906 medal came the designation of *hors concours*, which allowed Tanner to enter future Salon exhibitions without submitting works to the jury. In 1915 the African-American artist was awarded a gold medal at the Panama-Pacific Exposition held at San Francisco. The crowning point of Tanner's career came in 1923 when the French government presented him with the prestigious Cross of the Legion of Honor.[74]

After Tanner's death in 1937, recognition ranged from the issuance of a commemorative stamp by the U.S. Postal Service in 1973 to the designation of a professorship in his name at Morgan State University in Baltimore.[75]

Considering Tanner's widespread fame at the turn of the century, the absence of any evidence indicating his involvement with other famous emigré artists is most curious. From 1934 Tanner lived at 43 rue de Fleurus, near Gertrude Stein's residence at no. 27, where an "improbable mixture of types and nationalities" gathered,[76] and artists such as Matisse and Picasso often dined. There is no intention to imply that racism pervaded the expatriate community in Paris, yet we cannot say with certainty that Tanner met any of these luminaries. His contact with French artists in the avant-garde circle of Paul Gauguin (1848–1903) is discussed below, but the existing literature does not connect him with such Franco-American artists as his nearly exact contemporary Elizabeth Nourse (1859–1938);[77] his fellow Philadelphian and student at the Académie Julian, Aston Knight (1873–1948);[78] nor the expatriate Philadelphian and well-known Impressionist, Mary Cassatt (1845–1926).

But there is no question that Tanner was esteemed by his fellow artists. Their appreciation of his talent started well before he received substantial public recognition in 1897. His teacher at the Académie Julian, Jean-Joseph Benjamin-Constant (1845–1902), inscribed a picture to Tanner: "To my pupil Tanner from his teacher and friend, ever confident of the success of his accomplishments."[79] Benjamin-Constant's belief in Tanner's future success was emphasized when the older artist sought him out in Philadelphia during a trip to America in 1894.[80] Thomas Eakins painted Tanner's portrait in 1902, surely a sign of the two artists' warm relationship. Their friendship must have begun in the 1880s during Tanner's student years at the Pennsylvania Academy of the Fine Arts.

Correspondence during the late 1890s from Harrison S. Morris, managing director of the Pennsylvania Academy of the Fine Arts, sheds light on the artist's reputation among colleagues in the United States. Morris wrote to Tanner on April 16, 1897: "The picture *Daniel* was very much admired while it was in our exhibition and, especially, commended by Mr. William M.[erritt] Chase who spoke of it in a public address to his students and privately praised it very often."[81] Morris himself declared the next year: "In offering my sincerest congratulations on your continued success I feel naturally proud in being your fellow countryman."[82] In the same letter the Academy director requested Tanner to annotate Paris Salon catalogues with his comments on the best American pictures. Then, during the early summer, he referred to the reception of Tanner's *Annunciation* at the Salon, writing that the painter Walter Gay (1856–1937) "tells me that not since Sargent's early triumphs has there been anything like it."[83] Gay was to maintain his high opinion for forty years, later remarking, "Tanner is a great painter."[84]

The sculptor Hermon MacNeil, a longtime friend who shared a studio with Tanner in the 1890s, touched on the high regard and affection in which fellow artists held Tanner. MacNeil wrote to him on December 9, 1930: "Just a little reminder that we are occasionally thinking of you. . . . Last evening at the Arts Club Roundtable dinner I was sitting beside Roy Brown chatting about your good self. . . . Various of your friends here often speak of you in a more choice way. I will not stop to make you blush at this time. I am simply sending you the most pleasant greetings that I am able to wish for a pleasant holiday."[85]

The esteem in which Tanner was held by his fellow artists was not limited to views expressed in the intimacy of letters. He was elected by his peers as an associate member of the National Academy of Design in New York in 1909 and as a full academician in 1927. Between these years, he was invited to serve on the Pennsylvania Academy of the Fine Arts jury for the selection of its annual exhibition.[86] By the summer of 1914, Tanner was elected by his colleagues as President of the Société Artistique de Picardie. The artist and critic Clara T. MacChesney delineated Tanner's status among his colleagues: "H. O. Tanner . . . has long been a member of the Trépied colony and is president of the Art Society of Picardy, Le Touquet. His delightful home is the centre of the colony, and the artist or student from Etaples, of Le Touquet, Paris-Plage, is always sure of a welcome."[87]

Tanner's "delightful" colony home was open to young African-American artists seeking advice and encouragement. Hale Woodruff (1900–80), a black artist from Cairo, Illinois, visited Trépied in 1928; Tanner engaged him in a discussion about art in general and viewed his portfolio.[88] Woodruff recalled: "It was a brisk day in the late winter, or early spring of 1928, when I took the train from Paris bound for that small town. . . . I was soon to discover that I was on my way to meet a remarkable man of profound intelligence and scholarship, and, as I was also to learn, a man of personal dignity and elegance."[89]

Sudden changes in the world economy and radical shifts in modern aesthetics would force Tanner into relative obscurity by the end of his life. But his art, and his generous and spiritual nature, remained a major source of inspiration for younger painters. The renowned African-American artist Romare Bearden (1914–88) found the quality of self-exploration apparent in Tanner's work to be "vital and transcendent."[90] The strength and resonance of Tanner's inner vision, which remained constant throughout his career, ultimately account for the lasting relevance of his art.

DEWEY F. MOSBY

The Tanner family, c. 1890. *Left to right:* Isabella, Halle, her
daughter Sadie, Henry, Bishop Tanner, Carlton, Mrs. Tanner,
Bertha, Sarah, and Mary.

THE TANNER FAMILY:

A GRANDNIECE'S CHRONICLE

On a cold March evening in 1859 some of the citizenry of Pittsburgh gathered to hear a lecture in the Masonic Hall. Benjamin Tucker Tanner, a twenty-three-year-old black man of medium height and stocky build, was among those in attendance. As Tanner was taking his seat, U.S. Deputy Marshal Bernard Dougherty stepped forward and told him he could not sit in what was designated a white section. When young Tanner refused to move to the black section, Dougherty threw him out of the hall.

For many the matter would have ended there, but Tanner was indignant over his treatment. He hired a lawyer and sued the deputy marshal for assault and battery. A local newspaper supported Tanner's contention, calling him a "young colored man of good character, an intelligent, industrious, sober, young man . . . a native of this city; his father was a native of this city, and his grandfather lived here in 1792."[1] The paper noted that "long before Mr. Dougherty's parents had thought of his existence in the Green Isle, Tanner's father was a citizen of the country."[2] Court records of the lawsuit were destroyed by fire at the turn of the century, so we don't know its outcome. But Benjamin Tanner's outrage tells us a lot about his character: he was a man of dignity who challenged any form of racial abuse or denial.

The Tanners can trace their origins in the city of Pittsburgh to the eighteenth century through Benjamin Tanner's father (Hugh S. Tanner), grandfather (Herman Tanner), and great-grandfather (Richard Tanner), but other details of the family's history are sketchy.[3] Benjamin Tucker Tanner was born on Christmas Day in 1835. Reared in a deeply religious and socially committed family, Benjamin at an early age witnessed his parents' activism and resolve regarding problems of race and class. Hugh, a laborer, and Isabella Tanner were determined that their twelve children would acquire the best possible education. We do not know if his siblings were as fortunate, but Benjamin received a formal education, attending Avery College, a school founded for African-American students by a white abolitionist, Charles Avery, in Allegheny, Pennsylvania.[4] To help pay his tuition, Benjamin worked as a barber. It was perhaps at Avery College that Benjamin met his future wife, Sarah Elizabeth Miller, who was also a student there.

Sarah Miller's origins are not clear. Marcia Mathews, the biographer of Henry Ossawa Tanner, states that Charles Miller, Sarah's father, left Winchester, Virginia, in

Benjamin Tucker Tanner, c. 1870.

Sarah Elizabeth Miller Tanner, 1892.

1846 "for the free state of Pennsylvania, taking his family with him in an oxcart."[5] The family account, as told to me by my mother, Sadie Tanner Mossell Alexander, a granddaughter of Benjamin and Sarah Tanner, reports that Sarah, born on May 18, 1840, was one of eleven children born to a slave named Elizabeth. Six of Elizabeth's children were fathered by Charles Miller, a freedman who wanted to marry her; five of her children were fathered by the slave master who owned the plantation. Each time Miller saved enough money to purchase Elizabeth's freedom, the slave master increased the price. Finally Elizabeth contacted agents of the Underground Railroad. With their assistance, she put Sarah and her other children in one of the master's double-team wagons, stocked it with food, and sent them away at midnight, never to see them again. When the children arrived in Carlisle, Pennsylvania, they were met by members of the Pennsylvania Abolitionist Society. Shortly thereafter, the children were divided among various families. Sarah was sent to Pittsburgh.[6]

With his friends and associates, Benjamin Tanner was often stoic, circum-spect, and austere. But when he was with Sarah, whom he affectionately called Sadee, he was talkative, relaxed, and attentive. The two were soon engaged. On June 5, 1857, Benjamin wrote to Sarah professing his love and asking reassurance that if they faced a "maelstrom," she would not turn to another. He signed his letter, "Yours now and forever and no one else."[7] They were married on August 19, 1858, in Pittsburgh.

Upon graduation from Avery College, Benjamin enrolled at Western Theologi-cal Seminary in Allegheny, where his three years of study in a classical curriculum included Greek and Latin. In 1858 he was licensed to preach, and two years later he was ordained into the ministry of the African Methodist Episcopal Church. Founded in 1816 in Philadelphia by Richard Allen, the A.M.E. Church was, according to W. E. B. Du Bois, "the greatest Negro organization in the world."[8]

Henry, the Tanner's first child, was born June 21, 1859. His middle name, Ossawa, was derived from Osawatomie, the town in Kansas where in 1856 the white militant abolitionist John Brown launched his antislavery campaign. John Brown's heroic struggle symbolized for black people their quest for freedom. Thus, for Benjamin and Sarah, Ossawa embodied the hope for emancipation. A few months after Henry's birth, Brown was hanged for leading an antislavery raid on Harpers Ferry.

The Reverend Tanner was ever mindful of the fragility of life. Several children had died who were about the same age as Henry, including his sister Charlotte's daughter Florence, who was just eight months old. Writing in his daybook on January 21, 1860, Tanner said: "Whether the preservation of Henry's life and health will prove a blessing the Lord only knows. For how can I, a mortal man look into the future and see his life, and see whether he will love God and man, or whether he will be an enemy of both. The Lord give us, O give us wisdom to bring him up if at all in the understanding and admonishment of God."[9]

Soon after Henry's first birthday, Tanner was assigned by Bishop Daniel A. Payne of the A.M.E. Church to be a "supply and interim minister" at the prestigious Fifteenth Street Colored Presbyterian Church in Washington, D.C. When Tanner arrived in the city to assume his duties, free blacks comprised 15 percent of Washington's 75,000 residents. The slave population numbered 3,100. Although blacks were subject to the oppressive Black Codes, which restricted their civil rights and severely limited the areas in which they could purchase or rent property, they were still able to form a closely knit and cohesive community.

As the Reverend Tanner pastored his flock, the political climate in Washington grew ominous; a decade of mounting passion over the issue of slavery was tearing the Union apart. Presidential elections were on the horizon. Although neither black nor white Washingtonians could vote in the election, enthusiasm was high. Everyone knew that the man elected president would decide the fate of the nation. On November 7, 1860, Benjamin Tanner wrote in his daybook: "Abraham Lincoln is elected President of the U.S. As far as I am judge it is for good great excitement. So much so that I was advised not to have church."[10]

One week after the election, Washington's real estate market collapsed, and a few days later the local banks suspended specie payments. Although the economy was unstable, on November 19, Tanner sent a check for sixteen dollars to Sarah, who had remained in Pittsburgh, to help pay her passage to Baltimore. Nine days later he met her and young Henry there. After breakfast and a brief rest at the home of "Bro. Read's," a member of his congregation, he and his family took the train to Washington. The brief trip was marred by what Tanner referred to as "American prejudice," the racial discrimination that placed black travelers at the mercy of white passengers and indifferent conductors.

During his eighteen months as minister in Washington, the Reverend Tanner spent long hours reading and preparing his sermons. Early in his career he had established a pattern of hard work, diligence, and a meticulous concern for detail. As an extension of his ministerial duties, in 1861 he founded the Sabbath School for Freedmen in the U.S. Navy Yard. A year later Tanner established the Alexander

Mission for Freedmen on E Street in Washington, the first such mission during the Civil War. In rapid succession he became the pastor at Georgetown in 1863; at Frederick, Maryland, in 1864, and at Bethel A.M.E. Church in Baltimore in 1866.

Tanner wrote on January 10, 1866: "I was in my study this morning at six, having been kept up late last night. 5 o'clock is the time usually for me to be at my studies. This morning I devoted as usual to my languages, the Latin, Greek, and Hebrew."[11] In another daybook entry on January 26, he wrote of how much time his studies consumed and how they interfered with his responsibilities as a pastor: "Ten hours of the 24 are spent in my study. I have a burning desire to feel as I know a Priest ought to feel: but, my studies, they consume me, and I am compelled to it."[12]

Tanner was writing a manuscript on the A.M.E. Church, and it was probably the demands of this important task, coupled with his waning interest in the ministry, that caused him to leave the pulpit of Bethel Church in 1866 and return to Frederick, Maryland, for a new post as principal of the A.M.E. Conference School of Freedmen. The Freedman's Society also secured his services in organizing a common school. While Tanner moved from one assignment to another, his family grew: Halle was born in 1864; Mary Louise, my grandmother, in 1865; and Isabella in 1867.

By this time Tanner had completed his first book, *An Apology for African Methodism* (1867). An impressive volume of 468 pages, it presented one of the first intellectual and theological accounts of the schisms between the black and white Methodist churches. Tanner also briefly outlined the history of the A.M.E. Church, and the confluence of its African heritage, the Methodist form of worship, and the Episcopal hierarchical structure.

A critical success, Tanner's book was enthusiastically received by the religious community. Within the A.M.E. Church he was highly respected and viewed as a brilliant ecclesiastical scholar. It was not surprising therefore that the general conference of the A.M.E. Church, meeting in 1868, elected Tanner to be editor of the denomination's widely influential newspaper, the *Christian Recorder*, a post he would hold until 1884. The Tanners moved to Philadelphia and settled in a home on Third and Pine streets, just a few blocks from the building that housed the offices of the newspaper.[13]

With Tanner as editor, the *Christian Recorder* now turned from a solely religious outlook to encompass secular topics. Through his editorials Tanner addressed the major issues facing African-Americans in the nineteenth century. Between 1870 and 1880 the black population in Philadelphia had increased 68 percent. Blacks were attracted to the city because of jobs but found themselves in direct competition with European immigrants. In the pages of the *Christian Recorder* Tanner followed the changing demographics of the community and railed against the loss of jobs by African-Americans to the new arrivals from Europe. These were mostly jobs "in service," and although Tanner envisioned more skilled jobs for blacks, he was "realistic when these may be the only jobs we can get to feed our families."[14] A series of articles he wrote on the immigration of blacks to Africa revived an old controversy. Tanner opposed emigration, believing that blacks with training and education were needed in America to help build a strong middle class. A contrary view was taken by an eminent black nationalist, Bishop Henry McNeal Turner of the A.M.E. Church. The heated exchange between the two thinkers soon expanded to include prominent black spokesmen such as Frederick Douglass (1817–95), who generally subscribed to

Tanner's position. Most African-Americans opposed emigration, concluding that after suffering the ravages of slavery, black people in America would not be aided by sending their most talented professionals to live and work in Africa.[15]

Tanner's ecclesiastical and secular writings won him the recognition of his undergraduate school, Avery College, from which he was given an honorary M.A. degree in 1870. That same year another son, Carlton, was born to the Tanner family, which by now had grown too large for their little house on Pine Street. In 1872 Tanner purchased an eight-room house at 2908 Diamond Street in North Philadelphia. Two more daughters followed — Sarah Elizabeth, born in 1873, and the last child, Bertha, in 1878. (Two other children did not survive infancy.) Although she was busy caring for her family, Sarah Tanner found time to organize the Mite Missionary Society of the A.M.E. Church, one of the earliest societies of black women in America.

The Tanner home soon became a place for leading black and white clergymen to participate in learned discussions on theological and secular matters. Noted black historian Dr. Carter G. Woodson deemed the home "the center of the black intellectual community in Philadelphia,"[16] and within this stimulating atmosphere the seven Tanner children were encouraged to succeed. Later, during the early years of Henry's artistic career, Reverend Tanner's professional circle provided his son with ready encouragement and support. He spent one winter sketching and painting in Florida as the guest of Bishop Daniel A. Payne, his father's friend and superior in the A.M.E. Church. Henry benefited also from his association with Bishop Joseph Crane Hartzell, another of his father's colleagues. Bishop Hartzell and his wife, whom Henry met in Atlanta, helped him secure a teaching position in 1889 at Clark University, and later sponsored the first exhibition of his works at the Methodist Book Concern in Cincinnati.

My mother, who lived with her grandparents as a small child, recalled some of the more quotidian details of the Diamond Street household:

> Food was never considered a matter on which one should spend precious hours of his life. I can so well remember that we children were not even allowed to discuss what we enjoyed eating. The attitude of our grandparents was that food was to be eaten only to keep the body well, so that one could work, not give pleasure. My maternal grandfather (Benjamin T. Tanner), a prolific writer, would eat only fruit, cereal, tea and/or milk in the morning. Frequently, we children would have to wait until almost 2:00 p.m. for the noon day meal, because Grandpa was writing in his study and would not stop, saying that if he stopped to eat, his mind would become dull because the blood previously supplying his mind would be used to help the stomach take care of the food.[17]

Along with these daily measures of discipline, the Reverend Tanner also showed a loving side. To celebrate Halle's eighteenth birthday, he wrote a poem joyfully recounting the progress of her years, and encouraging her to "be, my daughter, like the river/be an earnest, happy liver."[18]

In 1881 the Reverend Tanner went to London to attend the Ecumenical Conference of Methodism. His visit lasted three months and was chronicled in the *Christian Recorder.* Perhaps the most poignant account was written on Tanner's return to Philadelphia, when he contrasted his life in Europe with that in America. In words laced with anger, he spoke of being denied service with whites in a restaurant and of being unable to sit in a railroad car next to white women or children in the

Carlton Tanner, c. 1890.

United States, but that while in Europe he had been unencumbered in his travels. Tanner mused about a time in the future, perhaps "fifty years hence and caste will be dead. The grandchildren of the present generation will experience little, if any, of it [discrimination]."[19]

Henry too experienced the hardships of racism, especially when white art teachers in Philadelphia refused to take him as a pupil. He found support for his ambitions from men such as Jacob C. White, principal of the Roberts Vaux Grammar School and an important leader in the local African-American community, as well as from his father and the pages of the *Christian Recorder*. In the early 1870s, Henry might have read there about the travels and studies of the artist Edmonia Lewis, whose sculpture Tanner would see in 1876 at the Centennial Exposition, along with paintings by the black artist Edward Mitchell Bannister. Benjamin Tanner, writing in the *Christian Recorder*, had expressed his concern that black artists be included in the exposition.

The Reverend Tanner completed a major book on African Methodist Episcopal Church history in 1884 and later that year launched the *A.M.E. Church Review*. One of the first church magazines published by blacks for a national audience, the *Review* provided its readers with a rich variety of articles on social and political issues of particular interest to African-Americans. William J. Simmons described the *Review* as "one of the most scholarly productions of the age, and its list of writers includes all classes of thinkers and writers of all denominations, male and female."[20]

Nearly all of Benjamin Tanner's time was devoted to editing the *Review*. His oldest daughter, Halle, worked in the magazine's office, but her mind was not always on her work. She had fallen in love with a tall handsome man, Charles E. Dillon, from Trenton, New Jersey, and following a brief courtship they were married in the Tanner home in June 1886. The bride was elegant and beautiful with "many richly dressed ladies in attendance."[21] A year later Halle and Charles became the proud parents of a little girl, Sadie. The first grandchild of the Reverend and Mrs. Tanner, Sadie was naturally showered with affection. But tragedy struck this young family when Charles Dillon died. Their joy and tranquillity shattered, Halle and her daughter moved into the house on Diamond Street.

After several months, Halle set aside her grief, and at twenty-four she entered medical school at Women's Medical College in Philadelphia. Women's Medical was established in 1850 because no orthodox medical school in the city would train female students. The school graduated its first black student, Rebecca Cole, in 1867, but only a few blacks graduated in the interim; Halle was the only black student in her class.

In 1888, Benjamin Tanner was elected a bishop of the A.M.E. Church. He could no longer act as editor of the *Review*, but his appointment did not curtail his output of scholarly publications, and he continued to be an ardent evangelist for his emancipated people.

Before Henry left Philadelphia in 1891 to study art in Europe, the Tanners posed for a family portrait. Benjamin Tanner is seated in the center of the photograph in a high-back, brocaded chair, his eyes fixed. His wife is to his left; the seven Tanner children and the first grandchild, each elegantly dressed and strikingly handsome, surround the bishop and Sarah.

In 1891 Halle completed her three-year course of study at Women's Medical. Before graduation, she had written to Booker T. Washington, founder and president of Tuskegee Normal and Industrial Institute, asking him to consider her for a job at the school. Washington offered her the position of resident physician, informing Halle that the job paid "$600 a year with board for twelve months' work, including one month of vacation."[22] Moreover, he added, "This is with the understanding that you would teach two classes a day, if necessary, and take full charge of the health department. We should expect you to compound your own medicine as far as possible."[23] Halle and Washington met in Philadelphia in the spring of that year, and he assured her and her father that the institute would be the right place for a young black woman doctor to begin her career.

Halle Tanner, c. 1890.

At the beginning of August, Halle arrived in Tuskegee, Alabama, a small town of three thousand, half of whom were black. This was a long way from her cosmopolitan hometown. Halle must have been viewed by the students and residents not only with curiosity but with pride, since she was the first woman physician most had ever met. After becoming acquainted with the facilities, Halle left several days later for Montgomery to prepare for the medical board tests. Washington had arranged for her to study for the strenuous exams with Dr. Cornelius Nathaniel Dorsette, who practiced medicine in Montgomery and was the first black physician to pass the Alabama medical boards.[24]

In a letter to Washington, Bishop Tanner expressed his concern for Halle's success: "Of course, we are all anxious about the Doctor. Not that we have any misgivings as to her ability to pass any reasonable and just examination. But we know that both her sex and her color will be against her."[25] Washington accompanied Halle to the capitol building on the first day of the exhausting, difficult exams, which lasted ten days. But Halle passed, with a score of 78.8,[26] to become the first woman ever admitted on examination to practice medicine in Alabama.[27]

From 1891 to 1894 Dr. Dillon served as resident physician of Tuskegee Institute. Attempting to address social inequities, she charged her private patients only twenty-five cents for medicines — many of which she prepared — and ten cents for a house call.[28] White physicians charged two dollars per mile for a visit, with an additional fee for medicine.[29] During her tenure at Tuskegee Dr. Dillon also established the Lafayette Dispensary and Nurses' Training School. In 1894 she married the Reverend John Quincy Johnson, and they eventually moved to Nashville. Halle bore three sons and died in childbirth in April 1901.

While Halle was establishing herself as a doctor, Henry was maturing as an artist and traveling between Europe and the United States, with occasional side trips to the Middle East. These productive times for the young artist were given yet another exciting dimension when he met Jessie Macauley Olssen in 1898. A white woman of

Henry Ossawa Tanner, c. 1900.

Jessie Tanner, c. 1905.

Swedish-Scottish ancestry, Jessie was born in San Francisco, where her father was in the shipbuilding industry. She was a tall, attractive woman whose sparkling, ebullient personality was a pleasant complement to Henry's quiet reserve. Henry, however, balked at marriage, but while on his second trip to the Near East in 1898–99, he received a telegram from Jessie which read: "Come to me."[30] If Henry had any uncertainty about marrying a white woman, it vanished, and on December 14, 1899, they were married in London. Jessie's sister, Elna, and a Dutch friend, Gerhoodt C. Mars, served as witnesses. Their parents were unable to attend the wedding but sent their blessings. About four years later, on September 25, 1903, the couple's son and only child, Jesse Ossawa Tanner, was born in New York City.

Henry was increasingly acclaimed as an artist, and his rising celebrity caused aspiring artists to seek his assistance and endorsement. During the fall of 1899 the niece of a Philadelphia friend came to Paris to study at the Ecole des Beaux-Arts. The young artist, Meta Vaux Warrick (Fuller), became famous for her remarkable sculpture. Henry had planned to meet Warrick at the station, but for some unknown reason he did not appear. She took a taxi to the American Girls Club, but when the resident director saw Warrick, she exclaimed: "Why didn't you tell me you were not a white girl?" Henry was contacted, and he immediately secured her a room at a small hotel. Warrick was the first of many black artists who called on Henry for advice, support, and fellowship—which he gave based on ability, not race.

While Henry was winning prizes and selling paintings, his father was as active as ever. In September 1901 he was in London as a delegate to the Third Ecumenical Conference on Methodism, where he read a paper on the "Elements of Pulpit

Effectiveness." Henry and Jessie visited London during the bishop's stay, and they found him strong and vigorous at sixty-six years of age.

The rest of the family was settling down. Mary Louise, Henry's favorite sister and my grandmother, who was thirty-five years old at the turn of the century, was married to Aaron Mossell, a young lawyer from Lockport, New York. Mossell was the first black person to graduate from the University of Pennsylvania Law School. He would later abandon Mary and his three children and move to Cardiff, Wales. One of Mary's daughters, Sadie, my mother, was distinguished in her own right, becoming the second black woman in America to receive a Ph.D., and the first in economics. She was not only the first black woman to graduate from the University of Pennsylvania Law School but the first to pass the bar and practice in the state. She married Raymond Pace Alexander, with whom she established a lifelong law practice. My father, an eminent jurist, was also an outstanding city councilman in Philadelphia.

Jessie Tanner holding Jesse, October–November 1903.

Carlton Tanner, who had attended theological school, was by this time in South Africa working as managing editor of the *South African Christian Recorder*. Subsequently he would write a number of books on the history and polity of his church. He married Frances Stanford, a trained nurse, who was unstinting in her support of Carlton's ministry. Isabella Tanner had married the Reverend Noah Temple and was living in Pittsburgh. Bertha Tanner had married Samuel Patterson Stafford, a member of the first four-year class in medicine at the University of Pennsylvania, and had settled in St. Louis. Sarah Elizabeth married Lewis B. Moore, the first black to receive a Ph.D. from the University of Pennsylvania. Later, at Howard University, Dr. Moore was instrumental in organizing the Teacher's College. The Moores' son, Lewis, was educated at Storer College and Bates, and received a law degree from Temple University. A daughter, Sarah Moore Pride, taught school in New York.

Given Henry's growing stature and the bishop's demanding schedule, it is little wonder that several years passed before the entire family assembled once again. They finally gathered in the winter of 1908 to celebrate Bishop and Mrs. Tanner's fiftieth wedding anniversary. It was a festive occasion, although no doubt the race riots that had marred the summer were discussed. Those relatives who could not attend sent warm regards to the patriarch and his wife, including the bishop's three living sisters, Nancy, Mary, and Charlotte.

Nancy was married to the Reverend Lewis Woodson, a minister in the A.M.E. Church who had been a teacher at a popular school for African-Americans in Pittsburgh before the Civil War. Mrs. Woodson had eleven children, most of whom rose to distinction. Mary, the bishop's youngest sister, was also married to a minister, the Reverend John Russell. Mary and her husband were committed to religious and educational work, and all of their children attended college.

The bishop's niece, Arrena, was married to Charles H. Brown, a teacher in the St. Louis public schools for more than half a century. Of her four children, Maudelle would achieve the most acclaim. She married Midian O. Bousfield, who was a colonel in the army during the Second World War. She graduated from the Mendelssohn Conservatory of Music, and after teaching at several schools in Chicago, St. Louis, and Baltimore, Maudelle served as dean of girls at Phillips High School in Chicago and later became the first person of her race to be named principal of a Chicago public school. Maudelle earned a national reputation, particularly for her exemplary work with the large number of black migrants who flowed into Chicago from the South. She demonstrated to many skeptical white educators that a black woman could function successfully not only as a teacher but also as a supervisor.

Bishop Tanner died on January 15, 1923, several months before the family received the good news that Henry had been made a chevalier of the Legion of Honor. Henry considered his citation by the French government to be the greatest honor of his illustrious career. Another joyous family event took place that year when the bishop's nephew, Benjamin T. Johnson, Halle's son by the Reverend J. Q. Johnson, married Mary Parker of Boston.

Two years after his father's death, however, Henry faced another loss: his beloved Jessie died on September 8, 1925. His son, Jesse, was his only consolation, but he was completing his education at the London School of Mines. Within a year the two were reunited as Jesse returned home to care for his father and to recover from his own mental exhaustion. Henry's concern about his son's health forced him to set aside his own despair. Soon he was painting with greater regularity and anticipating a round of New York exhibitions. He would continue working, albeit with decreasing vigor, until his death on May 25, 1937.

Henry Ossawa Tanner was a complex man who was unwilling to compromise his integrity or his humanism. In the same way that his family fought for civil rights in America, Henry waged a determined struggle against the social and historical factors that sought to limit his artistic expression. His residency in Europe was not a retreat from the political issues facing his people; he needed this distance to paint freely the stories he had heard at his father's knee and in his father's churches. "In his religious painting," the late artist Romare Bearden commented, "Tanner tells us much of what he thinks about the world and of man's place in it. This kind of self-exploration when integrated by a personality of real proportion can be both vital and transcendent."[31]

Bearden's perception was echoed and extended by my cousin, Jesse O. Tanner. He recalled: "My father always worked very hard on his pictures and they were painted very slowly. If you study them, you keep discovering new things about them — a new form is revealed, a new star seems to shine, a new shadow stretches out — in a word, his pictures are very much alive. A Tanner can do more than give you enjoyment, it can come to your rescue, it can reaffirm your confidence in man and his destiny, it can help you surmount your difficulties or console you in distress."[32]

Having explored the Tanner roots in the United States, I set out in 1984 to discover the Tanner connection in Europe. My mother's memories had been silenced due to severe illness, so I turned to historical records and the reflections of other relatives. One of the first I sought was Jesse. From his correspondence with my mother, I knew that he was eighty-one years old and lived in Le Douhet, a small village in southwest France. Of course the letters did not change the fact that Jesse and I were strangers. He knew nothing about me and little about the rest of his relatives in America, and perhaps he wanted to keep it that way.

I wrote to Jesse and suggested a meeting, which he discouraged by various strategies. But I was determined, even after he wired a telegram saying that it would not be possible for me to visit him. When we did meet, he still seemed to resent my presence, as if he were fearful of opening old wounds, or of having to probe once more into the reality of who he was and his own ambivalence about his family. Eventually though, over some delicious potato soup and a few fond memories, he warmed to me and slowly began to reveal portions of our common ancestry. Jesse opened his arms to me and, speaking for all of my French relatives, said, "We have grown to love you." Like the thread Ariadne gave Theseus to solve the labyrinth, Jesse, with a smile and soft words, provided me with both encouragement and with an aperture through which to survey my family's origins.

It was my good fortune to meet and talk with Jesse when I did; in May 1985 he died. In the end he had shared some of his private feelings and allowed me to forage among his father's diaries and documents. From this vast assortment of memorabilia I learned that Henry Tanner was not so absorbed in his work that he ignored the plight of other artists. He often opened his home and studio to black American artists, such as William Henry Johnson, Meta Vaux Warrick Fuller, Laura Wheeler Waring, Aaron Douglas, and Hale Woodruff, all of whom sought his advice and counsel when in Paris. While reading a passel of his letters, I discovered that my granduncle never considered himself an expatriate; in fact he eschewed the word. He believed he did not have the luxury of being an expatriate, a privilege, as James Baldwin would suggest years later, accorded only to white Americans.

Henry Tanner was a quiet, self-effacing, and talented man whose work influenced the development of black art in America. He made it possible for generations of black artists to compete in the world of art, giving them an example of how to create without capitulating to rampant racism. In myriad ways he was continuing a legacy passed on to him by his noble father. There is much to glean from the exemplary life of a man who would brook no compromise and insisted, as his son wrote of him, "that man has an active role to play and should not submit passively to his fate."[33] I am convinced that there was neither submission nor surrender in the art and life of Henry Ossawa Tanner.

RAE ALEXANDER-MINTER

CHRONOLOGY

KATHLEEN JAMES

SYLVIA YOUNT

Thomas Eakins, *Portrait of Henry O. Tanner*, 1900, oil on canvas,
24 1/8 × 20 1/4", The Hyde Collection, Glens Falls, New York.

1858   August 19. Benjamin Tucker Tanner (1835–1923), minister in the African Methodist Episcopal (A.M.E.) Church, marries Sarah Elizabeth Miller (1840–1914).

1859   June 21. Henry Ossawa Tanner born to Benjamin and Sarah Tanner.

1860   B. T. Tanner ordained deacon and then elder in A.M.E. Church. Family moves to Washington, D.C., where Tanner briefly serves as minister of Fifteenth Street Colored Presbyterian Church.

1861   B. T. Tanner founds Sabbath School for Freedmen, Washington, D.C.

1862   B. T. Tanner becomes director of Alexander Mission for Freedmen, Washington, D.C.

1863   B. T. Tanner serves as pastor of A.M.E. Church, Georgetown, Washington, D.C.

1864   B. T. Tanner serves as principal of A.M.E. Conference School in Frederick, Maryland, until 1865.

Halle Tanner born (d. 1901).

1865   Mary Louise Tanner born (d. 1935).

1866   B. T. Tanner briefly serves as pastor of Bethel A.M.E. Church in Baltimore, then becomes full-time principal of A.M.E. Conference School for Freedmen in Frederick, Maryland.

1867   Isabella Tanner born (d. unknown).

1868   Family moves to Philadelphia, "near Third and Pine." B. T. Tanner is appointed editor of the *Christian Recorder* (begun 1854), weekly journal of A.M.E. Church, a position he holds until 1884.

Henry attends Lombard Street School for Colored Students (known as James Forten School, 1871–1933) for two years.

Spring. Family moves to house at 631 Pine Street which also serves as office of the *Christian Recorder*.

1869   Henry enters Roberts Vaux Consolidated School for Colored Students. (In 1876 the school becomes Roberts Vaux Grammar School, then the only secondary school for black students in Philadelphia.)

1870   Carlton M. Tanner born (d. 1933).

1872   Family buys house at 2908 Diamond Street (later Park Avenue) in Philadelphia.

While walking with father in Fairmount Park, Henry sees an artist at work and is motivated to begin painting.

1873   Sarah Elizabeth Tanner born (d. 1900).

1876   Earliest dated work, *Harbor Scene*, painted in Atlantic City.

1877   July 6. Graduates from Roberts Vaux Grammar School with class of ten and delivers valedictory address entitled "Compulsory Education."

Apprenticed to family friend in flour business; by 1878, after severe illness, gains parental consent to pursue artistic career.

1878   Paints earliest Adirondack landscapes during convalescent trip to Rainbow Lake, New York; also visits Florida.

Bertha Tanner, last child of B. T. Tanner, born (d. 1962).

1879	December. Begins studies at Pennsylvania Academy of the Fine Arts, Philadelphia, with Thomas Eakins; remains student sporadically through 1885.
1880	April 29. The *Christian Recorder* reports that Henry "will be sent to Rome by some interested gentleman to study the works of the old masters" (although Tanner does not travel to Europe until 1891).
1881–82	While living with parents in Philadelphia, attempts to establish himself as painter.
	Serves as Sunday school superintendent at Morris Brown Mission.
	June–September. Benjamin T. Tanner travels to London to attend Ecumenical Conference of Methodism; also visits Paris.
	November–March. Henry is ill with "hemorrhage of the nose."
1882	Summer. Convalesces in Adirondacks at Rainbow Lake.
	July. Four illustrations commissioned by Judge Albion Tourgee, editor of *Our Continent*, for Louise Stockton's "In the Days of Witchcraft"; three of the four appear in the August 30 edition of *Our Continent*.
1884	Benjamin T. Tanner founds quarterly periodical *African Methodist Episcopal Church Review*; serves as editor until 1888.
1886–87	September. Henry rents studio at 927 Chestnut Street, Philadelphia.
1887	May. Henry is one of two artists (with E. M. Bannister) included in *Men of Mark: Eminent, Progressive and Rising*, dictionary of 177 biographies of prominent African-Americans, by William J. Simmons, president of Kentucky State University, Louisville.
	November. Attends A.M.E. conference in Jacksonville, Florida, where he spends coming winter painting; also visits Enterprise, Florida.
1888	January 10. Single illustration for Kate Upson Clark's "Old Win-ne-wan's Star" appears in *Harper's Young People*.
	February. Returns to Philadelphia from Florida.
	March. Models and casts bust of his earliest patron, Bishop Daniel A. Payne of A.M.E. Church.
	May. Benjamin T. Tanner elected eighteenth bishop in A.M.E. Church; serves in Eleventh Episcopal District, which included Canada, West Indies, British Guiana, and South America.
	Summer. Family resides at retreat cottage, Atlantic City.

Insofar as possible, painting titles appear as they did in contemporary sources. They do not necessarily correlate to present-day titles. When a title is not given, the exhibited work is unknown.

1880   February. Philadelphia, window of Meade and Robbins Jewelry Store, Chestnut Street.

April. Philadelphia, window of Meade and Robbins; work sold.
April. Philadelphia, Pennsylvania Academy of the Fine Arts. *Hazy Morning at Narragansett, Pursuing Calvary.*

October. Louisville, Kentucky, World's Industrial and Cotton Centennial Exhibition. *Point Judith.*

November. Philadelphia, Workingmen's Art Exhibition (African-American artists and artisans). *Atlantic City I Let [sic] House.*

1881   April. Philadelphia, Pennsylvania Academy of the Fine Arts. *Point Judith, Burnt Pines — Adirondacks.*

1881–83   Sells *Boy and Sheep Lying under a Tree* (1881) the first of three works sold to Edward Lawrence Scull, Philadelphia, before 1884; not shown publicly.

1882   December. Philadelphia, window of Meade and Robbins.

1884   March. Philadelphia, Hazeltine's Gallery. *The Battle of Life.*

December. New Orleans, World's Industrial and Cotton Centennial Exhibition, "Coloured Races" Department. *The Battle of Life.*

1885   April. New York, National Academy of Design. *Lions at Home* (sold).
October. Philadelphia, Pennsylvania Academy of the Fine Arts. *Back from the Beach.*

1886   April. New York, National Academy of Design. *Back from the Beach.*

1887   March. Philadelphia, Pennsylvania Academy of the Fine Arts. *A Scouting Incident.*
April. New York, National Academy of Design. *A Dusty Road.*

1889   January. Moves to Atlanta and opens photography gallery and "art room"; venture is unsuccessful.

Summer. Visits the Highlands, North Carolina, for his health.

Fall. Serves as drawing instructor at Clark University, Atlanta, position secured through efforts of a trustee, Bishop Joseph Crane Hartzell, M.E.; receives first portrait commission (Professor William H. Crogman).

1891   January 4. Departs for Rome via London and Paris. Decides to remain in Paris; begins study with Jean-Joseph Benjamin-Constant and Jean-Paul Laurens at Académie Julian.

Joins American Art Students' Club of Paris through which he makes the acquaintance of Rodman Wanamaker, head of Paris branch of family retail firm.

Rents studio-apartment at 12 rue de Seine, Paris, through 1892.

Summers in Pont-Aven, Brittany.

1892   Summers in Concarneau, Brittany.

1893   Spring. Shares studio with sculptor Hermon A. MacNeil at 15 rue de Seine.

Summer. Possible visit to Brittany.
Summer. Returns to United States to recuperate from typhoid fever.

August. Visits Chicago to present paper, "The American Negro in Art," at the Congress on Africa, an auxiliary congress at the World's Columbian Exposition.

1894   January. Finishes bust of Bishop Payne; advertises through the *Christian Recorder*. Tanner sees his instructor from the Académie Julian, Jean-Joseph Benjamin-Constant, who visits Philadelphia.

February. Attends A.M.E. conference in Tallahassee, Florida.

May. Attends commencement ceremony at Hampton Institute, Virginia, in company of Robert C. Ogden, early Philadelphia benefactor and partner in Wanamaker firm. Ogden donates *Lion's Head* to institute's library and loans *The Bagpipe Lesson* for exhibition.

Summer. Possible visit to Brittany.

August. The *Christian Recorder* reports that Henry is in Chicago to "fill an order" for a painting.

October. John T. Morris, Philadelphia patron, purchases *The Thankful Poor* and lends it to Pennsylvania School for the Deaf. Henry uses income to return to Paris.

November. Robert C. Ogden donates *The Banjo Lesson* to Hampton Institute.

1895   Rents studio-apartment at 51 boulevard Saint-Jacques, through 1904.

Studies with Eugène Frémiet.

Fall. Joins American Art Association of Paris (Rodman Wanamaker, president, and Hermann Dudley Murphy, vice-president).

Henry Ossawa Tanner on horseback in the Highlands, North Carolina, July 30, 1889.

1889   January. Philadelphia, Pennsylvania Academy of the Fine Arts. *Early November.*

1890   May. The *Christian Recorder* reports that Tanner sells a work for $700, "no color lines on it."

December. Cincinnati. First solo exhibition of paintings at headquarters of Board of Education, Methodist Episcopal Church, organized by early patrons Bishop and Mrs. Joseph C. Hartzell.

Académie Julian, c. 1891–93. Tanner is in the last row, fourth from the left.

1893   August. Chicago, World's Columbian Exposition, special exhibition of one hundred American art students. *The Bagpipe Lesson;* one of forty works illustrated in catalogue.

October. Philadelphia, Earle's Galleries, genre painting show. *The First Lesson* [*The Banjo Lesson*].

December. Philadelphia, Pennsylvania Academy of the Fine Arts. *The Bagpipe Lesson.*

1894   April. Philadelphia, Earle's Galleries, with Thomas Hovenden. *The Bagpipe Lesson, Bois d'Amour, Evening, Evening on the Saint John's, The Foster Mother, Lake Monroe, October, Orange Grove, Return of Fishing Boats, Rocks at Concarneau, Scrub-Pine Land, Spring Morning, Study of Head—Italian Woman, A Sudden Squall, The Thankful Poor, Young Orange Trees.*

May. Paris, Salon de la Société des Artistes Français (Salon). *La Leçon de Musique* [*The Music Lesson* (*The Banjo Lesson*)]. From this year through 1914, Tanner will exhibit at the Salon annually.

September. Philadelphia, Wanamaker's Art Gallery. *The Bagpipe Lesson.*

1895   May. Paris, Salon. *Intérieur Bretagne* [*Brittany Interior*], *Le Jeune Sabotier* [*The Young Sabot Maker*], pastel of New Jersey coast by moonlight.

September. Atlanta, Cotton States and International Exposition. *The Bagpipe Lesson.*

October. Philadelphia, Earle's Galleries. *The Young Sabot Maker.*

December. Philadelphia, Pennsylvania Academy of the Fine Arts. *The Young Sabot Maker.*

1896   May. Paris, Salon. *Daniel dans la Fosse aux Lions* [*Daniel in the Lions' Den*], awarded honorable mention.

October. Chicago, Art Institute. *Daniel in the Lions' Den, In the Desert.*

December. Philadelphia, Pennsylvania Academy of the Fine Arts. *Daniel in the Lions' Den, In the Desert.*

1897
January. Bishop and Mrs. Tanner and family move to Kansas City, Kansas, where the bishop serves in Fifth Episcopal District (Missouri, Kansas, Colorado).

January–April. Henry travels to Palestine and Egypt at expense of Rodman Wanamaker; returns via Italy with stops in Naples, Rome, Pisa, Florence, and Venice.

June. Makes brief visit to England.

July. Arrives in Philadelphia, then visits parents in Kansas City where he paints *Portrait of the Artist's Mother.*

September. Returns to Paris via Philadelphia.

Campground shared by Tanner and Sandor Landeau in Palestine, c. 1899.

1898
Meets future wife, Jessie Macauley Olssen (1873–1925) of San Francisco, first at Barbizon and later in Paris.

October. Second trip to Near East, through March 1899; again funded by Rodman Wanamaker.

1899
July. Booker T. Washington visits Henry in Paris and writes an article about trip for *Washington Colored American.*

December 14. Marries Jessie Macauley Olssen at Saint Giles-in-the-Fields, Bloomsbury, London; honeymoon at Martigues, in the south of France.

Old American Art Club, boulevard Montparnasse, Paris, c. 1900. Tanner is seated in the first row, fourth from the left.

1900
January. Henry and Jessie rent apartment on rue d'Assas, Paris, overlooking Luxembourg Gardens.

January. Bishop and Mrs. Tanner and family return to Philadelphia from Kansas City, Kansas.

April. First major article on Henry, "A Negro Artist of Unique Power," by E. F. Baldwin, appears in the *Outlook.*

June. "Henry O. Tanner, Painter," by Helen Cole, appears in *Brush and Pencil.*

July. Henry and Jessie reside in Trépied, near Etaples, Pas-de-Calais (Normandy).

1901
September. Henry visits with Bishop Tanner in London, where the bishop serves as delegate to Third Ecumenical Conference of Methodism.

1897   May. Paris, Salon. *La Résurrection de Lazare* [*The Resurrection of Lazarus*]; awarded third-class medal and purchased by French government for Musée du Luxembourg.

Summer. Munich, International Art Exhibition. *Daniel in the Lions' Den.*

June. New York, Wanamaker's Art Gallery. *The Bagpipe Lesson.*

September. Philadelphia, Earle's Galleries. *The Young Sabot Maker.*

1898   May. Paris, Salon. *L'Annonciation* [*The Annunciation*].

October. Chicago, Art Institute. *The Annunciation, Lions.*

November. Pittsburgh, Carnegie Institute. *The Jews' Wailing Place.*

Henry Ossawa Tanner in his studio at 51 boulevard Saint-Jacques, Paris, c. 1900. On the easel is a lost work, Christ among the Doctors, exhibited at the 1900 Salon. Charles Grafly's portrait bust of Tanner stands in the corner.

1899   January. Philadelphia, Pennsylvania Academy of the Fine Arts. *The Annunciation, The Jews' Wailing Place, Jerusalem, Lions.*

March. New York, Century Club. *The Annunciation.*

May. Philadelphia, Pennsylvania Museum and School of Art, Wilstach Gallery, Memorial Hall. *The Annunciation*; purchased for collection.
May. Paris, Salon. *Nicodème Venant Voir Jésus* [*Nicodemus Visiting Jesus*].
May. Paris, American Art Association. *And He Vanished Out of Their Sight.*

November. Pittsburgh, Carnegie Institute. *The Flight into Egypt, Judas.*

1900   January. Philadelphia, Pennsylvania Academy of the Fine Arts. *Hills near Jerusalem, Judas, Nicodemus Visiting Jesus*; latter awarded Lippincott Prize and purchased for Temple Collection.

May. Paris, Salon. *Marie* [*Mary*], *Christ parmi les Docteurs* [*Christ among the Doctors*].

Summer. Paris, Exposition Universelle. *Christ among the Doctors, Daniel in the Lions' Den*; latter awarded silver medal.

November. Pittsburgh, Carnegie Institute. *Christ among the Doctors, The Departure into Egypt.*
November. Philadelphia, Art Club. *Night Scene.*

Christ among the Doctors, 1899–1900, location unknown.

1901   January. Philadelphia, Pennsylvania Academy of the Fine Arts. *"And He Vanished Out of Their Sight," Christ among the Doctors, Departure into Egypt, Mary, Night.*

May. Paris, Salon. *La Nuit* [*Night*].
May. Buffalo, Pan-American Exposition. *Daniel in the Lions' Den*; awarded silver medal.

November. Pittsburgh, Carnegie Institute. *Night.*

1902   August–November. Henry and Jessie reside with patrons and friends Atherton and Louise Curtis at Mount Kisco, New York, in small community planned by Curtises.

September. First installment of the "Mothers of the Bible" series (*Sarah*) appears in the *Ladies Home Journal*; subsequent installments (*Hagar, Rachel, Mary*) are published through January 1903.

December. "Henry Ossian [*sic*] Tanner," by W. S. Scarborough, appears in *Southern Workman*.

Jessie Tanner, c. 1905.

1903   January–March. Henry and Jessie reside briefly in Granada, Spain, and London before returning to Paris.

June. Henry and Jessie return to Mount Kisco.

August. Henry invited to serve on eleven-person jury for Pennsylvania Academy of the Fine Arts 1904 annual exhibition.

September 25. Son, Jesse Ossawa, born in New York City.

1904   April. Tanners return to Paris.

Spring. Purchases summer house, "Les Charmes," at Trépied; helps found Société Artistique de Picardie, in the artist colony at Le Touquet, Paris-Plage, Pas-de-Calais.

October. Henry rents studio at 70 bis rue Notre-Dame-des-Champs, Paris, which he maintains until 1912.

Tanners reside with Jessie's recently retired parents, Bessie and John Olssen, at Sceaux, Hauts-de-Seine.

1905   August. Henry invited to serve on three-person Paris selection jury, with Walter MacEwen and Charles Morris Young, for Pennsylvania Academy of the Fine Arts 1906 annual exhibition.

1906   November. "Henry O. Tanner," by Florence L. Bentley, appears in the *Voice of the Negro*.

Bessie Olssen dies. Tanners and John Olssen move into 70 bis rue Notre-Dame-des-Champs, Paris.

Jesse Tanner, Jessie Tanner, and John Olssen, c. 1906.

1902   May. Paris, Salon. *La Musique* [*Music, Chamber Music*].

September. Minneapolis, Society of Fine Arts. *Mary.*

Hermann Dudley Murphy, *Henry Ossawa Tanner,* c. 1891–95, oil on canvas, 37 × 28″, Art Institute of Chicago, gift of the Friends of American Art.

1903   January. Philadelphia, Pennsylvania Academy of the Fine Arts. *Hagar* and *Mary* from the "Mothers of the Bible" series.

1904   January. Philadelphia, Pennsylvania Academy of the Fine Arts. *Peter after the Denial.*

March. New York, Society of American Artists. *Christ and His Disciples on the Road to Bethany, Daniel in the Lions' Den.*

April. St. Louis, Louisiana Purchase Exposition. *Daniel in the Lions' Den;* awarded silver medal.

1905   January. Philadelphia, Pennsylvania Academy of the Fine Arts. *Job and His Three Friends.*

March. New York, Society of American Artists. *Job and His Three Friends.*

April. Paris, Salon. *Le Bon Samaritain* [*The Good Samaritan*], *Le Christ Lavant les Pieds de ses Disciples* [*Christ Washing the Feet of the Disciples*].

Summer. Liège, Exposition Universelle. *On the Road to Bethany.*

June. Portland, Lewis and Clark Exposition. *Mary.*

October. Chicago, Art Institute. *Abraham's Oak, The Good Samaritan.*

November. Pittsburgh, Carnegie Institute. *Judas Covenanting with the High Priests.*

1906   January. Philadelphia, Pennsylvania Academy of the Fine Arts. *Christ Washing the Feet of the Disciples.*

Winter. Paris, American Men's Club. *Two Disciples at the Tomb.*

April. Pittsburgh, Carnegie Institute. *Judas Covenanting with the High Priests;* purchased for permanent collection.

May. Paris, Salon. *Les Pèlerins d'Emmaus* [*The Disciples at Emmaus*], *Le Retour de la Sainte Femme* [*Return of the Holy Women*]; former awarded second-class medal and purchased by French government. Tanner designated *hors concours.*

Jesse Tanner, Jessie Tanner, maid, artist
Myron Barlow, and Henry O. Tanner in
their garden at Trépied, c. 1908–1909.

1907   August. Henry invited to serve on
three-person Paris selection jury,
with Alfred Maurer and Florence
Esté, for Pennsylvania Academy of
the Fine Arts 1908 annual
exhibition.

1908   Joins Paris Society of American Painters.

February–March. Henry visits Algiers.

May. Bishop Tanner, first A.M.E. bishop to
receive pension, retires on half pay.

August–mid-September. Tanners visit United
States on occasion of Benjamin and Sarah Tanner's golden wedding anniversary.

October. An unsigned article, "An Afro-
American Painter Who Has Become Famous in
Paris," appears in *Current Literature*.

November. Visits the United States for first
solo exhibition at American Art Galleries,
New York; remains until May 1909.

December. "Henry O. Tanner, Exile for Art's
Sake," by William R. Lester, appears in *Alexander's Magazine*.

Bishop Benjamin Tucker Tanner, c. 1900.

1909   April. Elected associate member of National Academy of Design (along with Mary
Cassatt and George Bellows).

June and July. Henry's autobiographical "The Story of an Artist's Life" appears in two
issues of the *World's Work*.

Fall. Jesse attends Hillcrest School at Folkestone (Kent), England, through 1914; funded
by Atherton Curtis.

1906   Summer. Paris, American Art Students' Club. *Two Disciples at the Tomb*.

October. Chicago, Art Institute. *Two Disciples at the Tomb*; awarded Harris Prize for "the most impressive and distinguished work of art of the season" and purchased for permanent collection.

1907   January. Philadelphia, Pennsylvania Academy of the Fine Arts. *Return of the Holy Women, Two Disciples at the Tomb*.
January. Paris, Société Internationale de Peinture et Sculpture. *Christ at the Home of Mary and Martha, The Disciples See Christ Walking on the Water, Hebron*.

April. Pittsburgh, Carnegie Institute. *Christ at the Home of Mary and Martha, Nicodemus*; former purchased for permanent collection.

October. Chicago, Art Institute. *Judas Covenanting with the High Priests*.

November. St. Louis, City Art Museum, exhibition of six American artists resident in Paris. *Daniel in the Lions' Den, The Disciples See Christ Walking Upon the Water, Escape of Paul, Hebron, Moonlight, Jew of Jerusalem, Judas*.

1908   January. Chicago, Art Institute, exhibition of six American artists resident in Paris (see November 1907, St. Louis).
January. Philadelphia, Pennsylvania Academy of the Fine Arts. *Nicodemus*.

April. Pittsburgh, Carnegie Institute. *The Ox-Cart*.

May. Paris, Salon. *Les Vierges Folles et les Vierges Sages* [*The Wise and Foolish Virgins*]; hung in Salon d'Honneur.

Summer. Antwerp, Triennial Exhibition, Paris Society of American Painters. *Moise et le Buisson Ardent* [*Moses and the Burning Bush*].

October. Chicago, Art Institute. *Ruth and Naomi*.
October. Kansas City, Missouri, Fine Arts Institute. *Two Disciples at the Tomb*.

December. New York, American Art Galleries, first major solo exhibition. *Abraham's Oak, Behold, the Bridegroom Cometh, Christ and Nicodemus, Christ at the Home of Mary and Martha, Christ on the Road to Bethany, Christ Washing the Disciples' Feet, Daniel in the Lions' Den, Death of Judas, The Disciples See Christ Walking on the Water, Escape of Paul, Flight into Egypt* (2), *The Good Shepherd, He Vanished Out of Their Sight, Head of Old Jew, Hebron, The Hiding of Moses, Hills near Jerusalem, Jerusalem Types* (4), *Judas Covenanting with the High Priests, Mary, Mary Pondered All These Things in Her Heart, Moonlight—Hebron, Moses and the Burning Bush, Nicodemus, Night (After the Denial by Peter), Night of the Nativity, On the Road to Emmaus, Return of the Holy Women, Two Disciples at the Tomb, The Wise Men*.
December. Paris, Société Internationale de Peinture et Sculpture.

1909   January. Philadelphia, Pennsylvania Academy of the Fine Arts. *Behold the Bridegroom Cometh, The Hiding of Moses*.

April. Pittsburgh, Carnegie Institute. *The Hiding of Moses*.

May. Buffalo, Fine Arts Academy. *Behold, the Bridegroom Cometh, Two Disciples at the Tomb*.

June. Seattle, Alaska-Yukon Pacific Exposition. *Christ and Nicodemus*.

September. St. Louis, City Art Museum. *The Wise and Foolish Virgins, Two Disciples at the Tomb*.

Jesse Tanner, January, 1911.

1911   January. "Henry O. Tanner" entry appears in eleventh edition of *Encyclopaedia Britannica*.

Janaury–April. Visits United States to attend solo exhibition at Thurber Art Galleries, Chicago; also visits Philadelphia and New York.

March. "Henry O. Tanner's Biblical Pictures" by F. J. Campbell appears in *Fine Arts Journal*.

1912   Tanners return to former studio-apartment at 51 boulevard Saint-Jacques, which Henry will keep until 1934.

March–June. Travels to Tangier and other cities in Morocco.

Purchases land at Trépied, Picardy.

1913   January–March. Visits United States to attend solo exhibition at Thurber Art Galleries, Chicago; also visits Muskegon, Michigan, Milwaukee, Philadelphia, and New York.

January. Henry and Jessie attend annual conference of National Association for the Advancement of Colored People in Philadelphia.

Elected president of Société Artistique de Picardie, Le Touquet, Paris-Plage.

Sarah Elizabeth Miller Tanner, c. 1914.

1914   August 14. Sarah Elizabeth Miller Tanner dies.

August. With outbreak of war, Trépied evacuated. Tanners travel to England to reenroll Jesse in Hillcrest School.

1909   October. Chicago, Art Institute. *The Hiding of Moses.*

December. Indianapolis, Art Association, John Herron Art Institute. *Ruth and Naomi.*

1910   January. Buffalo, Albright Gallery. *Return of the Holy Women.*

May. Paris, Salon. *La Fuite en Egypte* [*Flight into Egypt*], *Les Trois Maries Approchant le Tombeau* [*The Three Marys Approaching the Tomb, The Three Marys*].
May. Berlin, Akademie der Künste. *Two Disciples at the Tomb, Mary Visiting Elizabeth.*
May. Pittsburgh, Carnegie Institute. *Mary, The Disciples See Christ Walking on the Water.*

September. St. Louis, City Art Museum. *Return of the Holy Women.*

October. Chicago, Art Institute. *Behold, the Bridegroom Cometh, Flight into Egypt, The Three Marys.*

December. Washington, D.C., Corcoran Gallery of Art. *Return of the Holy Women, The Three Marys.*

1911   February. Chicago, Thurber Art Galleries, solo exhibition. *Aldernay, Christ Learning to Read, Christ Walking on the Water* (2), *Disciples on the Sea of Galilee, Dunes near Etaples, Hebron, Hiding of Moses, Hills near Jerusalem, Holy Family, Mary Visiting Elizabeth, Morocco, Sand Dunes, Three Marys, Women of Bethlehem, A Yemen Jew.*

April. Pittsburgh, Carnegie Institute. *The Three Marys, Return of the Holy Women.*
April. Rome, Esposizione Internazionale. *The Supper at Emmaus.*

October. St. Louis, City Art Museum. *The Disciples.*

1912   November. Chicago, Art Institute. *Etaples Fisher Folk.*

December. Washington, D.C., Corcoran Gallery of Art. *Christ Learning to Read, Etaples Fisher Folk.*

1913   February. Chicago, Thurber Art Galleries, solo exhibition. *Christ at the Home of Lazarus, Christ Learning to Read, A Covered Street, Disciples on the Sea, Entry of El Mokri into Tangier, Entry to Kasbah, Foggy Moonrise, Hayricks at Trépied, Jew of Marakasch, Moonlight – Hebron, Moonlight – Old Buildings Outside* (2), *Moonlight – Palace of the Governor of Tangier, Moonlight – Road to Etaples, Moonrise – East Gate of the Kasbah, Moonrise near Kasbah, Moonrise – Walls of Tangier, The Mosque – Main Street, Road to Etaples, Street in Tangier, The Sultan's Stables* (2), *Windy Day at Trépied, Windy Moonlight.*

April. New York, Knoedler's Gallery, solo exhibition. *Christ at the Home of Lazarus, Christ Learning to Read, Entry of El Mokri into Tangier, Entry to Casbah, Etaples Fisher Folk, Foggy Moonrise, Hayricks at Trépied, Moonlight – Old Buildings Outside* (2), *Moonlight – Palace of the Governor of Tangier, Moonlight – Road to Etaples, Moonrise – East Gate of the Casbah, Moonrise – Walls of Tangier, Road to Etaples, The Sultan's Stables* (2), *Windy Day at Trépied, Women of Bethlehem.*

July. Le Touquet, Paris-Plage, Société Artistique de Picardie. *Mary, Etaples, Tangier* (4).

Fall. New York, emancipation celebration exhibition with African-American artists Clyde T. Boykin and Richard Lonsdale Brown, who also served as curator.

November. Chicago, Art Institute. *Palace of Justice, Tangier, Jesus Learning to Read.*

1914   January. Chicago, Art Institute. *A Street in Tangier.*

April. Pittsburgh, Carnegie Institute. *Miraculous Haul of Fishes.*

May. Paris, Salon. *Christ dans la Maison de Lazare* [*Christ at the Home of Lazarus*], *Marie* [*Mary*].

1914   September. Return to Trépied, where Tanners become involved in relief work.

Henry becomes member of American Negro Academy, Washington, D.C.

1915   January–April. Visits Philadelphia, New York, and Chicago.

May–June. Brief visit to England.

1916   Winter. Tanners reside at Vittel, health resort in Vosges Mountains.

May. Jessie returns to Trépied, where she remains primarily until the end of the war.

1917   December. Henry serves in American Red Cross, France, until June 1919, first as lieutenant in Department of Public Information then as assistant director of Farm and Garden Services.

1918   Winter. Submits proposal, subsequently accepted, to American Red Cross, Bureau of Hospital Farms and Gardens, that calls for utilization of vacant land around hospitals and base depots for raising of potatoes and other garden vegetables by convalescent patients.

Fall. Makes sketches of Red Cross activities in the region of Vittel and Neufchâteau, Vosges.

1920–21   Tanners sell Les Charmes and build Edgewood, another summer house, at Trépied.

1921   Fall. Jesse enters Cambridge University to study mining engineering; again funded by Atherton Curtis.

Tanner, then lieutenant in the Red Cross, Vosges, France, 1918.

1914   July. Le Touquet, Paris-Plage, Société Artistique de Picardie.

August. Muskegon, Michigan, Hackley Art Gallery. *Holy Family*.

September. Shepherd's Bush, London, Anglo-American art exhibition. *Daniel in the Lions' Den*.

1915   February. San Francisco, Panama-Pacific Exposition. *Christ at the Home of Lazarus*; awarded gold medal.

1916   November. Chicago, Art Institute. *Return of the Holy Women*.

1917   Summer. Los Angeles, Museum of History, Science and Art, Harrison Collection Exhibition. *Moonrise, Walls of Tangier*.

1919   March. New York, Knoedler's Gallery, group exhibition of American artists; circulated to several Eastern and Midwestern cities.

October. Paris, Musée du Luxembourg, Exposition des Artistes de l'Ecole Americaine. *Les Pèlerins d'Emmaus*. Serves on Paris selection committee.

1920   June. Los Angeles, Museum of History, Science and Art. *Daniel in the Lions' Den*.

1921   January. Boston, Vose Galleries, solo exhibition. *The Arch, Christ and Nicodemus, Flight into Egypt* (2), *Governor's Palace, Tangier, Head of a Bethlehem Girl, Home of Jeanne d'Arc, Moonrise in Tangier, Old Gateway, Tangier, Return of the Holy Women*.

April. Pittsburgh, Carnegie Institute. *Christ at the Home of Lazarus, Old House, Neufchâteau, Vosges*.
April. Detroit, Institute of Arts. *Return of the Holy Women*.

August. New York, Public Library, 135th Street branch, first major exhibition of African-American artists in U.S. *Christ Washing the Feet of the Disciples, The Good Shepherd*.

Philadelphia, Wanamaker's Art Gallery. *Wise and Foolish Virgins, Flight into Egypt*.

1922   Washington, D.C., Dunbar High School. Tanner included in exhibition of African-American artists, organized by Tanner Art League, a group of artists and teachers, in studios of school.

April. Des Moines, Association of Fine Arts, solo exhibition. *The Arch, Christ in the Home of Lazarus, Christ Learning to Read, Christ Walking on the Water, Les Fêtes des Morts, Paris, Portrait of Booker T. Washington*.
April. Pittsburgh, Carnegie Institute. *The Hiding of Moses*.

September. St. Louis, City Art Museum. *Christ and Nicodemus*.

October. Kansas City, Missouri, Art Institute. *Le Touquet*.

1923   January 15. Bishop Benjamin Tucker Tanner dies.

Henry elected chevalier of Legion of Honor by French government.

December. Visits United States for last time, and remains until March 22, 1924. Rents studio at 246 Fulton Street, Brooklyn. Accepts commissions for a bronze tablet for Bethel Church, Philadelphia, and for a painting of *Nicodemus Coming to Christ* for Cheyney Training School for Teachers, Cheyney, Pennsylvania.

1924   Jesse graduated from Cambridge University and enters Royal School of Mines, London.

April. "Henry O. Tanner," by Jessie Fauset, appears in the *Crisis*.

1925   August. Cover of the *Crisis* features drawing of Tanner, together with W. E. B. Du Bois, Frederick Douglass, Alexandre Dumas, Paul Laurence Dunbar, and Samuel Coleridge-Taylor.

September 8. Jessie Macauley Olssen Tanner dies at Etaples, Pas-de-Calais; buried at Sceaux, Hauts-de-Seine.

1926   June. Jesse completes study in London and accepts position with geophysical department of Anglo-Persian Oil Company; a case of "nervous exhaustion" forces him to leave in October.

1927   October. Henry elected full academician of National Academy of Design.

Cover of the *Crisis*, August 1925, designed by Albert Alex Smith and featuring portraits of Henry O. Tanner, W. E. B. Du Bois, Frederick Douglass, Alexandre Dumas, Paul Laurence Dunbar, and Samuel Coleridge-Taylor.

1922 November. Richmond Public Art Gallery, Indiana. *Christ and Nicodemus*.

December. Columbus, Ohio, Gallery of Fine Arts. *Christ and Nicodemus*.

1923 March. New York, Grand Central Art Galleries, opening exhibition of Cooperative Gallery of Painters and Sculptors Association. *The Three Marys*.

April. Pittsburgh, Carnegie Institute. *Christ Learning to Read*.

September. St. Louis, City Art Museum. *Miraculous Haul of Fishes*.

November. Chicago, Art Institute. *Christ and Nicodemus*.

December. Washington, D.C., Corcoran Gallery of Art. *The Hiding of Moses*.

1924 January. New York, Grand Central Art Galleries, solo exhibition. *The Arch, Christ and Nicodemus, Christ at the Home of Lazarus, Christ in the Garden of Gethsemane, Christ Learning to Read, Flight into Egypt (2), The Futile Guard, Gateway—Tangier, The Good Shepherd (Lost Sheep), Governor's Palace, Tangier, Head of a Bethlehem Girl, The Hiding of Moses, Holy Family, Market Place, Tangier, Morocco, Mary, Miraculous Haul of Fishes, Moonrise in Tangier, The Other Disciple, Salomé*.

October. Chicago, Art Institute. *Miraculous Haul of Fishes*.

1925 October. Pittsburgh, Carnegie Institute. *Two Disciples at the Tomb*.
October. Paris, Galerie Charpentier, Exposition des Artistes Americains de France.

1926 April. Buffalo, Albright Art Gallery. *Two Disciples at the Tomb*.
April. Washington, D.C., Corcoran Gallery of Art. *Fisher Folk*.

October. Chicago, Art Institute. *Two Disciples at the Tomb*.
October. Pittsburgh, Carnegie Institute. *Arc de Triomphe*.

December. San Francisco, California Palace of the Legion of Honor. *Holy Family*.

1927 February. New York, National Arts Club. *Flight into Egypt (At the Gates)*; awarded bronze medal.

October. Chicago, Art Institute. *Etaples Fisher Folk*.

November. New York, National Academy of Design. *Miraculous Haul of Fishes*.
November. Chicago, Art Institute. *Flight into Egypt, The Poor Ye Have With You Always, The Three Marys, Two Disciples at the Tomb*.

December. Chicago, Carson, Pirie, Scott Art Gallery. *The Poor Ye Have With You Always*.

1930   Joins European chapter of American Artists Professional League.

1932   Joins Allied Artists of America, New York.

1934   June. Moves to last studio-apartment, 43 rue de Fleurus.

Henry Ossawa Tanner, early 1920s.

1937   May 25. Henry Ossawa Tanner dies in Paris; buried at Sceaux, Hauts-de-Seine.

1928   October. Chicago, Art Institute. *Christ at the Home of Lazarus.*
October. Washington, D.C., Corcoran Gallery of Art. *Destruction of Sodom and Gomorrah.*

1929   October. Chicago, Art Institute. *Destruction of Sodom and Gomorrah.*

November. New York, Grand Central Art Galleries.

1930   May. Venice, Esposizione Biennale Internazionale d'Arte. Included in American pavilion organized by Grand Central Art Galleries.

November. New York, Grand Central Art Galleries. *Etaples Fisher Folk;* awarded Walter L. Clark prize.

1931   February. New York, Art Centre, Harmon Foundation exhibition.

April. New York, Grand Central Art Galleries. *The Arch* [*Arc de Triomphe*].

1932   October. New York, International Art Center of Roerich Museum.

1933   April. Brooklyn, Brooklyn Museum, twentieth annual exhibition of Allied Artists of America. *Etaples Fisher Folk.*

May. Chicago, Art Institute. *Two Disciples at the Tomb.*

June. Paris, Simonson Galleries, American Artists Professional League. *The Good Shepherd, The Governor's Palace, Tangier, Moonlight.*

1934   April. Brooklyn, Brooklyn Museum, twenty-first annual exhibition of Allied Artists of America. *Destruction of Sodom and Gomorrah.*

1935   March. Washington, D.C., Corcoran Gallery of Art. *Return from the Cross.*

May. New York, Fine Arts Building, twenty-second annual exhibition of Allied Artists of America.

1936   Rockford Art Museum, Illinois. *Two Disciples at the Tomb.*

NOTE TO USE OF THE CATALOGUE

The entries that follow represent the authors' best efforts to establish a fresh chronology for Tanner's works. This task is complicated by the artist's tendency throughout much of his career to return to similar subjects and often identical titles for his paintings, and by his working methods, which, particularly toward the end of his life, did not preclude reworking earlier canvases. When the title under which a picture was first exhibited is known, it is used; in a few cases new titles are proposed based on close reading of the subject matter. Traditional or alternative titles are given in parentheses. The chapters that precede each group of entries give an overview of the artist's development during five periods in his life; their titles indicate the focus of his work during that time. The entries themselves appear in chronological order, except where it seems appropriate to group several works because of the common subject matter they address or their special role in Tanner's oeuvre.

Height precedes width for all measurements.

Notes to the catalogue as well as provenance and exhibition history during Tanner's lifetime for each work can be found at the back of the book, beginning on page 290.

CATALOGUE

CHAPTERS BY

DEWEY F. MOSBY

CATALOGUE ENTRIES BY

DEWEY F. MOSBY AND DARREL SEWELL

STUDENT YEARS

AND EARLY CAREER

1873–1890

At the age of forty, Henry Tanner recalled about his childhood: "Like many children, I had drawn upon my slate to the loss of my lessons,"[1] and "Never had it crossed my mind that I should be an artist, nor had I even wished to be."[2] Nothing in Tanner's early background suggested that he would develop into an artist of international renown: his father was a minister, and Henry was not exposed to art and artists as a young boy. Furthermore, there were virtually no African-American artists of an older generation to set an example.

The young Tanner's artistic educational milieu was quite different from that of other artists who would later play a role in his life. For example, one of his future teachers, Thomas Eakins (1844–1916), attended Central High School, the most prestigious in Philadelphia and the only one to include a formal drawing course in its curriculum.[3] Tanner's Roberts Vaux Consolidated School for Colored Students offered drawing only as a practical skill, useful for developing elegant penmanship, and making maps and mechanical drawings. Joseph Pennell (1860–1926), a nearly exact contemporary of Tanner from Philadelphia, began his artistic training with watercolor lessons from his father at around age four.[4] One of Tanner's later colleagues in Paris, a painter of delicate interior views, Walter Gay (1856–1937), from Hingham, Massachusetts, would remember watching his uncle W. A. Gay (1821–1910) paint and listening to him talk about France.[5]

In the summer of 1872, around the time of his thirteenth birthday, Tanner was walking with his father in their neighborhood at Fairmount Park when they saw a painter at work. He vividly recalled that "the subject the artist had chosen was a middle distance hillside with a magnificent elm in bold relief."[6] He watched for an hour and decided on the spot to become an artist. With encouragement from his mother and fifteen cents, Henry acquired basic art supplies and embarked upon a course of self-training as a landscape painter. He recollected:

> I went straight to the spot where I had seen the artist of the day before. Don't you suppose a boy, trying to hold a canvas between his knees and mix dry colors upon a pasteboard palette, might be liable to get things mixed? Well, I did. Whether I got the most paint upon the canvas, upon myself, or upon the ground, it would be hard to tell. But I was happy, supremely so, there can be no doubt.[7]

During the ensuing school year Tanner's enthusiasm did not wane. He began to study works by professional artists exhibited on Chestnut Street at James S. Earle and Sons and in the window of Bailey's Jewelry Store. Returning home, he would make renditions from memory of the pictures he had seen. Tanner also perused art journals, probably in his father's substantial library; he reported that he "decided to become America's great marine painter"[8] based on an article he had read.

By 1875 Tanner recognized that he needed formal training, a decision accompanied by great consternation. He had felt the bitter sting of racial discrimination from time to time during his childhood but now it would affect his chosen profession:[9] "No man or boy to whom this country is a land of 'equal chances' can realize what heartaches this question caused me, and with what trepidation and nervousness I made the round of the studios. The question was not, would the teacher have a boy who knew nothing and had little money, but would he have someone like me, or would he keep me after he found out who I was?"[10] Tanner's worst fears were realized when one studio master informed him that he "had other pupils."[11] However, Isaac L. Williams (1817–95), a painter of landscapes and interiors, agreed to take him for two dollars a session, which offered the prospect of twenty-five lessons because Tanner had saved fifty dollars for this purpose.[12] But the exercises set by Williams proved so prosaic that Tanner quit after one lesson and continued on his own: "I plodded along as best I could without instruction."[13]

Tanner's career as an artist began in earnest in the summer of 1876. He was in Atlantic City, New Jersey, where a black resort industry with many seasonal employees was developing,[14] and his work caught the attention of Henry Price, an amateur artist spending the summer there. He treated Tanner with kindness and received him in his Philadelphia home to live and work for over a year.[15] Tanner expressed his interest in attending the Pennsylvania Academy of the Fine Arts, which had just reopened in a new building, but Price discouraged him. Eventually Price ended the relationship abruptly, and Tanner was again without an art teacher.[16]

During this period, Tanner continued his general education. He noted modestly that he left school in the regular course of events,[17] but in fact Tanner was valedictorian of his class of ten, graduating on July 6, 1877, from Roberts Vaux Grammar School. The subject of his valedictory address was compulsory education.[18]

After Tanner's graduation, the Reverend Tanner was reluctant to allow him to pursue the uncertain career of an artist. Instead he was placed with a family friend to learn the flour business. Tanner's determination to become an artist did not wane: "But belief in myself did not fail, nor my ardor flag. To do any painting now, I had to be up with the dawn to seize the precious minutes of light before seven, when I had to be off to the humbler, though more useful, avocation of selling flour."[19] This proved to be too strenuous, and he became severely ill. His parents acquiesced and not only supported Henry's effort to become an artist but assisted him financially, as they would for several years.[20] Benjamin Tanner's later admiration for his son's tenacity seems evident in a passage in his *Hints to Ministers* of 1902: "All men who have amounted to much or even a little in this world, have had as it were a guiding star— some omnipresent object, which has been their thought by day and dream by night. In the eyes of some it has been money; in others medicine; in others art."[21]

Sometime in 1878–79, Tanner recovered from his illness at Wardner's Rainbow Lake Inn in the Adirondack Mountains. The inn was widely advertised as a haven for health seekers, and it was inexpensive,[22] but perhaps even more appealing was the resort's location in the area where Gerrit Smith, an abolitionist, had celebrated the twelfth anniversary of British emancipation of the West Indies on August 1, 1846, by offering free blacks 100,000 acres of his Adirondack land on easy terms.[23] Also significant for the Tanner family must have been the proximity of John Brown's farm, established in 1848 amid the black colony at North Elba (Keane, New York), not far from Rainbow Lake;[24] Benjamin Tanner was an officer of a committee of black people in Pittsburgh who had resolved in the year of Henry's birth to honor "John Brown, a hero, patriot and Christian."[25]

During his stay at Rainbow Lake, Tanner was exposed to the work of the successful painter Arthur Fitzwilliam Tait (1819–1905), who lived and worked at Long Lake in the Adirondacks for most of the second half of the nineteenth century. Paintings made by Tanner at the time of his Adirondack sojourn show a predilection for animal and hunting themes favored by Tait (cat. no. 5).[26]

The trip to the Adirondacks worked wonders for Henry's health. He wrote: "That some change was desirable, and even necessary, cannot be doubted, so much so that, when my dear mother, who was used to my more or less delicate health, finally saw me off on my journey, she never expected, as she afterward told me, to see me return alive. But I did get there and return alive, and I must always believe that it was the good God who opened the way and gave me good friends, thus filling me with confidence in the future which never deserted me in those darkest days."[27]

Tanner was back in Philadelphia by November 1879, when he inscribed *Ship in a Storm* (cat. no. 4) to Bishop Daniel A. Payne (1811–93), a family friend and the founder of Wilberforce University in 1856. Around this time, Tanner probably made the acquaintance of Christopher High Shearer (1840–1926), a landscape painter from Reading, Pennsylvania, who became a close friend, confidant, and a source of professional inspiration.[28]

It could have been through Shearer that Tanner met William Wilson Cowell (1856–1920). Tanner noted in his autobiography: "How well I remember 'A Foggy Morning' by Cowell — in whose studio I afterward worked."[29] Cowell's studio seems to have provided Tanner with his first experience of a professional artistic ambience, although Tanner was not Cowell's pupil in any formal sense. Tanner's desire to study at the Pennsylvania Academy of the Fine Arts was rekindled, perhaps as a result of his tenure at Cowell's and a long article illustrated with works by Academy students which appeared in an 1879 issue of *Scribner's Monthly*.[30]

Tanner registered as a student in the antique class at the Academy on December 4, 1879.[31] The Academy did not prohibit attendance by blacks; in a letter of more than a year earlier, on September 30, 1878, Fairman Rogers, chairman of the Academy's Committee on Instruction, had concluded: "My own opinion is that the time has passed for such distinctions to be recognized."[32] Yet admission of an African-American student still seemed controversial enough that the next year the chairman reopened the matter for discussion. A passage in the autobiography of illustrator Joseph Pennell almost certainly applies to Tanner. Pennell and a group of obstreperous friends had been expelled from the Pennsylvania Museum and School of Industrial Art in Philadelphia in late November 1879, and they enrolled in the Academy at about the same time as Tanner:

There was every kind of man and boy, from sixty to twenty, in that class, except black men, and one day the Chairman of the School Committee appeared [with] a solemn announcement that he was coming. . . . [The] Chairman came in state, accompanied by the Secretary, other members of the Committee, and the Professor [Thomas Eakins]. And he said something like this. A drawing has been sent in and passed. The person who made it has been notified that he is admitted to the school. He has come and the Secretary has seen him. He is a colored man. Now there is no rule in the Pennsylvania Academy of Fine Arts excluding people of color from the school. But, knowing the feeling on the subject, I have placed the matter before the Antique Class; and I wish the Life Class to meet and decide whether he should be admitted. We met, and we decided that we had no objection. I do not remember a dissenting voice.[33]

Pennell, a self-described "conceited prig" and an overt racist, continued:

He came, he was young, an octoroon, very well dressed, far better than most of us. . . . He worked at night in the Antique, and last of all, he drew very well. I do not think that he stopped long in the Antique—the faintest glimmer of any artistic sense in a student, and he was run right into the Life. He was quiet and modest, and he "painted too," it seemed, "among his other accomplishments." We were interested at first, but he soon passed almost unnoticed, though the room was hot.[34]

When Tanner entered the Pennsylvania Academy, tuition was free once a student passed the entrance examination. The curriculum was divided into antique, life, modeling, and composition classes, and lectures.[35] Thomas Eakins, a charismatic teacher who was named director of the Academy in 1880, was in charge of the courses that dealt with drawing from antique casts and painting from live models.[36] Academy students were not initiated to the classes; in the life course, for example, "one just went in at the beginning of the pose, drew a number, sat down and began to work."[37] The professors did not attend classes every day but appeared intermittently to provide critiques and demonstrations.[38] Tanner recounted an incident which had a profound impact on his artistic formation:

About this time, Mr. Thomas Eakins, under whom I was studying at the Pennsylvania Academy of Fine Arts, gave me a criticism which aided me then, and ever since; it may apply to all walks of life, I will "pass it along." I had made a start on a study, which was not altogether bad, but very probably the best thing I had ever done. He encouraged but, instead of working to make it better, I became afraid I should destroy what I had done, and really did nothing the rest of the week. Well, he was disgusted. "What have you been doing? Get it, get it better, or get it worse. No middle ground of compromise."[39]

Thomas Hovenden (1840–95), another successful painter in Philadelphia who became an instructor at the Academy after Eakins's dismissal in 1886, also played a pivotal role in Tanner's development as an artist.[40] W. S. Scarborough, a friend of the Tanner family, recounted in 1902 that Hovenden infused in Tanner "a comprehension of and sympathy with the broader and deeper things of life and art."[41] Hovenden's narrative genre paintings of the 1880s might have intrigued Tanner, especially for their sympathetic and dignified treatments of African-Americans.

Tanner's exact tenure at the Pennsylvania Academy of the Fine Arts is difficult to determine. After his initial registration on December 4, 1879, his name appears once more in Academy records, on January 4, 1881, in the list of students in the life class, but not after that. The Academy began to charge tuition in the fall of 1882, and perhaps Tanner, like a number of other students whose names disappear from the rolls at this time, could not afford the fee. However, the minutes of the Committee on Instruction for January 30, 1884, show that Eakins successfully petitioned the committee to admit Tanner as a free student in the life class. Tanner himself recalled that he had been a student of Eakins "for four or five years."[42] Perhaps he attended the Academy informally in the intervening years or received private criticism from Eakins. In any case, Eakins evidently took a personal interest in Tanner. The sensitive, eloquent portrait that Eakins painted of Tanner in 1902 (page 34) suggests a closer acquaintance between the two men than customary between teacher and student.

Tanner exhibited several (unidentified) works in the window of Meade and Robbins Jewelry Store, on Chestnut Street, in February and April of 1880. He made his debut in a museum exhibition in April 1880 at the prestigious Pennsylvania Academy of the Fine Arts annual, which Academy students could enter without submitting to the jurying process that screened the work of established artists. He showed two works, *Pursuing Cavalry* and *Hazy Morning at Narragansett* (locations unknown). These paintings caught the attention of an unidentified gentleman who, according to the *Christian Recorder* for April 29, 1880, offered to send Tanner "to Rome . . . to study the work of the old masters."[43] Although this trip did not materialize, study in Europe was clearly one of Tanner's goals. In 1881 he sent two more works to the Academy annual, and between 1881 and 1883 he made one of his first sales, to the local collector Edward Lawrence Scull (see cat. no. 8). Tanner continued as an enrolled student at the Academy, where he also learned bronze casting and photography.

Despite his progress as a painter, by November 1881 Tanner was "lying very ill, suffering from hemorrhage of the nose."[44] Perhaps his malaise was associated with the prejudice he encountered from racist individuals such as Joseph Pennell and his circle.[45] Pennell recalled an incident in his autobiography some forty-five years later: "One night we were walking down Broad Street, he with us, when from a crowd of people of his color who were walking up the street, came a greeting, 'Hullo, George Washington, howse yer gettin' on wid yer White fren's?' Then he began to assert himself and, to cut a long story short, one night his easel was carried out into the middle of Broad Street and, though not painfully crucified, he was firmly tied to it and left there. And this is my only experience of my colored brothers in a White school; but it was enough. Curiously, there never has been a great Negro or Jew artist in the history of the world."[46]

Pennell's account of this disgraceful event helps us to understand Tanner's own anguish: "I was extremely timid, and to be made to feel that I was not wanted, although in a place where I had every right to be, even months afterward caused me sometimes weeks of pain. Every time any one of these disagreeable incidents came into my mind, my heart sank, and I was anew tortured by the thought of what I had endured, almost as much as by the incident itself."[47]

Tanner was ill until the spring of 1892, but the good care of his mother and the vigilance of many friends aided his recovery.[48] Christopher Shearer was among the friends Tanner cherished and clearly was the antithesis of Pennell. Tanner remembered:

> I can never too highly appreciate his personal service to me and how his kindly nature and gentle disposition helped to reduce the bitterness I (at times) had in my life, and gave me a more hopeful view of my own individual situation; in fact, a visit to him

always renewed my courage, not that courage which was necessary for my work but the courage that was necessary to overcome some of the unkind things I had to struggle with. . . . It was he who first gave me the idea that I might have qualities that, cultivated, would be of great help in the battle of life. And it was done in a manner hardly to be calculated upon. It was by believing in me, and how necessary it is to have some one (besides one's family) to believe in you.[49]

Tanner's first published notice from an art critic came in response to the display of one of his paintings in the window of Hazeltine's Gallery on Chestnut Street in March 1884. The review of *The Battle of Life* (location unknown), a picture of an elk attacked by wolves, appeared in the *Philadelphia Press*: "The painting is attracting attention, not only for its real merit, but for the fact that it was painted by a young colored man, a student at the Academy of Fine Arts . . . [and] has received many favorable criticisms from prominent artists."[50] The reviewer concluded with an account of Tanner's racial awareness: "Mr. Tanner thinks that his race has an adaptability to art, if only it is given an opportunity."[51] The notice also contained a revealing observation on Tanner's goal in early 1884: "It is his ambition, and he thinks his forte, to become an animal painter, and he is certainly making good progress."[52] Tanner later described his aim: "I met a young animal painter, J. N. Hess (now dead), and learned from him that animal painters were even less numerous than good marine painters, and that we were even less well represented in this field—so, in order that America should not always be in such a deplorable plight, I renounced this inviting field of [marine] painting to become an American Landseer."[53] Tanner's decision could have also been prompted by the fact that his teacher and friend Thomas Eakins was a passionate animal lover.[54]

Tanner sent *The Battle of Life* to the World's Industrial and Cotton Centennial Exhibition in New Orleans, which opened in December of 1884, where it was seen by the Reverend William J. Simmons, an organizer of the African-American section. Simmons wrote an important statement on the artist for his book, *Men of Mark*, published three years later: "His pictures take high rank. No favoritism is shown in the selection to enter the academies and galleries of this country. Each specimen must pass the committee of eminent men, who are art critics of long standing. This is stated lest many think he is patronized by rich men, or through the influence of his father, or because someone takes pity on him, trying to help a colored man to rise. No! It is merit; let that be understood at once. Perseverance, pluck and brains is my young man's capital."[55]

Tanner's New York debut came in April 1885 at the National Academy of Design, followed by the sale of a painting entitled *Lion at Home* (location unknown). In September of 1886 he opened his own studio at 927 Chestnut Street, not far from Thomas Eakins's studio and the Art Students' League.

The picture that emerges of Henry O. Tanner by the mid 1880s is one of individualism. He had gained control over the tools of his profession as taught at the Pennsylvania Academy, but he never became an imitator of his teachers' styles or their subject matter. Tanner was so inspired by his successes up to this point that he decided to take on his first historical subject, traditionally among the most ambitious for a painter. He chose the tale of Androcles (see cat. no. 12), which proved to be beyond his present ability, although he noted: "I learned some things in my failures."[56]

In July of 1882 Tanner was commissioned to complete drawings for illustrations in *Our Continent* (cat. nos. 10, 11), and throughout the 1880s he sent black and white drawings every month or so to New York publishers.[57] His first success with these random submissions came in 1887 when *Harper's Young People* accepted an illustration for Kate Upson Clark's "Old Win-ne-wan's Star" (cat. no. 9). In November 1887 Tanner attended the African Methodist Episcopal Church conference in Jacksonville, Florida, and stayed on with Bishop Daniel A. Payne to "spend the winter in sketching and painting such natural objects as may arrest his attention."[58] The painter also traveled to Enterprise, Florida, on Lake Monroe north of Orlando. Titles of untraced pictures suggest that the African-American artist returned to marine themes: *Evening on the St. John's* and *Lake Monroe.*[59] Tanner returned to Philadelphia by February 1888, and his family spent the next summer in Atlantic City, where the artist painted one of his most beautiful landscapes (cat. no. 15).

In January 1889 Tanner attempted to unite business with art by opening a photography studio in Atlanta.[60] His biographer, Marcia Mathews, attributed the selection of Atlanta to the fact that the city was a center for African-American education and the site of Morris Brown College, which was founded in 1880 by the African Methodist Episcopal Church.[61]

Tanner expected that the business would leave him with time to paint, but he recalled: "I had so much more leisure than I had calculated upon, and this so distressed me, that I could not work."[62] No paintings (or photographs) have been identified as belonging to this Atlanta sojourn.[63] Tanner was able to meet expenses with earnings from the studio, but eventually he sold it with great satisfaction. The most significant result of this venture was meeting Joseph Crane Hartzell, a bishop in the Methodist Episcopal Church. He and his wife provided moral support for Tanner and were soon to become his patrons.[64]

In the summer of 1889 Tanner traveled from Atlanta to the Highlands, North Carolina, southwest of Asheville, with the thought that he could make a living with his camera and, at the same time, profit from the mountain air. He had very little money and got by on a diet of cornmeal and applesauce. His situation improved with a commission to photograph a small cottage: "I made photographs of the whole immediate region, a most lovely country, and, as no photographer had ever visited it before, they were a success, and my hard times—very hard times—vanished as the mountain mist before the sun."[65] Tanner's use of the camera may account for the paucity of drawn and painted sketches of North Carolina, but the beautiful region did yield a few finished paintings such as *Mountain Landscape, Highlands, North Carolina* (cat. no. 13).

While in the Highlands, Tanner made the acquaintance of the family of Wesley N. Clifford, with whom he became lifelong friends.[66] Clifford taught at Clark University and might have worked with Bishop Hartzell to secure a post there for Tanner. When Tanner returned to Atlanta in the fall, he taught drawing at Clark. It has been suggested that the artist remained at the black Methodist institution until 1893;[67] however, this notion is incorrect, and no real documentation confirms what

Tanner did at the college. He did make contacts that led to an opportunity to attempt a new genre: Professor William H. Crogman commissioned a portrait (location unknown).

Tanner probably missed the artistic ambience that he had enjoyed in Philadelphia, and he clearly had little contact with local artists. Bishop Hartzell wrote: "While Tanner was in Atlanta he encountered a former schoolmate and personal friend from the days of the Pennsylvania Academy. He was the leading White artist in Atlanta. Unfortunately, however, since the southern mores rigidly prohibited any social intercourse between Whites and Negroes, the two surreptitiously arranged to meet secretly in the room of the White artist whereupon he eagerly sought Tanner's criticism of his works."[68] Carlyn G. Crannell Romeyn has identified Tanner's friend in Atlanta from the Pennsylvania Academy as Harry Wilson Barnitz (1863–1914)[69] and also connected Tanner with the successful Atlanta portrait painter James Field.[70] Field left for Europe in 1890 to study at the Académie Julian in Paris, and his departure must have rekindled Tanner's own desire for European travel.

To raise funds for his trip, Mrs. Hartzell suggested an exhibition of Tanner's work in her hometown of Cincinnati, where the A.M.E. Church had its board of education.[71] Tanner's first solo exhibition was arranged for two or three weeks in December 1890. A warm review effectively summarized the African-American artist's early career:

> Mr. H. O. Tanner is a young colored man on his way to Rome, who has some good things on exhibition at the Methodist Book Concern. The gem of the collection is a marine, the surf dashing over the break-water at Atlantic City, a picture in which he has water that has a feeling of wetness to it. A scene in Western North Carolina — some hemlocks with a storm just breaking — is a somber but impressive picture. Another fetching thing represents an old colored man taking his little cotton to market on a rattle-trap ox-cart. It is a thing containing some good drawing and excellent coloring. Deer coming to drink in the Adirondacks form the subject of another piece of work.[72]

When, despite this critical interest, nothing sold from the exhibition, Bishop and Mrs. Hartzell bought the entire collection for a sum sufficient to permit Tanner to travel to Europe.[73] Whether Tanner went to Cincinnati for the exhibition is unknown, as is the date that he left Atlanta, but he was certainly back in Philadelphia before the end of the year, when he sat for a Tanner family photograph (see p. 22). He recalled receiving seventy-five dollars for a commission from a Mr. E — in order to help with European expenses,[74] raising the tempting speculation that Thomas Eakins was the source; Eakins was known to aid his students financially in exchange for work rendered.[75]

December 1890 marked the end of Tanner's formative American period. He was a well-trained artist who had enjoyed a modicum of public acclaim. But, as was the case for numerous American artists before and after him, he was lured by European study and the glamour surrounding it. After a farewell party given by his parents in Philadelphia,[76] Tanner set sail on the *City of Chester* for Rome, via Liverpool and Paris, on January 4, 1891.[77]   DFM

1

HARBOR SCENE
1876
Oil on canvas board glued to Masonite
14 × 20" (35.56 × 50.8 cm)
Signed and dated lower left: monogram signature/1876
John Quincy Johnson, Sharon, Massachusetts

2

SEASCAPE — JETTY
c. 1876–79
Oil on canvas
12 × 17" (30.48 × 43.18 cm)
Signed lower left: monogram signature
Estate of Sadie T. M. Alexander

3

SEASCAPE
c. 1876–79
Oil on canvas board
12 × 8" (30.48 × 20.32 cm)
Signed lower right: monogram signature
Private collection

4

SHIP IN A STORM
1879
Oil on academy board
10 1/16 × 6" (25.56 × 15.24 cm)
Signed and dated lower right: monogram signature/79
Inscribed verso: *Compliments of Henry O. Tanner to Bishop Daniel A. Payne, November 5, 1879*
Mr. and Mrs. E. T. Williams, Jr., New York

Writing in 1909 about his first paintings, Henry Tanner recalled, "After school, I would often go down on Chestnut Street, to see the pictures in Earle's Galleries, or in the window of Bailey's jewelry store. How well I remember 'A Foggy Morning,' by Cowell—in whose studio I afterward worked; or 'A Morning at Long Beach,' by Senat; how much better the numerous 'Storm at Sea,' by Hamilton, and still more numerous 'Breezy Day off Dieppe,' by Briscoe; how, after drinking my full of these art wonders, I would hurry home and paint what I had seen, and what fun it was!"[1]

Tanner's paragons at this time, when he was about thirteen, were painters of marine subjects. His interest was more than casual: "This was not a matter of chance, it was choice—caused by the fact that at this time . . . I had decided to become America's great marine painter. This decision had been prompted by an article I had seen in some art journal to the effect that the crying need of America was a great marine painter."[2]

Among the men Tanner mentioned, Prosper Senat (1852–1925), W. W. Cowell (1856–1920), and Franklin Dulin Briscoe (1844–1901) were all local artists, then relatively young. They devoted much of their careers to marine subjects in the manner of their teacher, Edward Moran (1829–1901). Inspired by the more conservative seascapes of England's J. M.W. Turner (1775–1851), Moran was well known for expansive views of ships scudding through white-capped green waves set against blue skies and billowing clouds, or heroic scenes of men in small boats rescuing the crews and passengers of ships foundering in stormy weather (fig. 1). The most famous artist Tanner listed is James Hamilton (1819–78) who, with Moran, set the standard for marine painting in Philadelphia in the mid-nineteenth century. Hamilton was influenced by the more expressionistic aspects of Turner's style, and his depictions of sea battles and storms at sea, and his thickly textured, loosely painted canvases, with their vivid color, won him the title of "the American Turner" even before he had seen Turner's work firsthand.

Five marine paintings by Tanner are known to survive, and while they demonstrate his early abilities as an artist, they provide few clues to his development over the three-year period they represent. Tanner's first known painting is *Harbor Scene* (cat. no. 1), dated 1876. Benjamin T. Johnson, grandson of Halle Tanner Dillon Johnson, Tanner's sister, to whom he gave this painting, referred to it in his will as "my Atlantic City painting," perhaps providing a more specific locale for the subject, and establishing a date for an event Tanner described in his autobiography: "The next school vacation, while at Atlantic City, a sketch of a wrecked schooner driven ashore during a great storm, seemed to have enough in it to attract the attention of Mr. X —, an amateur artist, spending the summer at this place."[3]

Harbor Scene shows in the distance a tall masted ship docked at a warehouse, smaller boats sailing on an inner channel, and in the foreground, the marshy edge of the harbor with a two-story structure at the right. Rowboats and a sailboat are moored in channels between the narrow fingers of swampy ground; a man strains against a rowboat line; and two men gather around a smoky fire in the middle distance. Vignettes of harbor life appear as details in paintings by Briscoe and Senat; this unprepossessing backwater view suggests that the young painter's shyness precluded a busier vantage.

The range of colors used in *Harbor Scene* is extremely limited, the technique of laying on the paint is tentative, and difficulties with perspective misconstrue the building to the right and a foreground rowboat. Yet the color harmonies are nicely considered, with little similarity to the palette conventions of the Philadelphia marine painters. The complexities of a spacious view with many boats, buildings, and figures in action were an ambitious undertaking for a young painter. While naive in many ways, *Harbor Scene* stands as evidence of Tanner's artistic potential at the age of sixteen or seventeen.

This painting might be the work exhibited as *Atlantic City I Let House* [sic] at the Workingmen's Art Exhibition in Philadelphia in 1880. Because it so clearly defines a style at the beginning of Tanner's career, *Harbor Scene* raises the question of whether the work entitled *After the Storm* (Washington, D.C., Evans-Tibbs Collection), which could be the "sketch of a wrecked schooner," was painted during the same visit to Atlantic City, or whether, considering its

2 SEASCAPE—JETTY

greater technical competence and unified color scheme, it was made during another visit a year or two later.

Seascape—Jetty (cat. no. 2) and *Seascape* (cat. no. 3) might be exercises in mastering the palettes and techniques of other Philadelphia marine painters. Approximately the same size, both works display a similar color range and address the problem of depicting waves breaking against rocks. Neither appears to be a directly observed view; they might have been done while Tanner was working in Cowell's studio. *Seascape* is more sophisticated, with bold brushstrokes individually placed to indicate patterned ripples in the water, the rugged texture of shoreline rocks, and streaks of clouds in the sky. As a technical study, it takes a step beyond the tentative, comparatively undefined brushwork of *Seascape—Jetty*, which seems closer to the 1876 *Harbor Scene*. Especially in its treatment of foam-capped waves, however, *Seascape—Jetty* is similar to the later *Ship in a Storm*, dated 1879 (cat. no. 4), which must have been painted near the end of Tanner's early preoccupation with marine subjects.

Ship in a Storm is inscribed on the back to Daniel A. Payne, Benjamin Tanner's superior in the A.M.E. Church and a friend of the Tanner family. An early supporter of Tanner's artistic efforts, Payne "admired most heartily and encouraged steadily this budding genius."[4] Tanner would have wanted to present Payne with one of his best works, yet the limited colors of the small canvas and its conventional subject, probably derived from another artist's work, are much less ambitious than *Harbor Scene* of three years before. Bishop Payne gave three seascapes (now lost) to Wilberforce University; in 1902 W. S. Scarborough, vice-president of the school, described one as "somewhat 'Turneresque' in its dashing impressionist style of representing a storm at sea, the other two, small panels, rich in coloring, giving thus a hint of future excellence."[5] One wonders whether *Ship in a Storm* is the painting described as "Turneresque," or if Scarborough was referring to a more elaborate and more accomplished work, still untraced.   DS

3 SEASCAPE

4 SHIP IN A STORM

5

FAUNA
c. 1878–79
Oil on canvas
38³/₈ × 29³/₄" (97.47 × 75.57cm)
Signed lower right: monogram signature
Hampton University Museum, Virginia

Fig. 2 Henry O. Tanner, *Flora*, c. 1880, oil on canvas, 38³/₈ × 29³/₄", Hampton University Museum, Virginia.

Fig. 3 Arthur Fitzwilliam Tait, *At Home*, 1893, oil on canvas, Springfield Science Museum, Massachusetts.

After Tanner graduated from high school in July 1877, his parents placed him in a flour business owned by a friend of his father. The work was too arduous for him, his health collapsed, and he was sent to Rainbow Lake in the Adirondacks to recuperate, although his mother later told him she never expected to see him return alive.[1] Tanner was then eighteen, so the year would have been 1878 or 1879.

Through friendship with a young Philadelphia painter, James N. Hess (1859–90), Tanner had learned that animal painters in America were even scarcer than marine painters "so, in order that America should not always be in such a deplorable plight," he determined "to become an American Landseer."[2]

Fauna (cat. no. 5), Tanner's first known animal subject, owes less to the example of the English-born Edwin Landseer than to the American animal painter Arthur Fitzwilliam Tait (1819–1905). Tanner made another convalescent trip to the Adirondacks in 1882, but stylistically the painting appears to come at this earlier point in his career, when he had gained some confidence and experience as an artist but before he entered the Pennsylvania Academy of the Fine Arts in December 1879.

Although *Fauna* and a companion painting known as *Flora* (fig. 2) were most likely inspired by Tanner's Adirondack stay, the present titles do not identify a location. *Flora* might be the painting Tanner exhibited at the Academy in 1881 under the name *Burnt Pines, Adirondacks*, and *Fauna* the work described as "deer coming to drink in the Adirondacks" in a review of an exhibition Tanner had in Cincinnati in December 1890.[3] Tanner probably stayed at Wardner's Rainbow Lake Inn, and he there apparently became acquainted with Tait's work. A well-established and popular painter of animals, birds, and hunting scenes, Tait spent his summers at nearby Long Lake. Although there is no specific evidence that the two met, a successful artist whose subjects coincided with Tanner's current enthusiasm surely would have been of interest. Tanner could have known Tait's work through many available prints, but the strong similarity between *Fauna* and a work by Tait such as *At Home* (fig. 3) suggests more than indirect contact.

The motif of deer surprised as they step out of a wooded hillside to drink at a stream is characteristic of Tait, although Tanner did not attempt to emulate his color scheme or smoothly finished surface. Stiff brushwork and anatomical awkwardness in the deer mark *Fauna* as an early painting; nonetheless the subject is boldly if naively painted, and the rich browns and greens of the forest floor create a softly glowing reflected light distinctive of Tanner's work.

A search of the exhibition records of the National Academy of Design in New York, where Tanner exhibited regularly during the 1880s, does not reveal a painting that might be *Fauna*. A review of a painting (now unlocated) shown at Hazeltine's Gallery in March 1884 indicates that Tanner did move on, at least temporarily, to works that followed Landseer's example in ennobling their subjects: "There is a picture that is attracting considerable attention at the Hazeltine's Gallery on Chestnut Street above Fifteenth. It is of an elk in a Western Canyon, surrounded by a pack of grey wolves. The noble beast has been wounded in the side and his life's blood is staining the drifting snow into which he has sunk; but he is game to the end, makes savage lunges with his huge horns at the yelping wolves."[4] This description suggests the influence of one of Landseer's most renowned works, *The Stag at Bay* (fig. 4), which was widely circulated through engravings. According to the *Christian Recorder*, Tanner's painting was "attracting attention, not only for its real merit, but for the fact that it was painted by a young colored man. This picture he studied and modelled in the Zoological Garden where there are excellent specimens of elks and wolves. It is his ambition, and he thinks his forte, to become an animal painter, and he is certainly making good progress. This picture had received many favorable criticisms from prominent artists. Mr. Tanner thinks that his race has an adaptability to art, if only it is given an opportunity, which it can now have."[5]

Tanner displayed a painting with the Landseer-like, moralizing title of *The Battle of Life* in the "Coloured Races" Department at the World's Industrial and Cotton Centennial Exhibition, held from December 16, 1884, to May 31, 1885, in New Orleans, where it was seen by Tanner's first biographer, William J. Simmons: "It attracted my attention at the time on account of its size and naturalness."[6] Simmons set the animal subject into a spiritual context, no doubt echoing Tanner's point of view: "His taste is somewhat on the order of that of Landseer and Bonheur, who love animals. These artists did not look upon them simply as so many bones, with hide, horns and other necessary parts thrown in, but they delighted to portray their nature, habits, affections, symmetry and beauty. This is indeed an exaltation of their Maker and the dignifying of God on canvas, by employing their genius in portraying the characteristics mentioned."[7]   DS

Fig. 4 *The Stag at Bay*, 1853, engraving by Charles Mottram after a painting by Sir Edwin Landseer.

6

"POMP" AT THE ZOO

c. 1880
Oil on canvas
20 × 16″ (50.8 × 40.64 cm)
Signed lower right: *H. O. Tanner*
Private collection

7

LION LICKING ITS PAW

(After Dinner)
1886
Oil on canvas
30 × 36″ (76.2 × 91.44 cm)
Signed and dated lower right: monogram signature/*1886*
Allentown Art Museum, Pennsylvania, gift of Mr. and Mrs.
Philip Berman, 1962

The would-be Landseer took full advantage of the dramatic potential of the wild animals in the Philadelphia Zoo. Extant paintings and exhibition records indicate that Tanner produced more studies of lions than of any other animal, an interest he maintained after moving to Paris, where he made several versions of *Daniel in the Lions' Den* (cat. no. 87) and at least one painting of lions in the desert (cat. no. 44).

Awkwardness in the foreshortening of the figures and a certain crudeness in the application of paint suggest that *"Pomp" at the Zoo* (cat. no. 6) is an early, naive effort. Yet the arrangement of eight figures in an interior space is far more original and ambitious than his marine subjects or the animal painting *Fauna* (cat. no. 5). The narrative aspects of the scene, the gestures and expressive attitudes of the onlookers, and the lion's single-minded concentration on the chunk of meat about to be flung through the bars are acutely observed and amusingly presented. The shy little girl who clutches her hands at her chest and stands well back, a perceptive image of timidity even though her face is entirely hidden, shows Tanner's talent for illustration and suggests why he later ventured to make his living as an illustrator. Perhaps, in fact, it is an early attempt from his first years at the Pennsylvania Academy of the Fine Arts in 1880 or 1881; the foreshortening in the figures is slightly less accomplished than in the drawings Tanner made for illustrations commissioned for *Our Continent* in July 1882 (cat. no. 11). In any case, the latest possible date for the painting is established by the title that has descended in the Tanner family: "Pomp," the nickname of Pompeii, a popular lion acquired by the zoo in 1874, died in May 1884. Tanner's friend James N. Hess, who had interested him in animal subjects, also made a painting of Pompeii which is now lost.[1]

One of the first paintings Tanner sold was *Lion at Home*, purchased from the 1885 exhibition of the National Academy of Design in New York for eighty dollars.[2] Heartened by this success, he began a historical scene of Androcles and the lion (see cat. no. 12). Tanner abandoned it as beyond his talent, and apparently returned to simpler presentations such as *Lion Licking Its Paw* (cat. no. 7). Confidently painted, with a clear understanding of volume and anatomy, this painting perhaps offers some idea of what *Lion at Home* looked like, for it shows the animal lazily tidying up after a meal, and its alternate title, *After Dinner*, reinforces the domestic note.

6 "POMP" AT THE ZOO

Lion Licking Its Paw must be the painting described by William J. Simmons in 1887. The "gallery" Simmons mentions was probably Tanner's studio at 927 Chestnut Street, which he occupied only in 1886: "I visited his gallery and was shown quite a number of his pictures, especially was I pleased with one of a lion in his den, where it was shown that he was eating bloody meat. It was truly life-like and the lion's head with all its fierceness, seemed so natural that one would almost feel like looking toward the door for egress. . . . Let me explain here that the picture was out of its frame and was standing upon its edge upon the floor, leaning against the easel. The lion's massive paw, seemed as if he were about to lift it and reach out for the meat just before him."[3]   DS

8

BOY AND SHEEP LYING
UNDER A TREE
1881
Oil on canvas
17 ³/₈ × 27″ (44.13 × 68.58 cm)
Signed and dated lower left: *Tanner/81*
Grace Scull Sawyer, Philadelphia

Tanner's paintings from the decade before his departure for Europe in 1891 are relatively scarce and so varied that they do not give a clear picture of his artistic development. *Boy and Sheep Lying under a Tree* (cat. no. 8) and two smaller paintings — one of a young girl and two calves standing in a meadow, the other an enigmatic but vigorous depiction of a dog, a goat, and a stone wall — convey an unusually sharp image of Tanner at a distinct moment in his early career. *Boy and Sheep Lying under a Tree* was purchased around 1883 by Edward Lawrence Scull, an artist and wool merchant whom Tanner used to visit to "talk over his painting."[1] All three paintings were in Scull's possession when he died in 1884, thereby establishing the latest possible date for their production.

Compared to works painted only a few years earlier, such as *Ship in a Storm* (cat. no. 4) of 1879 or *Fauna* of approximately the same date (cat. no. 5), *Boy and Sheep Lying under a Tree* reveals a remarkable change in Tanner's interests and abilities. Painted in his second year at the Pennsylvania Academy of the Fine Arts, the work suggests the stimulating effect of Tanner's studies. The courses taught at the Academy under Thomas Eakins's direction were famous, even notorious, for emphasizing the study of human anatomy and direct painting from nude models, but no known examples of figure studies from this time survive among Tanner's work. Only a small bust-length portrait inscribed "Sister Sarah," similar in treatment to Eakins's own early portraits of his sisters, is a possible example of Tanner's figure work at the Academy.

Eakins instructed his students in mammalian anatomy, bringing horses and cows into the studios and taking his students to the country to see farm animals. He also encouraged them to sketch at the zoo. In the early 1880s Eakins himself was occupied with a series of landscape paintings that usually included human figures but also contained animals, such as the geese in *Mending the Net* (fig. 5) or the cows in *The Meadows, Gloucester, New Jersey* (c. 1882, Philadelphia Museum of Art).

Eakins's exhortations to observe and paint a variety of beasts no doubt accorded well with Tanner's earlier decision to become the American Landseer. Tanner even purchased a sheep: "Do you know what it means to possess and try to educate in artistic habits a lone solitary sheep? . . . While a flock of sheep is the personification of peace, docility, and all that is quietude, from my (unscientific) study, I have come to the conclusion that *one* sheep has none of the qualities of a flock of sheep, no, not one, except, it may be, their stupidity."[2]

Fig. 5 Thomas Eakins, *Mending the Net*, 1881, oil on canvas, 32 ¹/₈ × 45 ¹/₈″, Philadelphia Museum of Art, gift of Mrs. Thomas Eakins and Miss Mary Adeline Williams.

Fig. 6 Henry O. Tanner, *Georgia Landscape*, 1886, oil on canvas, 16 × 25″, Mr. and Mrs. D. Scott Mahoney, Atlanta.

Tanner conceived the figures in *Boy and Sheep Lying under a Tree* as concrete objects existing in space and defined by light, no doubt the result of Eakins's insistence on the representation of specific, solid form. In his earlier paintings, light effects are generalized, light sources are unspecific, objects are differentiated by color, and the lightness or darkness of a subject is considered a tonality within a scheme of subdued, limited colors, as though Tanner were closely following a set example. The solidity of forms, the bright, varied colors, and the play of dappled light over this scene imply Tanner's expanded awareness of the means by which to achieve artistic goals. In his effort to distinguish objects, Tanner has given them individual textures; even spots of light are heavily impastoed. Thick and thin areas of paint show that Tanner worked and reworked the canvas to produce the result he desired. The lively play of light and decorative touches, such as flecks of color to indicate flowers in the grass, are entirely new. Areas of opaque color in the sky and grass around the trees, man, and animal—a device Tanner would use throughout his career—were no doubt influenced by Eakins's landscapes, but the sunny, brightly colored appearance of the painting more closely resembles the work of Thomas Anschutz (1851–1912), one of Eakins's assistants.

Tanner's next known landscape with animals, dated 1886, is also a painting of sheep in a pasture (fig. 6). The picture displays the subdued harmonies of color and increasingly coherent technique that define his work just before his trip to Atlanta in 1889. DS

9

IT MUST BE MY VERY STAR,
COME DOWN TO BROOKLYN,
AFTER ALL

From "Old Win-ne-wan's Star," by Kate Upson Clark
Published January 10, 1888, in *Harper's Young People*,
vol. 9, no. 428
Wood engraving
6 1/2 × 9 1/4" (16.51 × 23.5 cm)
Signed lower right: monogram signature
The Free Library of Philadelphia

1 0

THE WITCH HUNT
c. 1882–88
Gouache on board
13 × 20" (33.02 × 50.8 cm)
Signed lower right: *Tanner*
Sheldon Ross Gallery, Birmingham, Michigan

1 1

WAITING FOR THE LORD

From "In the Days of Witchcraft," by Louise Stockton
Published August 30, 1882, in *Our Continent*, vol. 2, no. 8
Wood engraving
4 1/2 × 5 1/8" (11.43 × 13.02 cm)
Signed lower right: *Tanner*
H. M. Snyder after H. O. Tanner
The Free Library of Philadelphia

"I was sending black and white drawings every month or so to New York publishers. As fast as they would be returned with thanks by one, they were off to another. Very few stayed, but I remember the first one that did, and the check for forty dollars that came with the letter of acceptance made me wonder how they could pay such 'big prices.'"[1]

Until recently, the only engraving known to have been made from a drawing by Tanner was one that appeared in *Harper's Young People* in January 1888, illustrating a story by Kate Upson Clark entitled "Old Win-ne-wan's Star."[2] Drawings such as this were seldom made on speculation but were commissioned by the publisher to illustrate a particular story. In this tale, a young girl and her brother are given a fawn, Star, by an old Indian, Win-ne-wan, during a vacation in the Catskill Mountains. Disappointed when they are unable to take the fawn home, the children are later reunited with her at Brooklyn's Prospect Park Zoo. The engraving after Tanner's drawing, titled *It Must Be My Very Star, Come Down to Brooklyn, After All* (cat. no. 9), depicts a scene in which the children coax the fawn to come closer.

Although a published engraving of the *Witch Hunt* drawing (cat. no. 10) has not been found, it too was probably made to illustrate an article: its narrative character and its black and white rendition on a buff background would readily translate into the black and white tones of the wood engravings used to illustrate popular publications of the day. A drawing in the collection of the Historical Society of Pennsylvania (fig. 7), in the same technique and proportionally sized, appears to represent an earlier moment in the same narrative: a toothless crone sits reading a large book by firelight, observed by a black cat and a raven perched on her chair, while a bearded face peers in amazement through a window.

Wood engravings after the gouache drawings appeared in *Our Continent* for August 30, 1882, as illustrations for a story entitled "In the Days of

9 IT MUST BE MY VERY STAR, COME DOWN TO BROOKLYN, AFTER ALL

10 THE WITCH HUNT

11 WAITING FOR THE LORD

Witchcraft" by Louise Stockton. In this melancholy tale an impoverished old woman, Nurse Ann, struggles against the temptations and mockeries of the devil and longs for death as her only salvation. She is appeased by comforting friends: "'And you'll see I die in my bed, Mollie,' continued the old woman. 'You'll never let me be burned?' Mollie shivered. 'We never do such things in Pennsylvania,' she said, 'and you couldn't be that wicked any where, nurse, and I want you to come home with me.'"[3]

Three of Tanner's drawings illustrate the story; the engraving after the Historical Society drawing is titled *Waiting for the Lord* (cat. no. 11). *The Witch Hunt*, a modern title that does not accurately describe the content of the story, was not used, probably because the incident depicted does not appear in the printed version. Nevertheless, *The Witch Hunt* is clearly related to the other three illustrations. Its omission may account for the good condition of the drawing, since it was not subjected to the rigors of the engraver's studio.

A paragraph in the Personal column of the *Christian Recorder* of July 27, 1882, quoting the *Chicago Conservator*, noted that "Henry O. Tanner, the talented colored artist of Philadelphia, has sold four fine black and white crayons. They are to be used in illustrating *Our Continent*. We call to mind no other colored artist whose work has found so high and valued a recognition."[4] On August 31, the Personal column reported, "Those crayons executed by H. O. Tanner appeared in *Our Continent* of Philadelphia, the 29th [*sic*] of August issue. In presenting these to the public, Judge Tourgee [the publisher] said it gave him especial pleasure."[5]

William J. Simmons, writing in 1886–87, confirmed Tanner's activity as an illustrator: "This young man, then, will gain a widespread influence if he continues to supply illustrations to Harper Brothers, for *Harper's Young People* and for Judge Tourgee's paper *Our Continent* as he has done." And he notes, "The firm of Harper & Brother does much to encourage colored men, and employing Mr. Tanner deserves here to be mentioned."[6]

Tourgee's magazine lasted only two years, from 1882 to 1884. Not all of its illustrations are signed, and no others can be attributed to Tanner by outside documentation; it is unknown if he made further contributions. *Our Continent* had been out of print for three years at the time Simmons discussed Tanner's work for the magazine; one wonders to what degree the author was simply boosting the young artist's career. Nonetheless, the 1882 date signals that Tanner had begun to make his way as an artist. *The Witch Hunt* is most likely one of his first efforts at illustration after his year and a half of study at the Pennsylvania Academy of the Fine Arts. Possibly Tanner's interest in illustration was aroused by Thomas Eakins, for Eakins himself made magazine illustrations in the previous decade, and he taught a course in the subject at the Academy to provide his students with a commercial but artistic means of earning a livelihood.   DS

Fig. 7 Henry O. Tanner, *Waiting for the Lord,* 1882, gouache on board, 13 1/2 × 12″, Historical Society of Pennsylvania, Philadelphia.

1 2

STUDY FOR ANDROCLES

(Study of a Male Nude with Beard)
c. 1885–86
Oil on canvas
31 × 18″ (78.74 × 45.72 cm)
Signed upper right: *Tanner*
Estate of Sadie T. M. Alexander

Fig. 8 Thomas Hovenden, *The Last Moments of John Brown*, 1884, oil on canvas, 77 3/8 × 63 1/4″, The Metropolitan Museum of Art, New York, gift of Mr. and Mrs. Carl Stoeckel, 1897.

Nudes are extremely unusual among Tanner's painted oeuvre even though the study of anatomy from live models was an important part of the curriculum at the Pennsylvania Academy of the Fine Arts and central to the tutelage of Thomas Eakins. In his studies drawn from models, including those sketched in the early 1890s at the Académie Julian in Paris (cat. nos. 16–18), Tanner did not emphasize the carnal nature of the nude body, probably as a result of his religious upbringing. His father wrote in *Hints to Ministers*: "The body is sanctified, when its instincts and wants are ruled and regulated by the spirit through the soul, and its members are made altogether instruments of holiness."[1]

The model's striking pose suggests that the picture is more than a simple study of the male body, although the stool and the easel in the background indicate a studio setting. The old man's facial expression, extended hand, and dropped front knee strongly suggest a supplicant. Broad, liquescent brushstrokes and crisp lights and darks call attention to each telling aspect of the pose. A subtle line of light on the brow and nose accents the beseeching expression, and the splendid light underneath the model's forearm accentuates the finely drawn hand, which is cast in darker values. Sharp patches of light on the knee and foot emphasize the figure's imploring posture.

This male nude echoes the attitude and agonized countenance of the African-American figure restrained by a soldier in the left foreground of *The Last Moments of John Brown* (fig. 8) by Thomas Hovenden, one of Tanner's mentors. This picture was widely discussed after 1884, and particular mention was made of the length of the beard that Hovenden placed on Tanner's namesake, John Brown of Osawatomie.[2] The long beard on Tanner's nude

Fig. 9 Jean-Léon Gérôme, *Christian Martyrs' Last Prayer*, 1883, oil on canvas, 34 1/2 × 59″, Walters Art Gallery, Baltimore.

12 STUDY FOR ANDROCLES

is one indication that he absorbed compositional ideas and motifs from works he admired.

This vigorous canvas is here claimed to be more than a simple classroom exercise; it is conceivably a study for the figure of Androcles in a major composition that Tanner began at this time: "I sold a painting, 'A Lion at Home,' [location unknown] . . . and was encouraged to commence a most ambitious canvas of 'Androcles.' I . . . did not finish the picture; it was beyond me."[3]

According to legend, Androcles, a Roman slave, escaped and took refuge in a cave. A lion entered, in obvious pain, and Androcles extracted a large thorn from its paw. Later the slave was captured and thrown to the beasts in a Roman arena, whereupon he was recognized by the same lion, who caressed rather than attacked him.

Tanner would have had several reasons for selecting this theme, many of them rooted in his African-American heritage. His father was well versed in ancient history, especially as it related to the descendants of Ham, and he most likely knew this story. Androcles found refuge in Africa, and the second-century Roman author of the tale, Aulus Gellius, was considered by many to have been African.[4] Yet another source of inspiration could have been a work by Jean-Léon Gérôme (1824–1904), one of Thomas Eakins's teachers. Gérôme's painting *Christian Martyrs' Last Prayer*, 1883 (fig. 9), shows a lion waiting for his prey, a long-bearded old man surrounded by kneeling supplicants. The setting is the Circus Maximus in Rome, also the site of Androcles' reprieve.

Tanner was faced with more than one closely connected issue when he decided to attempt his first history painting. His religious upbringing, which emphasized human rights, came into play: the Androcles story can be related to the Christian belief that good deeds are rewarded. The issue of slavery is obvious; Androcles journeyed by his own "underground railroad" from Rome to Africa. Slavery was a fact of life in many parts of the United States when Tanner was growing up, and the scars that it left were widely discussed in the black community during the years after the Civil War. Even more significant is the fact that Tanner's mother was born a slave. Aulus Gellius' tale of Androcles dealt with public execution as did the story of John Brown. But this complex mix of issues was apparently beyond the scope of Tanner's youthful talent. His ambitious plans for a picture did not go beyond this eloquent oil sketch and, perhaps, *Lion Licking Its Paw*, 1886 (cat. no. 7), which can be seen as the wounded lion that shared Androcles' cave.   DFM

1 3

MOUNTAIN LANDSCAPE, HIGHLANDS, NORTH CAROLINA

(Cumberland Foothills)
c. 1889
Oil on canvas
22 × 36″ (55.88 × 91.44 cm)
Signed lower left: monogram signature
Berea College Art Department, Kentucky

1 5

SAND DUNES AT SUNSET, ATLANTIC CITY

c. 1886
Oil on canvas
29 1/4 × 58 3/4″ (74.37 × 149.23 cm)
Signed lower left: monogram signature
Estate of Sadie T. M. Alexander

1 4

GEORGIA LANDSCAPE

1889–90
Oil on canvas
17 3/4 × 32 1/4″ (45.08 × 81.91 cm)
Signed lower left: monogram signature
The Morris Museum of Art, Augusta, Georgia

Fig. 10 Edward Moran, *A Windy Day on Coney Island*, 1871, oil on canvas, 17 1/2 × 29 1/2″, Philadelphia Museum of Art, gift of Harry S. Dion.

Along with the illustration for "Old Win-ne-wan's Star" published in 1888 (cat. no. 9), these three landscapes stand as the most complete examples of Tanner's mature style before his departure for Europe in January 1891. They show that he did not pursue the avant-garde interests in proto-impressionist effects, high-keyed color, and exaggerated light seen in *Boy and Sheep Lying under a Tree*, 1881 (cat. no. 8), but chose instead a more conservative approach to landscape that combined Tonalism's subtle light and color effects with touches of bravura painting to delineate vegetation and other natural elements. These canvases express the possible influence of the work of Edward Moran (fig. 10) or the style of—and possibly lessons from—his friend Christopher Shearer, a landscape artist who trained in Düsseldorf and Munich. The titles of these works are not necessarily the original ones, and the dates assigned to them are based on circumstantial evidence. But they are linked to the years before Tanner left the United States by their style, which clearly predates the definitive changes seen in Tanner's landscapes once he settled in Paris (cat. nos. 19, 25).

The mountain landscape traditionally described as *Cumberland Foothills* (cat. no. 13), an area Tanner is not known to have visited, can be reidentified on the basis of a watercolor of a similar view (Washington, D.C., National Museum of American Art) inscribed "Highlands North Carolina"; its date is based on the assumption that Tanner's stay in the North Carolina mountains, as described in his autobiography,[1] occurred in the summer of 1889.

Identification of the other two works is more problematic. Tanner seemingly would have been eager to exhibit such large, decorative, and presumably commercially appealing works, yet a search of exhibition records up to the time of Tanner's departure for Europe has not turned up titles approximating the present captions. On the basis of its subject matter, the painting now called *Georgia Landscape* (cat. no. 14) might be a work entitled *Early November*, which Tanner showed at the Pennsylvania Academy of the

13 MOUNTAIN LANDSCAPE, HIGHLANDS, NORTH CAROLINA

14 GEORGIA LANDSCAPE

15 SAND DUNES AT SUNSET, ATLANTIC CITY

Fine Arts in January 1889, the same month he moved to Atlanta to set up a photography studio. No other known work by the artist seems to fit this title, and Tanner could have had the painting sent to Atlanta to serve as an advertisement for his new venture. Since no specific geographic features determine its setting, the painting could have been renamed by Tanner or a subsequent owner to increase its appeal to a local audience. Such speculations indicate how little is known about Tanner's career during the second half of the 1880s, and how few of his paintings from this time have been solidly identified.

By the similarity of its color scheme and technique to a signed and dated painting (see fig. 6), *Sand Dunes at Sunset, Atlantic City* (cat. no. 15) can be dated to about 1886. It is possibly the same painting that Tanner exhibited as *Back from the Beach* at the Pennsylvania Academy of the Fine Arts in October 1885 and in New York at the National Academy of Design in April 1886. Certainly the painting is of the important size and technical accomplishment by which the artist would choose to represent himself at such major exhibitions, and again, no other known work by Tanner fits the title. "Back from the Beach," however, seems to imply a genre scene, not a painting of a beach. Perhaps Tanner never exhibited *Sand Dunes at Sunset, Atlantic City* publicly (although this would have been uncharacteristic), but instead gave it to his parents, who spent at least part of their summers at a cottage in Atlantic City.[2] In any case the painting was definitely painted on a beach: a considerable amount of sand was brushed into the wet paint.

The largest and most ambitious of these three American landscapes, *Sand Dunes at Sunset, Atlantic City* is the most distinctive. Although a harsh cleaning and repainting of the sky has somewhat distorted the overall tonality of the picture, Tanner's perception of light and atmosphere is acutely rendered. The view looks across the cool gray of a shadowed beach to dunes made pink by late sunlight; a low haze over the water partially hides the sun. This painting alone indicates that even without the benefit of European study, Tanner would have become an accomplished, distinctive, though conservative artist.   DS

PARIS, RACIAL AWARENESS,

AND SUCCESS

1891–1897

Tanner arrived in Liverpool on January 18, 1891, traveled briefly to London, then set out for Rome via Paris. There he was welcomed by friends, most probably including his cohort from Atlanta, James Field, who helped to settle the artist into a student hotel at 12 rue de Seine in the Latin Quarter, near the Ecole des Beaux-Arts. He was depressingly lonely at first, his room was cold, and he longed for an American breakfast. But Tanner remarked, "After having been in Paris a week, I should find conditions so to my liking that I completely forgot that when I left New York I had made my plans to study in Rome."[1]

Tanner enrolled at the Académie Julian, where Field had been studying since 1890. This private academy, actually a group of studios, was founded by the painter Rudolphe Julian (1839–1907) in 1873 and flourished for many years. Julian's work was exhibited at the Salon des Refusés in 1863 and at the Salon itself from 1865 before he concentrated on teaching, which would win him the Legion of Honor in 1881.[2] His curriculum emphasized working from live models and weekly critiques by celebrated artists, who were always members of the Institut Nationale des Sciences et des Arts, a government establishment with widespread influence over the arts. Julian himself supervised the day-to-day activities of the studios and established the life model's pose for the week on Monday mornings.[3]

Tanner and other newcomers to the academy were broken in gently: there was no hazing such as occurred at the official Ecole des Beaux-Arts.[4] New students were expected to pay a *bienvenue*, or footing, which usually took the form of punch and brioche.[5] The ages of the students varied greatly: Shirley Fox, a British pupil, enrolled in the 1880s at the age of twelve.[6] Many Americans studied at the academy, and their interactions would make a special study unto itself. John Milner clarified why so many artists were attracted to Julian's:

> [The academy] provided an invaluable introduction to the discipline of drawing and painting from the life-model, contact with other artists, informed criticism both from Julian and respected tutors. ... Aesthetic considerations aside, Julian's Academy was for many years an invaluable start for a career as an artist, guaranteeing a model, tuition, experience and contacts for little outlay and without difficult entrance requirements. Progress was competitive but open to all.[7]

Fig. 11 Jean-Joseph Benjamin-Constant, *Moorish Procession*, 1880, oil on canvas, 39 × 52 ½", Forbes Magazine Collection, New York.

Tanner did not record much information about the art that he made at Julian's. He did note the extraordinary level of tobacco smoke in the rooms, and that his religious upbringing was at odds with the studio practice of having the weekly *concours*, or competitive examination, on Sundays. He recalled that the *massier*, or senior art student in charge of the studio, who had become a friend, allowed him to complete the assignments on Mondays. One of Tanner's efforts, devoted to the time-worn *concours* subject of the Deluge (location unknown), was awarded one of two prizes.[8] Tanner pointed out: "I was never in the least brilliant in the work of the school and, save for my sketches for proposed pictures [unidentified], my work never in the least attracted any attention."[9]

Examples of Tanner's drawings from live models (cat. nos. 16–18) reveal his accomplishment as a draughtsman. Indeed these works are of the type that one would expect from a Julian pupil, and despite Tanner's self-disparaging remarks, a contemporary source observed: "His charcoal studies were admired, even before it was known that he had such skill as a painter. In the schools he carried away many honors, and was considered a 'strong man' at Julien's [*sic*] before his first salon picture."[10]

Beginners most often started by drawing from plaster casts before they moved on to the life room,[11] however, no evidence suggests that the thirty-two-year-old Tanner, after all an

Fig. 12 Henry O. Tanner, *Horse of the Khedive*, c. 1902, oil on canvas, 19 ½ × 25 ¾", F. M. Hall Collection, Sheldon Art Gallery, Lincoln, Nebraska.

Fig. 13 Jean-Paul Laurens, *The Excommunication of Robert the Pious*, 1875, oil on canvas, 51 ¹/₄ × 85 ³/₄″, Musée d'Orsay, Paris.

alumnus of the Pennsylvania Academy of the Fine Arts, was required to go back to plaster casts. He was assigned to the visiting Institut team of Jean-Paul Laurens (1838–1921) and Jean-Joseph Benjamin-Constant (1845–1902).[12] Tanner became closest to Benjamin-Constant,[13] better known of the two today, and an accomplished painter of portraits and of North African and Near Eastern scenes.[14] Tanner seems to have been only indirectly influenced by these teachers. As with Eakins and Hovenden some ten years before in Philadelphia, Tanner apparently borrowed figures and compositional ideas from his French instructors, but he did not imitate their styles. For example, the horse and burnoose-clad figure in Benjamin-Constant's *Moorish Procession* of 1880 (fig. 11) could have been a source for Tanner's *Horse of the Khedive* (fig. 12), which was painted around 1902, the year of Benjamin-Constant's death. Similarly, the 1875 *Excommunication of Robert the Pious* (fig. 13) by Laurens might have been one prototype for the angular spatial arrangement of the African-American artist's *Daniel in the Lions' Den*, 1895 (fig. 16).

An individualist and remarkably independent in his development, Tanner avoided direct copying. He visited the Louvre, but the museum's archives reveal that he did not apply for permission to copy there,[15] a popular practice by which many artists supplemented their studies. Thomas Eakins had done so in 1866 during his Paris years, and Henri Matisse added to his formal academic pursuits in 1891 by copying a painting by Chardin.[16] Julie Manet—daughter of the Impressionist artist Berthe Morisot and niece of Edouard Manet—recorded in her diary that on the morning of November 16, 1897, an array of major figures including E. A. Carolus-Duran, the poet Stéphane Mallarmé (accompanied by Whistler), Zandomeneghi, and Renoir were at the Louvre when permission was given to copy.[17] But no direct copies after earlier artists' work have been found or recorded in Tanner's oeuvre.

An important aspect of Tanner's time at the Académie Julian was the benefit he derived from friendships with fellow students.[18] From his colleagues, Tanner discovered that Parisian art students spent their summer holidays in the country. In

1891 he retreated to the little village of Pont-Aven on the Brittany coast, both for the opportunity to improve his French and "because board could be had for $11 a month."[19] Tanner might have been influenced by more than economy when he chose Pont-Aven. Thomas Hovenden, a friend and mentor from Philadelphia, had been there as early as 1876. By the time Tanner had arrived in Paris in 1891, Paul Gauguin (1848–1903) had emerged as something of a cult figure among artists who summered at Pont-Aven. On March 23, 1891, a banquet was given in Gauguin's honor at the Café Voltaire, which was attended by many young artists connected with the Académie Julian.[20]

Regardless of the motivating forces that took him to Brittany, Tanner had contact at Pont-Aven with the latest artistic ideas that excited France following the advent of Impressionism. In 1889 a show of work by Pont-Aven artists had been held at the Café Volpini on the Champ-de-Mars in Paris. Announced as an "Exhibition of Paintings of the Impressionists and Synthetist Group," it was dominated by Gauguin's recent Synthetist work.[21] Synthetism, or Symbolism, roughly defined, sought to express ideas, mood, and emotion without particular attention to naturalistic representation. Space was flattened, and colors were often bright and separated by black lines. Paintings in this mode tend to be both decorative and the abstraction, or "synthesis," of the subjects that inspired them.

Alas, Tanner did not speak about the art that he made during his first trip to Brittany. Two small pictures have recently come to light (cat. nos. 20, 21) that show Tanner recorded local scenes, but their styles and palettes do not reflect the innovations going on around him.

Tanner returned to Paris, apparently unswayed by the Symbolist experiments taking place at Pont-Aven. In the ensuing months he determined to enter the Salon, the vast, official annual exhibition held at Paris each spring.

> As I now look back, it seems curious to me that I should have been able to arrive at [about] thirty years of age with two years of that time in Paris and never to have heard of the Salon or, having heard of it, not to have at all realized its importance in the art world. Its discovery came to me in this manner: I had been to Dr. Thurber's church, and was on my way home when, near the Palais d'Industrie, I saw great crowds making their way into [a] building.
>
> To my question, it was Le Salon and, to see for myself, I joined that good-natured throng. What a surprise awaited me!...The paintings — thousands of them — and nearly all of them much more to my taste than were the old masters of the Louvre — not that they were really as fine, but they were more within my range.[22]

Tanner's discovery of the Salon counts among the most important events of his career. As a result of his first chance visit, he set a goal for himself in purely artistic terms. On that afternoon in Paris Tanner began to think like an artist instead of merely wanting to be one: "Here was something to work for, to get a picture here. This now furnished a definite impetus to my work in Paris — to be able to make a picture that should be admitted here — could I do it."[23]

Tanner pursued his new-found aim during the summer of 1892 in the little Brittany fishing village of Concarneau. He had made an excursion there in 1891 and may have returned on the advice of fellow Académie Julian student Armand Séguin

(c. 1869–1903), a native of the region and an artist in the orbit of Gauguin.[24] The result of Tanner's efforts in Concarneau was a picture described by the artist as of an apple orchard, which has been identified as *The Bagpipe Lesson* (this work in fact was never accepted at the Salon, see cat. no. 25). In this painting Tanner interpreted the peasants and landscape of the region according to a more traditional, American-informed vision rather than the new Symbolism, or even Impressionism in its most advanced state.

There is no reason to believe, as some writers have suggested, that Tanner himself made an impression in Brittany as a result of the novelty of his skin color and gold teeth.[25] The artist had friends from the Académie Julian in the area and had already won a *concours*. The closest that we can come to a contemporary account of racial awareness in 1892 at Brittany's art colony is Henry Bataille's positive recollections of the region's Celtic past, popular poetry, life among the peasants, and his reference to visits by Gauguin and his Javanese mistress ("sa Négresse") to Huelgoat.[26]

By 1893 Tanner was renting a studio at 15 rue de Seine and had developed friendships with American artists such as Hermon MacNeil and Hermann Dudley Murphy.[27] Around this time, Tanner joined the American Art Club in Paris and made the acquaintance of Rodman Wanamaker, of Philadelphia's prominent merchant family. Wanamaker was interested not only in promoting art and artists but, like his famous father, John (1838–1922), in improving the lot and living conditions of Native Americans and African-Americans.[28] He was to figure prominently in the advancement of the artist's career.

Tanner began studies in 1893 for another picture of Breton life, *The Young Sabot Maker* (cat. nos. 31–33). These works continue *The Bagpipe Lesson*'s theme of teaching and introduce the suggestion of a religious motif: Jesus in the carpentry shop of Joseph. Tanner lowered the vantage point of these compositions in accord with recent notions in French painting and moved toward a shallower representation of space. This is not to imply that Tanner is a hither-to unrecognized member of the progressive Symbolist group centered around Paul Gauguin. But, in his early thirties, he was not too old to learn or to search for a personal style within the context of prevailing modes. James A. Porter, who interviewed the artist during his lifetime, summarized the recognizable impact of Tanner's first experiences in France as giving him a sense of greater personal freedom, expanded manhood, and a consciousness of self-responsibility that fed his ambition and energy.[29]

In the first part of 1893, Henry came down with typhoid fever.[30] He was treated successfully at the Hôtel Dieu hospital. He wrote: "The third year I had typhoid fever, which was no doubt caused by too much work and too little food of the proper kind....When I was well enough to travel, I returned to Philadelphia for a convalescence, and to 'recoup' a depleted treasury."[31] This recollection, which condenses the events of about one year, offers little insight into the total and remarkable change during this period from the relatively conventional style of *The Bagpipe Lesson* to the more fluid, lyrical one of *The Banjo Lesson* (cat. no. 27), also completed in 1893. A number of events in Tanner's life, however, point to a possible explanation for the shift seen in *The Banjo Lesson* to genre subjects dealing with African-Americans.

Precisely when Tanner returned to Philadelphia is not clear, but he was in the United States no later than early August 1893, when he was an invited speaker at the Congress on Africa held from August 14 to 21 at the World's Columbian Exposition in Chicago. This symposium addressed African-American life, as well as that of Africa, some thirty years after the Emancipation Proclamation, and provided the first real overview of black leadership and African-American aspirations across the nation.[32] The complete text of Tanner's presentation has not been found, but a good idea of its content is given in a report on the congress in *Our Day*: "Professor Tanner...[on August 15] spoke of Negro painters and sculptors, and claimed that actual achievement proves Negroes to possess ability and talent for successful competition with white artists."[33]

The Chicago conference must have had a profound impact on the artist's racial awareness and his search for subject matter. As Tanner himself stated, he was inspired at this time to concentrate on sober, sympathetic depictions of African-American life to offset a history of one-sided comic representations.[34] *The Banjo Lesson*, in which an older black man instructs a young lad, is the first painting that can be ascribed to Tanner's new desire. Among the several artists and writers participating in the World's Columbian Exposition was the twenty-one-year-old African-American poet and genius Paul Laurence Dunbar (1872–1906). He read from his work, but it is not known whether he recited "A Banjo Song," which had been published in 1892 in a volume called *Oak and Ivy*.[35] The third stanza of the poem creates a tender picture of family love and joy close to the sentiment of *The Banjo Lesson*:

> Den my fam'ly gadders roun' me
> In de fadin' o' de light,
> Ez I strike de strings to try 'em
> Ef dey all is tuned er-right.
> An' it seems we're so nigh heaben
> We kin hyeah de angels sing
> When de music o' dat banjo
> Sets my cabin all er-ring.[36]

Another critical factor in Tanner's increased sense of racial identity was the influence of his father's *Theological Lectures*, delivered in 1893 at Tuskegee Institute and published in 1894. The bishop wrote, following Xenophanes of Colophon (570–480 B.C.): "If oxen or lions had hands and could work in men's fashions, and trace out with chisel and brush their conception of Godhead, then would horses depict gods like horses and oxen like oxen, each kind the divine with its own form and nature endowing."[37] This passage accords with Henry's feeling that "he who has most sympathy with his subjects will obtain the best results," an attitude embodied in his tender representations of black Americans.[38]

When Tanner decided to render African-American subjects, he was also pondering his approach to painting in other terms, "whether it was better to do a few things — one picture, for instance — and bring it to a fairly successful conclusion, or to do many pictures, trusting to some chance that one of them would be better than any continued and more or less labored effort could be."[39] This quandary might account in part for the relatively few black images that Tanner completed during this period of

Fig. 14 Henry O. Tanner, *Aix-en-Provence*, c. 1894, oil on panel, 9 3/8 × 13", Merton Simpson, New York.

Fig. 15 Paul Gauguin, *Washerwomen at Pont-Aven*, 1886, oil on canvas, 28 × 35 1/2", Musée d'Orsay, Paris.

avowed commitment to the theme. He continued to render other subjects and did not return to African-American genre scenes after 1894, but he never abandoned the sensitivity to social issues inherent in his "desire to represent the serious and pathetic side" of black life.[40]

During his prolonged stay in Philadelphia, Tanner most likely made the acquaintance of both Robert C. Ogden (1836–1913) and Harrison S. Morris (1856–1948). Ogden was a partner in John Wanamaker's dry-goods business, an advocate of African-American public education,[41] and the eventual purchaser of *The Banjo Lesson*. Morris was the managing director of the Pennsylvania Academy of the Fine Arts. Both men would figure prominently in Tanner's career over the next ten years.

Just how far Tanner had advanced since his days as a fledgling artist in Philadelphia is revealed by the fact that he shared an exhibition in 1894 with Thomas Hovenden. The show was held at James S. Earle and Sons Gallery on 816 Chestnut Street from April 28 to May 5.[42] Earle's was the very establishment at whose windows the teenaged Tanner had eagerly studied pictures in the 1870s. The exhibition included a variety of subjects: genre, figure studies, and landscapes done in Brittany and Florida. W. S. Scarborough, vice-president of Wilberforce University at the time, pointed out that Tanner exhibited both old and recent works.[43] When the exhibition was reviewed in the *Daily Evening Telegraph*, one of Tanner's new black subjects was singled out for special praise: "On the side wall a centre is made by a pathetic group entitled 'The Thankful Poor'—an important work, rendered with conscientious care, and qualities of atmospheric perspective, what our French friends call envelopment, and in truth of values one of the most satisfactory productions of Mr. Tanner's brush."[44]

The artist later recalled that at the end of his successful visit to the United States "an auction sale of all the pictures I could lay my hands upon furnished a few hundred dollars, and with this and 'promises' (never fulfilled) I returned again to Paris."[45] (The "auction sale" could very well have been the show at Earle's.)[46] Tanner would have been eager to return to France: *The Banjo Lesson* had been accepted by the Salon jury of 1894.

The importance of acceptance into the Salon should not be underestimated. The *vernissage* was a great social event in Paris, and the Salon was an immense marketplace for the work of European and American artists, visited by thousands.[47] In spite of the sheer difficulty of having their work noticed among the canvases hung from floor to ceiling, artists gained the attention of art critics and opportunities for public success. The critic Théodore Duret, an advocate of the Impressionists, wrote to Camille Pissarro in 1874 to urge his participation: "You will be seen by fifty dealers, patrons, critics, who would otherwise never look you up and discover you."[48] *The*

Banjo Lesson, however, does not appear to have attracted any special critical notice. Moreover, Tanner recalled that the hanging committee "skied" his painting, installing it extremely high on the wall.[49]

Tanner's return to Paris was brief; it is proposed here that during the summer of 1894 he might have been back in Pont-Aven in the company of old friends. Gauguin was there from April to November, and Judy Le Paul states that "close links were formed at Pont-Aven between...British painters, the American Henry Ossawa Tanner, and Gauguin's group: Filiger, Séguin, Verkade, Sérusier, and the poet Alfred Jarry."[50] Tanner knew Séguin and Sérusier from his initial trips to Brittany, and his intimacy with the group is illustrated by the fact that he sat for a portrait by Séguin during this period (location unknown).[51]

Only a few works clearly document Tanner's activity at this time. However, his proximity to the circle of Gauguin could suggest a flirtation with Symbolism or at least a continuation of the brand of Impressionism that he had explored in the first half of 1893. Among the paintings firmly dated to 1894 are two pictures inscribed with that year in the DuSable Museum of Afro-American History, Chicago: *Pont-Aven* and *River Landscape in Brittany*. Perhaps the sunlit picture called *Aix-en-Provence* (fig. 14) also belongs to this group.[52] Nothing suggests that Tanner visited this town in southern France, but certain aspects of the scene suggest Pont-Aven, and specifically the Ty-Fleur mill, which is seen from a different vantage point in a work by Gauguin, *Washerwomen at Pont-Aven*, 1886 (fig. 15). Unnaturalistic, red shadows underneath the loosely rendered trees in *Aix-en-Provence* are consistent with the Symbolist approach to color; nevertheless, it is not easy to understand why Gustave Loisseau (1865–1935), who was among this circle of friends at Pont-Aven in 1894, claimed that Tanner was clearly influenced by Symbolism.[53]

By early 1895 Tanner had taken an atelier at 51 boulevard Saint-Jacques in a district of many artists' studios. Although he did not pursue Symbolism, he did continue to paint Breton subjects. He completed a definitive version of *The Young Sabot Maker* (cat. no. 34) and painted *The Bagpipe Player* (cat. no. 26) and *Brittany Interior*, which has not been traced. His efforts were rewarded again by the Salon jury — *The Young Sabot Maker*, *Brittany Interior*, and a pastel called *New Jersey Coast by Moonlight* were exhibited, but did not attract the attention of critics. The latter work is probably the picture now titled *Marshes in New Jersey* and inscribed "Paris, 1895" (Washington, D.C., National Museum of American Art).

Around the middle of 1895 Tanner made another marked shift in subject matter with *Daniel in the Lions' Den* (fig. 16). Turning to more traditional narrative themes for the first time since his aborted composition of *Androcles* (see cat. no. 12), Tanner chose a biblical story possessing some of the sentiments inherent in his African-American scenes. The Bible forcefully espouses equality, as has been pointed out by theologians N. C. Cooper-Lewter and H. H. Mitchell,[54] and slaves "knew that the Bible, like their root culture, was loaded with support for the equality of persons."[55] Certainly issues of social justice must have been on Tanner's mind after the Chicago congress of 1893. Informed by his family background and his desire to represent profound issues of black life, Tanner now looked to the Bible for some of his most vital themes.

Fig. 16 Henry O. Tanner, *Daniel in the Lions' Den*, 1895,
oil on canvas, location unknown.

In *Daniel in the Lions' Den*, Tanner returned to matters he had attempted to address in *Androcles*: slavery, false accusations, execution, and martyrdom. W. S. Scarborough pointed out in 1902: "Of this picture [*The Resurrection of Lazarus*] there could be said what was said of the 'Daniel' — 'there was race in it,' a quality that one critic avers to be new to Biblical painting. Be that as it may, Mr. Tanner studied to put 'race in it.'"[56] In his 1894 *Theological Lectures*, Bishop Tanner identified Daniel as recognizing the children of Ham — the black race.[57] Could Tanner have seen himself in the figure of the lonely, persecuted Daniel? There is no evidence to suggest that he would have experienced such feelings during the summer of 1895. But the highly controversial Dreyfus affair might have fanned the painter's interest in issues of race and persecution: late in 1894, a young Jewish French military officer, Alfred Dreyfus, was found guilty of spying and sentenced to life imprisonment in a degrading trial based on meager evidence. Tinged with virulent anti-Semitism, the affair was frequently discussed in the newspapers.[58]

While Tanner was completing *Daniel in the Lions' Den*, the Cotton States and International Exposition was held in Atlanta, where Booker T. Washington gave an inaugural speech that was hailed as "the beginning of a moral revolution in America."[59] The art exhibition was an impressive event at which medals were awarded to Thomas Eakins, Mary Cassatt, and Winslow Homer,[60] as well as Tanner's friend and colleague from the Académie Julian, James Field. Tanner sent three paintings to the exhibition; only *The Bagpipe Lesson* has been clearly identified, and it won a medal.[61] But the artist did not exhibit with his compatriots Eakins, Cassatt, and Homer as he was now accustomed to doing at the Paris Salon: instead his work was shown in the special Negro Building of the exposition. Tanner's paintings were placed there at the urging of his patron Robert C. Ogden, who rationalized this recommendation in a letter of October 17, 1895, to Booker T. Washington: "They would have lost their distinctive race influence and character if placed in the general art exhibition. My purpose was to get the influence of Mr. Tanner's genius on the side of the race he represents and at the same time I did not want it degraded by inharmonious associations with inferior work."[62]

Ogden's mention of a "distinctive race influence and character" in Tanner's pictures suggests that the other two works shown might have been *The Banjo Lesson* and *The Thankful Poor* (cat. no. 28), the only known paintings from this period that deal with black subjects. In spite of Ogden's good intentions, Tanner must have felt that his inclusion in the Negro Building, rather than in the main exhibition, was a racial affront. Moreover, during this period of Tanner's heightened race consciousness, he would certainly have been struck by the fact that *The Bagpipe Lesson*, with its white Breton denizens, was awarded a medal, while paintings of black genre scenes, if indeed *The Banjo Lesson* and *The Thankful Poor* were shown, were passed over.

Daniel in the Lions' Den was not only accepted for the 1896 Salon but secured Tanner's first Salon award, an honorable mention.[63] Tanner, shy and reserved, later understated the significance of *Daniel*'s recognition, but after 1880 only eighty-five prizes were awarded annually among the thousands of paintings accepted by the Salon jury.[64] He probably never knew that the painting was also considered (although finally not purchased) by the French government. Lists of purchase-prize artists for 1896 preserved in the Archives Nationales include a final addition, in pencil, of the name "Tanner," with the notation *"offre."*[65] Tanner was considerably motivated by the honorable mention alone:

> True it was but a "mention honorable," but it was an "honor." I could have all the confidence in myself possible. I could believe that I might do something some day, but I verified however small a part of that belief, that day was new hope given to me that I might also reach other "day dreams" which I would never have confessed even to my most intimate friend. So it was that this first little "mention honorable" gave me a courage and a power for hard work, and also a hope that I had never before possessed.[66]

Tanner next embarked on his most famous painting, *The Resurrection of Lazarus* (cat. no. 38). As with *Daniel*, Tanner found in this biblical subject a connection to social issues; in this case, the promise of Lazarus' renewed life paralleled the reborn hope offered to black Americans by the Emancipation Proclamation of 1863.

Tanner labored throughout the summer of 1896 on the canvas: "I had worked upon it all summer, because, in summer, models are not in such demand, and are willing to make 'terms,' and I very much needed all the 'terms' that could be made."[67] Following the advice of a friend, he abandoned an initial smaller-scale version to attempt a larger canvas:

In the making of this picture, I was helped by criticism, but several times I felt somewhat like Voltaire must have felt when he said, "I will take care of my enemies if the Lord will deliver me from my friends." I nearly made a shipwreck trying to follow the advice of a friend who counselled that a canvas that gave as much promise "as this small-sized one should be much larger." He prevailed—very likely it flattered my vanity—and I bought a canvas six by ten feet. After working upon it quite a long time, I came to the conclusion that I could only make a very much "watered" edition of the smaller one and I recommenced work upon my "first love," accepting radical criticism with more caution.[68]

Toward the end of the year Rodman Wanamaker paid a visit to Tanner's boulevard Saint-Jacques studio to see the completed painting. He was impressed by the work, but found its pleasing "Orientalism" to be "a fortunate accident." He offered to send Tanner to the Holy Land for his own firsthand glimpse: "One should go there every two or three years, at least, to keep in touch with the Oriental spirit."[69]

Tanner spent six weeks, beginning in early 1897, in Egypt and Palestine.[70] He was deeply impressed by the Near Eastern countryside, but his impressions were not immediately reflected in his work other than in *The Jews' Wailing Place* (see cat. no. 43) and a sketch preserved in his account book.[71] It should be noted that several paintings by Tanner that have been ascribed to the late 1890s bear old titles related to North Africa; these are either mislabeled or incorrectly dated. Tanner would not visit North Africa until 1908.

Tanner was still traveling when Harrison S. Morris wrote on April 16, 1897, about the reception of *Daniel in the Lions' Den* at the 1896 annual exhibition of the Pennsylvania Academy of the Fine Arts:

> The picture "Daniel" was very much admired while it was in our exhibition, and especially commended by Mr. William M. Chase, who spoke of it in a public address to his students and privately praised it very often. I may say to you privately that it very nearly received the Walter Lippincott Prize of $300.00. I am very sorry that more substantial results should not have been produced by it; but I know that you will persevere in your course and someday there will be a better outcome.[72]

Little did Morris know that the French government had secured an even "better outcome" for another work. Tanner was in Venice and on his way home when he received word in early May that *The Resurrection of Lazarus*, which had been accepted for the 1897 Salon—his third consecutive acknowledgment by the artistic hierarchy of France—was to be purchased for the Musée du Luxembourg, where it would join other celebrated works by living artists such as Whistler's portrait of his mother and Gérôme's *Combat de Coqs*. Tanner hastily returned to Paris, to rave reviews from art critics on both sides of the Atlantic. Virtually overnight he had become an artist of international renown.

On the heels of these heady experiences, Tanner planned a three-month trip to Philadelphia to commence June 18, 1897,[73] with a brief stop in London first.[74] During his sojourn in the United States he traveled to Kansas City, Kansas, where Bishop Tanner was on assignment. Henry's major undertaking during his visit, a portrait of his mother (cat. no. 41), might be seen as a challenge to works by other masters of his time, such as Whistler and Eakins. As early as the eighteenth century, theorists in

French art suggested to young artists the practice of competition: by surpassing recognized works, challengers demonstrated their imaginative powers and proclaimed their own genius.[75] Tanner's new-found, well-deserved fame for *The Resurrection of Lazarus* could have encouraged his own competitive spirit; a few months later, he apologized to Morris for sounding rather egotistical about his work.[76] During the nineteenth century, a premium was placed on originality but with an approach that acknowledged existing works without servile imitation.[77] Tanner was certainly aware of this tradition; a reviewer of the 1897 Salon pointed out in the *Gazette des Beaux-Arts* that *Lazarus* contained a "recollection of Rembrandt," but that it "does not displease us because it does not obscure the personal sensibility of the artist."[78]

By the end of 1897 Tanner was no longer a raw recruit to the art of painting. His search for his own subject matter, style, and approach was reaching resolution, and he had come to terms with racial consciousness on several levels. Around this time he met Atherton Curtis, a wealthy expatriate with a fortune derived from patent medicine who would become a lifelong friend and financial benefactor,[79] and Harrison S. Morris wrote to him on November 29 about "the possibility of a commission through the Mayor [of Philadelphia]."[80] This commission was never realized, but the recognition it implied must have encouraged Tanner as he embarked on the next phase of his career — religious painting. DFM

16

HALF-LENGTH STUDY OF
A NEGRO MAN

c. 1891–93
Charcoal on paper
19¹/₂ × 9³/₈″ (24.6 × 23.9 cm)
Detroit Institute of Arts, Founders Society Purchase,
African Art Gallery Committee Fund

17

HALF-LENGTH STUDY OF A
BEARDED MAN WITH LONG
HAIR

c. 1891–93
Charcoal and pencil on paper
10¹/₁₆ × 6¹/₂″ (25.56 × 16.51 cm)
Merton Simpson, New York

18

BUST-LENGTH STUDY OF A
BEARDED MAN WITH SHORT
HAIR
(Study for Christ)
c. 1891–93
Charcoal on paper
12 × 9¹/₂″ (30.48 × 24.13 cm) sheet, 11¹/₂ × 7¹/₄″
(29.21 × 18.42 cm) plate
Schomburg Center for Research in Black Culture, The New York
Public Library, Art and Artifacts Division

Little attention has been paid to Tanner's drawings, in part because of his fame as a colorist but also because relatively few of his works on paper survive. The three superb sheets presented here, however, suggest that his power as a draughtsman could not have gone unrecognized. Indeed, Helen Cole wrote as early as 1900 in *Brush and Pencil*: "His charcoal studies were admired, even before it was known that he had such skill as a painter. In the schools he carried away many honors, and was considered a 'strong man' at Julien's [*sic*] before his first salon picture. Even now what gives his work its solidity and character is the absolutely good drawing in it."[1]

These works are pure drawings in the sense that they are "academies," studies of a nude model executed solely for purposes of instruction or practice. An academy drawing is considered an independent object, as opposed to a study made for a larger composition. *Bust-Length Study of a Bearded Man with Short Hair* (cat. no. 18) appears not to be a preparatory study for any known painting, despite its traditional title of *Study for Christ*. Tanner's sheets hint at his father's influence and his religious upbringing; the figures' genitals are not shown, although in such drawings they often are.

Given their proficiency, these drawings were almost certainly executed during Tanner's study in the early 1890s at the Académie Julian under the direction of Jean-Joseph Benjamin-Constant and Jean-Paul Laurens (1838–1921) rather than at the Pennsylvania Academy of the Fine Arts under Eakins during the early 1880s. The basis for study at the Académie Julian was the nude model. Studies from life covered the walls and filled the racks of stacked paintings in the studio. Seated on low stools or positioned at easels, Julian's

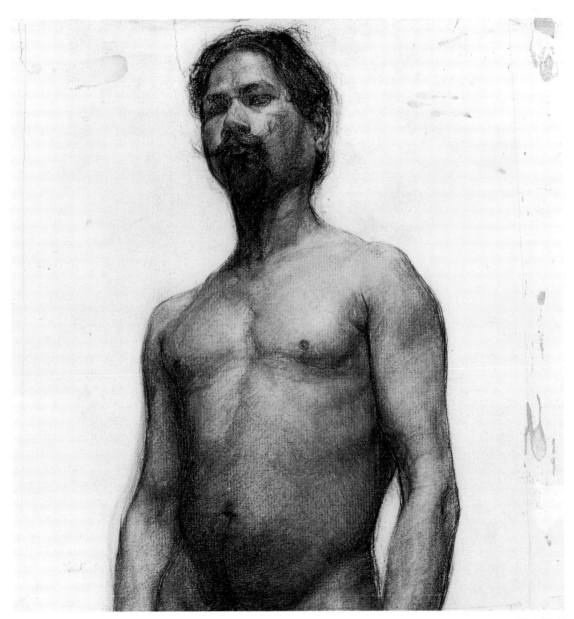

16 HALF-LENGTH STUDY OF A NEGRO MAN

17 HALF-LENGTH STUDY OF A BEARDED MAN WITH LONG HAIR

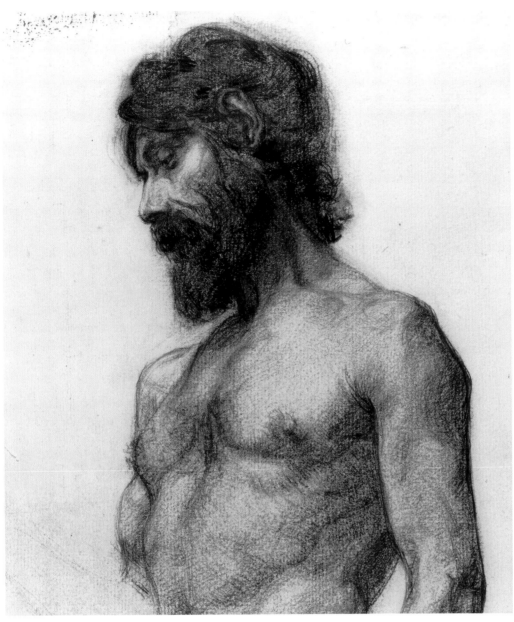

18 BUST-LENGTH STUDY OF A BEARDED MAN WITH SHORT HAIR

students learned to analyze and observe form and light by working from professional models.[2] The vantage from which *Half-Length Study of a Negro Man* (cat. no. 16) is drawn suggests that Tanner had a seat down front and to the right of the handsome subject.

All three pictures are characterized by strongly rendered facial expressions and beautifully observed light. A noteworthy aspect of Tanner's drawing method is the graceful, flowing contour line of the limbs and torsos of the figures, which is drawn with an absolutely sure touch. But his style does not depend on outline for its effect. Instead Tanner conceived his figures as masses of darks and lights by using the broad side of charcoal and crayon sticks, closely connected lines and hatching, and rubbing with his fingers or implements, as is particularly evident in the torsos. His approach provides an internal or even self-contained luminosity, which permeates the drawings and evokes a feeling of serene beauty.　　　　　　　　　　　　　DFM

1 9

HORSE AND TWO DOGS
IN A LANDSCAPE
(*Animal Troupe*)
1891
Oil on canvas
28 × 33 1/2" (71.12 × 85.09 cm)
Signed, inscribed, and dated lower left: monogram
signature/*Paris/1891*
Inscribed, signed, and dated verso: *12 rue de Seine/*
Henry O. Tanner/1891
Private collection

Fig. 17 Alexandre-Gabriel Decamps,
A Boy Leading His Animal Troupe, n.d.,
watercolor over light pencil sketch, 6 1/2 ×
9¹⁵/₁₆", Sterling and Francine Clark
Art Institute, Williamstown, Massachusetts.

Fig. 18 Thomas Eakins, *The Fairman Rogers
Four-in-Hand*, 1879, 24 × 36", Phila-
delphia Museum of Art, gift of William
Alexander Dick.

This painting was executed during Tanner's first year in Paris. Its ample size and high degree of finish suggest that he began work on it soon after arriving in the French capital, while studying at the Académie Julian. At first glance, the prominent horse seems an anomaly; Tanner's animal subjects up to this point had included only deer, sheep, and lions. But the study of horses had figured in Tanner's training at the Pennsylvania Academy of the Fine Arts a decade earlier:

> From the 1880–81 season on, a horse was used as a model in the modeling class for a six or seven weeks' pose.... At the same time a dead horse was dissected.... Every winter or early spring Eakins took a class to a suburban bone-boiling factory where they dissected horses in the slaughterhouse; and in summer they continued with studies of the living animal, modeling and painting and studying its movements, at Rogers' farm.[1]

Tanner absorbed these lessons well, as can be seen in the strong modeling of the horse and in the drawing of the dogs. The three beasts display individual personalities and carry on a dialogue that arouses the viewer's sympathy with the artist's presentation. This approach suggests Tanner's quick adoption of and improvisation on the *petit savoyard* motif of young gypsy urchins, supposedly from Savoy, who roamed the streets of Paris begging.[2] They would sing, play instruments, or present a small circus with a troupe of animals in exchange for alms. Tanner included a *petit savoyard* in this painting but removed it: a pentimento of such a figure is visible just behind and to the right of the large dog. The theme had a long tradition in French art, originating with Jean-Antoine Watteau (1684–1721) about 1708 and continuing with such nineteenth-century artists as Alexandre-Gabriel Decamps (1803–60) (fig. 17) and François Bonvin (1817–87). When Tanner painted the subject, however, it was no longer current, thus he was taking up recent historical genre.[3]

Although the subject and attitude of this work are at their core French, the composition might also reflect Tanner's study under Thomas Eakins. Eakins's *The Fairman Rogers Four-in-Hand* (fig. 18) could have provided a precedent for the glossy bay horse and the park setting. The tilt of the head of the second horse and Eakins's color scheme of greens, browns, and tans, with red accents, is echoed in Tanner's painting. However, Tanner used a lighter palette than did Eakins, and his contrasts of lights and darks are less emphatic.

This diffused light is yet another technique that the newly arrived artist learned from the art around him in Paris. Tanner's depiction of a gypsy troupe is far removed from Eakins's leisurely, middle-class ride in the park. As far as can be determined, this painting was neither discussed in the contemporary literature nor exhibited. One might speculate that it is the picture exhibited as *Spring Morning* at Earle's Galleries in Philadelphia in 1894. Eakins's own title for *Four-in-Hand* was *May Morning in the Park*.

In 1902 in his discussion of the Philadelphia show, W. S. Scarborough mentioned that Tanner's *Spring Morning* was a scene from Chester County, Pennsylvania.[4] But Tanner clearly indicated in an inscription on the back of the picture that it was executed in Paris in 1891, three years prior to the Earle's Galleries exhibition. No firm conclusion can be drawn about its presence there. DFM

BOIS D'AMOUR
1891
Oil on canvas
11⁷⁄₈ × 13⁷⁄₈" (30.16 × 35.24 cm)
Signed lower left: *H. O. Tanner*
Benjamin T. Johnson, Jr., Berkeley, California

CONCARNEAU
1891
Oil on canvas
10 × 17" (25.4 × 43.18 cm)
Signed, inscribed, and dated lower left: *H. O. Tanner/*
Concarneau/91
William Randolph Dorsey, Silver Spring, Maryland

Fig. 19 Roget Viollet, *The Bois d'Amour*, c.1900, postcard, Collection Boyle-Turner.

Tanner spent his first summer in France in Brittany: "As the summer approached, the students in Paris began to wend their way to the country. I wished to go to a rather isolated district so that I might improve my French. . . . Upon deciding to go to Pont-Aven on the Brittany coast, what was my surprise and disappointment to find that it had a large, a very large, English and American colony."[1] While at the coast Tanner made at least "half a dozen pleasant plein-air studies of subjects near Pont-Aven and Concarneau."[2] Among these were views of the Bois d'Amour and its tree-lined paths.

Bois d'Amour (cat. no. 20) was not executed on the spot like other of Tanner's sketches; its composition appears to draw instead on a contemporary postcard (fig. 19). Tanner often made use of diverse sources without resorting to direct copying; here he reversed the position of the figures and placed them closer together. He also straightened the clump of trees on the left and reorganized the right side of the composition. The overall treatment of the terrain and leaves, green with dappled patches of blue highlights, harks back to *Boy and Sheep Lying under a Tree*, 1881 (cat. no. 8). However, the brushwork is looser, and the handling of light and color much bolder, which certainly had to do with Tanner's exposure to French Impressionism and Post-Impressionism.

During this summer Tanner made an excursion to Concarneau, 15 kilometers south of Pont-Aven, where he painted a small, fluid depiction of rocks and water (cat. no. 21). Such scenes were very popular as postcard images and with the artists who frequented Brittany, including Tanner's friend Paul Sérusier. But Sérusier's pictures, in keeping with the prevailing aesthetic of Paul Gauguin, are much more linear than Tanner's newly found but relatively conservative form of Impressionism. As with *Bois d'Amour*, in this view of Concarneau Tanner looked back to his American training and experience for inspiration or, perhaps, safe solutions to artistic problems even while in the midst of a new breed of artists.

Neither landscape study was mentioned by the *Daily Evening Telegraph* when Tanner's show at Earle's Galleries was reviewed in April 1894. But insight into contemporary appreciation of this type of picture can be gained through the reaction, a few years later, of W. S. Scarborough to a similar work:

> On the writer's wall hangs one of the bits of the results of his first studies in Concarneau, that picturesque spot in Brittany where painters flock to paint the quaint scenes and dresses of this chief center of sardine fisheries. It is a morning scene — "The Going Out of the Fishing Boats from Concarneau." It is a bright, cheery one — a sandy strip and a brown spit of rock in the foreground with a narrow, dim shore line stretching out against the sky in the background, nearly encircling the broad, blue expanse of water on which, near the horizon, rests a misty fleet of departing sails.[3]

DFM

20 BOIS D'AMOUR

21 CONCARNEAU

22

EDGE OF THE FOREST
(*Bois d'Amour*)
c. 1893
Oil on wood panel
7 1/4 × 10 1/2" (18.42 × 26.67 cm)
Signed lower right: *H. O. Tanner*
N. N. Serper, courtesy of Rosenfeld Fine Arts, New York

At Pont-Aven in 1891, Tanner was attracted to the beech tree alleys of the Bois d'Amour both for their popularity with local inhabitants and for their beauty as landscape subjects. It appears that Tanner returned to Pont-Aven, before going to America by August 1893, to solve certain artistic problems through the study of nature. This desire would certainly have been intensified by the rejection of *The Bagpipe Lesson* (cat. no. 25) by the Salon jury and encouraged by his involvement with the circle of Paul Gauguin.

At first glance, the title of the present work, *Edge of the Forest* (cat. no. 22), seems apt. The site appears generalized past easy identification, but closer observation reveals trees on either side of a path, suggesting that the subject is again the Bois d'Amour. Moreover, a village can be discerned beyond the trees, and water, perhaps the Aven River, is in the distance.

Tanner demonstrated his originality in selecting this unusual view of Pont-Aven from the Bois d'Amour. The diagonal of the trail in the left foreground helps to hold the warm colors of the background in place. This line can be read as an arch whose form is repeated in front of the alley, which in turn forms a diagonal that is played off against the horizon. Tanner orchestrated these shapes with a palette of pinks, pale greens, and blues, presaging the hues of *The Banjo Lesson* (cat. no. 27), presumably painted shortly thereafter. Tanner handled the paint loosely, and the even, natural light is much more sophisticated in *Edge of the Forest* than the patches of light in *Bois d'Amour* of 1891 (cat. no. 20). Tanner's informality and freedom of brushwork here move him closer to Impressionism.   DFM

22 EDGE OF THE FOREST

23

STUDIO INTERIOR
1893
Pen and ink with ink washes on paper
10 1/2 × 7 1/2" (26.67 × 19.05 cm)
Inscribed and dated lower left: *15 rue de Seine with
H. MacNeil/at Paris 1893*
Archives of American Art, Smithsonian Institution, Washington, D.C.

Until brought to light in the course of work on the present exhibition, this sheet with its fresh drawing had gone unrecognized as an important document. The subject is the atelier that Tanner shared with the sculptor Hermon MacNeil on the rue de Seine in the Latin Quarter. Tanner lived across the street at 12 rue de Seine upon his arrival in Paris in 1891. The inscription on this sheet, in Tanner's hand at the lower left, corrects previously held notions that he had an atelier in 1893 in the more fashionable quarter of the rue de Reine.

Judging from Tanner's composition, the studio was located on the ground level, below the *rez-de-chaussée*. The entry door is of the poorest type, and the viewer is forced to look up and out through the windows, which seem to yield little interior light. The promise of more light beyond is held in the highlights at the door's base and at the windows.

Tanner employed three different perspectives, viewing the overall room at eye level, looking down on the crack of light below the door and the stack of paintings on the right, and looking up at the recessed framework of the windows. His fine pen lines, hatching, and wash are more relaxed than in his academy drawings (cat. nos. 16–18) executed in the formal setting of the Académie Julian, where he was a student around this time. The technique of *Studio Interior* can be constructively compared to that of *Study for the Young Sabot Maker* (cat. no. 32), where the use of hatching has seemed an anomaly in Tanner's oeuvre.   DFM

15 rue de Seine with H. MacNeil
at Paris 1893

23 STUDIO INTERIOR

24

STUDY FOR THE
BAGPIPE LESSON
1892
Oil on paperboard
5 × 5 ¹⁵/₁₆″ (12.7 × 15.08 cm) sheet
Signed and inscribed in ink lower left: *H. O. Tanner/Study for—*
The Bagpipe Lesson—in Brittany
Inscribed verso: *To my friend* [illegible]
National Museum of American Art, Smithsonian Institution,
gift of Mr. and Mrs. Norman B. Robbins

25

THE BAGPIPE LESSON
1892–93
Oil on canvas
45 × 68 ³/₄″ (114.3 × 174.63 cm)
Signed and inscribed lower left: monogram signature/
Concarneau Brittany
Hampton University Museum, Virginia

Fig. 20 Aston Knight, *May Blossoms*, c.
1910, oil on canvas, 31 ¹/₄ × 24 ³/₄″, The
Picker Art Gallery, Hamilton, New York,
gift of Mary C. Colgate.

Fig. 21 Camille Pissarro, *Landscape—*
Fields, 1885, oil on canvas, 29 × 23 ⁵/₈″,
Philadelphia Museum of Art, W. P.
Wilstach Collection.

In the season after his summer vacation of 1891 at Pont-Aven in Brittany, Tanner discovered the existence of the Salon, the most prestigious annual juried exhibition held in Paris. The paintings that he saw there suited his personal taste, and he felt that admission to the Salon was within the range of his talent: "Here was something to work for, to get a picture here. This now furnished a definite impetus to my work in Paris—to be able to make a picture that should be admitted here—could I do it? The next summer I worked in Brittany at Concarneau, upon a picture of an apple orchard."[1]

Presumably Tanner was speaking of *The Bagpipe Lesson* (cat. no. 25). The works catalogued here are the only known paintings by Tanner that can be described as depicting an apple orchard. Moreover, *Study for the Bagpipe Lesson* (cat. no. 24) is very close in handling to the overall green palette and daubing brushwork with patches of colored highlights that Tanner employed the year before in *Bois d'Amour* (cat. no. 20). The tree trunk on the left of the wonderfully fresh study and the lad blowing into the bagpipe on the right provided the basic ingredients for the finished work. *The Bagpipe Lesson* was certainly Tanner's most ambitious and fully realized undertaking to date. Its size, nearly 4 feet high by 6 feet wide, eclipses by far any of the artist's previous attempts.

Tanner's fellow pupil at the Académie Julian, the future playwright Henry Bataille (1872–1922), spent the summer of 1892 at Huelgoat in Brittany near Concarneau, and he wrote about an old man and young boy, *chanteurs populaires*, who roamed the region presenting impromptu entertainments.[2] Tanner depicted two such characters, along with a bonnet-clad woman, in *The Bagpipe Lesson*. Brittany peasants had been popular as subjects since the admirable figure paintings of Jean-François Millet (1814–75) in the 1850s to 1870s and of Jules Breton (1827–1906), such as *Great Pilgrimage*, 1868 (France, private collection). However, representations of bagpipe players from the region are rare.

Tanner arranged the three principal figures of his final composition in a pyramidal format with the woman as the apex. The imaginary line linking this figure, the front knee of the boy, and the sabot-clad foot of the old man imparts volume to the pyramid and anchors the group. The curving movement of the arms of the boy and man unifies the group and is reinforced by the circle of the wheel on the left. The angle of the young lad's back plays against the line of the tree trunk and its branches and the handles of the wheelbarrow. A diagonal path on the right, strewn with apple blossoms, leads to a barely

discernible, mysterious figure of a child at the upper right. Her position calls attention to the vaguely defined buildings of a village in the distance. These contrasting geometric shapes, coupled with the exaggerated facial features of the figures and the play of crisp against ambiguous images, account for the tremendous and somewhat unsettling energy of *The Bagpipe Lesson*. Tanner's drawing of the figures is superb, as seen in the complex foreshortening of the old man's pose. The deliberate comedy in their expressions is unusual in Tanner's work and suggests that his models may indeed have been performers.

Tanner employed the same basic green and white palette in the finished painting that he used for the study. The overall appearance of the work reflects a lingering Franco-American version of Impressionism in the manner of Daniel Ridgway Knight (1839–1924) and Aston Knight (1873–1948), as can be seen in Aston's *May Blossoms* (fig. 20),[3] rather than the tendency toward abstraction that can be seen in a work by Camille Pissarro (1830–1903) (fig. 21). (Aston Knight began his studies at the Académie Julian in 1891, the same year as Tanner.) However, the tilted perspective of the path in *The Bagpipe Lesson* reflects a Japanese compositional device adopted by many contemporary French artists. The odd dreamlike child at the end of the path calls to mind the figures of the Symbolist painter Odilon Redon (1840–1916), who was well known to the artists working in Brittany. Tanner would not fully explore these French tendencies until the summer of 1894.

The artist was pleased enough by *The Bagpipe Lesson* to make it his first *envoi* to the Salon in 1893 (which indicates that it was certainly completed by

25 THE BAGPIPE LESSON

the end of April), but despite his best efforts, it was refused. Tanner confused his own chronology by stating: "Two years afterward, in 1895, it was accepted, but no impression was made."[4] The artist's Salon submissions accepted in 1895 are well documented, and *The Bagpipe Lesson* was not among them. The work could not have been shown in Paris in 1894; during the Salon season it was on view in Philadelphia at Earle's Galleries and remained there throughout the year. The painting listed as *La Leçon de Musique* in the 1894 Salon catalogue (no. 1710) must have been a work painted a little later, *The Banjo Lesson* (cat. no. 27), which was not shown in the 1894 spring exhibition at Earle's.[5] For all its ambition, *The Bagpipe Lesson* was a relatively conservative production and, in spite of its date, does not represent a direct stylistic link to *The Banjo Lesson*, although they share the theme of teaching to which Tanner would return throughout his career.

Although refused by the Salon, *The Bagpipe Lesson* was accepted into the competitive annual exhibition of 1893–94 held by the Pennsylvania Academy of the Fine Arts. It was exhibited thereafter at Earle's together with works by one of Tanner's Academy mentors, Thomas Hovenden. *The Bagpipe Lesson* held a special place in the installation and was singled out by a critic for the *Daily Evening Telegraph*: "In the same galleries [with Hovenden] Mr. H. O. Tanner is also holding a special exhibition. There are seventeen numbers in Mr. Tanner's catalogue, including landscape, genre, figure studies and composed subjects. His large picture, *The Bagpipe Lesson*, a scene in Brittany, recently seen at the Academy of the Fine Arts, occupies the central place in the collection."[6]

The Bagpipe Lesson played yet another role in Tanner's career. Unbeknownst to the artist, one of his major future benefactors and supporters, Robert C. Ogden, a partner in the Wanamaker dry goods company, wrote to Booker T. Washington on October 17, 1895:

> A proposition was made in this city some time ago for the colored people to purchase [Tanner's] large picture "The Bagpipe Lesson" and present it to the Academy of Fine Arts in this city. The movement did not make much progress, resulting in the collection of only about $100. . . . The amount needed is something over $1000. If you think this is a worthy matter, please give it your influence for at least the 25¢ subscriptions [for a good reproduction of the picture]. I have bestowed time, thought and money upon the plan and I certainly hope it will succeed.[7]

This plan did not succeed, but Ogden, who was also a trustee of Hampton University, bought the picture himself and donated it to the university by 1905. As a result, Tanner gained a sum some three times above his usual income,[8] and Hampton, which already owned *The Banjo Lesson*, acquired its second major work by Tanner.   DFM

2 6

THE BAGPIPE PLAYER
1895
Oil on canvas
21¹/₂ × 18¹/₂" (53.34 × 47 cm)
Signed, inscribed, and dated lower left: *H. O. Tanner/Paris 95*
Private collection

The Bagpipe Player must be based on Tanner's stay at Pont-Aven in 1894. Tanner dealt with the same subject in his more ambitious *The Bagpipe Lesson*, 1892–93 (cat. no. 25). This type of peasant musician harks back to the street entertainer theme (cat. no. 19) but was not a frequent subject of nineteenth-century French artists.

A young bagpipe player is placed in a shallow space with a wood-paneled wall as a backdrop. The boy wears recognizable dress from the Breton region but not its more decorative ceremonial costume,[1] and he seems about to go off to perform. He holds with his left hand a deflated *biniou*, a bagpipe unique to Brittany; a simple pewter water pitcher sits on a bench to the left.

Tanner captured in his subject's face the modest pleasure that an ordinary person might feel as a result of such singular attention. The artist's sympathy for this large-eared, big-handed Breton is perhaps not inconsistent with his expressed desire to show the "warm big heart" of contemporary blacks.[2] Tanner conveyed the inner temperament of the bagpipe player through a deft use of light and shadow. A strong light from the upper left falls gently on the pewter jar and accents the figure's smiling head, relaxed hands, and inert *biniou*. The lack of cast shadows behind the figure and objects clarifies the overall image, and the straightforward palette of dominant blue and brownish maroon colors adds to the uncomplicated, friendly nature of the work.

Tanner rarely, if ever, invented subjects or compositions, although he freshly interpreted what he observed in nature and what he saw in the renderings of other artists. He might have known the model for *The Bagpipe Player* at Pont-Aven, or he could have seen the subject in a postcard. The strong three-dimensional modeling of the figure owes a debt to Thomas Eakins, and the commonality of pose and light suggests that *The Bagpipe Player* can be interpreted as a deliberate variation of Eakins's 1880 *Portrait of General George Cadwalader* (fig. 22). For instance, the stern-faced military man stares out at the viewer, while the rustic musician inclines his head with a gentle smile. The collarless uniform and glowing buttons in Eakins's picture have softer counterparts in Tanner's painting. Finally, the highlighted hands in the foreground play similar roles, albeit reversed in the compositions.

The Bagpipe Player, a pleasant picture both visually and emotionally, offers further testimony to the manner in which Tanner sought a working method by experimenting with various approaches rather than depending solely on his past training or present environment. The shallow space and simplicity of the brown paneled background were precursors of later pure portraits (cat. nos. 41, 42, 86).   DFM

Fig. 22 Thomas Eakins, *Portrait of General George Cadwalader*, 1880, oil on canvas, 38 ¹/₂ × 24 ¹/₂", The Butler Institute of American Art, Youngstown, Ohio.

26 THE BAGPIPE PLAYER

Fig. 23 Henry O. Tanner, study photograph for *The Banjo Lesson*, Jacques Tanner, Le Douhet, France.

Recovering from a bout with typhoid fever, Tanner left Paris and returned to Philadelphia sometime in the summer of 1893. It has been assumed that he came home in the fall of 1892,[1] but by Tanner's account, he contracted typhoid during his third year in Paris, which would have been 1893. *Studio Interior* (cat. no. 23) and a pastel study for *The Young Sabot Maker* (cat. no. 31), both signed and dated "Paris, 1893," offer additional evidence.

Tanner delivered a paper on "The American Negro in Art" in August before the World's Congress on Africa, held in Chicago in 1893 in conjunction with the World's Columbian Exposition.[2] The text of his speech has not been found, but a summary was published in a report on the congress in *Our Day*: "Professor Tanner (American) spoke of negro painters and sculptors, and claimed that actual achievement proved negroes to possess ability and talent for successful competition with white artists."[3] This statement echoes sentiments Tanner expressed in an interview almost ten years earlier.[4] Perhaps more of the speech's content can be gleaned from a statement Tanner wrote (in the third person) in Philadelphia about a year later:

> Since his return from Europe he has painted mostly Negro subjects, he feels drawn to such subjects on account of the newness of the field and because of a desire to represent the serious, and pathetic side of life among them, and it is his thought that other things being equal, he who has most sympathy with his subject will obtain the best results. To his mind many of the artists who have represented Negro life have only seen the comic, the ludicrous side of it, and have lacked sympathy with and appreciation for the warm big heart that dwells within such a rough exterior.[5]

27 THE BANJO LESSON

In early October 1893 at Earle's Galleries, where he had admired marine subjects during his student days, Tanner exhibited *The Banjo Lesson* (cat. no. 27), a painting of an African-American subject that has since become his most famous work. Following the tenets of academic figure compositions, Tanner selected a large canvas and arranged two figures as dominant elements in the composition. But the high point of view and the cut-off ceiling compress the scene, emphasizing the figures and concentrating attention on their interaction in a manner very different from the more fully defined space and relaxed narrative of conventional genre painting.

A gray-haired man sits in a sparsely furnished interior on a straight-back chair, a young boy standing between his legs. With the man's help, the boy plays a banjo; both are absorbed by his effort. The youngster's right hand is isolated against the round sounding board of the instrument, the focus of the painting. Against the background wall, a plank table is partially covered with a white cloth and laid with plates and a white pitcher. Two small pictures and a shelf hang on the wall. To the left, a coat is draped over the back of a chair; another garment hangs on a side wall. Visible at the lower right, a portion of a stone hearth is set into the bare plank floor. A volume of space is created around the man and boy by a rough circle of objects—an iron skillet, a stoneware crock, and a tin coffeepot on the hearth at the right, and a hat and pipe on the floor at left.

A notice of the painting, then titled *The First Lesson*, appeared in the *Christian Recorder* for October 5, 1893: "We visited Earle's Art Gallery on Chestnut Street to see 'the first lesson' a remarkable life-sized oil painting by Prof. H. O. Tanner, on exhibition there. We found the picture surrounded by a large crowd of spectators and it seemed to be the most admired of all others, and was decided by the best critics to be a very superb picture."[6]

Two days later the *Daily Evening Telegraph* devoted a long paragraph to Tanner and the painting, noting that he had "opened a studio in this city and proposes to remain here during the coming winter." The writer characterized Tanner as a landscape painter working in the Impressionist mode, although not "dominated by the 'blue bug' craze so far as to sacrifice his perception of color, and [he] has kept a place on his palette for other tints besides yellow and purple."[7] The writer depended on racial stereotypes to describe the man and boy, but otherwise the account is informed, perceptive, and sympathetic:

> In a present venture Mr. Tanner has entered upon a field new to his endeavor, so far as this public is aware his first exhibit of a figure subject of importance being now on view. . . . This is a large upright entitled, "The First Lesson," a composition of two figures. . . . An old Uncle Ned, bald and venerable, has a bare-footed little darkey of seven or eight years between his knees, and is earnestly instructing the youngster how to finger the strings of an ancient banjo. The figures are firmly modelled and well "enveloped," each occupying its own space and place and each bearing the stamp of individuality. The heads are especially well drawn, that of the child being a study Mr. Tanner may well be proud of, and the faces are informed with intelligence and expression. On its literary side the picture is in every way to be commended, its simple and rather pathetic story being told very cleverly and with interesting effect.[8]

A striking technical aspect of *The Banjo Lesson*, which Tanner would use in only one other painting, is the illumination of the scene by two light sources beyond the edges of the picture: daylight from a window at the left, and firelight from a fireplace at the right. The *Daily Evening Telegraph* critic admired the ambition of this device but would have preferred a more unified effect:

> Technically speaking, the artist has set himself a problem fraught with difficulties that might perhaps better be avoided except for study purposes. He has posed his figures between the chimney and the window, with warm firelight illuminating one side of his group, and cold daylight striking sharply against the other side. To paint his details in these two hostile lights, to make them blend where they come together, and to harmonize the whole . . . is an exceedingly trying task which he grappled manfully and with marked success, but which is, after all, evidently enough not the happiest way in which the subject might have been treated. Students will be attracted and pleased by the searching distinctions he makes and the skill with which he brings the two discordant schemes of his picture into unity and bids them pull together; but picture-lovers will wish he had closed the window-blinds and let the glow of the fire shine all through the room, throwing deep shadows into the far corners.[9]

Despite the critic's disapproval, the two light sources allowed Tanner to depict the effect of warm and cool illumination on the figures' dark skin. These light effects, together with the heightened pinks and ochres in the background, convey Tanner's profound study of the beauty to be found in the scene. Something of the same seriousness and intense observation can be found in Thomas Eakins's watercolor *Negro Boy Dancing* (fig. 24), but the rich color keyed to the values of the subjects' skin is unique to Tanner.

It has been suggested that *The Banjo Lesson* was based on sketches and paintings inspired by Tanner's experiences in the Highlands of North Carolina during the summer of 1889,[10] although no such work has been found. Apparently, at least one painting of a black genre subject (now lost) resulted from Tanner's years in Atlanta; a newspaper account of an exhibition of Tanner's work held in Cincinnati in 1890 describes one canvas as "an old colored man taking his little cotton to market on a rattletrap ox-cart. It is a thing containing some good drawing and excellent coloring."[11]

The theme for *The Banjo Lesson* might well be the result of Tanner's North Carolina visit, but he developed the painting from posed models. A recently discovered photograph, probably taken by Tanner (fig. 23), shows a man and boy posed much as they appear in the finished painting, with the boy holding what is obviously a studio prop — a roughly constructed cardboard banjo with lines drawn for the strings. What appears to be a canvas turned to the wall in the background suggests that the photograph was made in the artist's studio, and the cardboard banjo seems to indicate that Tanner intended his models to embody his specific idea. Recently it has been proposed that *The Banjo Lesson* was painted in Paris,[12] and certainly the ambition and complexity of the work suggest that it was made after a period of study in France. But in light of Tanner's statement that "since his return from Europe, he has painted mostly Negro subjects," Philadelphia seems a more likely locale for its production. Especially in the background, the brushwork of *The Banjo Lesson* is much looser, and strokes of color are more assertive than in his equally ambitious painting, *The Bagpipe Lesson* (cat. no. 25), completed in France in the same year. Tanner used this technique in two other large figure pieces (cat. nos. 28, 29) painted during his Philadelphia stay, but he abandoned it after his return to France; the effect is distinctive enough to suggest the

Fig. 24 Thomas Eakins, *Negro Boy Dancing*, watercolor, 1878, 18 1/8 × 22 5/8", The Metropolitan Museum of Art, New York, Fletcher Fund.

Fig. 25 *I's So Happy!*, engraving by Willy Miller after a painting by Thomas Hovenden, 1885, location unknown.

Fig. 26 Walter M. Dunk, *The Fruits of Genius*, c. 1883, engraving.

Fig. 27 Thomas Hovenden, *Their Pride*, 1888, oil on canvas, 31 × 40", The Union League Club, Frick Art Reference Library, New York.

definitive changes both in Tanner's location and in his artistic direction.

But the question remains: why did Tanner turn to African-American subjects in Philadelphia during 1893–94? A number of suppositions have been offered. After two and a half years abroad, and participation in the Chicago congress, Tanner would have again confronted racial issues that were less immediate than in Paris, and his reacquaintance with American prejudices might have inspired him to take up the black cause in art. Parallels existed between European depictions of rural peasants in genre scenes and portrayals of African-Americans by American artists,[13] and Tanner's experience of painting in Brittany, where local peasants were a favorite subject, and his study of rural scenes in the salons perhaps suggested that American black subjects would fit within an established, widely accepted art tradition. Tanner might have turned to African-American subjects in response to a challenge, stated or unstated, from his father "to demonstrate that he could make positive statements about his race from the canvas just as effectively as his father could from the pulpit."[14]

Although Tanner was the first African-American artist to produce black genre works,[15] some white American artists had been incorporating black figures in genre scenes since the 1820s. African-Americans had figured in the work of William Sidney Mount (1807–68) and Winslow Homer (1836–1910), prominent artists whose paintings Tanner might have known.[16] Tanner's teachers and friends Thomas Eakins and Thomas Hovenden and his contemporaries Thomas Anschutz and Walter M. Dunk had painted black genre scenes in Philadelphia in the 1880s (fig. 26). Hovenden and Eakins, especially, are recognized today for their serious and individual treatments of their subjects without the elements of caricature or grotesquerie that pervaded popular imagery and even the work of other important artists (fig. 27). Recent interpretations of Eakins's and Hovenden's black subjects, however, have suggested that even their work reflects racial stereotypes,[17] and perhaps Tanner had in mind certain examples of their work, as well as that of others, when he commented that many artists represented only "comic" or "ludicrous" aspects of black culture.[18]

In choosing the theme of *The Banjo Lesson*, and later *The Thankful Poor* (cat. no. 28), Tanner did not break new ground. The banjo-playing black man was a standard figure in paintings of African-Americans, from minstrel show parodies to domestic scenes such as Eastman Johnson's *Old Folks at Home* and portraits as sympathetic (despite its title) as Hovenden's *I's So Happy!* (fig. 25), which might have inspired Tanner to take up the subject. In fact, it has been suggested that Tanner deliberately selected a cliché to show that he could render a compassionate reinterpretation.[19] In a departure from conventional treatments, Tanner distinguished between musical entertainment and education, recognizing that "images of men teaching were not that common in the American genre tradition."[20] The painting reveals a genuine and profound sympathy for the subject, and even more than his written testimony, *The Banjo Lesson* demonstrates that while in Philadelphia Tanner thought intensely about the relation of his race to his own art.

Tanner intended to return to Paris as soon as he had regained his health and sold some paintings to finance further studies. From the first notice in October 1893 to the last in September 1894, newspaper accounts mentioned his plans to go abroad again. It seems reasonable to assume that Tanner would

28 THE THANKFUL POOR

Fig. 28 Thomas Eakins, *Spinning*, 1881, watercolor on paper, 15 5/8 × 10 5/8″, private collection.

Fig. 29 Thomas Hovenden, *Breaking Home Ties*, 1890, oil on canvas, 52 1/8 × 72 1/4″, Philadelphia Museum of Art, gift of Ellen Harrison McMichael in memory of C. Emory McMichael.

have painted at least the major works of his Philadelphia stay with the Paris Salon in mind. Certainly in its size, ambitious figure composition, and complex lighting, *The Banjo Lesson* is the kind of painting he would have sent to the Salon, but until recently exactly which painting Tanner submitted from Philadelphia has been unclear. The 1894 Salon catalogue lists Tanner's entry as *La Leçon de Musique*, and it has been assumed that this was *The Bagpipe Lesson*, also a large academic figure piece and the most elaborate painting Tanner had completed before leaving Paris. But Tanner showed *The Bagpipe Lesson* at the Pennsylvania Academy of the Fine Arts from December 1893 through February 1894 and also at Earle's Galleries in late April and early May, so it could not have been in Paris during May, when the Salon was held. On April 26, the *Christian Recorder* announced that one of Tanner's paintings would be shown at the Salon, and the *Philadelphia Inquirer* of April 29 stated that Tanner had just sent *The Banjo Lesson* to the Salon.[21] Still, evidence that the painting actually went to Paris was not entirely solid, and it has recently been suggested that the painting was sold before going to Paris.[22] A third notice, however, in *Southern Workman* for November 1894, appears to confirm its presence at the Salon: "[*The Banjo Lesson*] won an honorable place in the Paris Salon, and received high praise from the celebrated French artist, Mr. Benjamin-Constant, under whom Mr. Tanner has studied."[23]

Perhaps Tanner, in sending *The Banjo Lesson* to the Salon, was trying to gauge the reaction to African-American subjects as a direction for his work after his return to Europe. The painting did not attract the attention of critics, and other than praise from Benjamin-Constant, Tanner's teacher at the Académie Julian, there is no record of the painting's reception.

A newly discovered work by Tanner, dated 1894, and here titled *Spinning by Firelight — The Boyhood of George Washington Gray* (cat. no. 29), is closely related to *The Banjo Lesson*, with the crucial difference that its subjects are white. In 1894, the Reverend Gray, a minister in the Methodist Episcopal Church, was living in Evanston, a suburb of Chicago, and this might be the painting referred to in the *Christian Recorder* for August 23, 1894: "Artist H. O. Tanner has returned from Chicago where he filled an order for one of his valuable pictures with a gentleman of wealth and prominence in that city."[24] According to family tradition, the painting represents a scene from Gray's childhood; the fact that it was a commissioned work on a specific subject might account for the notice's unusual phrasing that Tanner had "filled an order" for a painting.

George Washington Gray was born December 6, 1834, on a farm near the small town of Piqua, Ohio. Tanner depicted the interior of Gray's childhood home with the same fireplace, rough walls, and plank floor that appeared in *The Banjo Lesson*, examples of which he might have studied during his stay in the mountains of North Carolina. In this painting, however, more sophisticated objects such as the gold-framed looking glass and the tall case clock are combined with homemade items and suggest the austerities of a settler's household rather than the deprivations of the rural poor. (These objects might have remained in Gray's possession, as did the spinning wheel, which is still owned by his descendants.)

Although less dramatic because both light sources are visible and perhaps because Tanner did not find white skin to be as rich a ground for reflected colors, the light effects, palette, and technique of the two paintings

29 SPINNING BY FIRELIGHT — THE BOYHOOD OF GEORGE WASHINGTON GRAY

are the same. The larger, more completely defined architectural setting of *Spinning by Firelight* allows a more spacious composition, and instead of a single complex group, as in *The Banjo Lesson*, three centers of interest form around the individual figures. Probably based on Gray's recollection, the scene depicts his father seated near the table against the back wall, himself as a boy building a tower of corncobs on the hearth, and his mother at a spinning wheel in the center foreground. No doubt Tanner hired models to pose as he worked on the picture, but the figure of the woman spinning is similar, especially in costume and pose, to the spinning subjects Thomas Eakins painted in the early 1880s (fig. 28), when Tanner was one of his students.

Confronted with the need to illustrate his patron's memories, Tanner recalled the work of another of his Philadelphia mentors, Thomas Hovenden. Instead of *The Banjo Lesson*'s concentrated emotional force, *Spinning by Firelight* tells its story in a series of anecdotes, like a conventional genre scene, and although the preoccupation of Tanner's three figures is different from the interaction of the characters in Hovenden's work, the extended narrative is similar to his approach in such elaborate compositions as *Breaking Home Ties* (fig. 29).

Sometime in 1894, before the Earle's Galleries exhibition, Tanner painted *The Thankful Poor*, his second known black genre subject and another highly regarded image. For his subject, Tanner again selected a familiar convention from European peasant and African-American genre painting, in which piety, humility, and poverty were frequently portrayed.[25] In the case of *The Thankful Poor*, Tanner possibly had a direct source of inspiration in a work by his contemporary, Elizabeth Nourse (1859–1938), who had won a gold medal at the 1893 Chicago world's fair for her depiction of a French peasant

Fig. 30 Elizabeth Nourse, *Le Repas en Famille*, 1891, oil on canvas, location unknown, photograph from E. Nourse *Scrapbook I*, Richard W. Thompson, courtesy Mary Alice Heekin Burke.

family gathered around a table, entitled *Le Repas en Famille* (fig. 30).²⁶

In some ways *The Thankful Poor* is a less ambitious composition than *The Banjo Lesson*. An old man and a boy are shown half length and separated by a table, rather than full length and united in a complex interaction. Space is more limited; a single large volume is solidly defined by the perspective of the tabletop on which the pitcher, plates, utensils, and cups stretch the spatial boundaries of the flat plane. These might be the same objects and table with white cloth that Tanner used in *The Banjo Lesson*, but the placement of the table in a corner, framed by a curtain to the left, the blank back wall, and a closer point of view create the effect of a much smaller room—possibly an urban space instead of the rural setting of *The Banjo Lesson*.

Although similar in technique, *The Thankful Poor* appears simpler and presents a more concentrated image than the earlier painting. Whether or not in response to criticism of the two light sources in *The Banjo Lesson*, Tanner limited himself to one light source, which unifies the scene and emphasizes the stillness of the man and boy in prayer.

Yet while different in many details, *The Banjo Lesson* and *The Thankful Poor* are alike in that Tanner rendered his subjects as individuals, not as representatives of a class. The care Tanner took in the arrangement and depiction of the scene and his persistent, nonjudgmental study of the models create deep sympathy with his subject, an approach that echoes the artistic goal of Thomas Eakins. Even more than in *The Banjo Lesson*, Tanner makes the emotional content of the scene, rather than its visual aspect, his subject. The dignified portrayal of the old man and boy at prayer transcends any other image of black Americans in American art.

In his autobiography, written more than fifteen years later, Tanner devoted only two sentences to his 1893–94 stay in Philadelphia, describing only his attempts to raise money to return to Paris. Yet this period marks the beginning of Tanner's career as an established artist in the United States. He sold three major paintings and widely exhibited a fourth that later sold, and other works might have sold. Exhibitions attracted the attention of individuals who would be instrumental in promoting and buying Tanner's paintings for the next few decades: Harrison S. Morris, then head of the exhibitions committee at the Pennsylvania Academy of the Fine Arts, John T. Morris, a local philanthropist, and Robert C. Ogden, a board member of Hampton University who arranged for several of Tanner's paintings to be donated to the school. Meanwhile, Ogden, together with Booker T. Washington, began a campaign to inform African-Americans about Tanner's achievement as an artist and to encourage them to buy his work, or photographs of it.

In light of these successes and his declared aim to represent African-American subjects in art, the question of why Tanner abandoned these themes after his return to Paris takes on additional importance, although there is little evidence to support a definitive answer. An article in the *Daily Evening Telegraph* on September 17, 1894, offers a partial explanation: "Like other painters of ability, he can do better, financially speaking, in Paris than he can in Philadelphia, and consequently he will presently be going abroad again."²⁷ It might be that Tanner, perhaps acting on the advice of Benjamin-Constant, or of fellow students in Paris who had observed public response to *The Banjo Lesson* at the Salon, simply concluded that he could not prosper in France as a painter of black culture.

But the eloquence with which Tanner called for a broader understanding of the subject and his demonstration of that sympathy in his paintings suggest his decision was based more on personal than commercial reasons. Tanner offered only one oblique reference on the topic in his autobiography. Writing about the years 1895–96 in Paris, he said, "A gentleman who had enabled me to gain a little by writing up art notes in Paris now withdrew this work because he thought I should come to America and paint 'American subjects.' I refused to come home and paint things I was not drawn to, nor did I like the idea of quitting the helpful influences by which I was surrounded."[28] Whether or not "American subjects" is a euphemism for African-American themes, or whether Tanner included them in the much larger range of American subjects, it is remarkable that he would have rejected the whole field just a few years after he had made a plea for its serious treatment.

In making sympathetic pictures of blacks, did Tanner discover that his real artistic interests lay elsewhere? Did he realize that the conventions of European peasant genre were inappropriate or inadequate in portraying blacks? Or did a new understanding of his own social level in relation to that of his subjects disillusion Tanner with genre painting in general? Perhaps Tanner felt a need for innovation in his work that lay outside the possibilities offered by his depictions of African-Americans. Whatever the reason, after completing *The Young Sabot Maker* (cat. no. 34), which he had started before leaving Paris, Tanner would paint only a handful of genre scenes over the next thirty years.

Certainly Tanner was aware of pressure to become the creator of a new, distinctively African-American art. In 1902, W. S. Scarborough, a friend of Tanner and his father, addressed this issue in an article in *Southern Workman*: "When 'The Banjo Lesson' appeared many of the friends of the race sincerely hoped that a portrayer of Negro life by a Negro artist had arisen indeed. They hoped, too, that the treatment of race subjects by him would serve to counterbalance so much that has made the race only a laughing-stock subject for those artists who see nothing in it but the most extravagantly absurd and grotesque. But this was not to be."[29] Scarborough suggested that Tanner's rejection of black subjects was due to the strength of his religious convictions and his father's desire for him to paint religious scenes. "The fact had not been taken into consideration that his early home atmosphere had always been strongly religious, neither was it generally known that it had long been the wish of his father's heart that his son should paint Biblical subjects — turn his genius into religious channels and thus make his art serve religion, since neither his pen nor his voice was to be employed in such service."[30]

Although Tanner was evasive about his father's influence on his decision to paint biblical themes, clearly something during his Philadelphia stay determined his choice of religious rather than African-American subjects. In his autobiography and in other articles and interviews, Tanner never mentioned *The Banjo Lesson* or *The Thankful Poor*, and perhaps even more noteworthy, he seems not to have requested them for exhibitions of his work, including his first retrospective in New York in 1908. Perhaps in religious scenes Tanner saw the opportunity to create paintings of more profound universal significance than any genre subject could have, no matter the strength of his personal feelings or the sensitivity of his interpretation.   DS

3 0

FLORIDA
1894
Oil on canvas
18 1/2 × 22 1/2" (46.99 × 57.15 cm)
Signed, inscribed, and dated lower right: *H. O. Tanner/Florida 94*
Walter O. Evans, M.D., Detroit

On February 15, 1894, the *Christian Recorder*, a weekly publication of the A.M.E. Church, announced that Tanner had left Philadelphia for the A.M.E. conference in Florida. Perhaps, as in the past, Tanner was traveling to improve his health; he also was employed on unspecified church business. On April 19, the editor of the *Christian Recorder* commented: "A splendid work was that done by Prof. H. O. Tanner, for this department at the recent Florida conferences, and, best of all, the cash, with a clean-cut statement was sent promptly. That is the sort of agent we are looking for every time."[1]

During his sojourn in Florida, Tanner found time to paint several landscapes. All are about the same size, with paint broadly brushed and rubbed into unprimed, coarsely textured canvas in high-key, Impressionist tonalities, producing glowing colors in the diffused sunlight seen through high clouds in the Florida winter sky. Tanner showed these paintings in an exhibition of seventeen works done in France and the United States at Earle's Galleries in late April 1894. In an article of 1902, W. S. Scarborough mentioned the Florida paintings: " 'Scrub-Pine Land' and 'Evening on the St. John's,' both from studies near Enterprise, Fla.; 'Lake Monroe' and 'Orange Grove,' studies in the same state."[2] *Florida* (cat. no. 30) is probably the work Scarborough names as "Orange Grove"; two other paintings from the same series have descended in the Tanner family.

DS

30 FLORIDA

3 1

STUDY FOR THE YOUNG
SABOT MAKER
1893
Pastel and ink on paper, mounted on paperboard
10⁵/₁₆ × 8⁵/₁₆" (26.19 × 21.11 cm) sheet
Inscribed and signed in brown ink lower right: *To my
friend/Murphy/Tanner*; and dated lower center: *Paris 1893*
National Museum of American Art, Smithsonian Institution,
Washington, D.C., gift of H. Alan and Melvin Frank

3 2

STUDY FOR THE YOUNG
SABOT MAKER
1893
Pen, brush, and ink with charcoal and white gouache
on artist's board
15¼ × 10¼" (38.74 × 26.04 cm)
Signed and dated lower right: monogram signature/93
The Metropolitan Museum of Art, New York, purchase, Erving
Wolf Foundation gift and Hanson K. Corning gift, by exchange,
1975

3 3

STUDY FOR THE YOUNG
SABOT MAKER
c. 1894–95
Oil on canvas
16¼ × 13" (41.28 × 33.02 cm)
National Museum of American Art, Smithsonian Institution,
Washington, D.C., gift of Mr. and Mrs. Norman B. Robbins

3 4

THE YOUNG SABOT MAKER
1895
Oil on canvas
41 × 35" (104.14 × 88.9 cm)
Signed and dated lower left: *H. O. Tanner/1895*
Estate of Sadie T. M. Alexander

Fig. 31 Elizabeth Nourse, *The Sabot
Makers*, 1900, oil on canvas, 15½ ×
19³/₁₆", Cincinnati Art Museum, gift of
Melrose Pitman.

In addition to the landscape of the Brittany region, during the summers of
1891–93 Tanner was attracted by the life of the indigenous people of Pont-Aven
and Concarneau. He found subjects for his art in the region's bagpipe players
and the fabricators of wooden shoes, or sabots. No direct evidence indicates
that Tanner visited the sabot maker's shop or knew its occupants personally,
but it was a logical topic: sabots were *de rigueur* footgear for local residents. It
was not a widely popular theme, although the American painter Elizabeth
Nourse also rendered a similar scene several years later (fig. 31).

The four images of *The Young Sabot Maker* catalogued here should be
seen as two distinct pairs, in spite of their many common details. In the
National Museum of American Art pastel (cat. no. 31) and the Metropolitan
Museum gouache (cat. no. 32), the positions of the principal figures are the
reverse of those in the final painting (cat. no. 34) and its study (cat. no. 33). The
first pair of drawings must have been studies for an abandoned first attempt at
the composition, which Tanner altered when he returned to the subject.

The verso of Tanner's famous *The Thankful Poor* (cat. no. 29) contains
the beginning of a painting (fig. 32) that shows the young sabot maker on the
right side, as seen in the two drawings. The painting would have been nearly 4
feet tall by 3 feet wide, but by August 1893 Tanner had turned to depicting the
serious side of African-American life, and he reused the canvas for *The
Thankful Poor*. The two studies for the unrealized version of *The Sabot Maker*
point to the fact that, after two years in France, the thirty-three-year-old artist
was adding to his working methods. Thomas Eakins encouraged his pupils to
make compositional sketches in oil, but here Tanner executed one of his first
studies in pastel. He was pleased enough with the sketch to give it to his friend
and fellow artist Hermann Dudley Murphy.

31 STUDY FOR THE YOUNG SABOT MAKER

32 STUDY FOR THE YOUNG SABOT MAKER

Whereas the pastel can be seen as a preliminary study for the placement of the figures and the fall of light, the Metropolitan Museum gouache is much more ambitious. Tanner worked on facial expressions, contrasting the energetic action of the young boy with the calm benevolence of his old mentor, and above all, he tackled problems of light and dark. Allover pale gray washes reflect the light that shines through the splendidly rendered window. Lines of hatching in pen and brush — which the artist also used in *Studio Interior* (cat. no. 23) — add to the activity of the scene.

The preliminary studies for *The Young Sabot Maker* pursue the theme of age instructing youth begun in *The Bagpipe Lesson* (cat. no. 25) and pave the way for *The Banjo Lesson* (cat. no. 27). The acceptance of the latter work by the 1894 Salon jury could have impelled Tanner to retake the sabot-maker theme toward the end of 1894 and early 1895. Tanner was quite pleased with his effort; a letter of May 23, 1895, to John S. Durham sheds light on the dating of the picture: "Dear Friend, your kind note of Dec. 20 . . . arrived a long time ago. It found me very busy in the midst of work mainly upon the picture now exhibited in the Salon, 'Le Jeune Sabotier.'"[1]

The oil study for the final version (cat. no. 33) does not offer a great deal beyond the Metropolitan Museum drawing, although the figures are reversed and the hearth is given less emphasis. Tanner's fond recollection from his

Fig. 32 Henry O. Tanner, *Oil Study for the Young Sabot Maker*, verso of *The Thankful Poor*, c. 1894, oil on canvas, 35 × 44", William H. and Camille O. Cosby.

33 STUDY FOR THE YOUNG SABOT MAKER

infancy in Pittsburgh of "a great Dutch oven"[2] in his family's house might account in part for the prominence of the hearth in this drawing and in later works such as *Etaples Fisher Folk* (cat. no. 90).

The definitive Salon version of *The Young Sabot Maker* (cat. no. 34) incorporates and resolves all the elements of the studies and introduces new touches. The young sabot maker himself, perhaps because of the success of *The Banjo Lesson*, has been transformed into a lad of African-American heritage; crisp light emphasizes his facial features. Tanner used the shavings and sabot remnants on the floor of the shop, along with the vessels on the table in the left background and on the windowsill, to yield beautifully painted still lifes. The dominantly green and brown palette is applied with clean, descriptive brushstrokes.

Reviewers of the 1895 Salon did not single out *The Young Sabot Maker* for special praise. But exhibition of the picture was a welcome sign of official recognition by the French art world.   DFM

34 THE YOUNG SABOT MAKER

35

LES INVALIDES

1896
Oil on canvas
13 × 16 1/4" (33.02 × 41.28 cm)
Signed and dated lower left: *H O Tanner/96*
Terra Museum of American Art, Chicago, Daniel J. Terra
Collection

36

THE MAN WHO RENTED BOATS

c. 1900
Oil on canvas mounted on plywood
9 1/4 × 12 3/8" (23.5 × 31.43 cm)
National Museum of American Art, Smithsonian Institution,
Washington, D.C., gift of Mr. and Mrs. Norman B. Robbins

37

THE SEINE

c. 1902
Oil on canvas
9 × 13" (22.86 × 33.02 cm)
Inscribed, signed, and dated lower left: *To* [illegible]—
/*H.O T/July 10, 1902*
National Gallery of Art, Washington, D.C., gift of the Avalon
Foundation, 1971.57.1

Fig. 33 Frederick Childe Hassam, *Notre Dame Cathedral, Paris*, 1888, oil on canvas, 17 1/2 × 21 1/2", The Detroit Institute of Arts, Founders Society Purchase, Robert H. Tannahill Foundation Fund.

Fig. 34 Henry O. Tanner, *Venetian Bridge*, c. 1897, oil on canvas, 8 x 10", N. N. Serper, courtesy of Rosenfeld Fine Arts, New York.

These three canvases are among Tanner's few known depictions of the contemporary urban scene in Paris. Perhaps he made them as diversions from the intense work of composing elaborate biblical subjects intended for the Salon. When W. S. Scarborough visited Tanner's studio in 1902 he observed this mixture of subjects: "On one easel stood an evening sketch from near Paris—a bit of night with trees and dark blue skies. There was also the 'Preparation for the Flight into Egypt.'"[1]

By the 1890s France's monuments had become vastly popular subjects in such scenes as *Notre Dame Cathedral, Paris* (fig. 33) by Frederick Childe Hassam (1859–1935), who preceded Tanner as a student at the Académie Julian. Throughout his life, Tanner was drawn to specific sites and buildings, from the inn at Rainbow Lake where he lodged during a convalescent trip to the Adirondacks around 1878, to bridges across the canals of Venice where he stopped briefly in 1897 (fig. 34), to the many identifiable landmarks he painted on later visits to the Near East. Much later in his career, in July of 1919, Tanner himself would paint another landmark, the Arc de Triomphe (New York, The Brooklyn Museum).

In painting *Les Invalides* (cat. no. 35), which once served as a home for disabled military veterans and is now the repository of Napoleon's remains, Tanner depicted not only an important French monument but a more generalized symbol of unfortunate people. The composition is skillfully conceived. Seen from along the Seine, the building is set off to the right, offered in an uncluttered view across a nearly empty foreground where a woman in black strolls. The positioning of figures on a diagonal suggests movement and the presence of additional strollers beyond. The painting's technique shows the decided influence of Impressionism; broken brushstrokes, myriad colors, and even light cause the building and main figure to appear almost weightless. Considering Tanner's interest in social issues at this time, one wonders if he is presenting a soldier's widow in mourning, gazing at this great institution of

35 LES INVALIDES

36 THE MAN WHO RENTED BOATS

37 THE SEINE

charity, or if this is a wealthy woman on a casual stroll with her poodle, giving cursory recognition to the memory of Napoleon.

Whether one of the rare examples of Tanner sketching in oil as he observed a scene or a study for a larger work made in the studio, *The Man Who Rented Boats* (cat. no. 36) is remarkable for the acuteness with which it is observed and the fluency of its technique. The work depicts a typical French city park, edged with trees and surfaced with gravel. A man dressed in a long gray smock offers a toy sailboat to a small boy watched by a woman wearing a light-colored dress. More boats for rent stand at the base of a tree at the right, observed by three children. In the distance, beyond a woman in a black dress and bonnet who acts as a spatial marker, much as the woman in *Les Invalides*, the white sails of other small boats float on an ornamental basin. Apparently painted all at once, with no hesitation or afterthought, the picture maintains an even degree of detail. Although the people are featureless, the narrative of the scene is clearly rendered by their expressive postures.

Tanner presented a rather straightforward composition in *The Seine* (cat. no. 37), looking across an expanse of water to the Pont Royal and two towers of the Louvre. The diagonals of dock and boat play off the strong and varied brushstrokes of the water, the horizontals and arches of the bridge and landscape, and the verticals of the towers. Passages of reflected light and color establish the time of day—twilight—and create a sense of gentle movement.

Few informal paintings of this sort by the artist are known, and he did not send such works to public exhibitions. Yet these pictures provide a glimpse into an intimate side of Tanner's work. DFM/DS

38

THE RESURRECTION OF
LAZARUS
1896
Oil on canvas
37 3/8 × 47 13/16" (95 × 121.5 cm)
Signed and dated lower left: *H. O. Tanner/1896*
Musée d'Orsay, Paris
(Not in exhibition)

39

STUDY OF A MAN FOR THE
RESURRECTION OF LAZARUS
1896
Charcoal on paper
24 1/2 × 17 1/2" (62.23 × 44.45 cm)
Inscribed lower right center: *Knee*; and inscribed and dated
lower left center: *Resurrection of Lazarus/Paris 1896*
Estate of Sadie T. M. Alexander

The raising of Lazarus was one of the most dramatic miracles performed by Jesus (John 11:1–44). Mary and Martha sent word to Jesus that his friend, their brother Lazarus, was ill in the village of Bethany. When he arrived, Jesus found that Lazarus had already been dead for four days, but he ordered the stone at the mouth of the burial cave removed. Jesus raised his voice in a great cry, "Lazarus, come forth," and the dead man came to life.

Tanner's extraordinary painting of this miraculous event established his reputation as an artist (cat. no. 38). The precise scene rendered is difficult to reconcile with John's text. Tanner appears to have shown the moment when Lazarus begins to stir to life, not the commonly depicted scene in which Jesus raises his hand to command him to rise (fig. 35). Tanner's Jesus is calm, with his hands slightly raised, almost in the manner of Rembrandt's etching of the subject (fig. 36).

Tanner's profound conviction that religious themes should be persuasive as works of art is evident in this powerful, carefully balanced composition,[1] in which he created groups with subtle pyramidal configurations. In the foreground, Mary kneels on the left — identifiable by her long hair, with which she later wiped oil from Jesus' feet — Jesus stands in the middle, and Martha kneels on the right, their positions forming a volumetric triangle that is reinforced by the upper torso of Lazarus. The tall, turbaned black man in the background connects with the figure between the timbers on the left and with Jesus to form a similar shape; the kneeling Mary reinforces this pyramid. Tanner confined the movement of the large crowd of onlookers by placing them inside the cave/tomb. These subtle compositional devices link all the participants to the event both in arrangement and emotion. The figures are united further through bursts of light and richly textured surfaces, which Tanner might have admired in such paintings by Rembrandt as *The Woman Taken in Adultery* (1664, London, National Gallery). The somewhat monochromatic palette, so appropriate for the interior of a cave, also unifies these witnesses in their vivid recognition that the raising of Lazarus was indeed a miracle.

Tanner worked on *Lazarus* for about six months. One of the surviving compositional studies for it (fig. 37) is rather rough and difficult to interpret. Another study, a charcoal sketch of the figure supporting the head of Lazarus (cat. no. 39), demonstrates the difference between Tanner's studies for figure paintings and his academy drawings (cat. nos. 16–18). The artist's characteristic flowing contour lines prevail in both, but the preparatory charcoal is sketchily rendered and emphasizes an active pose rather than analysis of lights and darks.

Fig. 35 Carel Fabritius, *The Raising of Lazarus*, oil on canvas, 82 11/16 × 55 1/8", Muzeum Narodowe w Warszawie, Warsaw.

Fig. 36 Rembrandt van Rijn, *The Raising of Lazarus*, 1642, etching, first state, 6 × 4 1/2", Museum of Fine Arts, Boston, Catherine E. Ballard Fund.

Fig. 37 Henry O. Tanner, *Study for the Raising of Lazarus*, n.d., oil on plywood, 6 × 7⁷/₈″, National Museum of American Art, Smithsonian Institution, gift of Mr. and Mrs. Norman B. Robbins.

Fig. 38 Benjamin West, *The Raising of Lazarus*, 1780, oil on canvas, 101 × 130″, Wadsworth Atheneum, Hartford, Connecticut, gift of J. Pierpont Morgan.

Fig. 39 James Tissot, *It Is Finished*, c. 1886–94, gouache on paperboard, 11⁵/₁₆ × 7³/₄″, The Brooklyn Museum, purchased by public subscription.

In addition to studies from life, Tanner may have put to work his memory of a major composition of 1884 by his Pennsylvania Academy mentor Thomas Hovenden, *The Last Moments of John Brown* (see fig. 8). The group that enters Lazarus' tomb echoes the one leaving John Brown's place of imprisonment both in its lack of realistic perspective and in the portraitlike nature of the faces in the crowd. Tanner's awestruck, turbaned woman on the far left, looking skyward, finds a counterpart in the gazing woman on the extreme left in Hovenden's picture. The young girl agape just to the right of the second support beam in *Lazarus* calls to mind the staring figure behind the mother who offers her child to John Brown. The imploring figure who leads Tanner's group serves the same compositional role as Hovenden's sheriff with the death warrant in his hand; the true heroes of the scenes are just to the right and below the latter figures. Tanner consistently displayed an aversion to directly copying other artists' works, but an inclination to refer specifically to Hovenden's image is not surprising. The famous abolitionist was Tanner's namesake, and the artist was profoundly aware of issues of social justice during the 1890s.

When Tanner decided to tackle the subject of Lazarus, during the summer of 1896, he did not have a massive visual tradition upon which to draw.[2] The celebrated Anglo-American artist Benjamin West (1738–1820) painted several versions of Lazarus (fig. 38). Delacroix painted the subject once (1850, Basel, Kunstmuseum), and Vincent van Gogh produced a painted variant of a Rembrandt etching of Lazarus (1890, Amsterdam, Vincent van Gogh Foundation). The individualism of Tanner's approach is evident when compared to the treatment of a similar theme, *Christ Exorcising the Possessed*, by Sandor Landeau, Tanner's companion to the Holy Land in 1898. Landeau's work is more in line with the prevailing mode of biblical painting as practiced by James Tissot (fig. 39).

Considering the relative paucity of a visual tradition, why did Tanner choose the resurrection of Lazarus as a subject? An answer to this question might be found in an astute claim by W. H. Burgess III, who wrote: "[Tanner] fervently believed that the Biblical myths could illustrate the struggles and hopes of Black Americans."[3] In a similar light, and keeping in mind that Tanner's father was a minister, the noted theologian H. H. Mitchell discussed the African-American pulpit tradition and the manner in which black preachers "simply engage in interpretation which unites ancient biblical insights with modern experience to give some firm word about God's will for today."[4] Mitchell used Luke's reference to the beggar Lazarus (16:19–31) to illustrate his point.

The stories of the raised Lazarus and the beggar Lazarus (which were sometimes linked by commentators) deal with new life and redemption, as does the Emancipation Proclamation of 1863, which provided a rebirth for black slaves. Tanner might not have had many visual antecedents on which to draw for the Lazarus theme, but in the black church he did have a tradition rooted in the equality of persons.

The Resurrection of Lazarus was accorded a superb critical reception when it was shown at the Paris Salon of 1897. While it was still in the studio, Tanner's patron Rodman Wanamaker remarked that "there is Orientalism in the 'Lazarus,' but it was a fortunate accident."[5] Wanamaker was so impressed with the religious feeling, however, that he offered to pay Tanner's expenses to

38 THE RESURRECTION OF LAZARUS

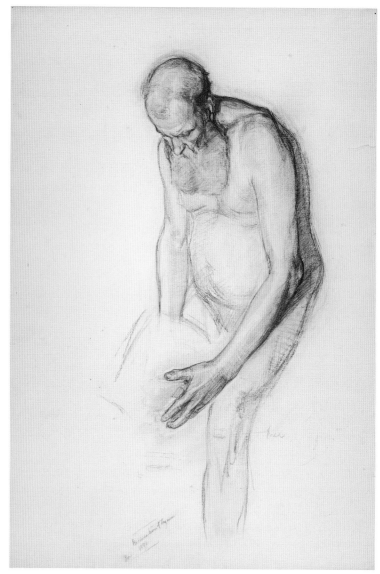

39 STUDY OF A MAN FOR THE RESURRECTION OF LAZARUS

the Holy Land for a firsthand look at the setting of the biblical stories he painted;[6] Tanner left for the Near East in January 1897. Albert Maignon, critic for the *Gazette des Beaux-Arts*, paid particular attention to the painting:

> Just a word about the "Resurrection of Lazarus," by Tanner, the remarkable work of a young American, whose ability greatly surpasses what the painter had shown us at previous Salons. The recollection of Rembrandt, which can be sensed in the understanding of the action, does not displease us because it does not obscure the personal sensibility of the artist. The painting retains a truly biblical feeling; we will remember the name of the artist as one of those which, tomorrow, will become famous.[7]

The critic for *Harper's Weekly* was equally impressed:

> When an artist's sense of responsibility to himself and his times prompts him to put his technical skill at the service of a great theme, he wins our respectful attention. Such a one is Mr. Henry O. Tanner, whose picture "The Raising of

Lazarus'' was exhibited in this year's Salon. In pleasant contrast to many Salon exhibitors, Mr. Tanner has not relied upon more extent of canvas or been contented to make only a clever exhibition of craftsmanship. His picture is comparatively small, but its seriousness of attention is very marked.[8]

The Resurrection of Lazarus was such a success that it was purchased by the French government's Department of Fine Arts for the Musée du Luxembourg, then the museum for living artists. Tanner, returning from his trip to the Near East, was on a stopover in Venice when he received word of the acquisition on May 3, 1897: "I sent a long telegram of acceptance which nearly 'broke the bank.'"[9] (In fact, it was a one-line telegram, followed by a letter.)[10] News of the purchase spread quickly, and on June 4, Harrison S. Morris, managing director of the Pennsylvania Academy of the Fine Arts, wrote to France's Director of Fine Arts requesting the painting for the academy's "Annual Exhibition, which is now the leading art exhibition in this country."[11] The French agreed to the loan with the stipulation that no mention be made in the label or catalogue of the work's ownership by the French state.[12] Morris made arrangements to have the picture sent to Philadelphia for the period from December 1, 1897, to March 1898, but for some unknown reason the picture was not shipped. In December of 1910 Morris requested Tanner's Disciples at Emmaus (see fig. 71) for the 1911 Esposizione Internazionale in Rome, at which Tanner was one of several American artists to be included. But Lazarus was sent to Rome instead, and there is no evidence that the French shipper (Lucien Lefebvre-Foinet) could have switched the works.[13]

In view of the success of The Resurrection of Lazarus, it is surprising that Tanner seems never to have taken up the subject again, except for an etching produced around 1913. However, he published a fascinating account in 1898 of a visit during his first Holy Land trip to the site thought to be the original tomb.[14]   DFM

4 0

BISHOP BENJAMIN TUCKER TANNER
1897
Oil on canvas
13 × 9 ¹/₄″ (33.02 × 23.49 cm)
Inscribed, signed, and dated lower right: *a hurried study*
of my dear/Father/H. O. Tanner/Kan. City/Sep, 1897
Dr. Rae Alexander-Minter, New York

Fig. 40 Benjamin Tucker Tanner, 1898,
photograph by Curtiss, Kansas City.

Fig. 41 Henry O. Tanner, *Mother of Henry
O. Tanner*, n.d., oil on plywood, 13 ×
9 ³/₄″, National Museum of American Art,
Smithsonian Institution, gift of Dr. Nicho-
las Zervas.

Tanner never exhibited a portrait, and he was apparently not very interested in the potential of portraiture either for study or as a source of income. He painted a few works of his family and friends before he left for Europe in 1891; he later sculpted a small bust of his father in 1894, and made the well-known portrait of his mother (cat. no. 41) and two small portraits of his parents (cat. no. 40, fig. 41) in 1897. A charcoal drawing of his artist friend Harry Boddington in fancy dress was made around 1910. He frequently employed his wife as a model in biblical subjects and had his son pose at least once (see figs. 81, 82), but he did not paint them as themselves, although family albums attest that he made many photographs of them. Apparently Tanner painted only two self-portraits, once depicting himself as an onlooker in *Chamber Music* (see fig. 47), shown at the Salon in 1902, and later as Lazarus in the large painting *Christ at the Home of Lazarus* (see fig. 76), his Salon entry of 1914.

Tanner sculpted a small bust of Bishop Daniel A. Payne, an early supporter, and painted a modest, possibly unfinished double portrait of his patrons Mr. and Mrs. Atherton Curtis (Washington, D.C., National Museum of American Art). He later used this image in a curious painting in which he placed the Curtises with the figure of Christ in another version of *Christ at the Home of Lazarus* (see fig. 70). A portrait, now lost, of the distinguished Clark University professor William H. Crogman was one of his first commissions during his stay in Atlanta in 1889–90. After his Atlanta sojourn, however, Tanner no longer sought portrait commissions, although he painted a posthumous portrait of Booker T. Washington in 1917, and in a 1913 article Clara MacChesney reported that Tanner had painted portraits (locations unknown) of the khedive of Egypt and of Rabbi Stephen Samuel Wise (1874–1949).[1]

Perhaps to celebrate his recent Salon triumph, in the summer of 1897 Tanner visited his parents in Kansas City, Kansas, from where the bishop presided over the Fifth Episcopal District of the A.M.E. Church from 1897 to 1900. During this stay he painted the two small, bust-length portraits of his parents, showing them against dark red backgrounds. A photograph of Bishop Tanner (fig. 40), taken in Kansas City the following year, shows that Tanner emphasized the strong structure of his father's head and made his intelligent and firm expression somewhat more severe. DS

40 BISHOP BENJAMIN TUCKER TANNER

41

PORTRAIT OF THE ARTIST'S MOTHER

1897
Inscribed, signed, and dated lower right: *To my dear Mother/H. O. Tanner/1897*
Oil on canvas
29 1/4 × 39 1/2" (74.29 × 100.33 cm)
Estate of Sadie T. M. Alexander

Fig. 42 James Abbott McNeill Whistler, *Arrangement in Gray and Black No. 1: Portrait of the Artist's Mother*, 1871, oil on canvas, 56 3/4 × 64", Musée d'Orsay, Paris.

While visiting his parents in Kansas City, Kansas, in 1897, Tanner painted a large portrait of his mother, Sarah Elizabeth Miller Tanner. In choosing a seated pose, Tanner referred to James Abbott McNeill Whistler's *Arrangement in Gray and Black No. 1: Portrait of the Artist's Mother* (fig. 42). Each painting shows a woman at full length, seated in an armchair, in profile against a background of carefully balanced geometric shapes. The portion of a framed, matted print visible in the upper left corner of Tanner's canvas is an explicit clue that Tanner had Whistler's work in mind. Tanner may have recalled the painting from his student days in Philadelphia, where it was shown at the Pennsylvania Academy of the Fine Arts in 1881 in the exhibition *Paintings by American Artists at Home and in Europe,* or he could have seen it in Paris at the Musée du Luxembourg, where it was displayed after its purchase by the French government in 1891. In any case, Tanner's desire to associate his mother's portrait with Whistler's painting, a famous, even notorious image of contemporary art by an established, though controversial artist, might have been a humorous reference to his own recent success at the Salon. Certainly it was the kind of gentle intellectual joke that would have been appreciated by the Tanner family.

Tanner's robust academic technique has little to do with the refined aesthetic principles of Whistler's work. Tanner relaxed Whistler's austere geometries: his mother's chair is not exactly parallel with the wall; the background space appears in two layers rather than one; and Mrs. Tanner's chair sits firmly on the floor, the plane of which is defined in academic fashion by a drape falling from the chair. In place of Whistler's carefully limited color range, which abstracts the composition, Tanner presented his mother as a dramatically lighted, solid figure against a shadowy background. The naturalistic effect is enhanced by the position of her hands: in her right she holds a palm leaf fan, and with her left she cradles her cheek. The result, less rigorous than Whistler's, is an affectionate, more evocative portrait of a sensitive, thoughtful personality.   DS

41 PORTRAIT OF THE ARTIST'S MOTHER

4 2

PORTRAIT OF BISHOP JOSEPH
CRANE HARTZELL
1902
Oil on canvas
47 × 36" (119.38 × 91.44 cm)
Inscribed, signed, and dated lower right: *To My Dear Bishop
and Mrs. Hartzell/in souvenir of earlier days of* [trial?]/
H. O. Tanner/1902
Hampton University Museum, Virginia

Portrait of Bishop Joseph Crane Hartzell is the only large formal portrait by Tanner that is known to exist, and apparently, as the inscription suggests, it was made as a token of friendship: "To my dear Bishop and Mrs. Hartzell in souvenir of earlier days of [trial?]." Hartzell (1842–1928), a minister in the Methodist Episcopal Church, and his wife, Jennie Culver Hartzell, had befriended the artist during a visit to Atlanta, and Hartzell, a trustee of Clark University, probably arranged for Tanner to teach there. In December 1890, with the aim of raising money to send Tanner abroad, the Hartzells organized an exhibition of Tanner's paintings at the Methodist Episcopal board of education headquarters in Cincinnati, where Hartzell was serving as secretary of the Freedman's Aid and Southern Education Society. The works did not sell, so the Hartzells bought the entire lot, providing Tanner with enough money to pay for his first trip to Europe. The Hartzells and the artist kept in touch, and when Tanner and Jessie Macauley Olssen were married in December 1899, the Hartzells gave the newlyweds a large, leather-bound presentation Bible.

In 1896 Hartzell was appointed missionary bishop for Africa, a post in which he served with zeal for twenty years, winning many honors for his work. Tanner's richly colored painting gives the bishop the attributes and accoutrements of official portraiture in the grand tradition. He stands beside a globe turned to the African continent. His right hand rests firmly on a sheaf of paper lying on a book, symbolizing learning and the missionary's oratorical and writing skills; his uplifted head and farseeing gaze signify both a visionary planner and a man of faith. With boldly brushed strokes of rather liquid paint, Tanner rendered the strong planes of his face and his handsome white hair and muttonchop whiskers.

Apparently Tanner retained an affectionate interest in Bishop Hartzell over the years; among his papers he kept a copy of "The Wreck of the Schooner Storm," published in 1891, a poem celebrating an event from the bishop's school days when he rescued four men in a storm on Lake Michigan. And a letter from Bishop Hartzell in January 1928, "in his eighty-sixth year," indicates that Tanner had offered to make a small memorial portrait of Mrs. Hartzell.[1] Considering that Tanner was then mourning his own wife, his offer to his old benefactor and friend is especially touching.   DS

42 PORTRAIT OF BISHOP JOSEPH CRANE HARTZELL

CELEBRATED SALON ARTIST

AND RELIGIOUS PAINTER

1897–1907

The great success of *The Resurrection of Lazarus* in 1897 laid the foundation for Tanner's work over the next decade. He would devote himself largely to the rendition of religious themes, a preference that must have been inspired by his personal background. Bishop Tanner wrote about the relationship of art to religion: "By the presentation of visible objects to the eye, divine truths may be most vividly photographed upon the soul. . . . In representation man does not, like the great Originator, create by his own fiat, his world of mental objects. What he reproduces or constructs anew is in some way dependent upon what he has personally experienced."[1]

In 1902 Professor W. S. Scarborough, vice-president of Wilberforce University in Ohio and a family friend, gave a succinct account of Tanner's new direction:

> When *The Banjo Lesson* appeared many of the friends of the race sincerely hoped that a portrayer of Negro life by a Negro artist had risen indeed. They hoped, too, that the treatment of race subjects by him would serve to counterbalance so much that has made the race only a laughing-stock subject for those artists who see nothing in it but the most extravagantly absurd and grotesque. But this was not to be. The fact had not been taken into consideration that his early home atmosphere had always been strongly religious, neither was it generally known that it had long been the wish of his father's heart that his son should paint Biblical subjects — turn his genius into religious channels and thus make his art serve religion, since neither his pen nor voice was to be employed in such service. So Mr. Tanner turned, at this point in his career, to what promises to be his life work.[2]

Harlem Renaissance novelist Jessie Fauset interviewed the artist for the *Crisis* in late 1923 or early 1924, and gave the following account: "A man came to the artist not long ago and said: 'I want you to tell me the truth of this story. I understand that years ago your father wanted you to be a minister, but you replied: "No, father, you preach from the pulpit and I will preach with my brush." Now is that true?' "[3] Fauset reported that Tanner responded, "That's a pretty story — I won't destroy it."[4]

The resounding critical and financial success of *The Resurrection of Lazarus* should not be overlooked in considering why Tanner concentrated on biblical themes around 1898. Moreover, his decision to adopt a new source of subject matter followed an established pattern. As a fledgling artist during the 1870s, Tanner heard that

America needed a great painter of marine scenes, and seized upon this as his career objective.[5] In the early 1880s he learned that the United States lacked a significant animal painter, and so he set about to become an American version of Britain's esteemed Sir Edwin Landseer (1802–73).[6] Tanner decided around 1893 to devote himself to portraying the serious aspects of contemporary African-American life,[7] and after 1908 he would turn to the Near East as a source for the settings of his religious paintings.

When Tanner decided to specialize in religious painting, a Catholic revival was taking place in France. The fin de siècle offered the repeated spectacle of the most unlikely converts returning to the church after experiencing visions of mystic innocence and miraculous revelation, usually recorded by the grateful recipient in fervent, even hysterical terms. Catholicism in this form went hand in hand with a powerful belief in spiritualism and the materialization of the dead.[8] The Catholic Church, however, did not again become a bountiful source of commissions for artists. The major official activity affecting religious art was the French government's decoration of the Panthéon with monumental works depicting the life of Sainte-Geneviève, the patron saint of Paris,[9] a program of which Tanner was aware.[10]

As an African-American artist with a Methodist background, Tanner was not drawn into the Catholic revival. He was described in 1900 as "a mystic, but a mystic who has read Renan and studied with Benjamin-Constant."[11] Ernest Renan (1823–92), a French historian and philosopher, presented in his *Vie de Jésus*[12] a lyrical picture of the carpenter's son as a youth in Galilee but totally rejected any supernatural elements in his life. The writings of Tanner's father, who also read Renan, separated the public ministry of Jesus from his performance of miraculous events.[13]

At the turn of the century Tanner was among the few innovative artists in the field of religious painting, which was still ripe for commercial exploitation. He did not face a great deal of serious competition, although the annual salons in Paris and major exhibitions in the United States continued to include a number of religious paintings. No single uncontested painter of biblical themes reigned near the end of the century, although James Tissot (1836–1902), who was in his sixties when Tanner took his own decision, came closest. Tissot experienced a vision in 1885 and from then on devoted his art to a celebration of the life of Christ. He traveled to Palestine to add historical accuracy to his scenes,[14] painting an extended series of 365 small gouaches on the life of Christ, which were exhibited in Paris in 1894 and 1896 to great acclaim. Another of the most frequently mentioned contemporary French painters of biblical scenes was Pascal-Jean Dagnan-Bouveret (1852–1929), whose mild influence Tanner acknowledged.[15] But most of Dagnan-Bouveret's subjects were genre scenes of peasant piety drawn from the Franche-Comté and Brittany regions, and his later career was spent making official portraits.[16]

In the late 1890s Tanner began to focus on completion of one major work at a time. His primary undertaking of late 1897 was the beautifully painted and emotionally compelling *Annunciation* (cat. no. 45), which set the course Tanner would follow in his biblical paintings over the next ten years. His approach was summarized in 1911 by F. J. Campbell, editor of the *Fine Arts Journal*: "Mr. Tanner told me that one of his aims was to present the simple domestic side of biblical personages. He said that

Fig. 43 James Tissot, *Annunciation*, c. 1886–95, gouache on paperboard, 6 ⁵/₈ × 8 ¹/₂", The Brooklyn Museum, purchased by public subscription.

Fig. 44 Carl Gutherz, *Light of the Incarnation*, 1888, oil on canvas, 77 × 114", Memphis Brooks Museum of Art, gift of Mr. and Mrs. Marshall F. Goodheart, 68.11.1.

the Bible was full of suggested domesticity. He is not painting actual incidents, as they have a thousand times been represented, but that quiet suggestion of Bible characters as we might imagine them to be."[17]

The Annunciation, clearly successful in this aim, was novel among religious paintings executed during the last years of the nineteenth century, being happily devoid of the photographic historicism found in Tissot's last works (fig. 43). Neither *The Annunciation* nor other biblical works by Tanner embraced the heavy-handed symbolism found in the religious painting of the Swiss-born, American painter Carl Gutherz (1844–1907). Gutherz's most famous undertaking, a large canvas entitled *Light of the Incarnation* (fig. 44), is so crowded with symbolic emblems that the artist wrote an interpretive text to go along with the painting.[18] Like Tissot, Gutherz rendered images that reflected his personal mystical beliefs and actually applied imitation pounced gold leaf to the halos of his figures in an extravagant Symbolist stylization.[19]

Tanner's domestic treatment of the annunciation captured the imagination of both art critics and fellow painters. Harrison S. Morris, managing director of the Pennsylvania Academy of the Fine Arts, wrote to Tanner on June 13, 1898: "I have been hearing unbounded praise of your Salon picture. Mr. Alexander Harrison was here last week and said 'Tanner has made another ten-strike.' [Walter] Gay tells me that not since Sargent's early triumphs has there been anything like it."[20]

The Annunciation made a triumphal tour of the United States in 1898 and 1899, with stops at the Art Institute of Chicago, the Carnegie Institute in Pittsburgh, and the Pennsylvania Academy. The growing esteem for Tanner in America was further attested by his first sale to a major public collection in his native land: the Wilstach Collection, the forerunner of today's Philadelphia Museum of Art. About this time Morris employed Tanner to select and make annotated comments on the best pictures by American artists in the Paris Salon as guidance in choosing works for the Academy's annual shows.[21]

Around 1898 Tanner executed a painting, *And He Vanished Out of Their Sight* (fig. 45), based on the Gospel of Luke (24:28–31) in which the resurrected Jesus eats supper with two of his disciples, who do not recognize him. When Jesus blessed their bread, "their eyes were opened, and they knew him, and he vanished out of their sight." Gabriel Paulin, an art writer for *Brush and Pencil*, reviewed the picture when it was exhibited at the American Art Association in Paris in May of 1899. He described "a vaporing form, indicating where the Savior was seated,"[22] a device not unlike the burst of light Tanner used to depict the angel in *The Annunciation*. The novelty of Tanner's approach can be understood when compared to a traditional rendition of the scene at Emmaus such as that by Rembrandt, in which a corporeal Jesus is shown breaking bread (fig. 46).

The majority of Tanner's biblical themes deal with the events of the nativity, crucifixion, and resurrection. The notions of birth and rebirth inherent in these subjects are easily linked to messages of human rights and social justice, and they relate to issues of equality:

> African Americans survived in part because of a profound and unshakable confidence that God did not will them to be enshackled or considered unequal. Although slaves were hardly allowed to read the Bible, they knew that the Bible, like their root culture, was loaded with support for the equality of persons. Their underground network of literates spread the word that God shows no respect for race or class.[23]

According to Tanner's son, writing in 1969, the artist "felt there was a unity in human aspirations and revealed faith."[24] This sentiment is revealed in his view of Jerusalem's Wailing Wall (see fig. 54), in which Tanner's sympathy for the devout worshipers is apparent.[25]

In the fall of 1898, Rodman Wanamaker planned a second trip for Tanner to the Holy Land to coincide with a visit by the German emperor to Palestine.[26] Tanner recalled: "It seemed to me that this might be a great pageant, or that there might be incidents not easily to calculate upon that might arise, which would give a chance for a very interesting picture."[27]

Fig. 45 Henry O. Tanner, *And He Vanished Out of Their Sight,* c. 1898, location unknown.

Fig. 46 Rembrandt van Rijn, *The Disciples at Emmaus,* 1648, oil on canvas, 26 ³/₄ × 25 ⁵/₈", Louvre, Paris.

The journey of the German emperor William II and Empress Augusta Victoria to Palestine to inaugurate new foreign policies occupied about a month, beginning in the middle of October 1898.[28] Tanner was accompanied on his trip by the Hungarian-born painter Sandor Landeau (b. 1864), a fellow student at the Académie Julian. Tanner lamented that "our hoped-for picturesqueness of the entry of the Emperor into Jerusalem did not materialize. The police regulations were too severe, the whole affair was, as it were, at a gallop, and at no time was it in any way an event of any beauty."[29]

Tanner and Landeau remained in the Near East throughout the winter of 1899, painting around Jerusalem and the region of the Dead Sea.[30] Tanner's stay yielded a number of successful efforts that disclose new insights into the country and the character of its people. *Flight into Egypt* (cat. no. 49), *Nicodemus Visiting Jesus* (cat.

no. 47), and several smaller canvases, such as *Road to Jerusalem* (New York, private collection), were the result of this sojourn.

Tanner was back in Paris by late March of 1899. His major undertaking of this year was *Christ among the Doctors* (location unknown). According to the Gospel of Luke (2:41–50), the twelve-year-old Jesus was separated from Mary and Joseph during a visit to Jerusalem for the Passover feast. His parents found him three days later seated among the teachers in the temple, astonishing everyone with his sagacity. This subject was not unusual in French art, but it would not recur in Tanner's work. He might have turned to this popular theme as a measure of his success against that of other painters who had attempted it.

Helen Cole described in detail the composition and color scheme of the lost painting in June 1900:

> The Christ seated in the middle is the least worked-out point of the composition; but, sketched in as it is, there is something very Rembrandtesque in the turbaned head and the attitude. The temple walls are a warm gray in tone, and the pillars, so cleverly composed that they do not divide the picture, are of richly tinted Oriental marble. There is a peculiar green-blue mosaic which I have only seen in the south of Italy. . . . Mr. Tanner has a slab of this, originally taken from some Oriental temple, and this he will use as a guide for his mosaic floor. Here and there are irregular patches of sunlight, and the whole tone of the picture is warm. At the right an old patriarch crouches on an orange mat, and suggestions of orange are to be carried throughout the picture. There is also a sort of purple tunic that he has put on one or two of the men; not a vivid, strong purple, but a deep warm, steeped-in-sunshine purple, a tone that I have never seen used by any other painter. . . . He paints for himself first, and for the public afterward. If they like it, *tant mieux* [so much the better].[31]

Tanner's efforts during the last years of the nineteenth century, which included another version of *Daniel in the Lions' Den* (location unknown) and a variation on the annunciation theme, *Mary* (cat. no. 50), met with mixed reviews from art critics. We learn more about the artist's lost works, and the prevailing attitudes of American criticism, through reviews of the Pennsylvania Academy of the Fine Arts annual exhibition in 1900–1901:

> Several canvases, and these of very unequal merit, by Henry O. Tanner are found in the present exhibition. Most important, perhaps, is that showing "Christ Among the Doctors" in which the artist has cast tradition to the winds and represented the youthful Jesus with the crisp blue black hair of the Jewish race. The same artist's "Mary" is an interesting and novel interpretation of a Biblical subject, as is "He Vanished From Their Sight" but Mr. Tanner's other contributions are interesting chiefly as studies in chiaroscuro rather than as finished pictures.[32]

Another critic stated: "One must not pass by Tanner's contributions, though the palette of rich, warm hues with color laid on some of the pictures as if a hectic flush at times seems to be mannerism and a harking back to other days and other ideals."[33]

Arthur Hoeber, of New York's *Commercial Advertiser*, wrote:

> The exhibition contains, too, much of an experimental nature of the latest develop-ments in the art way, the extremists increasingly finding favor with the jury. Most of

these, it must be confessed, are interesting rather for describing modern tendencies than from serious accomplishments, while a number are so freakish and so mannered as to count for little. Thus, for example, Henry O. Tanner, a man who has obtained much recognition abroad . . .[34]

Just before the turn of the century, a crucial event occurred in Tanner's life which would affect him both personally and artistically. On December 14, 1899, at Saint Giles-in-the-Fields, Bloomsbury, London, he married Jessie Macauley Olssen, a young white woman from San Francisco studying music in Europe. Jessie Olssen and Tanner had met a year earlier in Barbizon and shared many interests including music; their marriage was to be a singularly happy one. They spent their honeymoon in the south of France at Martigues before settling in Paris in an apartment on rue d'Assas, overlooking the Luxembourg Gardens in the Latin Quarter.[35]

The artist retained his studio at 51 boulevard Saint-Jacques, which had been renovated to his specifications. Helen Cole described it in 1900:

> This is a studio for work. . . .There are a few fine old pieces of furniture picked up at the Hotel Drouôt, for Mr. Tanner enjoys nothing more than a bargain in rugs or studio property, a few reproductions and photographs on the wall, but no half-finished pictures, no charcoal sketches, and no odds and ends. It is roomy and arranged in a way to quietly satisfy the eye, and is distinctly restful, and yet not a lounging or cigarette-smoking place.[36]

Contemporary descriptions and photographs of the studio disclose reproductions of heads by the Italian Renaissance sculptor Donatello and the German artist Hans Holbein. Among the furnishings were a Roman lamp and a chair that supposedly had belonged to the great Flemish painter Peter Paul Rubens. Tiles from Jerusalem and Oriental costumes, which Tanner bought from the studio sale after the death of the fashionable contemporary Hungarian painter Mihaly Munkácsy (1844–1900), were also evident.[37] The reproductions and furniture do not appear to have been used as props in Tanner's paintings, but the costumes might have been the basis for the attire in many of his religious pictures.

Helen Cole referred admiringly to Tanner's work habits: " 'Mr. Tanner does most of his work in the morning,' said a friend, in speaking of him, 'and he rises very early.' 'What does he do in the afternoons then?' was asked. 'Oh, he works.' "[38] Tanner set himself such a pace, in fact, that his Philadelphia patron Robert C. Ogden advised: "Allow me to caution you against overwork. Your art draws heavily upon your sympathies, and such work is always both mentally and physically exhausting. 'If you want to get there quick go slow.' "[39]

The intense work habits of the newlywed Tanner now included trying his hand again at illustration, a field he had essayed with some success in the 1880s (cat. nos. 9–11). During the second half of 1899 he worked on a picture based on the story of Barabbas (John 18:39–40), which was submitted for publication to the Lippincott Company but not accepted.[40] Harrison S. Morris attempted an explanation: "I fear the Barabbas illustration is hardly what was required. Illustration requires a more definite treatment than you have given this. I hope that you can make another venture and succeed with the work as I should be rejoiced to find you take a front in this growing American field."[41]

Undaunted, as early as November 14, 1900, Tanner proposed a group of six biblical illustrations to Edward Bok, editor of the *Ladies Home Journal*.[42] This series, intended to present revealing episodes in the lives of famous mothers of the Bible (cat. nos. 51–53), was Tanner's major undertaking during 1901 and almost met the fate of the illustration of Barabbas, again because Tanner's style was interpretive rather than factual. Bok worried that the pictures might be beyond his readers' comprehension and that they would be tricky, and expensive, to reproduce.[43] In the end, five images in the series were published, but the difficulties surrounding Tanner's efforts might account for the fact that he returned to illustration only once again, in a cover for the *Crisis* in December 1922.

The "Mothers of the Bible," according to the artist, "marked the commencement of my painting pictures containing all or nearly all female figures."[44] In September of 1901 the Tanners joined Henry's father in London, where the bishop was a delegate to the Third Ecumenical Conference of Methodism. During this trip Henry and Jessie visited the Somerset home of Catherine Impey (1847–1923), a feminist, temperance agitator, antisegregationist, and humanitarian worker, and the founder of *Anti-Caste*, a publication designed to argue against racial discrimination and segregation.[45] Impey's views might have heightened Tanner's sensitivity to the status of women in society.

The Tanner family was accompanied on this journey by Professor and Mrs. W. S. Scarborough. Scarborough reported:

Fig. 47 Henry O. Tanner, *Chamber Music*, 1902, location unknown.

> Tanner is ever a student, the close observer instantly feels. It was our personal pleasure . . . to accompany him and his father one day in London to view an exhibition of Spanish paintings at the Guildhall Art Gallery — a fine loan collection, chief among which was a series of paintings by Velásquez, mostly portraits, and the main attraction for Mr. Tanner. His appreciative comment made it very evident that nothing is allowed to escape his observation, in all that goes to make up technique in art.[46]

Regarded as a supreme realist and the father of modern art,[47] Velázquez and his technique were frequently discussed and admired at the end of the nineteenth century. Tanner was already familiar with Velázquez's art from his student days at the Pennsylvania Academy of the Fine Arts; Thomas Eakins held the Spanish master in great esteem.[48] Tanner might have had a special interest in him because in 1654 Velázquez allegedly freed his black slave, Juan de Pareja, who became an artist in his own right. The extent to which Velázquez's supposed act of emancipation might have been discussed during the period is unknown, but his *Portrait of Juan de Pareja* (New York, Metropolitan Museum of Art) was well known as early as 1650.[49]

By early 1902 Tanner was at work on a completely different type of painting, *Chamber Music* (fig. 47), an elegant, linear composition that calls to mind seventeenth-century Spanish painting. Its models included Jessie Tanner playing the cello, her sister, Elna Olssen Charles, at the piano, and Tanner himself standing in the shadows.[50] The artist sent the painting to the Salon of 1902, and a favorable review in the *New York Herald* shed light on Tanner's changing palette:

> Here is a surprise, a widely incredible thing. A painter, an American, has tried to revolutionize manner and shed his personality. It is Mr. Tanner, who used to concoct estimable works in a dark brown medium, and now astonishes us with a large painting, "Chamber Music", in which one sees a lady playing the cello. The quaint grace and amusing color of this large canvas make it one of the attractions of the Salon.[51]

In November 1900, Tanner's friends Atherton and Louise Curtis left France to take up residence in the United States. They asked Henry and Jessie to join them at Mount Kisco, an idyllic area just north of New York City.[52] A violent race riot had occurred in New York in August of 1900, and race relations were at their nadir in the history of African-Americans.[53] Perhaps in response to the dismal circumstances, the artist and his wife did not accept the invitation. However, the Tanners did join the Curtises at Mount Kisco in August 1902,[54] Tanner's first trip to the United States since the summer of 1897, in the aftermath of the great success of *The Resurrection of Lazarus*. The couple apparently moved about without trepidation, despite their interracial marriage. Henry continued to work at Mount Kisco, and it seems likely that while there he took up subjects that had become rare in his oeuvre: a horse (see fig. 12), a pure still life, and a formal portrait, of his early supporter Bishop Joseph Crane Hartzell (cat. no. 42). Although Tanner painted few portraits, all are of individuals committed to improving human welfare. Another of his sitters was the spirited orator and author Rabbi Stephen Samuel Wise (1874–1949).[55]

The extended Tanner family spent the 1902 Christmas season together at the Diamond Street homestead in Philadelphia,[56] certainly basking in the glory of the appearance of the "Mothers of the Bible" in the *Ladies Home Journal*. On December 31, 1902, Henry and Jessie sailed from Boston to Spain, where they resided in Granada for several months.[57] This interlude had a major impact on Tanner's style. He must have had ample opportunity to see additional works by Velázquez and to study pictures by El Greco (1541–1614). Tanner seems to have adopted the elongated figure style of El Greco, and it affected his works, off and on, for the remainder of the decade (cat. no. 56). This figure type can be seen in *Salomé* (fig. 48) and in an unfinished work on its verso, *Moses and the Burning Bush*.

From Spain the Tanners returned to Paris,[58] and by June 1, 1903, they were back in the United States.[59] Tanner's only child was born in New York City on September 25, 1903, and named Jesse Ossawa Tanner, revealing that the black artist continued to value his own namesake, the abolitionist John Brown of Osawatomie. With the new responsibility of fatherhood, Tanner seemed to acquire anxieties about

Fig. 48 Henry O. Tanner, *Salomé*, c. 1902–1903, oil on canvas, 46 × 35 1/4″, National Museum of American Art, Smithsonian Institution.

commercial concerns. In a letter of February 19, 1904, Booker T. Washington confidentially apprised Robert C. Ogden that Tanner was having financial difficulties, owing to "the large expense in connection with the sickness of his wife" and an inability to sell pictures in America,[60] and he inquired about procedures for publicizing pictures that Tanner would have on view at the National Arts Club in New York in April. Tanner hit upon his own fund-raising scheme in a letter of March 3 to Washington:

> I am sending a large picture "Daniel in the Lions Den" to the exhibition. . . . I am asking $3000 for it and Mr. Ogden would be willing to give $500 of this sum if the picture could be placed in the Metropolitan Museum of Art. This I should like if we could get others who would subscribe the balance. Of course I should first have to approach the authorities of [the] museum to see if the picture would be agreeable to them.[61]

Washington had secured the interest of William Jay Schieffelin and Stephen Arnold Douglas as patrons by late March, but a purchase for the Metropolitan Museum of Art did not occur. On March 2, 1904, Tanner complained to Harrison S. Morris that except for *The Annunciation* and *Nicodemus Visiting Jesus*, he had not sold a picture in Philadelphia in eight or ten years.[62] Morris replied: "Doesn't it seem a rather large exception to you that your principal picture and one other important one should have been sold to the Academy? If you leave these out of your entire record of sales it will make a big gap, won't it? How many have you ever sold from the Salon, anyhow, or from any other exhibition?"[63] Tanner smoothed over the spat with a gracious apology, but these seem to have been generally unhappy times. His correspondence with Morris during this period is usually unenthusiastic and does not mention work in progress. Moreover, lost works which seem to date to this period, such as *Peter after the Denial*, were considered below standard by many art critics.[64] Jessie Olssen Tanner was ill, certainly an added worry. These difficulties could account for the fact that Tanner decided rather abruptly to return to Paris. The Tanners made a farewell appearance in Philadelphia sometime after March 6, 1904,[65] and then sailed from New York harbor on April 18, 1904.

In Paris Tanner did not immediately return to painting full-time. He became occupied with finding suitable lodging for Atherton Curtis, who had decided to leave Mount Kisco.[66] Still hoping to increase his income, he corresponded again with Booker T. Washington, who would gently refuse this outright approach:[67]

> Do you know what I thought it might be possible for you to do for me. To bring my work . . . to the attention of some persons or person like Mr. Carnegie, who might be willing to give me for a period of 3 or 4 years $2000 (Two Thousand) dollars for the picture of the year the best I could do, and thus for this period the question [of] money would be settled and I would have a "square" chance to see what I really could do.[68]

Tanner now stepped up the pace of his artistic production, with handsome results. By early 1906 he had completed four major pictures, all of which turned away from the bright colors and elongated figures of the El Greco–inspired works. He instead looked to Velázquez and his own *Resurrection of Lazarus* for inspiration. One of these new pictures, *The Disciples at Emmaus* (see fig. 71), was shown in the 1906 Salon and purchased by the French government for 4000 francs,[69] or $760, joining *Lazarus* in the Musée du Luxembourg. One critic noted: "Tanner has had the honor to

which every artist who comes to Paris aspires—
two of his paintings are in the Luxembourg."[70]
In addition *Emmaus* was awarded a second-
class medal from the Salon. (First-class medals
could only be awarded to French citizens.) A
reviewer for the *Philadelphia Inquirer* placed
this award in perspective: "The jury of the
Salon des Artistes Français has awarded two
second class medals to Mr. Anson [sic] Knight
and Mr. Tanner, who are thus made *Hors Concours*....There are now eight Americans in
possession of the second class medals of the
Salon."[71]

Fig. 49 Henry O. Tanner, *Christ Washing His Disciples' Feet*, by 1906, location unknown.

Tanner also regained critical success in
America in 1906: *Christ Washing the Disciples'
Feet* (fig. 49) was widely acclaimed in the press,
and *Two Disciples at the Tomb* (cat. no. 59),
considered the most impressive and dis-
tinguished work of the season, was awarded the Harris Prize of $500 by the Art
Institute of Chicago and entered its permanent collection. The Carnegie Institute in
Pittsburgh, Tanner's birthplace, in 1907 acquired *Christ at the Home of Mary and
Martha* (cat. no. 58) for $500 and an exchange of *Judas Covenanting with the High
Priests* (c. 1904, location unknown).[72] Most art critics favorably reviewed the new
religious pictures. A writer for the *North American* in Philadelphia called *The
Disciples at Emmaus* "one of Tanner's best paintings,"[73] and *Two Disciples at the
Tomb* was described in New York's *Globe* as "a quite remarkable achievement of
strength, dignity, and impressiveness."[74] From sales of his work both in Paris and the
United States, Tanner must have amassed at least the $2000 he had sought to give
himself a "square chance" to see what he could do. Nor was he overlooked in
Philadelphia: Tanner had the honor of serving on the European jury for the 1908
annual exhibition of the Pennsylvania Academy of the Fine Arts.

Up to this point Tanner had not attempted a truly large picture on the scale of
the works by David and Delacroix that he could see at the Louvre, or the recently
completed monumental religious paintings at the Panthéon. But during part of 1906
and all of 1907, Tanner tackled the most ambitious undertaking of his career—*The
Wise and Foolish Virgins* (fig. 50), also known as *Behold! The Bridegroom Cometh*.
Measuring 10-by-15 feet, this huge painting was probably destroyed; it is difficult to
believe that such a large canvas could remain untraced.

The painting records a parable in which Christ warns that the hour of the
Second Coming cannot be foretold (Matt. 25:1–13):

> Then shall the kingdom of heaven be likened unto ten virgins, which took their lamps,
> and went forth to meet the bridegroom. And five of them were wise, and five were
> foolish. They that were foolish took their lamps, and took no oil with them: But the
> wise took oil in their vessels with their lamps. While the bridegroom tarried, they all
> slumbered and slept. And at midnight there was a cry made, Behold, the bridegroom
> cometh; go ye out to meet him. Then all those virgins arose, and trimmed their lamps.

Fig. 50 Henry O. Tanner, *The Wise and Foolish Virgins*, c. 1906–1907, 120 × 180", location unknown.

And the foolish said unto the wise, Give us of your oil; for our lamps are gone out. But the wise answered, saying, Not so; lest there be not enough for us and you: but go ye rather to them that sell, and buy for yourselves. And while they went to buy, the bridegroom came; and they that were ready went in with him to the marriage: and the door was shut. Afterward came also the other virgins, saying, Lord, Lord, open to us. But he answered and said, Verily I say unto you, I know you not. Watch therefore, for ye know neither the day nor the hour wherein the Son of man cometh.

Tanner depicted twelve life-size figures in a palatial interior. The wise virgins, the principal group, glide joyously toward the distracted women on the left. In front of the advancing maidens stands a herald who announces the coming of the bridegroom, a figure difficult to discern.[75] In the middle ground are other processions, described by a critic for the Scranton *Times* as "secondary scenes that greatly augment the interest of the principal."[76] Much of what is known about the composition's color and light effects comes from descriptions in the contemporary press. Tanner clad the wise maidens in white, airy drapery, and with a few telling brushstrokes suggested undulating folds of cloth and the movement of the figures.[77] Others wear mauve or blue tunics.[78] The faces of the wise women and the herald were characterized by remarkably individual expressions and evidently were painted from carefully selected models.[79] Light effects further enhanced the foreground figures and rendered the interior as a relatively shallow space. The flare of the burning lamps helped to establish a range of values.

The overall coloring of the picture was described as deliciously rich and grave, and the brushstrokes as forceful, drawing only enough to suggest motion or the lack of

Fig. 52 Godfried Schalcken, *The Five Wise and Foolish Virgins*, n.d., oil on canvas, 37 × 44 ⁷/₈″, Bayerische Staatsgemäldesammlungen, Munich.

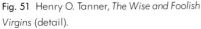

Fig. 51 Henry O. Tanner, *The Wise and Foolish Virgins* (detail).

it.[80] Another reviewer found the work to be "full of exquisite and very picturesque details. The necklace of red coral, the green scarf, a blue shade in the silky paleness of the scarf, and such easy, free and harmonious treatment."[81] The floor was checkered white and green, and a reddish brown drapery with garlands of laurel hung between the ceiling beams, beyond which a bluish mauve sky was visible, filled with golden stars.[82] The work must have been a visual feast of color, light, and movement. In this picture Tanner embraced new artistic treatments of the early twentieth century such as those seen in the work of Matisse, but the gigantic, roundly modeled figures reflect the tradition of nineteenth-century French art, and even that of his first Philadelphia mentors, Thomas Eakins and Thomas Hovenden.

Tanner would have found ample antecedents for the parable of the wise and foolish virgins, by no means a rare subject in the history of art.[83] One contemporary critic even suggested that he had based his work on a painting by Godfried Schalken (1643–1703),[84] a Dutch artist fond of complexly lighted nocturnal scenes (fig. 52). Tanner himself described his attempt to differentiate his work from earlier treatments by stressing the human emotion he hoped to evoke:

> In "Behold! the Bridegroom Cometh" I hoped to take off the hard edge too often given to that parable; how generally the wise virgins are made good but cold and unlovable; how I attempted to show that they were sympathetic for their sisters in distress, and that this sympathy was one of their beauties, in a marked degree, by the figure on the left on her knees — with her own lamp "bright burning" at her side — trying to bring to life the smoking lamp of her friend — in fact interpreting the whole parable in keeping with our knowledge of the goodness of God and what He considers goodness in us.[85]

It is not surprising that Tanner chose a well-known subject for the major undertaking of his career. Already a successful artist and nearly fifty years old when he began the picture, he surely would have wanted to be judged against the best in the field.   DFM

43

STUDY FOR THE JEWS'
WAILING PLACE
c. 1897
Oil on canvas
25¹/₂ × 19¹/₄" (64.77 × 48.9 cm)
Signed lower right: *H. O. Tanner*
Museum of Art, Rhode Island School of Design, Providence,
gift of Mr. and Mrs. Leonard Granoff

Fig. 53 Gustav Bauernfeind, *Lament of the Faithful at the Wailing Wall*, 1904, oil on canvas, 76³/₁₆ × 38⁹/₁₆", private collection.

Fig. 54 Henry O. Tanner, *Jews' Wailing Place*, 1897, oil on canvas, location unknown.

On his visit to the Near East in early 1897, Tanner was struck by some of the local sites. Among them was the Wailing Wall in Jerusalem, where orthodox Jews traditionally go to pray and bewail the capture of their city by the Romans and their present dispersion. This site attracted the attention of many other nineteenth-century artists; Peter E. Bergheim photographed it around 1870, and Gustav Bauernfeind painted it around 1904 (fig. 53). Tanner himself owned a photograph of the wall of the type sold to tourists, and he made his definitive painting of the picturesque subject in 1897 (fig. 54), a work now lost.

The Wailing Wall made a particular impression on Tanner: "Nor do I forget the deep pathos of the 'Jews Wailing Place' — those tremendous foundation stones of that glorious temple [of Solomon] that stood upon Mt. Moriah, worn smooth by the loving touch of tearful and devout worshippers from all over the world . . . ; nor the sight of those devout Russian pilgrims, with their primitive faith and religious ardor."[1]

In this study (cat. no. 43), Tanner used a plunging perspective, unlike his usual panoramic approach to space, to present a fairly realistic view. The yellow-brown color scheme with accents of red, green, and blue of *Study for the Wailing Place* is similar to other works such as *Lions in the Desert* (cat. no. 44), and the looser, thicker handling of paint is consistent with Tanner's contemporary sketches. The light is intense, but the shadows do not have the darkness of *The Resurrection of Lazarus* (cat. no. 38), which may be attributed directly to Tanner's firsthand experience of the brilliant Near Eastern sun. Tanner clad the figures in various costumes to show the universal nature of the worshipers in this sacred place.

In the definitive version of *The Jews' Wailing Place*, Tanner expanded the number of persons and poses seen in the study. A background figure from an early illustration in *Harper's Young People* (cat. no. 9) acted as a prototype for one of the enfeebled men in the foreground. The worshiping figures are intense and energetic, while the study is characterized by serenity.

Both the study and the final rendition of *The Jews' Wailing Place* may be seen in light of Tanner's continuing concern for human rights, addressed in the aborted *Androcles* (cat. no. 12) of a decade earlier and rendered successfully in *Daniel in the Lions' Den* (cat. no. 87) and *Lazarus*.   DFM

43 STUDY FOR THE JEWS' WAILING PLACE

LIONS IN THE DESERT
(*Lions*)
(*A Still Hunt: Kings of the Desert*)
1897–98
Oil on canvas mounted on plywood
15 1/2 × 29 3/8" (39.37 × 74.61 cm)
National Museum of American Art, Smithsonian Institution,
Washington, D.C., gift of Mr. and Mrs. Norman B. Robbins

Fig. 55 Henry O. Tanner, *Lion's Head*, 1892, oil on linen, 19 × 24", Hampton University Museum, Virginia.

Fig. 56 Jean-Léon Gérôme, *Lion on the Watch*, n.d., oil on panel, 28 × 39", The Cleveland Museum of Art, gift of Mrs. F. W. Gehring in memory of her husband, F. W. Gehring.

Beginning with early sketches made at the Philadelphia zoo, lions were a recurring theme in Tanner's art. He continued to study them at the zoo in the Jardin des Plantes after arriving in Paris in 1891,[1] as can be seen in *Lion's Head*, dated 1892 (fig. 55). In 1895 he took an animal anatomy course given by Emmanuel Frémiet (1824–1910) at the park's natural history museum.[2] Lions figured in such major subject pictures as the unrealized *Androcles* of about 1885–86 (see cat. no. 12) and in various renditions of *Daniel in the Lions' Den* (cat. no. 87). The African habitat of the lion may have held an added attraction for Tanner because of his family's interest and pride in the history and accomplishments of the biblical Hamitic races of African origin.[3]

The setting of *Lions in the Desert* (cat. no. 44) calls to mind Tanner's observation of the area around Jerusalem as a "barren, broken-cisterned, sterile" landscape.[4] It is highly unlikely that he actually came across such a scene with lions present; he simply cast the beasts in a Palestinian landscape. The painting recalls the horizontal, layered compositions with low vantage points that Tanner executed during the late 1880s in America (cat. nos. 13–15) and in Brittany during the early 1890s (cat. nos. 20–22). This picture can be identified as one exhibited at the Art Institute of Chicago (as *Lions*) in October 1898, the month Tanner departed for his second Near East trip. His landscape views became much more panoramic after this sojourn.

Lions in the Desert at first appears to be an array of sun-drenched browns under a blue sky. Closer examination reveals a warm palette of subtly modulated pinks, purples, blues, and yellows.[5] Strong oranges mixed with yellow in the heads of the lions call to mind the palette (if not the high degree of finish) of Jean-Léon Gérôme. The celebrated French artist, who painted several scenes with lions in the 1890s (fig. 56), was well known to Tanner.

Tanner's treatment of the subject avoids drama. The composition of horizontal and diagonal bands of animals, terrain, and sky is serene; the artist gave the viewer no reason to fear the customarily ferocious beasts. In fact, Tanner never rendered the threatening, physically troubling, or gory aspects of his chosen themes. Contemporary critical reaction to *Lions in the Desert* has not yet come to light, although Helen Cole reproduced the painting in a 1900 article on the artist.[6]   DFM

44 LIONS IN THE DESERT

THE ANNUNCIATION

(L'Annonciation)
1898
57 × 71 ¹/₂" (144.78 × 181.61 cm)
Oil on canvas
Signed and dated lower left: *H. O. Tanner/1898*
Philadelphia Museum of Art, W. P. Wilstach Collection

Fig. 57 Dante Gabriel Rossetti, *The Annunciation (Ecce Ancilla Domini!)*, 1850, oil on canvas, 28 ¹/₂ × 16 ¹/₂", The Tate Gallery, London.

The Annunciation was Tanner's first major painting following his trip to the Holy Land in 1897. It was his entry for the 1898 Salon, where it was bound to receive especially close attention after the remarkable triumph of *The Resurrection of Lazarus* (cat. no. 38) the year before.

Perhaps emboldened by his success, Tanner chose a large canvas for *The Annunciation*, one of the biggest of his career; he, like many artists submitting works, most likely hoped that the size of his painting would ensure its notice among the hundreds of pictures crowding the exhibition walls. Tanner found the first version of the painting to be "so unsatisfactory that there seemed no other way out of the difficulty than to commence a new one."[1] He may have begun again with a new compositional sketch, for the present version of *The Annunciation* is very close to the small preliminary study now in the National Museum of American Art.

Apparently Tanner took to heart a comment by Rodman Wanamaker, who sponsored his Near East trip: "In the Orient the light, both interior and exterior, the mannerisms of the people, the costumes and habits of living, all are vastly different from anything that could be imagined in the West."[2] In *The Annunciation* the artist introduced the textiles, ceramics, and white-washed, stone-floored architecture that would constitute the settings for his later interior scenes of biblical subjects. Tanner must have purchased some of these furnishings to be used as props; the distinctively patterned carpet, for example, appears again in *Christ Learning to Read* (cat. no. 70) of 1910–14.

A contemporary critic saw a reminder of Dante Gabriel Rossetti's *The Annunciation (Ecce Ancilla Domini!)* (fig. 57) in Tanner's work,[3] but comparison of the paintings emphasizes the realist origins of Tanner's approach and the tactile painterliness of his technique, modeled on that of his teacher Jean-Paul Laurens. The most striking contrast between the two works is Tanner's innovative use, possibly deriving from his fundamentalist religion, of a column of light to stand for Gabriel, the angel of the annunciation, whom Rossetti portrays as a human figure whose holiness is represented by a halo and small golden flames that lick at his heels. Another writer more aptly captured the mood of Tanner's interpretation of the subject: "The young Jewish peasant sit[s] on the edge of a couch, wearing the common striped cotton of the Eastern women of the poorer class, a costume which they have kept to the present day, no halo or celestial attributes about her, and only the flood of golden light to herald the approach of the angel."[4] It has been suggested that Tanner's fiancée, Jessie Olssen, posed for the figure of Mary,[5] but he more likely used a professional model, as Tanner probably did not meet Olssen until the summer after the painting was exhibited at the Salon.

45 THE ANNUNCIATION

Contemporary 1898 Salon reviews of *The Annunciation* have not been found, but other accounts suggest that the painting was received enthusiastically. According to one writer, it "proved one of the great successes of the year. . . . It is said that when this picture was brought before the jury of admission that a storm of 'bravos' burst forth."[6] The painting must have been mentioned in the press, for in a letter of May 16, 1898, Harrison S. Morris, managing director of the Pennsylvania Academy of the Fine Arts, congratulated Tanner and continued, "'The Annunciation' seems to be a fitting sequel to the 'Lazarus' and it is most gratifying to read the unstinted praise which you modestly enclosed."[7]

Morris had become acquainted with Tanner and his work during the artist's 1893–94 stay in Philadelphia, and followed his career with interest. He had urged Tanner to send *Daniel in the Lions' Den* to the Academy's sixty-sixth annual exhibition in 1896–97, and had been disappointed not to obtain *The Resurrection of Lazarus* for exhibition the following year, despite an energetic letter-writing campaign. Even before he knew the subject of Tanner's new painting, he wrote in January 1898, "While we are extremely sorry to be deprived of the picture [*The Resurrection of Lazarus*], yet if it inures to your benefit, we shall feel you are entirely justified in what you have done. . . . Next year you will doubtless have something else as good, and we hope that you will arrange in any case to let it come to us before its final disposition."[8] After receiving favorable reports of *The Annunciation* at the Salon, he wrote in May 1898, "Please believe that we earnestly want this new picture for the next exhibition, and after our abortive efforts of last year, you should let us have it without fail. You owe it to yourself and your growing fame that this second success should be seen in your native city and elsewhere in your native land which is becoming proud of you."[9]

Both Morris and Robert C. Ogden, an executive with the Wanamaker Company, were assiduous in their efforts to promote Tanner's reputation and encourage the sale of his work; both were keenly aware of Tanner's "pressing circumstances."[10] Ogden, especially, used his social, business, and philanthropic connections in New York to bring prospective buyers to see Tanner's works. In a letter to Morris, Ogden stated that he had a specific interest in the artist because of his race.[11]

The Annunciation was shown at the Art Institute of Chicago in October 1898, where Morris admired it as "very impressive and beautiful,"[12] and at the annual exhibition at the Pennsylvania Academy in early 1899. Whether or not through Ogden's efforts, *The Annunciation* in January of 1899 was sold to Rodman Wanamaker, a senior officer in the Wanamaker Company and a personal friend of Tanner in Paris. Correspondence indicates that the primary reason for the purchase was to provide income for Tanner.

When the painting was shown at the Academy, it was greeted by the *Philadelphia Inquirer* critic as a "brilliant masterpiece."

> Mr. Tanner's paintings have always been markedly serious, honest, even exalted, but he has never shown in this country anything which in commanding quality approaches this beautiful work. . . . The little figure [of the Virgin] is intensely human, and at the moment of painting the child-woman is divided between fear and exaltation. A beautiful picture it is—a sympathetic picture, a picture to be regarded, not critically—although it can bear criticism—but with appreciation. Americans may be proud that this country has produced a painter of Mr. Tanner's ilk. They are not numerous.[13]

The Annunciation was seen at the Academy by John Q. Johnson, a prominent Philadelphia connoisseur and collector who was then chairman of the acquisition committee of the Wilstach Collection, which had been established in 1895 by Mrs. W. P. Wilstach to purchase works of art for the city of Philadelphia. The collection acquired the painting from Wanamaker on April 5, 1899, for $1,750. The 1902 Wilstach Collection catalogue alluded to Tanner's African-American heritage, but made it clear that the work was sought for its quality:

> Son of Bishop Tanner, of the African Methodist Episcopal Church, this Philadelphia painter has already won a prominent place in the ranks of American artists and has overcome any possible prejudice, especially in Paris, where Art is sufficiently catholic to ignore the distinctions of race. Tanner has had the courage to choose scriptural subjects for his pictures, and has thus challenged comparison with the great painters of every age and race. His pictures having much of the simplicity and fervid religious feeling of the old masters, are yet more than servile imitations, and are distinguished by originality and nobility in conception and no ordinary skill in execution.[14]

In entering the Wilstach Collection, *The Annunciation* won a place in the Pennsylvania Museum and School of Art and became the first work by Tanner to be purchased for an American museum.   DS

4 6

A VIEW IN PALESTINE
c. 1898–99
Oil on canvas
23 × 37³/₄" (58.42 × 95.89 cm)
Signed lower left: *H. O. Tanner*
Vassar College Art Gallery, Poughkeepsie, New York, gift of
Margaret L. Weyerhaeuser '23, Elizabeth L. Weyerhaeuser '15,
and Sarah Weyerhaeuser ex '30, 46.3.3

A View in Palestine is based on Tanner's second visit to the Holy Land during the winter of 1898–99. The artist recorded his vivid impressions of the landscape during his first visit the previous year: "I saw for the first time Egypt and Palestine. . . . Those great barren hills that can blossom like a rose, with irrigation, were to me a natural setting, a fitting setting, to a great tragedy. The country, sad and desolate, is big and majestic."[1] He went on to describe his second trip: "We spent six months painting around Jerusalem and the Dead Sea, and this gave me an insight into the country and the character of the people that my shorter previous visit had only whetted my appetite for. Here it was that I made a study of the Mount of Temptation from which I afterward painted 'Moses and the Burning Bush.' "[2] It is interesting to note that Tanner's father pointed out in his *Theological Lectures* the words of the French philosopher and historian of religion, Ernest Renan (1823–92): "Seeing Palestine is the fifth gospel."[3]

Tanner's painting could serve as an illustration for his written description. A high vantage point reveals the complexity of the setting and draws the viewer into the picture along the irrigated hill on the left, which drops down to a plateau. The landscape tilts up in the manner of modern French painting and Tanner's own *Fishermen at Sea* (cat. no. 78). Even as it expands toward the horizon, the plateau stretches into infinity on the right side of the composition.

The dominantly brown, green, and blue palette is enriched with myriad other colors, causing the even light to dissolve in haze. The varied brushstrokes range from long, loaded strokes in the left foreground to quicker ones in the right middle ground that suggest the ruggedness of the terrain. These touches are contrasted with the more liquid application of pale greens and blue-greens in the trees which call to mind passages in *Fishermen at Sea*.

Tanner successfully turned his own powerful response to the region into a permanent memory in *A View in Palestine*. The work counts among the first pictures for which he felt no need to respond to the paintings or subjects of other artists.
                                                                          DFM

46 A VIEW IN PALESTINE

4 7

NICODEMUS VISITING JESUS

(*Christ and Nicodemus on a Rooftop*)

(*Nicodème Venant Voir Jesus*)

1899

Oil on canvas

33 ¹¹/₁₆ × 39 ¹/₂" (85.57 × 100.33 cm)

Signed, inscribed, and dated lower left: *H. O. Tanner/ Jerusalem 1899*

Pennsylvania Academy of the Fine Arts, Philadelphia, Joseph E. Temple Fund

4 8

HEAD OF A JEW
IN PALESTINE

1899 and c. 1918–20

Oil on canvas

24 × 21 ¹/₈" (60.96 × 53.66 cm)

Inscribed on paper label on lower left of stretcher: *January 28th 1920/Painted in oil/After 2 or 3 yrs./drying painted background in tempera/after rubbing back/ground with an/emulsion*

National Museum of American Art, Smithsonian Institution, Washington, D.C., gift of Mr. and Mrs. Norman B. Robbins

Fig. 58 Piero della Francesa, *Saint Jerome and Gerolamo Amadi*, c. 1450, panel, 19 ⁵/₁₆ × 16 ¹/₂", Galleria dell'Accademia, Venice.

As its inscription and date specify, *Nicodemus Visiting Jesus* (cat. no. 47) was made in Jerusalem during Tanner's second trip to the Near East. Actively exhibited and the subject of early published notices, the painting was among his most famous and the source of his first major honors in the United States. It won the esteemed Lippincott Prize at the sixty-ninth annual of the Pennsylvania Academy of the Fine Arts in 1900, "for the best figure painting in the exhibition by an American artist,"[1] and was purchased for the Academy's permanent collection from Rodman Wanamaker, who sponsored Tanner's travels to the Near East.

The story of Nicodemus visiting Jesus appears in the Gospel of John (3:1–3):

> There was a man of the Pharisees, named Nicodemus, a ruler of the Jews: the same came to Jesus by night, and said unto him, Rabbi, we know that thou art a teacher come from God: no man can do these miracles that thou doest, except God be with him. Jesus answered and said unto him, Verily, verily, I say unto thee, except a man be born again, he cannot see the kingdom of God.

Tanner started to think about this theme even before he went to the Near East. One of his patrons, Robert C. Ogden, wrote on June 15, 1896: "I hasten to congratulate you upon the distinction that your 'Daniel' has received from the judges of the Salon. Of the several religious subjects to which you have recently devoted yourself, I think the Nicodemus will stand the best chance of popularity, but I understand that at present recognition is more important than a market for your pictures."[2]

It is impossible to determine whether the artist actually started work on a painting as early as 1896. The subject deals with a number of themes important to Tanner including that of rebirth, also addressed in *Daniel in the Lions' Den*, 1895 (see fig. 16), and *The Resurrection of Lazarus* (cat. no. 38), both executed around the time of Ogden's letter. Moreover, it returns to the teaching motif of *The Young Sabot Maker* (cat. no. 34) and *The Banjo Lesson* (cat. no. 27), although here youth instructs age.

Tanner's father considered Nicodemus' visit to be one of three notable incidents of the second stage of Jesus' public ministry,[3] and indeed, the image of the rabbi coming to Jesus by night provided a biblical precedent for the worship habits of African-American slaves as well as for post-emancipation practices. Slaves were neither allowed to have formal church services nor to read the Bible,[4] and their clandestine religious activities were perforce con-

ducted at night. Many African-American and evangelical denominations continue to this day to have full-fledged Sunday night services.

Tanner returned from the Holy Land in 1897 by way of Venice, where he visited several art institutions including the Galleria dell'Accademia, and he could have seen *Saint Jerome and Gerolamo Amadi* (fig. 58) by the Italian Renaissance master Piero della Francesca (c. 1420–92). Piero's composition places his two protagonists with a tree to the right and a panoramic landscape as background; an open book on the saint's lap represents his learned status. The composition and the clear relationship between teacher and student might have been suggestive to Tanner.

In a small sketch (fig. 59), Tanner showed Nicodemus seated on a stool looking up at Jesus, who is distinguished by a bold halo. The foreground setting is the reverse of the final composition: here a tree and raised ledge appear on the left rather than the right, and the background depicts a plateau rather than mountains under a starry sky. The sketch could have been

Fig. 59 Henry O. Tanner, *Study for Nicodemus Visiting Jesus*, 1899, oil on canvas mounted on cardboard, 7 1/4 × 9 3/8", Merton Simpson, New York.

48 HEAD OF A JEW IN PALESTINE

conceived much earlier because it calls to mind the palette and handling of Tanner's studies made at Pont-Aven, and it might have something to do with the idea for a Nicodemus picture mentioned in Ogden's letter.

Tanner employed local models for the final painting. He wrote: "I still remember with pleasure the fine head of the old Yemenite Jew who posed for Nicodemus."[5] *Head of a Jew in Palestine* (cat. no. 48) could be the very model. The beard of this figure is not as flowing as Nicodemus', but Tanner later reworked *Head of a Jew*, which may account for its different appearance.

Tanner also reworked the definitive composition of *Nicodemus Visiting Jesus*. E. C. Parry III was among the first careful viewers to recognize changes in the picture:

> In raking light even an untrained observer can see a looming area of *pentimenti* just to the right of Christ. Glimpsed from a steep angle, one realizes that this area once contained a standing figure.... But at some point Tanner scraped the thickly built-up figure off and filled in the space.... Since this picture has been in the Pennsylvania Academy collection since 1900, it is obvious that the repainting must have taken place at an early moment.[6]

In the finished version of *Nicodemus Visiting Jesus*, the two figures gaze at each other across an empty space charged with kinetic energy. Their diagonal relationship, emphasized by the slope of the mountain in the background, is contained within the neutral area defined by the horizon and the horizontal, orangish registers in the stairs on the lower right. The simple diagonal of the stairwell leads to the vertical figure of Jesus, which stops the eye from plunging into the panoramic landscape and refocuses attention on the intense discussion between the two men. Despite the masterful treatment of the composition, the hands of Nicodemus and Jesus are clumsily drawn—a problem that plagued Tanner throughout his career.

Similar objections cannot be made about Tanner's skillful use of light, which is as well thought-out as the arrangement of figures, architecture, and landscape. An overall pattern of essentially horizontal bands begins in the foreground and moves along the left side to a gentle glow on the horizon. The shadows cast by the figures on the balcony floor indicate moonlight coming from the upper right, as do the highlights on Nicodemus. But the viewer observes warm highlights on Jesus' chest and face, and a gleam of cool light along his knee. To achieve this effect, Tanner brought light up through the open stairwell, illuminating Jesus from below. Bright orange touches on the stair risers accentuate this area and suggest an artificial light source within the house. Despite these logical reasons for the play of light on Jesus, Tanner not only induces the viewer to accept all the illumination as deriving from the presence of Jesus but also emphasizes his spirituality without resorting to the use of a halo.

The generally positive reception of *Nicodemus Visiting Jesus* apparently inspired Tanner to make three more renditions of the subject, two of which are lost. One, a vertical painting of Nicodemus alone (location unknown), was exhibited at Pittsburgh's Carnegie Institute in 1907. Another, commissioned by the Cheyney Training School for Teachers at Cheyney, Pennsylvania, in 1924 and delivered in 1927, shows Nicodemus sitting on a rug on the ground in a somewhat humbler pose. A small sketch that might be for this picture is preserved in the National Museum of American Art. A third painting of Jesus and Nicodemus, known only from a photograph, seems relatively close in composition to the Cheyney picture.

Not every contemporary viewer was entirely persuaded by *Nicodemus Visiting Jesus*. Helen Cole, a writer sympathetic to the artist, pointed out: "Tanner's picture of this year, 'Nicodemus Coming to Jesus,' is less striking than the 'Raising of Lazarus,' which is in the Luxembourg, but it is a masterly composition."[7]   DFM

4 9

FLIGHT INTO EGYPT
(*Departure into Egypt*)
1899
Oil on canvas
19 3/4 × 25 1/2" (50.17 × 64.77 cm)
Signed, inscribed, and dated lower left: *H. O. Tanner/*
Jerusalem 1899
Detroit Institute of Arts, Founders Society Purchase, African
Art Gallery Committee Fund

The flight of the Holy Family into Egypt and the theme of the good shepherd
were Tanner's favorite subjects. He rendered each of them more than fifteen
times with varied approaches. The artist noted in 1909 that he had already
painted four or five different versions of *Flight into Egypt* and that "the 'crop'
is not all harvested yet."[1] As far as can be determined, the Detroit painting is
his earliest rendition of the subject, and sets the emotional and visual
standard by which subsequent versions should be judged. This subject of a
biblical flight from persecution might have been linked in Tanner's mind with
the plight of contemporary blacks, especially those who migrated from
southern states to the North.

Although the artist was certainly familiar with the biblical account of
the flight into Egypt (Matt. 2:13–15), the environs of Jerusalem itself inspired
the present picture. Tanner later recalled a specific scene: "Nor do I forget a
ride one stormy Christmas night to Bethlehem. Dark clouds swept the
moonlit skies and it took little imagination to close one's eyes to the flight of
time and see in those hurrying travelers the crowds that hurried Bethlehem-
ward on the memorable night of the Nativity, or to transpose the scene and see
in each hurrying group a 'Flight into Egypt.'"[2] The lack of articulation in the
faces of the figures and the unemphasized Christ Child, who is seen only as a
bundle of cloth on Mary's lap, allows one to see them as ordinary people drawn
from the crowds that hurried toward Bethlehem. The biblical figures become
timeless travelers, whose anxious journey gives them a universality that
extends even to the African-American migrants of Tanner's time.

The overall composition calls to mind *Nicodemus Visiting Jesus*,
another night scene painted at Jerusalem in 1899. In both works, the figures
(and animals) are placed diagonally on a flat area with a tree to the right and a
panoramic landscape in the background. Unlike *Nicodemus*, the blue and
green palette of *Flight into Egypt* is permeated by a pearly gray, and the
quickly rendered brushstrokes provide a visual equivalent for the sense of
touch. Tanner used an overall light effect, with luminosity generated by
touches of pale colors over dark, yet the cast shadows of the figures and
animals emphasize their westward flight and fix further the time of night. The
basic attitudes of the two donkeys suggest Tanner had come to know the
beasts well (and probably rode them himself). However, he endowed them
with the trained gait of fancy horses, in the manner of Thomas Eakins's *The
Fairman Rogers Four-in-Hand* (see fig. 00). The landscape background of
Flight into Egypt also harks back to the terrain on the right side of *A View of
Palestine* (cat. no. 45).

The tree on the right of this picture and the figure of Joseph with his staff provided motifs for future renditions by Tanner (cat. no. 103). He also seems to have been at work in mid-1899 on another variation of the Holy Family's flight, which might be the painting now in Wilkie House (Des Moines). Helen Cole described it: "A picture which I saw the other day in his studio, and which he modestly calls a sketch, is to me simply and wholly beautiful in conception and treatment. It is the 'Flight into Egypt' — a mountain wall in the desolate part of Palestine, the Virgin clasping the babe in her arms, mounted on a mule, which Joseph, bent with care is leading."[3]

When the Detroit version was shown at the Carnegie Institute in Pittsburgh in 1899 and subsequently at the Pennsylvania Academy of the Fine Arts in 1901, it attracted the attention of several reviewers. Francis B. Shaefer wrote: "Mr. Tanner continues to paint biblical scenes. His two pictures in the Carnegie Galleries are 'The Flight into Egypt' and 'Judas.' These paintings are naive, and yet they have a strong sentiment, and a deal of honest fervor which leaves no place in one's judgement of them for anything but respect."[4] Just over a year later, an anonymous writer for the *Philadelphia Inquirer* noted: "The Tanner pictures — after the standard Mr. Tanner has set himself the past few years — are a trifle disappointing. . . .'The Departure into Egypt' is somewhat more nearly in his earlier manner."[5]   DFM

50

MARY
(*La Sainte-Marie*)
1900
Oil on canvas
34 1/2 × 43 1/4" (87.63 × 109.86 cm)
Signed and dated lower right: *H. O. Tanner/1900*
Salon label on recto top center of frame: *1252*
Lasalle University Art Museum, Philadelphia

Fig. 60 Pascal-Jean Dagnan-Bouveret, *Vierge au Rabot*, 1885, oil on canvas, location unknown.

With *Mary*, Tanner returned to the type of image that he rendered in *The Annunciation* (cat. no. 45). The newborn child, with a halo hovering above it, is virtually concealed under folds of cloth on a rug-covered floor. The scene has been interpreted as the repose of the Holy Family on their flight into Egypt,[1] a subject depicted by many artists over the centuries but not actually described in the Bible. Tanner's religious scenes, however, are nearly always derived from scriptural texts. Daniel Burke, in an interesting article that explores the treatment of the subject in relation to late nineteenth-century Catholic thought, has suggested that Tanner could very well have intended to depict Mary after the visit from the adoring shepherds, as she ponders the enormous responsibility placed upon her (Luke 2:15–19).[2] But the shepherds found the child lying in a manger, clearly not the case in the present painting.

Further clues to the identity of the subject might lie in Tanner's knowledge of the evangelists. The Gospel of Matthew tells that the three wise men visited Mary and the infant Jesus (with no mention of Joseph) in a house, not a stable (Matt. 2:11); the same chapter also provided the source for the artist's *Flight into Egypt* (cat. no. 49). Tanner had recently returned from Palestine when he painted *Mary*, and he most likely continued to draw upon his studies and memories of local settings occupied by ordinary people. His characterization of Mary and her surroundings fits this mold. The facial features of Mary recall those of Tanner's new bride, Jessie Olssen, and if she were indeed the model, it would account for the tenderness with which she is painted.

Tanner's composition for *Mary* is essentially a reversal of *The Annunciation*. Burke has made an interesting connection between *Mary* and *Vierge au Rabot* (fig. 60) by Pascal-Jean Dagnan-Bouveret (1852–1929),[3] an artist whom Tanner credited with a slight influence on his work.[4] Unlike Dagnan's approach, however, Tanner's deep, uptilted space recalls his exposure at Pont-Aven to the more contemporary compositional notions of the circle of Gauguin. The light on Mary and on the unadorned wall behind her is crisp and intense, clearly suggesting sunlight. The window on the right is more than a light source; Tanner used its brightness to balance the composition. Color does not play a major role here, but the mauve that dominates the background walls activates those surfaces and unites them with the foreground through additional touches on the infant's coverlet. The child's human characteristics are hidden underneath the folds of cloth, emphasizing the mysterious and spiritual nature of the newborn. Through the

handling of light, the pensive expression given to Mary, and the rather incongruous and old-fashioned halo, the artist turned the plain space of an ordinary Near Eastern household into something approaching a chapel.

When *Mary* was exhibited in America in 1901, it received mixed reviews. Francis J. Ziegler in the *Philadelphia Record* found that " 'Mary' is an interesting and novel interpretation of a Biblical subject."[5] On the other hand, Melville E. Wright said, "Mary is too severe to be pleasing."[6] Perhaps both views truly reflect the compassionate yet serious effect that Tanner set out to achieve. DFM

STUDY FOR ISAAC FROM THE
''MOTHERS OF THE BIBLE''
1901
Charcoal on paper
24⅝ × 15½" (62.55 × 39.37 cm)
Permanent collection, Howard University Gallery of Art,
Washington, D.C.

5 2

STUDY FOR RACHEL FROM THE
''MOTHERS OF THE BIBLE''
1901
Charcoal on paper
23⅛ × 13⅞" (58.74 × 35.24 cm)
National Museum of American Art, Smithsonian Institution,
Washington, D.C., gift of Mr. and Mrs. Norman B. Robbins

5 3

STUDY FOR MARY FROM THE
''MOTHERS OF THE BIBLE''
1901
Charcoal on paper
24 × 28" (60.96 × 71.12 cm)
Inscribed with color and shading notes on dress
Permanent collection, Howard University Gallery of Art,
Washington, D.C.

Fig. 61 Henry O. Tanner, *Sarah*, from the "Mothers of the Bible" series, *Ladies Home Journal*, vol. 19, September 1902, p. 9.

Fig. 62 Henry O. Tanner, *Rachel*, from the "Mothers of the Bible" series, *Ladies Home Journal*, vol. 19, November 1902, p. 13.

Between September 1902 and January 1903, Tanner published a series of four works featuring Sarah, Hagar, Rachel, and Mary, called the "Mothers of the Bible," in the *Ladies Home Journal*. The three charcoal sketches catalogued here are studies for figures in the final paintings, all of which are untraced to date.

Tanner wrote captions for the series to describe what he hoped to capture in each scene. *Study for Isaac* (cat. no. 51) relates to *Sarah* (fig. 61), for which the artist used a passage from Proverbs (31:18–19): "Her candle goeth not out by night. She layeth her hands to the spindle, and her hands hold the distaff." Tanner chose Sarah because "all the virtues of a true mother can be judged from the fact that the one sorrow of her life was that she was childless."[1] Tanner emphasized the importance of Isaac, born in Sarah's old age, by placing him in the foreground of the finished painting.

The elaborate and beautiful *Study for Rachel* (cat. no. 52) is a study for the swooning bride-to-be of Jacob (fig. 62). Tanner himself had been married less than three years at this time, and he turned to Genesis (29:10–11) "to present the story in the picture [as] a love story of Biblical times with the fresh human interest of all times preserved."[2] The tall model with a prominent nose could very well have been the artist's wife, Jessie Olssen.

Tanner seems to have used his wife again as the model for *Study for Mary* (cat. no. 53), her hair now worn in long braids. Jessie Tanner might also have posed for the so-called *Study of an Indian* (fig. 64), which is in fact a study for the figure of the teenaged Jesus which appears on the left in the finished painting of *Mary* (fig. 63). This scene depicts Mary pondering her son's assertion that he "must be about his Father's business," after finding Jesus in the temple in Jerusalem answering the questions of learned men (Luke 2:46–49). The theme echoes Tanner's earlier vision of *Mary* (cat. no. 50), where, "keep-

51 STUDY FOR ISAAC FROM THE "MOTHERS OF THE BIBLE"

52 STUDY FOR RACHEL FROM THE "MOTHERS OF THE BIBLE"

53 STUDY FOR MARY FROM THE "MOTHERS OF THE BIBLE"

Fig. 63 Henry O. Tanner, *Mary*, from the "Mothers of the Bible" series, reproduced in *Ladies Home Journal*, vol. 20, January 1903, p. 13.

ing all these sayings in her heart" (Luke 2:51), she reflects on her uncommon motherhood. In his extended caption for the illustration *Mary* published in the *Ladies Home Journal*, Tanner made clear his continuing interest in distinct ethnic groups:

> The physical characteristics of the child Jesus will always remain a point of discussion. No artist has ever produced a type, nor ever will that has in it all that the varying minds of all time will, acknowledge as complete. It was my chance in Jerusalem to run across a little Yemenite Jew. Where could a better type be found than this swarthy child of Arabia, of purest Jewish blood – nurtured in the same land, under the same sun, and never, neither he nor his ancestors, having quitted its (at times) inhospitable shores?[3]

The drawing style of these three sheets, plus the work here identified as *Study for Jesus*, shows that Tanner was well able to render volume through an economy of means. The sketch for the boy Isaac is much more detailed than the other works but not as elaborate as his drawings from the early 1890s (cat. nos. 16–18). The artist's command of his medium is illustrated by the flowing, multiple contour lines, with a minimum of shading, in *Study for Rachel* and *Study for Mary*.

Tanner did not exhibit these drawings (or apparently any others) during his lifetime. Their recent recognition as studies for important paintings and their innate beauty make them significant documents for our understanding of the artist. DFM

Fig. 64 Henry O. Tanner, *Study for Jesus (Study of an Indian)*, n.d., charcoal on paper, 11 3/4 × 9 1/4", Schomburg Center for Research in Black Culture, The New York Public Library.

5 4

THE GOOD SHEPHERD
c. 1902–1903
Oil on canvas
27 × 32″ (68.58 × 81.28 cm)
Signed lower right: *H. O. Tanner*
Jane Voorhees Zimmerli Art Museum, Rutgers, The State
University of New Jersey, New Brunswick, in memory of the
deceased members of the Class of 1954

The artist's son, Jesse O. Tanner, pointed out that the good shepherd was a favorite subject of his father,[1] and indeed Tanner painted it numerous times (cat. nos. 88, 89, 100–102). Jesse described his father's strong sense that Jesus watches over his flock, and that man and God together are needed to overcome evil.[2] These notions are powerfully expressed in the Twenty-third Psalm, which remains today an important part of African Methodist Episcopal liturgy, the denomination in which Tanner was reared.

The scriptural reference is from the Gospel of John (10:14–16): "I am the good shepherd, and know my sheep, and am known of mine. As the Father knoweth me, even so know I the Father: and I lay down my life for the sheep. And other sheep I have, which are not of this fold: them also I must bring, and they shall hear my voice; and there shall be one fold, and one shepherd." Tanner's interpretation of these last words should not only be seen as embracing Christianity as the one true faith. He certainly also saw the theme of the good shepherd in terms of racial and social equality, as did his father.

Tanner's first treatment of the subject seems to have been the vignette in the background of *Rachel* in his series the "Mothers of the Bible" (see fig. 62). The configuration of trees in *The Good Shepherd* is drawn from a work that Tanner probably made in the Holy Land (see fig. 65).

In this early version, a nocturnal scene, the figure and flock are only summarily suggested, but their movement and energy are evident. The limbs of monumental trees reach up toward the spacious sky and then control it by engulfing the beautifully treated moon, which breaks through the clouds with force. The palette is dominated by blues laid over greens, Tanner's celebrated blend. Shape and color, more so than the passage of the brush to articulate form, move the eye across the surface. The overall impact of the work recalls *Christ and His Disciples on the Road to Bethany* (cat. no. 55) and its kinship to the moonlit scenes of Millet (see fig. 66).

The painting was eloquently described by a contemporary reviewer:

> In the canvas called "The Good Shepherd" the sky is saturated with light, the ground has solidity, and the fine pattern made by the gnarled branches of the trees is extremely decorative. Moreover, in this picture, the execution has a particular beauty. The reduced palette and rather heavy pate, the closer drawing and more distinguished design, indicate a more than usually strenuous grapple with the inevitable difficulties attendant upon the translation of nature into terms of art.[3]

DFM

54 THE GOOD SHEPHERD

55

CHRIST AND HIS DISCIPLES ON
THE ROAD TO BETHANY
c. 1902–1903
Oil on canvas
37³/₈ × 47¹³/₁₆″ (95 × 121.5 cm)
Signed lower left: *H. O. Tanner*
Musée d'Orsay, Paris

Fig. 65 Henry O. Tanner, *Abraham's Oak*,
n.d., oil on canvas, 21³/₄ x 28³/₄″,
National Museum of American Art,
Smithsonian Institution, Washington, D.C.

Fig. 66 Jean-François Millet, *Shepherdess
and Flock at Sunset*, c. 1868–70, 14¹/₂ x
17³/₈″, Museum of Fine Arts, Boston, gift
of Quincy Adams Shaw through Quincy
A. Shaw, Jr., and Mrs. Marian Shaw
Haughton.

Christ and His Disciples on the Road to Bethany demonstrates the unique-
ness of Tanner's biblical scenes. As in the case of *Salomé* (see fig. 48) and
Return of the Holy Women (cat. no. 56), he used scriptural texts as a point of
departure, but he did not merely illustrate them in the stylized manner of
other contemporary painters. Tanner brought his sensitivity to his surroundings to bear on his depictions; here he was inspired both by his trips to the
Holy Land and by his father's interpretation of biblical texts. In his *Theological Lectures*, Benjamin Tanner stressed the evangelists' account of Jesus'
return to Bethany each night.[1]

Tanner wrote about this picture, which was owned by his friend and
patron Atherton Curtis:

> Very probably one of the most happy ideas is the one in "Christ and his Disciples
> on the Road to Bethany." I have taken the tradition that Christ never spent a
> night in Jerusalem, but at the close of day went to Bethany. . . . I have pictured the
> moon set in rather a blue sky high over the heads of Christ and four of His
> disciples, who are walking along a little roadway . . . while to the right a goat
> herder is returning with his herd of black goats. Recognizing in Christ a great
> prophet, he stops, places his hand upon his breast, and bows his head in reverence
> while Christ and His disciples pass.[2]

Christ and His Disciples on the Road to Bethany is composed along the
same principles as *Flight into Egypt* (cat. no. 49), and the tree at the right is
close to the rendering in *Abraham's Oak* (fig. 65). By this time Tanner's work
shows that he is clearly his own person: traces of his teachers' influences are
hard to detect, and his style is rarely compared to that of other artists in
contemporary reviews. As in *The Good Shepherd*, c. 1902–1903 (cat. no. 54),
however, it is difficult to ignore a kinship with the moonlit scenes of Jean-
François Millet, in which lonely shepherds with their flocks evoke a quasi-
religious feeling (fig. 66).

Christ and His Disciples was reviewed favorably during the black artist's lifetime. A characteristic notice appeared in the *New York Times* in
December 1908:

> The most successful combining of the pictorial scene with this emotional sig-
> nificance is seen in the "Christ on the Road to Bethany." Here the night land-
> scape is bathed in atmosphere. The vivid blue sky of the East, the trees massed at
> the left, grave in tone without heaviness, and the well-composed group of figures,
> the Christ returning from Jerusalem to his lodging in Bethany and the shepherd
> inclining his head in recognition of the spiritual eminence of the passerby, all
> combine to give an impression of quiet beauty quite without excess of symbol-
> ism or dramatic arrangement.[3]

DFM

55 CHRIST AND HIS DISCIPLES ON THE ROAD TO BETHANY

5 6

RETURN OF THE HOLY WOMEN

(Le Retour de la Sainte Femme)
1904
Oil on canvas
46 × 35″ (116.84 × 88.9 cm)
Signed and dated lower right: *H. O. Tanner/1904*
Inscribed on verso: *Study for a Grieving Woman with a Man*
Cedar Rapids Art Gallery, Iowa

Fig. 67 El Greco, *The Visitation*, c.
1607–14, oil on canvas, 38½ x 28½″,
Dumbarton Oaks Research Library and
Collections, Washington, D.C.

Fig. 68 Henry O. Tanner, *Ruth and
Naomi*, by 1908, oil on canvas, location
unknown.

Return of the Holy Women exemplifies Tanner's recurring interest in the themes of the crucifixion and resurrection, which replaced his teaching motif after the turn of the century. For the socially conscious African-American artist, the events in the life of Jesus were symbolic of the struggles of all the oppressed, as expressed by Julia Ward Howe in the monumental lines of the *Battle Hymn of the Republic*, "As he died to make men holy, let us die to make men free."

Tanner explained the effect he hoped to achieve in this work:

> It has often seemed to me that, when bowed by some sorrow, nature seemed more radiant than ever before. This apparent fact influenced largely "The Return of the Holy Women." The moon has risen, a shepherd returns with his flock, all unconscious of the terrible tragedy of the morning, or the sorrowing figures, one of them, Mary, supported by John, in front of him. All is tranquillity and loveliness, only within the souls of that sorrowing mother and those loving disciples is there turmoil and sorrow.[1]

Tanner's vision was drawn from the Gospel of John (19:25–27), which identifies the other two figures in this episode: "Now there stood by the cross of Jesus his mother, and his mother's sister, Mary the wife of Cleophas, and Mary Magdalene. When Jesus therefore saw his mother, and the disciple standing by, whom he loved, he saith unto his mother, Woman, behold thy son! Then saith he to the disciple, Behold thy mother! And from that hour that disciple took her unto his own home."

The style of *Return of the Holy Women* reflects the art Tanner would have seen during a trip to Spain in early 1903. The composition calls to mind the low vantage point—with a bird's-eye view of a distant landscape in the immediate background—of several Spanish artists including El Greco (fig. 67). Tanner's elongated figures, pushing against the vertical extremities of the format, reflect his admiration for seventeenth-century Spanish baroque painting. He took a similar approach in a lost painting, *Ruth and Naomi*, exhibited in 1908 (fig. 68). John's daggerlike fingers—at once reaching out to comfort the Virgin Mary and tenderly calling attention to his own aching heart—reflect the mannerisms of El Greco. But the headband worn by John is Tanner's own naturalistic shorthand for a halo, intended to prompt the viewer to recognize the subject's religious nature. He used the same device to identify the young Jesus in the painting *Mary* for the "Mothers of the Bible" series (see fig. 63). The pose of the younger Mary, on the left, is close to that of Tanner's *Salomé* (see fig. 48).

56 RETURN OF THE HOLY WOMEN

Tanner did not sacrifice complex color arrangements or atmospheric perspective in depicting the scene's nocturnal setting. The unseen moon emits a beautiful range of hues: blue, green, lavender, and rose. Tanner restrained these inherently bright colors with matte brushstrokes that recall a dry pastel technique. This handling of paint and the overall approach to the picture emphasize Tanner's ever-growing artistic diversity.

Tanner seems to have been hesitant about sending *Return of the Holy Women* or any other of his elongated figure compositions to public exhibitions. The work was not exhibited at the Paris Salon until two years after it was signed and dated, although he sent more conventional works such as *Job and His Three Friends* (cat. no. 57). If Tanner thought the picture was too daring stylistically, he was proven wrong by subsequent commentary. The critic for the *Public Ledger* said simply: " 'The Return of the Holy Women' presents an effect of moonlight admirable in its atmospheric depth."[2] David Lloyd, in *International Studio*, also commented favorably: "In this latter canvas the figures are seen ascending into the foreground from a hollow, whence the bluish mists are rising that give the predominant colour to the whole."[3]

DFM

5 7

JOB AND HIS THREE FRIENDS
c. 1904
Oil on canvas
41 × 49 ³/₄" (104.14 × 126.37 cm)
William H. and Camille O. Cosby

Paintings based on the Old Testament occur infrequently among Tanner's biblical subjects, but for *Job and His Three Friends* the artist turned to the celebrated story of the suffering of a righteous man and his eventual emancipation (Job 2:7–13). Job's ultimate acceptance by God and his regained wealth, even greater than before his tribulations, can be equated with the themes of rebirth and redemption to which Tanner was so frequently drawn:

> So went Satan forth from the presence of the Lord, and smote Job with sore boils from the sole of his foot unto his crown. And he took him a potsherd to scrape himself withal; and he sat down among the ashes. . . . Now when Job's three friends heard of all this evil that was come upon him, they came every one from his own place; Eliphaz the Temanite, and Bildad the Shuhite, and Zophar the Naamathite: for they had made an appointment together to come to mourn with him and to comfort him. . . . So they sat down with him upon the ground seven days and seven nights, and none spake a word unto him: for they saw that his grief was very great.

Two glowing lamps in the right foreground distinguish the scene as one of the seven nights of mourning mentioned in the scripture. Job reclines on a blanket in the middle of the composition; his feet, legs, arms, and face are bared, suggesting his suffering from boils. Two friends are seated on the left; a third kneels and comforts Job. A wall in the middle ground defines the enclosure, and to the right is a smoking, ricklike structure.

Tanner might also have been referring to a later passage in Job (42:7–9) in which the Lord is angry with Eliphaz and commands the three friends to make a burnt offering. The smoldering heap at the opening would be the sacrifice, and the man who comforts Job would be Eliphaz, whose prominent position in the center of the scene is further underscored by the portraitlike delineation of his head.

The life of Job was not a popular subject with nineteenth-century French painters, and Tanner would have had little precedent for this picture. Another intensely individual painter, Alexandre-Gabriel Decamps, chose to depict the subject several times around 1850 (fig. 69); Jules Laurens (1825–1901) made a lithograph after one of Decamps's versions. The *Job* by Léon Bonnat (1883–1922), shown in the Paris Salon of 1880, is almost shockingly realistic by comparison with the more poetic visions of Decamps or Tanner.

Tanner's composition is anchored by the diagonal, foreshortened figure of Job, which is balanced by the diagonal posture of Eliphaz on the right. The positions of the other two friends, only vaguely delineated on the left, act as vertical contrasts for the principal figures. The background wall focuses the viewer's eye on the central action. The arched opening at the right frames the smoke-filled sky; its curve is echoed in the jar in the left foreground.

Fig. 69 Alexandre-Gabriel Decamps, *Job and His Friends*, c. 1855, oil type on linen twill, 47 × 33 ³/₄", The Minneapolis Institute of Arts, gift of Mrs. Erasmus C. Lindley.

57 JOB AND HIS THREE FRIENDS

Tanner's handling of paint in this picture is much looser than his style of a few years earlier in paintings such as *Christ and the Doctors* (location unknown). A subdued palette of deep purplish browns, ochres, and grays conveys an appropriately somber mood. Brighter colors unite the sky with the foreground highlights on Job's garments and the glow of the lamps. Strokes of strong red punctuate the ground and define the contours of the blanket upon which Job reclines, reminding the viewer that he "sat down among the ashes." Further touches of red in the hero's body represent his sores.

Tanner captured Job's tragedy through the interaction of the figures, smoldering colors, and his individual approach to light sources. The oil lamps seem to cast light on Job's legs and account for the reflected highlights edging the robes of the two friends at the left. But the two little flames cannot account for all the light; embers from the ash heap also seem to glow. Yet another source, above and outside the picture plane to the right, seemingly behind even the viewer, generates the major illumination for the foreground and draws the viewer into the event. The light in the small section of sky visible beyond the enclosure is self-contained and does not fall on the figures; its brightness might even presage Job's future well-being. These four light sources, more than clever compositional devices, guide the viewer through different moments in the story.

Surprisingly this subtle and powerful image did not attract the attention of critics when it was shown at Philadelphia and New York in early 1905. In fact, Tanner's work of this period received severe criticism from Arthur Hoeber in his account of a Carnegie International exhibition in 1905:

> For some time he has fallen short of the interest earlier work inspired. Both on account of the artistic quality of certain pictures he sent back from abroad years ago, and from the fact that he was the first of his race — for Mr. Tanner is a Negro — to achieve artistic distinction, he was an entertaining personality in his profession and, confining himself almost entirely to Biblical themes, treated in a modern artistic manner, he attracted much attention. The virility of earlier performances, the personal note and the enthusiastic treatment of his canvases are quite gone, a certain indecision resulting instead, with indefinite colour and a way of handling his pigment that is far from agreeable. The intellectual quality of the composition once so marked is *nil* to-day and there is little health in the work.[1]

These negative comments were inspired by *Judas Covenanting with the High Priests*, a painting that Tanner himself seems to have found unsatisfactory,[2] and indeed, a number of his pictures of this period seem to have given him trouble. A mood of discouragement might explain why Tanner covered this compelling image of Job with the canvas for *Daniel in the Lions' Den* (cat. no. 87). Lost from view for nearly seventy years, it was only rediscovered during the restoration of *Daniel* in 1976. *Job and His Three Friends* can be judged today with fresh eyes. DFM

5 8

CHRIST AT THE HOME OF
MARY AND MARTHA
1905
Oil on canvas
50 × 39″ (127 × 99.06 cm)
Signed lower left: *H. O. Tanner*
The Carnegie Museum of Art, Pittsburgh

Fig. 70 Henry O. Tanner, *Christ at the Home of Lazarus*, n.d., location unknown.

Tanner continued to pursue his interest in depicting women from the Bible in *Christ at the Home of Mary and Martha*. He based the subject on the Gospel of Luke (10:38–42):

> Now it came to pass, as they went, that he entered into a certain village: and a certain woman named Martha received him into her house. And she had a sister called Mary, which also sat at Jesus' feet, and heard his word. But Martha was cumbered about much serving, and came to him, and said, Lord, dost thou not care that my sister hath left me to serve alone? bid her therefore that she help me. And Jesus answered and said unto her, Martha, Martha, thou art careful and troubled about many things: But one thing is needful; and Mary hath chosen that good part, which shall not be taken away from her.

Tanner seems to have chosen the moment when Jesus reproves Martha, who stands beside the table, frozen. The artist wrote that "very probably the most difficult effect I have ever undertaken is that in the picture, 'Christ at the Home of Mary and Martha,' now in the Carnegie Galleries."[1] Tanner might have been commenting on the complicated light sources in the painting, with a lamp on the table and a fire in the background, but a barely discernible figure standing behind the table, which is in fact a pentimento, raises questions about the exact nature of the subject. In another story set in the home of Mary and Martha, related in the Gospel of John (12:1–8), Mary anoints Jesus' feet with a costly perfume, and Judas Iscariot rebukes her for not giving the money for the unguent to the poor, thereby depriving him of an opportunity to pilfer the common purse. The "difficult effect" might have been Tanner's attempt to combine these two stories into one picture. Based on John's account, it would be Mary who is stunned by Judas' criticism, and the background figure would be Judas, here indeed rendered as a shadowy character.

This complex identification should not obscure Tanner's style and technique. The multiple light sources call to mind the interior of *The Banjo Lesson*, executed about ten years earlier (cat. no. 27), as well as *Nicodemus Visiting Jesus* of 1899 (cat. no. 47). The seated woman with a still life of fruit on the table to her right appears in another version of this subject as a portrait of his patrons Mr. and Mrs. Atherton Curtis (fig. 70). The shadowed interior and the quality of the whites in the tablecloth and Jesus' robe suggest Tanner's continuing interest in the art of Velázquez and other seventeenth-century Spanish artists.

Tanner wrote at length about his concern that religious paintings should be significant as works of art:

> It has often seemed to me that many painters of religious subjects (in our time) seem to forget that their pictures should be as much works of art (regardless of

the subject) as are other paintings with less holy subjects. To suppose that the fact of the religious painter having a more elevated subject than his brother artist makes it unnecessary for him to consider his picture as an artistic production, or that he can be less thoughtful about a color harmony, for instance, than he who selects any other subject, simply proves that he is less of an artist than he who gives the subject his best attention.[2]

Contemporary art critics seem not to have paid attention to *Christ at the Home of Mary and Martha* when Tanner exhibited it in Pittsburgh and New York in 1907 and 1908.   DFM

TWO DISCIPLES AT THE TOMB

c. 1905–1906

Oil on canvas

51 × 41 ⁵/₈″ (129.54 × 105.73 cm)

Signed lower left: *H. O. Tanner*

Art Institute of Chicago, Robert Waller Fund, 1906.300

STUDY FOR THE DISCIPLE
PETER

c. 1905

Conte crayon and charcoal on paper, mounted on paperboard

18 ⁹/₁₆ × 14 ³/₄″ (47.15 × 37.47 cm)

Signed in pencil lower left: *H. O. Tanner*

National Museum of American Art, Smithsonian Institution, Washington, D.C., gift of Mr. and Mrs. Norman B. Robbins

Two Disciples at the Tomb is the most widely discussed of Tanner's paintings. Even better known, especially in the United States, than the artist's crucial early painting *The Resurrection of Lazarus* (cat. no. 38), our image of the African-American artist has largely rested upon it.

Like the compelling and beautifully rendered *Annunciation* (cat. no. 45) and the ambitious *Nicodemus Visiting Jesus* (cat. no. 47) of the preceding decade, *Two Disciples* brought major recognition to Tanner in his country of birth. Florence L. Bentley described the picture's success at some length in 1906:

> To Henry O. Tanner, the famous Negro artist, has been awarded the Harris Prize of $500.00 for the best picture shown in the 19th Annual exhibition of American paintings now drawing towards its close at the Chicago Art Institute.
>
> The painting, "The Two Disciples at the Tomb," has carried off honors from an exhibition of unusual merit. The 350 pictures hung are all from artists of acknowledged ability. Quite a number have won prizes at other shows, while still a larger number had previously appeared at the walls of the exacting salons of Paris. After careful consideration of all this gathering of excellence, the jury of award was unanimous in selecting Mr. Tanner's picture as the best.[1]

Tanner based this picture on the Gospel of John (20:2–6):

> Then she runneth, and cometh to Simon Peter, and to the other disciple, whom Jesus loved, and saith unto them, They have taken away the Lord out of the sepulchre, and we know not where they have laid him. Peter therefore went forth, and that other disciple, and came to the sepulchre. So they ran both together: and the other disciple did outrun Peter, and came first to the sepulchre. And he stooping down, and looking in, saw the linen clothes lying; yet went he not in.

Peter, the bearded and older man, is on the left, and John, "whom Jesus loved," is on the right. A study for Peter (cat. no. 60) in Tanner's characteristic drawing style concentrates on the model's intense facial expression.

Tanner recorded that *Two Disciples at the Tomb* inspired his next major picture, *The Disciples at Emmaus* (fig. 71). Both paintings echo the yellowish brown palette and tight drawing, especially notable in *Lazarus*, that Tanner employed during the late 1890s. The model for the youthful John appears again in Tanner's more complex composition of *Emmaus*, and yet again in *Christ Washing the Disciples' Feet*, a lost painting of 1906 (see fig. 49). *Two Disciples* exemplifies Tanner's use of a varying palette within a short period of time. The color values of this picture are markedly different from those of *Return of the Holy Women* (cat. no. 56), which is nearly contemporary, yet they share an emphasis on the stylization of the figures.

Fig. 71 Henry O. Tanner, *The Disciples at Emmaus*, 1906, oil on canvas, 73¹/₂ × 83¹/₂″, Musée d'Orsay, Paris.

60 STUDY FOR THE DISCIPLE PETER

Florence Bentley provided a key to an understanding of *Two Disciples at the Tomb*, writing in eloquent detail:

> The picture shows the disciples, Peter and John, standing at the open sepulchre awaiting in tense expectancy the fulfillment of the promise made to them. From the opening streams a light which is strongly reflected on the faces of the men and showing that luminosity which is a peculiar quality of all Tanner canvasses. The men are very plain looking and of a strong Jewish type, and are dressed in dark nondescript clothes. That is all — an opening from which a stone has been rolled away from which light streams and two poor Jews gazing into the miraculous light. With this simple composition a master hand has told a human story which finds its way to every human heart.[2]

Nearly forty years later, the noted black art historian James A. Porter found himself equally moved by the painting:

> In this work Tanner comes as close to the real essentials of painting as he ever came. It is a bold, unusual conception of the theme, depending, like a cinematographic "close-up," on the power of the human face to convey pathos. The warm, glowing color is put on in brusque impasto technique, without fussiness or excessive modeling. This is the apogee of Tanner's religious paintings.[3]

DFM

6 1

NIGHT

(Return of the Fisherman)
c. 1905
Oil on canvas
26 ¹/₄ × 19 ³/₄" (66.68 × 50.17 cm)
Signed lower left: *H. O. Tanner*
Inscribed, signed, and dated verso: *Replica of Picture Owned/by*
Mr. and Mrs. Atherton Curtis/H. O. Tanner Paris 1905
Herbert F. Johnson Museum of Art, Cornell University, Ithaca,
New York, gift of Mrs. Stephen W. Jacobs, 79.29.1

In a letter written in 1920 to Helen Ogden Purves, the daughter of Robert C. Ogden, Tanner described the present picture as one that he had painted "in this little fishing village; and [it] is the return of father and son from the sea—I called it *Return of the Fisherman.*"[1] An inscription on the back further identifies the painting as a replica of a work originally called *Night*. The artist's good friends and patrons, Louise and Atherton Curtis, lent a version of this subject (location unknown) to the annual exhibitions at the Pennsylvania Academy of the Fine Arts (no. 65) and the Carnegie Institute (no. 219) in 1901. Tanner wrote to Harrison S. Morris on November 19, 1900: "I have sent you the picture you asked for and one—*Night*—that you have not asked for. It is I think the best small picture I have ever done, and so think my friends and I wished to exhibit it in Philadelphia.—Sir I hope it may not be unacceptable. It was made last summer and is the property of Mr. Atherton Curtis."[2] Arthur Hoeber, a reviewer for New York City's *Commercial Advertiser*, described the image shown at Philadelphia as a small pastel of a man carrying a lantern, clearly a prototype for the painting catalogued here.[3]

Beginning in the summer of 1900, Tanner spent his holidays in the rural village of Etaples in the Pas-de-Calais district of northwest France on the English Channel. *Night* surely represents a scene of this region, as evident in the barely discernible hayrick in the middle ground and in the costumes of the figures, which appear again much later in the firmly titled *Etaples Fisher Folk* (cat. no. 90). The simple cottage is characteristic of the rural architectural style of coastal France. In the subject of a man and a boy returning from fishing by lantern light, Tanner touched upon his frequent early theme of youth led by age, and the peasant types of *Night* are rooted in the French Barbizon tradition of Decamps and Millet.

The composition of this attractive painting balances the vertical figures with the diagonals of the cottage, and the horizontal background calls to mind elements of *Two Disciples at the Tomb* (cat. no. 59). The play of lines and shapes emphasizes the plodding, albeit decisive forward movement of the figures. Color has a minor role, but the illumination from the lantern is important: it leads the two figures and creates high-keyed passages in the nocturnal scene. At first glance, the glow framing the doorway seems to have its own source, but the tilt of the lantern accounts for this pattern and for the highlights on the boy's brow. Flares of light on the horizon animate the somber background and suggest other night fishermen still at sea.

61 NIGHT

Tanner's use of lamplight for this outdoor scene is striking; other similar works were most frequently illuminated by the moon (cat. no. 55). The bold artificial-light effects of Caravaggio and his followers might well have been on Tanner's mind when he rendered the pastel around 1900; he had seen the works of these artists during his visits to museums in Italy in 1897. Tanner also frequently took inspiration from observations of his immediate environment to launch a group of related works. He described such an occasion in his autobiography: "One evening, while riding in a jiggling ill-lighted omnibus in Paris, I was struck with the beauty of the effect around me. Inside, the figures dimly lighted with a rich cadmium; outside, the cool night with here and there a touch of moonlight."[4] Tanner's experience in the omnibus led to a painting, now lost, called *Judas Covenanting with the High Priests,*[5] but the contrasting illumination he observed also could have inspired his approach to *Night,* as well as another contemporary lantern-lighted scene, *Return at Night from the Market* (Clark Atlanta University).

Between the exhibitions at Philadelphia and Pittsburgh, the Curtises sent the first version of *Night* to the 1901 Paris Salon (no. 1906). Its active exhibition history brought the picture to the attention of art critics for several major publications, who gave it mixed reviews. A writer for the *New York Times* said: "A study in lantern light is H. O. Tanner's 'Night,' where the figures are all but invisible."[6] The critics for the *Philadelphia Inquirer* and *Philadelphia Ledger* countered: " 'Night,' lent by Atherton Curtis, is sombre, but beautifully treated,"[7] and, "He also shows a night scene, in which a lamplight effect is well rendered."[8] Arthur Hoeber disliked the experimental nature of much of the work in the Pennsylvania Academy exhibition and singled out Tanner's *Night* as especially freakish and mannered: "It is presumed that there is a man carrying a lantern, but this must be taken on faith, for the spectator sees only a dark mass of color from which glows a yellow spot and in vain does one seek to discover any form, color, or suggestion of humanity."[9] Toward the end of 1901, when the pastel was shown at the Carnegie Institute, Charles H. Caffin added a further negative note: "Henry O. Tanner, who has before now done some charming night pieces, shows here a 'Night' which in its excessive darkness is quite unintelligible. At least, it was so in the large gallery in Pittsburgh, where, to increase its disadvantage, it was skied."[10]

Although these reviews address the earlier version of this image, they are clearly relevant to the Cornell picture. Tanner himself thought well enough of the composition belonging to the Curtises to make this replica of it, perhaps as a token of friendship for Robert C. Ogden, thus linking two of his most loyal supporters. He painted yet another version (fig. 72) around 1930 with the enamellike surface that characterized his final years.   DFM

Fig. 72 Henry O. Tanner, *Fishermen Returning at Night,* c. 1930, oil and tempera on academy board, 9 3/8" × 7 1/2", Merton Simpson, New York.

62

THE DISCIPLES SEE CHRIST WALKING ON THE WATER

c. 1907
Oil on canvas
51 1/2 × 42" (130.81 × 106.68 cm)
Signed lower right: *H. O. Tanner*
Des Moines Art Center, gift of the Des Moines Association of
Fine Arts, 1921.1

Tanner's long-standing interest in marine painting reemerged in *The Disciples See Christ Walking on the Water*. Matthew dramatically described the scene (14:24–28):

> But the ship was now in the midst of the sea, tossed with waves: for the wind was contrary. And in the fourth watch of the night Jesus went unto them, walking on the sea. And when the disciples saw him walking on the sea, they were troubled, saying, It is a spirit; and they cried out for fear. But straightway Jesus spake unto them, saying, Be of good cheer; it is I; be not afraid. And Peter answered him and said, Lord, if it be thou, bid me come unto thee on the water.

The phantomlike vertical shape glowing in the upper left represents Jesus walking on water, and Peter stands tallest in the boat. Tanner did not depict the fury of the sudden storm, yet he was able to convey the awestruck feelings of the apostles through their postures. One figure in the front of the boat has just turned to witness the miracle, while another kneels with hands in prayer but seems to reel back from the approaching image. Two apostles standing in the rear of the boat hide their eyes. A faint outline around the rearmost apostle suggests the shaken state alluded to in the scripture.

In *The Disciples See Christ Walking on the Water* Tanner successfully attempted one of his most ambitious visual effects. The top of the composition is cropped below the actual horizon line, allowing the surface of the sea, which mirrors the cloudy sky, to fill the vertical format. Reflections in the water of the clouds, figures, mast, and rigging are rendered in a masterful fashion. Perhaps one of Tanner's most original ideas was to place the reflection of the moon in the water, at the lower left, making it the actual source of light, which fades as it recedes toward the right but sends a brighter glow toward the ghostlike figure of Christ. The overall unreality of the painting is enhanced by Tanner's mature palette of violet, blues, and blue-greens with a somewhat chalky surface.

Tanner retook this theme a few years later in *The Sea of Galilee*, now in the Toledo Museum of Art (fig. 73), although the figure of Jesus on the water has been painted out. In this later work Tanner also experimented with drying time to create a thick impasto. The Toledo picture and the one catalogued here can be compared with the dramatic, nonbiblical *Fishermen at Sea* (cat. no. 78).

The shroud of light symbolizing Jesus in *The Disciples See Christ Walking on the Water* is not as dramatic as the radiant glow that Tanner used for the angel in *The Annunciation* almost ten years earlier (cat. no. 45). This change in part had to do with Tanner's gradual stylistic move toward more abstract form.

Fig. 73 Henry O. Tanner, *The Disciples on the Sea of Galilee*, c. 1910, oil on canvas, 21 5/8 × 26 1/2", The Toledo Museum of Art, gift of Frank W. Gunsaulus, Chicago.

62 THE DISCIPLES SEE CHRIST WALKING ON THE WATER

The several reviews that appeared during Tanner's retrospective exhibition at the American Art Galleries in New York in 1908 did not single out this painting for special discussion, but it is the type of work that William R. Lester, following a critic for Paris *Figaro*, had in mind when he wrote of another nocturnal scene in 1908: "His figures are strongly grouped, energetically designed, tense in expression without gesticulation. The color scheme, with its tonality derived from the light [source], nowhere suggests the conventional tone of old paintings, and is rich and forceful throughout."[1]

DFM

NORTH AFRICA

AND ORIENTALISM

1908–1914

Henry O. Tanner spent the winter of 1908 in Algeria.[1] His visit might have been encouraged by the possibility of having his work subsidized for a few months: in 1907 the Villa Abd el Tif was founded in Algiers by Célestin Jonnart, governor of Algeria, for French artists wishing to work in the area.[2] Tanner's choice of Algeria illustrates the degree to which he had become immersed in French artistic traditions. Earlier trips had taken him to Egypt and Palestine, but the western coast of North Africa had been preferred by several generations of French painters.

For Orientalists, the "Orient" did not refer to Far Eastern countries such as China, Korea, or Japan; Orientalism in nineteenth-century art and literature was largely inspired by North Africa, Albania, Turkey, and the Holy Land. The French vogue for Oriental projects was first cultivated in the early nineteenth century by the mysterious artist and collector Monsieur Auguste (1779–1850).[3] During the 1830s a realistic vision of the region was created and popularized in the paintings of Alexandre-Gabriel Decamps (1803–60).[4] Another major formulator of Tanner's adopted tradition was the romantic master Eugène Delacroix (1798–1863), who expressed his attraction to the Near East in 1832: "If one has a few months free, it is necessary to come to Tangiers or any other city of North Africa, in order to see the natural, which is always disguised in our region, and to feel the precision and rare influence of the sun, which gives a penetrating light to all things."[5] Fascination with the Orient was not limited to French painters of the Romantic period, but was shared by artists over many decades such as Thomas Eakins's teacher Jean-Léon Gérôme, Tanner's Académie Julian master Benjamin-Constant, the Impressionist Pierre-Auguste Renoir, and, in the early twentieth century, the modernist Henri Matisse.

When Tanner arrived in Algiers in February 1908, he had already painted successful landscapes and moonlight effects in Palestine. Unlike his predecessors, he had not yet portrayed the local people or the characteristic architecture to any great degree beyond *The Jews' Wailing Place* (location unknown, see cat. no. 43), but several works from this sojourn show a changed emphasis. The fresh watercolor *In Constantine* (cat. no. 63) depicts a street scene in western Algeria, and local environs inspired the setting for *Christ with the Canaanite Woman and Her Daughter* (cat. no. 65). Also, the rugged terrain of the Saharan Atlas Mountains and its camelback travelers must have inspired the scene of the first version of *The Three Wise Men* (see cat. no. 97).

The titles of several works suggest Tanner visited Morocco during this stay at Algiers; moreover, these pictures share stylistic affinities with the Algerian works. Yet, John W. Cromwell, writing in about 1914, stated unequivocally that Tanner spent the winter of 1908 at Algiers.[6] This puzzle might be resolved by recalling Tanner's long-standing use of photographs and postcards as aide-mémoire (see cat. no. 20). A work like *Entrance to the Customs House at Tangier* (see fig. 78), for example, represents a fairly accurate rendition of the site, with some artistic license. *Flight into Egypt: Palais de Justice, Tangier* (cat. no. 64), where Moroccan architecture serves as a background for the biblical flight into Egypt, might also follow a photograph or postcard.

Tanner previously was thought to have first traveled to North Africa in 1910,[7] and recognition of his 1908 trip helps to sort out and, in some cases, redate works of multiple styles that appeared to coexist between 1910 and 1914. The stylistic differences among the large number of pictures that can now be dated to 1908 show that the painter was surveying a variety of working methods rather than concentrating on a single approach. For example, in *Entrance to the Customs House at Tangier*, Tanner returned to the elongated figures, loose brushstrokes, and bright palette of *Return of the Holy Women*, 1904 (cat. no. 56), techniques which he had moved away from somewhat in *Two Disciples at the Tomb*, 1905–1906 (cat. no. 59), and *The Disciples at Emmaus*, 1906 (see fig. 71).

Tanner was back in Paris by March 1908. Even before the official opening of the Salon in May, *The Wise and Foolish Virgins* (see fig. 50) was acclaimed in the press.[8] At the Salon, the painting was hung at an angle to the position of honor, which was occupied by Edward Detaille's gigantic canvas (about 50-by-40 feet), the patriotic *Chant de Départ* (location unknown).[9] *The Wise and Foolish Virgins* was greatly praised on both sides of the Atlantic and continued to be discussed and reproduced over the next five years. A review by William R. Lester is representative: "It would be difficult to conceive a more picturesque or expressive artistic ideal of the Saviour's pathetic parable. In composition, color, physical suggestion and mystic, creative atmosphere it discloses opulence of artistic resources, profound reverential feeling and wonderful sympathetic effect of pictorial narrative."[10]

The success of *The Wise and Foolish Virgins* might have caused Tanner to abandon temporarily his interest in Orientalism for his more traditional religious subjects. Before becoming absorbed by this body of work, he prepared for a long-awaited retrospective exhibition at the American Art Galleries in New York. A two-week showing of his religious paintings began on December 12, 1908. Thirty-three pictures were included, although neither *The Resurrection of Lazarus* nor *The Disciples at Emmaus* crossed the Atlantic from the Musée du Luxembourg, and the Wilstach Collection refused to send *The Annunciation* from Philadelphia.[11] Even with these stars of Tanner's oeuvre missing, the exhibition received highly favorable reviews, with headlines in the *New York Times* reading: "Religious Works in Tanner Exhibit: Emotional Picturesqueness Manifest in Paintings at American Art Galleries."[12] The *Times* reviewer proceeded:

Mr. Tanner's art, of which thirty-three examples are now on view at the American Art Galleries, is essentially a religious art.... These examples make it easy for the observer to realize that Mr. Tanner is interested not only in telling once more the story of the Christian religion, but in the mysterious qualities of nature as she appears to the human vision. We would like to see the landscape side of his accomplishment still further exercized.[13]

A writer for the *Independent* followed suit:

Of all the works of art that have been presented to the public of New York for inspection during the past month, there seem to be none more interesting and beautiful than those of that distinguished Negro painter, Mr. Henry O. Tanner.... To the special natural qualification that Mr. Tanner has brought to his work he has added culture. All his abilities, mental and technical, seem to be well under control.[14]

Henry and Jessie Tanner came to New York for the opening, and the artist took a studio at 14 West 22nd Street, where he planned to remain until April.[15] The fiftieth wedding anniversary of Bishop Benjamin Tucker Tanner and Sarah Miller Tanner,[16] and the bishop's retirement were celebrated at a Tanner family reunion. The younger Tanners seem to have been feted during their stay in New York. A reporter for the *Boston Herald* called attention to a party given in their honor: "A colored artist of distinction was the lion of the occasion when Bishop and Mrs. Alexander Walters of the African M.E. Church gave a reception this evening at their home in honor of Mr. and Mrs. Henry O. Tanner. Mrs. Tanner was one of the few white persons present."[17]

A long article with a portrait of Tanner appeared in the October 1908 issue of *Current Literature*,[18] and he began work on his own autobiography for *World's Work*, which appeared during the next summer. For this two-part article Tanner drew upon the characterizations of other authors who had profiled him, such as William J. Simmons in his 1887 *Men of Mark* and W. S. Scarborough in his *Southern Workman* article of 1902. Tanner's document articulated his firm conviction that form could not be separated from subject matter. He noted: "I believe most sincerely in a religious sentiment in religious pictures but, so far, have never seen it in a canvas which did not possess also artistic qualities."[19] In April 1909, Tanner was one of twelve artists, "headed by Mary Cassatt," elected as associate members of the National Academy of Design.[20]

Tanner was clearly at the height of his reputation in his native land. He had achieved a retrospective exhibition, widespread acclaim by art critics, and membership in a prestigious fine arts organization. If ever there was a time when he might have been attracted to stay permanently in the United States, it should have been then. But when Tanner returned in 1908, and throughout the duration of his visit, America was still recovering from the impact of a controversial incident that had as much significance as the Dreyfus affair had in France. The Brownsville affair "was an issue which no Black spokesman or voice dared ignore."[21] Late on August 13, 1906, a group of men went on a shooting spree in the streets of Brownsville, Texas, killing a resident. Members of a black infantry battalion stationed at nearby Fort Brown were accused as the culprits, although none could be identified by witnesses. President Theodore Roosevelt ordered the dishonorable discharge of the black soldiers despite the lack of sound evidence, incurring the indignation and outrage of the black press, pulpit, and public nationwide.[22]

Fig. 74 Henry O. Tanner, *Mary*, c. 1909–10, oil on canvas, 31¹/₂ × 25", Mr. and Mrs. Kendall Ide Lingle, Osprey, Florida.

When Tanner's exhibition opened at the American Art Galleries, intense hearings on the Brownsville affair were under way in the U.S. Senate. Whether the adult Tanner ever directly experienced the kind of legendary acts of racism that pervaded his era is not known; however, the hostile climate that produced such violent altercations helps to explain why he wrote a few years later: "This condition has driven me out of the country, but still the best friends I have are 'White' Americans and while I cannot sing our National Hymn, 'Land of Liberty,' etc., still deep down in my heart I love it and am sometimes sad that I cannot live where my heart is."[23]

In France Tanner found a more expansive and accepting environment, which he described in 1908: "There is a breadth, a generosity, an obsolete cosmopolitanism about her recognition of the fine arts, which bars no nationality, no race, no school, or variation of artistic method. All she asks is that the art shall be true, in other words that it shall set forth life."[24] During the final three decades of his life, Tanner continued to show his art in America as well as in France, but after returning to his adopted country in May 1909, he thereafter made only brief visits to the United States.

During 1909 and 1910, Tanner was actively painting, and he began to make variations on subjects and compositions from previous years. For example, *The Three Marys* (cat. no. 67) derives in part from *The Wise and Foolish Virgins*; its landscape recalls *The Good Shepherd* (cat. no. 54), and its architecture reflects Algeria. *Mary* (fig. 74) combines elements of Tanner's 1900 painting of the same title (cat. no. 50) with those of the famous *Annunciation* (cat. no. 45). When the artist turned to his local environment of Trépied in Picardy, where he owned a summer home, he painted

Fig. 75 Henry O. Tanner, *Le Touquet*, c. 1910, oil
on canvas, 51 × 42", Des Moines Art Center,
gift of Mrs. Florence Carpenter, 21.1.

subjects such as a faggot carrier (fig. 75) that had been popular at Barbizon and Pont-Aven during the nineteenth century.

A number of Tanner's biblical and Near Eastern scenes from these years were shown in a one-man exhibition at the Thurber Art Galleries in Chicago. Tanner attended the opening on February 1, 1911, and stayed in the United States until March 25, 1911.[25] The show received a long and favorable review by Harriet Monroe in the *Chicago Daily Tribune*:

> The present exhibition is the first [Tanner] has given in Chicago, and the pictures, with one exception are recent works now shown for the first time. . . . He is usually styled a religious painter, and sometimes his pictures achieve this quality, while others, even though bearing a Biblical title, have little or no religious feeling. In the present group, "The Holy Family" and "Christ Walking on the Sea" seem infused with this quality of spiritual mystery and poetry, while "Mary Visiting Elizabeth" and "Christ Learning to Read" are far less religious in their suggestion than some of the landscapes. . . . More important from the artistic point of view than the sacredness of the titles is the beauty of color, the clarity of light and shade, and the serene and lofty poetic feeling which the best of these pictures attain. These qualities are noticeable especially in "The Holy Family," an interior remarkable for the grace of its composition and for the soft richness and depth of its shadowy greenish tone crossed by a streak of yellow light, and that wonderfully transparent blue moonlight scene called "Morocco" [probably *Entrance to the Customs House*], which shows a group of oriental figures outside the dim white walls of a town. . . . "Hebron," another view of moonlit walls with cloaked figures is a poetic little picture, and the large landscape called "Hills Near Jerusalem" has a stern simplicity and grandeur.[26]

Tanner's stay in America must have made him particularly aware that even academic painters in America were creating narrative scenes in modified versions of Impressionist technique, which by 1911 had become a relatively conventional mode.[27] In the meantime, contemporary Europe was witnessing the further evolution of Cubism and the gradual development of abstract painting. The first Futurist

Manifesto was adopted in Milan in 1909, inciting artists to create pictures incorporating the sensation of movement and more dynamic effects.[28] Tanner was certainly aware of current trends, as Clara MacChesney reported in 1913:

> Mr. Tanner says that the ultimate effect of the new movement in art will be a good one. It will lift up the color scheme, induce greater individuality and freedom, and afford a looser and more open and spontaneous handling of pigments. He believes in acquiring new ideas from all schools and methods. Post-Impressionism is discarding all laws and is anarchistic in its belief. The pendulum now swings far to the extreme, but the ultimate end will be a good one.[29]

When Tanner returned to the Near East during the winter of 1912,[30] his attitude was quite different from that of his previous sojourns to Palestine and Algeria, and he surely had some awareness of modernism in mind. This time he went to Morocco and was based in Tangier. North Africa offered him a multiplicity of architectural motifs — arched doorways and windows, and interlacing borders of vegetation — and ample demonstration of the principle of continuous decor, in which surfaces are diversely decorated in vertical and horizontal registers. From Tangier Tanner went by mule to Tetuan to see an Islamic city uninfluenced by European civilization.[31] His desire to visit unspoilt areas suggests that he was after the Oriental aesthetic in purely artistic terms, in the manner of the French tradition which now included contemporary artists such as Henri Matisse, who was in Tangier from late January to mid-April of 1912.[32]

Although he painted the same type of street scenes that had attracted artists of the Romantic period in France, particularly Alexandre-Gabriel Decamps and Eugène Delacroix (cat. nos. 75–77), the paintings Tanner produced during this period show a contemporary grasp of the Oriental aesthetic. And unlike other American artists who absorbed the French Orientalist tradition, Tanner's observations of the Near East were rendered with detail based on firsthand observation, and not the "product of reminiscing fantasy and imagination."[33] *Entrance to the Casbah* (cat. no. 72) treats the plunging views, the people and their clothes, and the architecture as vehicles of new form and color. Although the composition is somewhat reminiscent of his 1898 *Jews' Wailing Place*, the flat, decorative surface, achieved through the thick buildup of paint, is completely modern. Around 1910 Tanner had begun to work out new methods by experimenting with pigments: "He finds that his results are more permanent, when working slowly, thus giving each glazed layer sufficient time to dry and harden."[34] This attention to process can be seen in part as a direct response to movements in contemporary art, which often literally forced attention to the surface of the canvas through the use of color, impasto, and collage.[35]

Tanner was back in Trépied by late summer, and the Tanner family was probably back in Paris at least by October 24, 1912. Edward Honor Coates, director of the Pennsylvania Academy of the Fine Arts, wrote to him about serving on the academy's Paris jury and including some of his own works in the academy's 1912 annual exhibition.[36] Tanner's response, if he made one, has not come to light.

The pictures resulting from Tanner's second voyage to North Africa reveal a preponderance of nocturnal scenes illuminated by moonlight, a motif he rendered with fluency. While visiting Tanner's studio in 1912, Clara T. MacChesney noted that "moonlight scenes appeal to him most,"[37] and went on to describe his recent work:

"His present style is much changed. Not only has he a greater breadth of vision, but his effects are cooler, grayer in tone and higher in key, not as black and brown in the shadows, or hot in color, as formerly. Thus his new canvases have a more spiritual, dreamlike quality. They are more poetical and show a great advance from earlier efforts."[38]

In April of 1913, following another show in Chicago at the Thurber Art Galleries, Tanner had an exhibition at New York's Knoedler's Galleries, his second one-man show in only five years. A lengthy review in the *New York Times* detailed the range of subjects displayed:

> One group includes views of Morocco, a number of moonlight scenes outside of the citadel, the smaller of which are tranquil and luminous, an "Entry to the Citadel," "The Sultan's Stables" and other subjects characteristic of the region. There are also several religious paintings, of which "Jesus Learning to Read" is the most satisfying. . . . "Woman of Bethlehem" is also informed with a gentle sentiment that does not exclude the suggestion of character, and the head is well placed in the envelope of atmosphere. . . . A little canvas showing a windy day in Trépied, with women wrestling with the pieces of clothing which they are trying to spread on the grass, gave the spirit of the domestic sphere with much vivacity.[39]

The *Times* critic was not alone in having a positive reaction to Tanner's exhibition. A writer for the *New York Tribune* was pleased by the artist's abandonment of the "brown sauce" that characterized Paris studio art: "In his show at Knoedler Gallery of Moorish and French subjects he demonstrates that he can exploit to some advantage an infinitely lighter key. . . . The result is capital and should convince Mr. Tanner that his old method is best left utterly behind him."[40] The art essayist for the *New York American* examined the actual manner in which Tanner applied paint and concluded: "It is [in] this way that Tanner introduced chromatic relations into the dark and light colors of his canvas and so draws them into a unity of vibrating and resonant harmony."[41] Tanner's exhibition came just after the International Exhibition of Modern Art, held at the Sixty-ninth Regiment Armory from February 17 to March 15, 1913, and the principal means by which modern art was introduced to the United States. Surely Tanner's new modernist pictures must have seemed in keeping with the lessons that American artists learned from the innovative European work seen in the Armory Show.

There is no evidence that Tanner traveled to the United States for his exhibition, and he apparently continued to work in France during 1913. He was actively involved with the Société Artistique de Picardie, founded in 1904, of which he was then president.[42] Tanner seems to have started to make prints, especially etchings, around this time. This dating is supported by the fact that several of these prints were based on more or less contemporary paintings (cat. no. 72, see fig. 83). Also, after a very successful phase at the turn of the century, with the encouragement of Booker T. Washington, Tanner made photographic reproductions of his work for general distribution.[43]

During 1914 Tanner continued to exhibit in America at Pittsburgh and Chicago, and in Europe at London and Paris, and the critics continued to sing his praises. This year marked his last showing at the annual Paris Salon, the initial source of his artistic motivation and fame during the 1890s. Yet another contemporary

Fig. 76 Henry O. Tanner, *Christ at the Home of Lazarus*, c. 1912, oil on canvas, location unknown.

account by Clara MacChesney described Tanner's last Salon *envoi*, *Christ at the Home of Lazarus* (fig. 76), and the culmination of his Oriental phase. She wrote for *International Studio* in November 1914:

> H. O. Tanner continues to be the poet-painter of Palestine. . . . Like many of his confreres, he paints in tempera. He sees and renders his impressions in blue and blue-green tones, generally high in key . . . in direct contrast to his "Raising of Lazarus." In this admirable picture, yellow and brown tones predominate. If I were to venture a criticism of Tanner's present work, which none more admires than myself, I would say he swings the pendulum now too far the other way. His large Salon picture shows Christ at supper in the home of Lazarus. Martha is standing and in the act of serving at the left. Christ is seated at the centre, a self-portrait of the artist is represented at the right with Mary at his side. In the figure of Martha, Tanner tries to raise her from the position of a worried housekeeper to that of a human and very sympathetic woman, lovingly serving her master. He considers this one of his most successful figures.[44]

Biblical subjects continued to be Tanner's basic theme even during his most active interest in Orientalism; however, his religious scenes gradually took on a different appearance as a result of his exposure to the Near East and his own version of modernism. MacChesney also foreshadowed what would happen during the next decade of the artist's career: "Tanner with his family, and other American artists of the region, had to fly precipitously to England last August. The artists' colony, the gardens filled with flowers, the orchards loaded with fruit, the studios with their unfinished canvases, were left to the mercy of the marauding peasants or the devastating Germans."[45] DFM

63

IN CONSTANTINE
c. 1908
Watercolor and gouache on paper
17 ³/₄ × 13″ (45.09 × 33.02 cm)
Signed lower left: *H. O. Tanner*
N. N. Serper, courtesy of Rosenfeld Fine Arts, New York

Tanner made his third trip to the Near East in 1908, traveling to Algeria, the North African country that had long attracted French artists. The title *In Constantine* suggests that he visited that city, and this view could well represent a corner of the place de Nemours, the commercial and social center of Constantine.

Tanner did not produce a large number of watercolors, although this work demonstrates his solid control of the medium. The multiple colors of the predominantly blue palette are blended by deft brushstrokes that echo his oil painting technique, while the bursts of light that bathe the building and alley on the left and inform the sky are to be found in the best uses of watercolor. The composition follows Tanner's familiar pattern of counterposing geometrical lines and shapes. The diagonal of the wall on the left dominates, and the acuteness of its angle is emphasized by the soaring vertical of the tower and by the horizontal tendency of the building on the right, which is accentuated by the windows and lines above its doorway. Figures also participate in this scheme. A person in a pale robe in the foreground echoes the verticality of the tower, while the seated figure to the left provides a counterpoint for the diagonal of the building against which it slumps. Suffused with light and color, these configurations provide a lively image of North Africa.

The history of *In Constantine* does not include contemporary exhibitions. It seems to have belonged to one of Tanner's earliest patrons, Rodman Wanamaker; a slide in the Harmon Collection shows it hanging above a mantel that might have been in Wanamaker's Philadelphia apartment.[1] It would have been appropriate and characteristic of Tanner's loyalty to make a gift of this beautiful work to Wanamaker, who funded his first trip to the Near East.   DFM

63 IN CONSTANTINE

FLIGHT INTO EGYPT: PALAIS
DE JUSTICE, TANGIER

(*Palace of Justice, Tangier*)
(*Flight into Egypt*)
c. 1908
Oil on canvas
25 ⁵/₈ × 31 ⁷/₈″ (65.09 × 80.96 cm)
Signed lower right: *H. O. Tanner*
National Museum of American Art, Smithsonian Institution,
Washington, D.C., gift of Mr. and Mrs. John Baxter

Fig. 77 Henry O. Tanner, *Moonlight,
Hebron*, c. 1907, oil on canvas, 25 ¹¹/₁₆ ×
31 ⁷/₈″, Milwaukee Art Museum, gift of
Mr. and Mrs. Thomas Whipple Dunbar.

Fig. 78 Henry O. Tanner, *Entrance to the
Customs House at Tangier (Port of Tangier)*,
1913–14, oil on board, 21 × 23″, N. N.
Serper, courtesy of Rosenfeld Fine Arts,
New York.

This work represents one of Tanner's favorite religious subjects, the flight into Egypt, as first suggested by Lynda Roscoe Hartigan.[1] The dominant architectural background of this rendition is the facade of the Mendoubia Palace, once the residence of the sultan's representative at Tangier. In the early twentieth century it became the law courts, or Palais de Justice.

As in many of Tanner's pictures, subtle arrangements of geometric shapes and lines underlie the composition. Emphasized by the movement of the sky above the massive walls and by the shapes of the fleeing figures and their shadows, the horizontal format is penetrated by the sharp diagonal of the windowless left side of the palace, which in turn slopes off into a less prominent angle. The vertical arched doorways, windows, and protruding architectural elements contrast with the squarish horizontal shapes above them. Two sharp passages of yellowish light on the ground, one running up the side of the building, and one emanating from an open doorway, play off diagonals and horizontals against verticals. A chalky, monochromatic color scheme and directional brushstrokes unify the diverse geometric elements. But not all is equal: the glow of light behind the figures, their green-blue cloaks, and the broken brushstrokes defining the terrain all call attention to the painting's subject.

This beautiful moonlit painting presents certain dating problems. Tanner traveled to Algeria in February of 1908, and the work *In Constantine* (cat. no. 63) suggests that he went to that city. Although there is no doubt that the buildings shown in the present picture (cat. no. 64) are located in the Moroccan summer capital of Tangier, no firm evidence places Tanner in Morocco at this time, and he most likely did not base his rendition on firsthand knowledge of the site. Tanner occasionally used photographs and postcards as departure points for his compositions, and he could have purchased postcards of Moroccan scenes while in Algeria.

Thus the date proposed here for *Flight into Egypt: Palais de Justice, Tangier* deserves discussion. Stylistically, the picture's palette and paint application are quite similar to that in *Moonlight, Hebron* (fig. 77) and *The Disciples See Christ Walking on the Water* (cat. no. 62), both of which can be safely dated to 1907 by their exhibition histories. In addition, *Flight into Egypt* has a strong kinship with *Entrance to the Customs House at Tangier* (fig. 78), which could be the work shown at Chicago in February 1911 under the title *Morocco*.[2] These paintings are all very different from those rendered during Tanner's documented trip to Morocco in the winter of 1912 as

exemplified by the signed and dated *Entrance to the Casbah* (cat. no. 72). After the turn of the century, Tanner worked on several pictures at the same time, and as a result, over a period of two to three years his paintings tended to have similar surface appearances.

An unidentified *Flight into Egypt* was shown at Tanner's retrospective exhibition held in New York City in 1908 along with the Detroit version (cat. no. 49). In 1913, around the same time that the present *Flight into Egypt* was sold, a painting simply called *Palais de Justice, Tangier* was shown at the Art Institute of Chicago. It is difficult to believe that Tanner would have exhibited an obviously biblical scene under such a purely genre title. Works exhibited during Tanner's lifetime were given specific titles that rarely changed from show to show, and when Tanner occasionally altered a name himself, as in the case of *The Wise and Foolish Virgins* (see fig. 50), which became *Behold! the Bridegroom Cometh* within the course of a year, the alternate title derived from the biblical passage on which the picture was based. The painting in the Chicago show was probably one of the Orientalist genre scenes painted around the time of the exhibition.   DFM

6 5

CHRIST WITH THE CANAANITE
WOMAN AND HER DAUGHTER

(*Christ and the Disciples*)
(*Christ and the Disciples before the Last Supper*)
(*Christ at the Door of a House*)
1908–1909
Oil on canvas
26 × 33″ (66.04 × 83.82 cm)
Signed lower left: *H. O. Tanner*
Spelman College, Atlanta

This picture has been known as *Christ and the Disciples*, but a more appropriate title, *Christ with the Canaanite Woman and Her Daughter*, is here proposed. The subject of the painting could have been derived from the Gospel of Matthew (15:21–28):

> Then Jesus went thence, and departed into the coasts of Tyre and Sidon. And behold a woman of Canaan came out of the same coasts, and cried unto him, saying, Have mercy on me, O Lord, thou son of David; my daughter is grievously vexed with a devil. . . . Jesus answered and said unto her, O Woman, great is thy faith: be it unto thee even as thou wilt. And her daughter was made whole from that very hour.

Jesus described himself in this section of scripture as looking for the lost sheep of Israel, and Tanner portrayed him with a shepherd's staff in his hand. The figure on the left with arms raised and hands clasped is the imploring mother, and the bedeviled daughter would be the figure standing in the dark doorway.

Tanner set the scene in a street with North African architecture, reflecting his trip to Algiers in early 1908. On the right side a seated figure drawn from the denizens of the crowded streets of Algiers, which appears in other works from this period (cat. no. 63), directs attention toward the central group. A vaguely rendered person on the far left further stresses the primacy of the main characters. As usual, the interaction of Tanner's personages is conveyed through the positions of their bodies rather than facial expressions. The treatment of their forms shows a return to the elongated figure type he had abandoned around 1904 (see cat. no. 56).

The overall composition is a straightforward arrangement of horizontals, verticals, and diagonals, with arched accents. Running across the ground and up the side of the building, the shadows of two trees, which are themselves unseen, hold the viewer outside the space, denying participation. The long, bluish shadows are a skillful variation of the device Tanner used in *The Disciples See Christ Walking on the Water* (cat. no. 62), in which not the moon but only its reflection appears. The shadows also recall the bright shafts of light in *Flight into Egypt: Palais de Justice, Tangier* (cat. no. 64).

65 CHRIST WITH THE CANAANITE WOMAN AND HER DAUGHTER

The shadows and the play of light are an integral part of the somewhat matte palette. The crouching figure casts a greenish shade, while the imploring mother's shadow is purplish. Both the color scheme and brushstrokes, which emphasize planar surfaces, are close to those found in *Flight into Egypt*.

The profound concern for social justice that pervaded Tanner's pictures of crucifixion and resurrection themes from the late 1890s until 1906 gave way somewhat in his later work to an emphasis on the specific miracles performed by Jesus. Tanner moved from universal human concerns to individual considerations, as seen in this painting.   DFM

66

THE HOLY FAMILY

c. 1909–10
Oil on canvas
35 × 42 3/4" (88.9 × 108.59 cm)
Signed lower left: *H. O. Tanner*
Muskegon Museum of Art, Michigan, Hackley Picture Fund

The Holy Family harks back to some of Tanner's earlier motifs, such as the simple interior space and thoughtful mood of *Mary*, 1900 (cat. no. 50). The setting is the workplace of Joseph the carpenter, as suggested by the wood shavings on the floor, and is probably located in Egypt, since Jesus is still an infant (Matt. 2:14–15). The theme of affectionate family life seems to have been on Tanner's mind at this time; in 1910 he also painted *Christ and His Mother Studying the Scriptures* (cat. no. 69) with his wife, Jessie, and son, Jesse, as models. Both works illustrate Tanner's propensity for rendering the parents of Jesus as everyday people.

The words of a contemporary critic speak well of Tanner's composition, palette, and use of light in *The Holy Family*. F. J. Campbell, editor of *Fine Arts Journal*, saw the picture in Chicago at Thurber Art Galleries in 1911:

> Tanner has painted a "Holy Family" in the suggested interior of a rude shop. There are some forms about the floor hinting at shavings and a bench with its worker, very suggestive. It is all in delicious color, still and gray, but an alive gray. Joseph in a dark blue long coat stands in shadow looking tenderly at Mary, who sits on a low seat covered with a rug of gray color and good pattern. The principal figure, the Madonna, occupies the middle of the picture. She is in profile and looks at a suggested window in the right hand wall. This window is partly concealed by a short portiere under which the light comes falling over the lower part of the picture. . . . Everything in the picture is vague, excepting [Mary], and one has to search a little to discover the babe's face appearing from the folds of a rug on the floor. . . . In it we still see Tanner's favorite management of light, and we see again how the concentration of this light in the lower part of the picture causes the face to swim in shadow. . . . The artist uses his color so variedly that we seem to find new combinations everywhere.[1]

In 1914 James William Pattison wrote upon the occasion of the opening of the Hackley Gallery, now the Muskegon Museum of Art: "One of the most important of the permanent collection is Tanner's 'Holy Family,' a remarkably fine picture."[2]

DFM

66 THE HOLY FAMILY

67

THE THREE MARYS
1910
Oil on canvas
42 × 50″ (106.68 × 127 cm)
Signed lower right: *H. O. Tanner*
Carl Van Vechten Gallery of Fine Arts,
Fisk University, Nashville

The Three Marys follows the account in the Gospel of Mark (16:1–4), in which Mary Magdalene, Mary, the mother of James, and Salomé, also called Mary Salomé, bring spices and perfumes to anoint the body of Jesus in his tomb. The long, flowing hair and headdress of the leading figure and her clinging, diaphanous gown, rendered by Tanner in a distinctive technique of isolated, feathery strokes, are traditional attributes of the Magdalene, but no distinguishing attributes offer positive identities for the other two women.

The scene is established by Mark: "And very early in the morning the first day of the week, they came unto the sepulchre at the rising of the sun." This time of day, with a setting moon and a few stars still visible in a dark blue sky, and the first rays of dawn illuminating the women, allowed Tanner to render the play of warm and cool light over the figures, one of his favorite color effects. His earliest experiment with mixed light sources is seen in *The Banjo Lesson*, 1893 (cat. no. 27), and he first used it in an outdoor setting in *Nicodemus Visiting Jesus*, 1899 (cat. no. 47).

In *Nicodemus Visiting Jesus*, the golden light falling upon Christ subtly emphasizes his divinity. In *The Three Marys*, the warm light signifies the moment of revelation when the two leading women, who gesture in amazement, discover that the massive stone has been rolled away from the entrance to the tomb: "And they said among themselves, Who shall roll us away the stone from the door of the sepulchre? And when they looked, they saw that the stone was rolled away: for it was very great."

In 1910 Tanner sent *The Three Marys*, along with *Flight into Egypt*, to the Paris Salon, and in 1911 it was exhibited in Chicago. Critic Clement-Janin, reviewing the Salon, not only expressed dismay at the paucity of religious painting but lamented the lack of spiritual quality in the few works exhibited.[1] Unlike many writers who believed Tanner had penetrated the spirituality of the people of the Bible,[2] Clement-Janin found Tanner and other artists lacking in religious aspiration and faith. He did, however, praise the marvelous color harmonies in *The Three Marys*. Tanner made a lithograph based on this composition around 1913.   DS

67 THE THREE MARYS

68

CHRIST AND HIS DISCIPLES ON
THE SEA OF GALILEE
(*Sea of Galilee*)
c. 1910
Oil on artist's board
10 × 14" (25.4 × 35.56 cm)
Signed lower left: *H. O. Tanner*
Richard C. Edgeworth, Chicago

Fig. 79 Eugène Delacroix, *Christ on the Lake of Gennesaret*, c. 1853, oil on canvas, 20 × 24", The Metropolitan Museum of Art, bequest of Mrs. H. O. Havemeyer,

Fig. 80 James Tissot, *Christ Stilling the Tempest*, after 1886, watercolor, 5 × 7 ¼", The Brooklyn Museum, purchased by public subscription.

Despite its size, this small painting is a complete work of art in itself, not a study for a larger picture. Between 1908 and 1914, Tanner exhibited a number of paintings depicting the miracles Jesus worked by the Sea of Galilee. Of this series, the picture catalogued here (cat. no. 68) is most similar to *The Disciples on the Sea of Galilee* (see fig. 73), purchased from the Thurber Art Galleries exhibition in 1911 and now in the collection of the Toledo Museum of Art. The two paintings display the same predominantly blue color scheme with a touch of orange indicating glancing sunlight, and they are more tranquil in mood than the turbulent *Fishermen at Sea* (cat. no. 78) and *Miraculous Haul of Fishes* (cat. no. 79) of a few years later. The high vantage of *Christ and His Disciples on the Sea of Galilee*, however, is more like the two later pictures.

This high viewpoint, looking down on figures in a boat isolated against water, suggests that Tanner must have been familiar with at least one of the versions of *Christ on the Lake of Gennesaret* (fig. 79) painted by Eugène Delacroix about 1853. Delacroix shows the boat tossed on a stormy sea with Christ placidly asleep in the midst of his panicked disciples, illustrating the Gospel of Matthew (8:24): "And, behold, there arose a great tempest in the sea, insomuch that the ship was covered with the waves: but he was asleep."

By contrast, Tanner depicted the scene after Christ miraculously stilled the waters: the sky is clearing, the sea rolls gently, and the disciples are bent to their oars. The remarkable feature of this painting is the pale, rather insubstantial but expressive figure of Christ, who stands facing the stern of the boat but with his head turned forward as though addressing the seated men with the famous words given to him by Matthew (8:26): "And he saith unto them, Why are ye fearful, O ye of little faith? Then he arose, and rebuked the winds and the sea; and there was a great calm."

James Tissot had painted a small version of this subject, entitled *Christ Stilling the Tempest* (fig. 80), some years before, but there is no evidence that Tanner ever saw it. His interest in the emotional significance of the scene has more in common with Delacroix's rendering than with Tissot's detailed, but static illustration.

DS

68 CHRIST AND HIS DISCIPLES ON THE SEA OF GALILEE

CHRIST AND HIS MOTHER
STUDYING THE SCRIPTURES

(Christ Learning to Read)
1910
Oil on canvas
48 ³/₄ × 40″ (123.83 × 101.6 cm)
Signed lower left: *H. O. Tanner*
Dallas Museum of Art, Deaccession Funds

CHRIST LEARNING TO READ

1910–14
Oil on canvas
52 × 41″ (132.08 × 104.14 cm)
Signed lower right: *H. O. Tanner*
Des Moines Art Center, gift of the Des Moines Association of
Fine Arts, 1941.16

Figs. 81, 82 Tanner's study photographs
of his wife and son for *Christ and His
Mother Studying the Scriptures*, c. 1910,
Archives of American Art, Smithsonian
Institution, Washington, D.C.

Tanner occasionally depicted biblical characters without referring to a particular story, as in these two paintings of Christ learning to read. At some time, probably in 1910, Tanner photographed his wife and son, Jesse, then seven or eight, in costumes resembling Middle Eastern garb as studies for a painting (figs. 81, 82). The finished works show how closely the artist adhered to his photographic models, although he may also have had his family pose as he painted.

The two works differ in details of furnishings as well as in color and lighting. An illustration published in the *Chicago Daily Tribune* for February 2, 1911, when *Christ and His Mother Studying the Scriptures* was first shown in the exhibition of Tanner's work at Thurber Art Galleries, confirms that the painting in the collection of the Dallas Museum of Art was the first version (cat. no. 69). Its relatively restricted palette is typical of Tanner's work at the time, and the figures are directly illuminated by a strong light source from the left. The result is appealing and uncomplicated, and stands as an affectionate tribute to his wife and child. Harriet Monroe, the poet and editor who was to found the influential magazine *Poetry* the following year, reviewed Tanner's exhibition and was unmoved by the painting, finding it lacking in "spiritual mystery and poetry" and "far less religious . . . than some of the landscapes."[1]

A reviewer for the *New York Times*, writing about Tanner's exhibition at Knoedler's Gallery in New York two years later, found Tanner's picture of Christ reading to be one of his "most satisfying" religious paintings: "The face of the mother and that of the child are entirely free from the cheaper form of idealization. Each is serious, deeply marked with character, and of the racial type. The composition also is well knit and agreeable, the long scroll drooping over the mother's knees and curling to the ground like a ribbon lending a graceful play of line to the simplicity of the grouping."[2] It is difficult to say which version of the subject the *Times* reviewer might have seen, for the exhibition history and provenance of the two paintings are unclear during these years. The Dallas version is not listed as the property of Rodman Wanamaker until 1921, and the Des Moines picture is not definitely established until 1916, when an illustration of it appeared in an article on J. S. Carpenter's painting collection.[3]

The *Times* reviewer might have found *Christ Learning to Read* less easily agreeable (cat. no. 70). Most probably sometime before the outbreak of war Tanner radically changed his conception of the scene. Instead of the direct light of the first version, Tanner showed the two figures in a shaded interior with just two areas of bright light at the left. This illumination of a shadowed

interior with a sliver of brilliant exterior light can be seen in *The Holy Family*, c. 1909–10 (cat. no. 66), and might represent a particular condition of light that Tanner observed during his trip to the Middle East in 1908. *The Holy Family*, however, like the Dallas picture, has a conventional color scheme, and its interior is merely shadowy and dim in contrast to the bright light source.

In the second version of the subject, the shaded interior is full of color, especially in the faces of Christ and the Virgin. The pink and green of the flesh tones are so pronounced and rendered with such firm and discrete strokes of paint that they almost go beyond an impressionist effect of reflected light to become an abstract color scheme in themselves. The exaggerated hues imply that Tanner was testing his own conceptions of representation and reality in his work. Within the conservative boundaries of his art, the Des Moines painting is a bold experiment, and perhaps in making it, Tanner was thinking of the Fauves' radical color schemes of a few years earlier. Considered with *Fishermen at Sea*, c. 1913–14 (cat. no. 78), which represents a similarly bold departure in composition, *Christ Learning to Read* suggests the artist's search for a new direction at the moment of his greatest success, just before World War I.

DS

70 CHRIST LEARNING TO READ

ANGELS APPEARING BEFORE
THE SHEPHERDS

(*Angels Appearing before the Wise Men*)
c. 1910–11
Oil on canvas
25 5/8 × 32" (65.09 × 81.28 cm)
Signed lower left: *H. O. Tanner*
National Museum of American Art, Smithsonian Institution,
Washington, D.C., gift of Mr. and Mrs. Norman B. Robbins

Tanner returned to his landscape views of Palestine of the 1890s (cat. nos. 44, 46) for the setting of *Angels Appearing before the Shepherds* (cat. no. 71). In this surprisingly literal painting, elongated angels hover above three tiny figures huddled around a fire; a town perches on a hilltop in the rugged landscape background. This work has been called *Angels Appearing before the Wise Men*; however, in the biblical account celestial messengers do not appear before the astrologers; God speaks to them in a dream (Matt. 2:11–12). Tanner seems to have followed the Gospel of Luke (2:8–16):

> And there were in the same country shepherds abiding in the field, keeping watch over their flock by night. And, lo, the angel of the Lord came upon them, and the glory of the Lord shone round about them: and they were sore afraid. . . . And suddenly there was with the angel a multitude of the heavenly host praising God. . . . And it came to pass, as the angels were gone away from them into heaven, the shepherds said one to another, Let us now go even unto Bethlehem, and see this thing which is come to pass, which the Lord hath made known unto us.

Linda Roscoe Hartigan's recent identification of the subject is surely correct.[1] Tanner's painting, a clear adaptation of the scripture, takes place at night. The tiny shepherds are awestruck and bathed in a heavenly light, and Bethlehem appears on the hilltop at the right. Unlike most renditions of the scene, there is a phalanx of angels rather than one because Tanner had seized upon Luke's phrase, "a multitude of the heavenly host."

The composition of *Angels Appearing before the Shepherds* is characteristic of Tanner's style during the first decade of the twentieth century. In a straightforward arrangement, the vertical figures of the angels balance the strong diagonal movement of the hillside terrain. The bluish palette is pervasive, outside of the pool of light around the shepherds, and the handling of paint is not as polished as in many of Tanner's other pictures. Also, the nearly literal human shapes of the angels are quite unlike the bursts of spiritual, textured light that Tanner used to symbolize the angel of *The Annunciation*, 1898 (cat. no. 45), or the figure of Jesus in *The Disciples See Christ Walking on the Water*, c. 1907 (cat. no. 62). Moreover, aside from its use of a specific landscape setting, the conception of this work is markedly different from the naturalism of Tanner's treatment of *The Holy Family*, c. 1909–10 (cat. no. 66), and *Christ and His Mother Studying the Scriptures*, 1910 (cat. no. 69).

Tanner retained this thinly painted picture of *Angels Appearing before the Shepherds*, his only known rendition of the story, in his studio until his death. He does not seem to have exhibited it during his lifetime, even though at least one version of all his other recorded paintings based on the scriptures was shown publicly. No record of his own evaluation of the painting exists, but Tanner never stretched another picture over it as he did in the case of *Fishermen at Sea* (cat. no. 78) and *Job and His Three Friends* (cat. no. 57), both of which were discovered beneath other finished canvases. Perhaps as time progressed, the mature Tanner felt satisfied with his approach to *Angels Appearing before the Shepherds*; certainly he never painted out the transparent angels, which give the picture such a mysterious atmosphere and make it so unusual within his oeuvre.   DFM

72

ENTRANCE TO THE CASBAH
(*Entrance of the Citadel*)
(*Entry of the Citadel*)
1912
Oil on wood pulp paper mounted on canvas
32 × 26 ¹/₂" (81.28 × 67.31 cm)
Signed, inscribed, and dated lower right: *H. O. Tanner*
Morocco 1912
Greater Lafayette Museum of Art, Indiana

Fig. 83 Henry O. Tanner, *Gate in Tangier,*
n.d., etching on paper, 9 ⁵/₁₆ × 7 ¹/₁₆",
National Museum of American Art,
Smithsonian Institution, Washington,
D.C., gift of Norman Robbins.

Entrance to the Casbah is rare among Tanner's renditions of North Africa in 1912 both for its large size and for its inscription as painted at Morocco. Since 1914 at least, the painting has carried variant titles referring to the entrance to the native section of a North African city. In 1913 Tanner sent several works to exhibitions in Chicago and New York with similar motifs, and sorting out the various versions is difficult. In other paintings (cat. no. 35) Tanner paid careful attention to the architecture of specific sites, without exercising artistic license. The crenellated molding of the principal gate of the Casbah in Morocco is more ornate than that shown in the present painting, as is evident from Tanner's own etching of the main entrance (fig. 83). The present picture probably depicts the less adorned East Gate.

Although the title of this work does not refer to a scene from the Bible, one comes to mind. The laden donkey and green-clad figure in the foreground and the person in white in the archway evoke the Holy Family arriving in Egypt from Bethlehem (Matt. 2:13–15), passing unnoticed by the group of figures along the wall on the left.

Tanner composed *Entrance to the Casbah* according to the Orientalist aesthetic of plunging views. He used the up-tilted perspective of the circle of Gauguin, learned during his early years in France, but here he closed off the space with massive walls. The lines and shapes on the right—with a triangle pointing to the white-robed figure, perhaps Saint Joseph—are antithetical to those on the wall on the left. Stark light and brilliant color are also at work: greens in the background join those in the foreground as do the bright red touches of the window frame and roof drain. Thick, painterly brushstrokes emphasize the direction of the composition's geometric planes and render little detail.

Despite its active arrangement of color, light, and planes, the mood of *Entrance to the Casbah* is serene. A reviewer for the *New York Times* may have had this painting in mind when he wrote: "Henry O. Tanner is showing a number of his recent paintings in one of the lower rooms of the Knoedler Galleries. One group includes views of Morocco . . . which are tranquil and luminous."[1]

DFM

72 ENTRANCE TO THE CASBAH

73

MAN LEADING A DONKEY IN
FRONT OF THE PALAIS DE
JUSTICE, TANGIER

(*Street Scene, Tangier*)
(*Man Leading a Calf*)
(*Moonlight – Palace of the Governor, Tangier?*)
c. 1912
Oil on paperboard
10 5/8 × 13 3/4" (26.99 × 34.93 cm)
Verso: oil sketch for what appears to be the Casbah at Morocco
National Museum of American Art, Smithsonian Institution,
Washington, D.C., gift of Mr. and Mrs. Norman B. Robbins

74

STREET IN TANGIER

c. 1912
Oil on fiberboard
13 7/8 × 10 1/2" (35.24 × 26.67 cm)
Signed lower right: *H. O. Tanner*
National Museum of American Art, Smithsonian Institution,
Washington, D.C., gift of James and Shirley Gordon

Fig. 84 Alexandre-Gabriel Decamps, *Donkey Attached to a Wall*, c. 1833, oil on canvas, 8 5/8 × 10 15/16", Musée de Ville, Evreux, France.

During his trip to Morocco in 1912 Tanner was attracted to the same type of scenes that were painted in the French Orientalist tradition by nineteenth-century artists such as Alexandre-Gabriel Decamps (fig. 84). Tanner depicted the place de Gouverneur, with the Palais de Justice, in *Man Leading a Donkey in front of the Palais de Justice, Tangier* (cat. no. 73) and perhaps rue des Siaghines in *Street in Tangier* (cat. no. 74). Both pictures conjure up biblical images. *Man Leading a Donkey*, for example, calls to mind events preceding the entry of Jesus into Jerusalem. The Gospel of Mark relates (11:2–4): "Go your way into the village over against you: and as soon as ye be entered into it, ye shall find a colt tied, whereon never man sat; loose him, and bring him. And if any man say unto you, Why do ye this? say ye that the Lord hath need of him; and straightway he will send him hither."

Street in Tangier can be imagined in the context of the Gospel of Luke (2:3–7), in which Joseph goes with Mary to register at Bethlehem. The two personages in the middle ground readily suggest Mary and Joseph approaching the inn's entrance as two figures flow out of the door.

Both works are about the same size and, with their quick handling of thick paint, could have been painted out-of-doors. Tanner was alert to selection of formats, opting for a horizontal structure for *Man Leading a Donkey*, with its repeated shapes of doors and windows, and a vertical format for *Street in Tangier*, which stresses the plunging view of the main street.

Although the paint is manipulated in a loose and spontaneous manner, and the color schemes are much more daring than in works of previous periods, the balance of color and light in these two pictures is pure Tanner. For example, in *Man Leading a Donkey* the bright orange on the animal's rump and in the man's shirt, which is reflected on the facade of the Palais de Justice, echoes the beautiful warm tones on the steps of *Nicodemus Visiting Jesus* (cat. no. 47). In both Moroccan scenes Tanner's use of brushwork and palette knife to construct his subjects is apparent. The steps of the Palais de Justice in

73 MAN LEADING A DONKEY IN FRONT OF THE PALAIS DE JUSTICE, TANGIER

74 STREET IN TANGIER

Man Leading a Donkey have a horizontal emphasis, while the walls of *Street in Tangier* are made up of vertical strokes. The lovely sunlight effects, which show the time of day, offer proof that Tanner's range stretched easily beyond his many renditions of moonlight.

The contemporary literature on Tanner does not specifically refer to these small, vivid studies, but they are important testaments to his ability and desire to record contemporary life with the same immediacy that energized avant-garde art in Europe and America around 1910.   DFM

75

NEAR EAST SCENE

(*Mosque in Tangier*)
c. 1912
Oil and casein on canvas
28 ³/₄ × 23 ¹/₂" (73.03 × 59.69 cm)
Signed lower right: *H. O. Tanner*
Des Moines Art Center, bequest of Edith King Pearson, 1964.76

76

SUNLIGHT, TANGIER

c. 1912–14
Oil on cardboard panel
10 ³/₄ × 13 ³/₄" (27.31 × 34.93 cm)
Signed lower right: *H. O. Tanner*
Milwaukee Art Museum, gift of Walter I. Frank

77

GATE TO THE CASBAH

(*Algerian Street Scene*)
1914
Oil on canvas
30 × 26" (76.2 × 66.04 cm)
Signed, inscribed, and dated lower left: *H. O. Tanner/Paris 1914*
Private collection

When the artist and critic Clara T. MacChesney visited Tanner's studio at Trépied in 1912, after he had returned from Morocco, she found him "completing twenty-five canvases for exhibitions shortly to be held in Chicago and New York."[1] Tanner had spent nearly three months making studies in Tangier, and like other artists, he was "tempted by the beauty of that unspoiled seaport town, with its entrancing mosques, alleys and narrow streets, its pink, pale mauve and ivory-colored plaster houses, and its picturesque people."[2]

MacChesney's description of the city can be applied to the group of paintings discussed here–*Near East Scene* (cat. no. 75), *Sunlight, Tangier* (cat. no. 76), and *Gate to the Casbah* (cat. no. 77). *Near East Scene* calls to mind genre painting in the French Romantic tradition such as *Street in Meknes* (fig. 85) by Eugène Delacroix (although his scene presented Moroccans in classic Renaissance poses: the young, cape-clad man on the left recalls any number of figures in paintings by Raphael). In contrast, the hard-bitten, poverty-stricken, and mysterious individuals in Tanner's street scenes have more to do with a realistic vision than one drawn from the ideal world of art. These three pictures do not conjure up images of biblical events, as do *Man Leading a Donkey* (cat. no. 73) and *Entrance to the Casbah* (cat. no. 72); they depict scenes of everyday life in the Near East.

In 1832 Delacroix advised artists to go to North Africa "to feel the precision and rare influence of the sun, which gives a penetrating light to all things."[3] Whether or not Tanner was aware of this counsel, he gave new meaning to Delacroix's phrase "penetrating light" in such works as *Sunlight, Tangier* and, as a result, modernized his palette. The milky whites, mauve shades and tints, and blues, greens, and yellows found in these pictures are highly characteristic of Tanner's style, but he now studied them under intense light. Tanner allowed almost unadulterated passages and touches of color,

Fig. 85 Eugène Delacroix, *Street in Meknes*, 1832, oil on canvas, 18 ¹/₄ × 25 ¹/₄", Albright-Knox Art Gallery, Buffalo, Elisabeth H. Gates and Charles W. Goodyear Funds, 1948.

75 NEAR EAST SCENE

76 SUNLIGHT, TANGIER

77 GATE TO THE CASBAH

Fig. 86 Henry O. Tanner, *Mosque, Tangier*, c. 1912–14, etching on paper, 7 × 9¼", National Museum of American Art, Smithsonian Institution, Washington, D.C.

especially green, to play dominant roles in all three compositions. The manipulation of the thick paint itself, with contrasting liquid and scumbled brushstrokes, animates their surfaces.

The similarity of the titles of many of Tanner's North African pictures, along with the paucity of contemporary descriptions and the many name changes made by subsequent owners, makes it extremely difficult to trace contemporary reactions to specific works. However, praise by James William Pattison of a particular Tangier painting sheds light on the manner in which reviewers must have responded to others:

> In the collection of Mr. Samuel O. Buckner, there is a picture by Henry O. Tanner, the celebrated painter of African extraction, called "A Street in Tangier." Tanner has an extraordinary talent. Not alone does he draw well, but in loose handling and great abandon in brushing, he is fond of putting colors together that are used by few painters; certain grey greens and violets. His draperies are also done in this same way floating in atmosphere and peculiar color. It cannot be denied that all this speaks loudly of his talent.[4]

Tanner's new modernist approach to light and color carried over into other works such as *Miraculous Haul of Fishes* (cat. no. 79) and *Christ at the Home of Lazarus* (see fig. 76), but it was not universally accepted. For instance, W. J. Peckham hoped that "such a good painter should take a more conventional line,"[5] and warned Tanner against becoming a Secessionist. MacChesney lamented, "If I were to venture a criticism on Tanner's present work, which none admires more than myself, I should say he swings the pendulum now too far the other way [from *Resurrection of Lazarus*]."[6]

Tanner had begun to make prints around this period, and most of their settings came from the environs of Tangier. One of his most ambitious etchings is a view of the Mosque of the Palms (fig. 86). In it, Tanner translated into black and white the intense light, color, architectural interest, and expressive poses found in his paintings such as the three under consideration here. DFM

7 8

FISHERMEN AT SEA

c. 1913–14

Oil on canvas

46 × 35 ¹/₄″ (116.84 × 89.54 cm)

Signed lower right: *H. O. Tanner*

National Museum of American Art, Smithsonian Institution,

Washington, D.C., gift of Jesse O. Tanner

One of Tanner's most boldly composed and freely painted works is also one of his most mysterious. The picture now called *Fishermen at Sea* (cat. no. 78) came to light when the canvas of another painting by the artist, *Salomé* (see fig. 48), was taken off its stretcher for conservation.[1] Two canvases mounted on one stretcher to reduce the cost of packing and transportation was not an unusual practice, but precisely when this double mounting occurred is impossible to determine. Both paintings are signed but neither is dated. A search of exhibition records shows that *Fishermen at Sea* seems never to have been shown, nor is it possible to confirm that its present title originated with Tanner. *Salomé* apparently was exhibited only once, at the Grand Central Art Galleries in 1924. Perhaps its canvas was placed over *Fishermen at Sea* at that time for shipment to the United States.

Salomé has been dated to around 1900 because of a study on its verso for a painting of Moses and the burning bush, which might be related to Tanner's trip to the Holy Land in 1898,[2] and because the work is similar in theme to other paintings that can be more firmly dated to around the turn of the century.[3] Of course, the position of *Salomé* as the topmost canvas does not necessarily signify an earlier date for *Fishermen at Sea*. The paintings remained in the Tanner family until they were given to the Museum of African Art by Tanner's son in 1975, so they could have been joined at any time over a long period, although most likely it occurred during the artist's lifetime. From its subject matter and style, *Fishermen at Sea* would appear to have been painted around 1913–14.

Beginning in 1907, Tanner exhibited several religious works with marine settings: *The Disciples See Christ Walking on the Water* (cat. no. 62) in 1907; another version of the same story (location unknown) and *The Disciples on the Sea of Galilee* (see fig. 73) in 1911; and *Miraculous Haul of Fishes* (cat. no. 79) in 1914. *Fishermen at Sea* has the high vantage point of the later *Christ Walking on the Water* and *Miraculous Haul of Fishes*, with which it shares the brighter palette and freer, more broadly brushed painting style that Tanner adapted after his trips to Algiers in 1908 and Morocco in 1912.

The dynamic composition of *Fishermen at Sea* is most similar to *Miraculous Haul of Fishes*, but unlike that painting and Tanner's other marine biblical scenes, the figures are so sketchily defined that it is impossible to tell if a specific story is intended. In fact, the large patches of color in the boat might have been placed there to obliterate figures. The narrative of *Miraculous Haul of Fishes* is emphasized by the large, hollow volume of the boat, in which men struggle with the catch. In *Fishermen at Sea* the vessel is shallower and the figures are negligible; the subject becomes the fragility of

the craft against the power of the ocean–effectively rendered by deep greens and blues in the foreground, the conflict of the boat's prow with the waves breaking over it, and the elimination of a horizon. The whole world of the boat is confined to the movement of the water. It is as if, instead of choosing a story with characters, Tanner has selected a moment that sets the scene, as in Matthew 14:24: "But the ship was now in the midst of the sea, tossed with waves: for the wind was contrary."

The lack of an overt narrative and the flattened composition suggest that Tanner was experimenting with a new direction for his art. Although Tanner's choice of subject and painting style were basically conservative, he incorporated certain avant-garde tendencies into his work. *Fishermen at Sea* might have appeared *retardataire* relative to the innovations of the Cubist painters around 1912, but it was a bold departure for a member of the established American art colony in Paris. The abrupt perspective of the scene shows that Tanner had not been oblivious to the flattened perspective of Japanese prints which he could have seen in the work of Paul Gauguin and his circle as early as 1891 and 1892 during his summers in Pont-Aven and Concarneau (fig. 87). Equally important is the picture's technique, in which many methods of paint application were used, including the assured manipulation of liquid paint with a palette knife. In the confidence with which it was planned and executed, *Fishermen at Sea* is one of Tanner's most distinctive paintings, and it remains as a signal work in his career before he confronted the new reality of the post–World War I era. To compare it with *Ship in a Storm* of 1879 (cat. no. 4) is to understand Tanner's growth as an artist over thirty-five years.   DS

78 FISHERMEN AT SEA

79

MIRACULOUS HAUL OF FISHES
(*Miraculous Draught of Fishes*)
c. 1913–14
Oil on canvas
38 × 47 1/2" (96.52 × 120.65 cm)
Signed lower right: *H. O. Tanner*
National Academy of Design, New York

Even while Tanner was preoccupied with scenes of Tangier and Morocco between 1912 and 1914, the Bible remained a source for many of his pictures intended for major American museum exhibitions and the Paris Salon. *Miraculous Haul of Fishes* is yet another of his adaptations of a biblical text into a marine scene (cat. nos. 62, 68). The event appears in the Gospel of John (21:3–7); the time is after Christ's resurrection. The apostles have come home with empty nets after a night of fishing, and they do not recognize the man who advises them, "Cast the net on the right side of the ship, and ye shall find. They cast therefore, and now they were not able to draw it for the multitude of fishes. Therefore that disciple whom Jesus loved saith unto Peter, It is the Lord. Now when Simon Peter heard that it was the Lord, he girt his fisher's coat unto him, (for he was naked), and did cast himself into the sea."

Tanner concentrated on the moment in which the apostles pull in the heavy net, so full of fish that the boat tilts to the sea. The water roils and ripples with unseen fish, unlike the mostly calm surface upon which another boat passes smoothly in the distance. A gleaming spot of sunlight falls where the fish gather. The principal standing figure, Simon Peter, mans an oar and is without a cloak; his light-encircled head inclines toward a bright mauve heap of cloth in the stern. Instead of the Gospel's designation of seven disciples, Tanner used nine figures, perhaps to underscore the geometrical aspects of the composition. The four net pullers on the port side of the vessel echo its shape; Peter and his oar and the other oarsman provide vertical and diagonal elements. The two disciples in the foreground who pull in the net and the figure behind and between them form a triangle. This pyramid is repeated in imaginary lines from the standing Peter, the apostle at the apex of the first triangle, and a figure on the boat's starboard side. Tanner might be calling attention to the inner circle of apostles, which included Peter, John, and James.

Tanner set the diagonal of the craft against crisp green lines in the water and the small boat in the background. Color passages of nearly pure green in the *Miraculous Haul of Fishes*, along with its exhibition history, help to date it to the period of Tanner's North African genre scenes (cat. nos. 72–77). Eugène Delacroix had adapted marine scenes to biblical subjects during the 1850s, and he often depicted boats adrift on expanses of green water. We have no evidence that Tanner knew particular marine works by him, but Delacroix was certainly an important part of the French artistic tradition that Tanner adopted at the turn of the century.

Apparently well satisfied by this picture, Tanner presented it as his reception piece to the National Academy of Design when he was elected full academician in 1927.   DFM

79 MIRACULOUS HAUL OF FISHES

8 0

LANDSCAPE

c. 1914
Oil on artist's board
10 × 13" (25.4 × 33.02 cm)
Signed lower left: *H. O. Tanner*
Inscribed on original backing board: *"France 1914"*
Sheldon Ross Gallery, Birmingham, Michigan

Throughout his years in Europe, Tanner painted numerous small pictures of trees in a landscape, possibly influenced by the Impressionist habit of studying changing light over a static object, a method he could have seen in works by his friends at Pont-Aven as early as 1891. Tanner's paintings of the motif range from trees against a sky at a specific site to extremely abstracted landscape forms that are obviously related to the work of his last decade. As it did for the Impressionists, this subject allowed Tanner a free hand for experimentation, more than his elaborately composed biblical scenes.

The spontaneous quality of this small panel suggests that it was made just before the war, during the most innovative period of Tanner's art. Inspired by his trips to Morocco and encouraged by his professional success, he was exploring a new palette of colors and a freer technique. The artist signed the panel, which must be evidence of his satisfaction with the result; however, nothing suggests that it was ever exhibited.   DS

80 LANDSCAPE

THE WAR YEARS

AND LATE WORK

1914 – 1937

The tremendous energy, stylistic change, and exploration of new media that characterized Tanner's career from 1911 came to an abrupt end in the late summer of 1914. By early August all the great powers of Europe were embroiled in the onset of World War I. President Woodrow T. Wilson proclaimed American neutrality, in line with the almost universal determination of United States citizens to stay out of the European conflict.[1] Wilson's proclamation reached Tanner and the other Americans living in Trépied; by late August they were evacuated from this village so near the advancing German front.

The Tanners with their teenaged son, Jesse, went to England on the 28th of August,[2] traveling to Rye, in East Sussex.[3] The German army occupied Amiens on August 30, 1914, but withdrew a few days later. Tanner was able to return to France after only two weeks, but by then he had lost any motivation to paint. He drafted a lengthy letter to his longtime friend Atherton Curtis on September 14, 1914:

> The Germans are on the retreat, Amiens evacuated, etc. — soon you can work say some of my friends — but how can I? What right have I to do, what right to be comfortable? In London I saw some of the Canadian contingent and many volunteers, fine, handsome, intelligent men going out to fight, to suffer and to die for principles which I believe in as strongly as they and sit down to paint a little picture, and thus make myself happy — No it cannot be done. Not after what I saw in London. . . . How many loving, carefully raised sons . . . how many fathers, how many lonely wives, mothers, children, sweethearts, waiting for the return that never comes. This waiting . . . waiting, waiting, with less light each day until despair puts out all light of life — and this is why I cannot work.[4]

Profoundly affected by world events, Tanner painted very few works between late 1914 and the latter part of 1918, and only one or two paintings can be ascribed to the early years of the war (cat. no. 81). Tanner tried at intervals to work but apparently with little success, a hiatus almost reminiscent of his unproductive Atlanta years of 1889–90.[5] Tanner's unhappiness was intensified by Sarah Miller Tanner's illness and death, on August 14, 1914. The desire to see his family after his mother's death must have been one reason for Tanner's return to Philadelphia in early 1915, a trip confirmed by an unpublished letter written at New York on April 18, 1915, to the collector Raymond Wyer.[6] This letter indicates that Tanner also went to Chicago to promote sales of his pictures, but the trip was not as successful as he had hoped. Moreover, he was not offering new works for sale; he referred only to *Return of the Holy Women* (cat. no. 56) and *Christ and His Mother Studying the Scriptures* (cat. no. 69), pictures painted years earlier.

For a few months Tanner was far from the disasters in Europe which had made him feel "like cursing the man whose fault this terrible war is."[7] But the war encroached even at home: on March 28, 1915, an American went down on a British ship; on April 29 a German airplane attacked a U.S. merchant ship; and 128 American lives were lost on May 7 when the *Lusitania* was sunk by a German submarine.[8] Tanner set sail for Europe despite these troubles on the high seas and was in England no later than May 31, when he departed from the channel town of Folkestone, arriving in France on June 1.[9]

The trip to the United States, the brief evacuation from Trépied, and the artist's sense of the triviality of his work in the face of the horrors of war combined to give Tanner little time or inclination to paint through early 1915, but his reputation continued to grow. *Christ at the Home of Lazarus* received a gold medal from the Panama-Pacific Exposition held in 1915 at San Francisco, and his name was favorably mentioned in a review of the exposition published in *Art and Progress*: "What may be called, for convenience sake, the newer Paris group [of American artists], is strongly represented by the notable canvases of Frederick Carl Frieske, H. O. Tanner, Lawton Parker, Max Bohm, Richard W. Miller, and Walter Griffin."[10]

The war continued to wear on Tanner's spirits during 1916, and weak sales from the year before could not have helped. In February the German government announced a renewal of submarine warfare on armed merchant vessels, and on March 24 the unarmed channel steamer *Sussex* was torpedoed without warning.[11] Germany's army occupied much of France. The artist's general state of depression must have been intensified by the news of Thomas Eakins's death on June 25, 1916.

Tanner's frame of mind is revealed in a letter from Atherton Curtis, clearly written, as Marcia Mathews has pointed out, in answer to a letter from Tanner. On July 29, 1916, just after Tanner's fifty-sixth birthday, Curtis wrote:

> In your special case today you must remember that you are living in times that are not conducive to artistic production. . . .You have been trying in these two years of awful anxiety and awful suffering to produce a work of art. It is not strange that at such a time, even more than ordinary times, your judgment should find itself at fault on your looking back on what you have done. It is naturally discouraging to be stopped suddenly this way. You will have to try to encourage yourself by thinking of the beautiful things done in the past by you and start again for the future.[12]

Tanner might very well have taken heart from Curtis's encouraging words and turned back to his earlier, successful work. He made a third rendition of *Daniel in the Lions' Den* (cat. no. 87), which he sold to a Los Angeles collector in 1917. The subject of Daniel had elicited his first official recognition in the Salon twenty years earlier. Another of the few works that can be safely dated to the war years is *The Good Shepherd* (cat. no. 88), again a repetition of an earlier motif.

A review in the 1916 March–June issue of *International Studio* might have brought yet more solace, although Tanner might not have known about the article until several months later due to uncertain mail delivery. Raymond Wyer wrote: "In this collection [of J. S. Carpenter] there are no less than four paintings by Henry O. Tanner....Tanner paints many old subjects but his conceptions are modern and individual and with his evident sincerity and sense of color and original brush work, he is one of the most important men in American art today."[13]

In 1917 Tanner received a commission from a women's group in Des Moines to paint a posthumous portrait of Booker T. Washington (cat. no. 86). In addition to the honor of depicting the great man, who had himself helped further the artist's career in the early 1900s, the commission provided Tanner with much-needed income.

Tanner's artistic production was again placed in abeyance when the United States entered the war in April of 1917. Henry was almost fifty-eight, which precluded his enlistment or conscription, but he found his own course of involvement to aid the war effort. His plan came to him during the winter of 1917, while he was in Vittel, where a field hospital was located. Seeing the unused land around the base and feeling sympathetic to the flagging morale of the wounded and recovering soldiers, Tanner proposed to raise fresh produce with the convalescing men as a work force.[14] Tanner's idea can be associated with his African-American heritage; it was the type of project that Booker T. Washington might have had in mind when he encouraged students to make use of idle time and develop pride through working with their hands.[15]

In November 1917, Tanner traveled to England, where he secured the support of Walter Hines Page, then U.S. ambassador to England, a friend of Booker T. Washington, and a supporter of W. E. B. Du Bois. As editor of *World's Work* for Doubleday and Company, "Page ran so many stories...that *World's Work* published more material about black people than any other national magazine."[16] Page had surely been responsible for publishing Tanner's "Story of an Artist's Life" in the same periodical in 1909. Page recommended Tanner's project to William G. Sharp, American ambassador to France, who presented it in turn to the Red Cross authorities in Paris. The scheme was put into effect, and Tanner was named assistant director of Farm and Garden Services for the American Red Cross.[17] For almost a year, the black artist's management of the program proved to be successful,[18] although Red Cross histories of the war era do not mention his practical contribution.[19]

On October 17, 1918, less than a month before the armistice, Tanner's American Red Cross supervisor, Captain William Gillespie, noted in response to a letter of October 14, 1918: "I am glad to hear that you have started on your own work, and rest assured that you have my very best wishes for entire success."[20] The painter's desire to resume making art had been rekindled as early as September, when he had applied to the Red Cross for permission to sketch scenes in the war zone. Tanner's request makes it clear that his immediate inclination was to record his own environment; ambitious pictures of religious subjects were temporarily suspended. On the very day of the armistice, November 11, 1918, the American Expeditionary Force authorized Tanner's travel to make sketches, subject to prevailing wartime censorship (cat. nos. 81–85).[21]

During the years following the war, Tanner again became active as an artist. He pursued earlier subjects but in new compositions with fresh effects of color and surface. His personal life was filled with sadness, but his reputation, particularly in the United States, expanded beyond all previous recognition.

In September of 1919, Robert C. Vose offered Tanner an exhibition in his Boston gallery, and a one-man show comprising ten works opened in January 1921.[22] Several prewar pictures appeared, such as *Return of the Holy Women* (cat. no. 56), but Tanner also included new renditions of a favored past theme, the flight into Egypt. One version shown in Boston depicted a weary Mary and Joseph mounted on plodding beasts (Houston, Museum of Fine Arts). The composition, less energetic than the artist's 1899 version (cat. no. 49), seems to reflect the artist's emotional malaise.

The Vose Gallery exhibition apparently did not generate much response in the press, but Tanner's work continued to be reviewed with varying degrees of enthusiasm. In June 1923 he received a lukewarm notice in the *American Magazine of Art*.[23] A critic of the 1926 annual exhibition in Chicago was more positive: "But what of the strange vision of Henry O. Tanner? As for [his] *Two Disciples at the Tomb*, little relates this remote blue-green scene to the yellow-lighted painting of the same name in the Institute's permanent collection, except the reverence, the mystery, the faith which breathes in all of Mr. Tanner's works."[24]

In 1922 a group of black artists and art teachers in Washington, D.C., organized the Tanner Art League and mounted an extensive exhibition in the studios of Dunbar High School.[25] Nothing is known about this show other than it contained works by Tanner, but its presentation at a school named for Paul Laurence Dunbar — the noted author whose poem "A Banjo Song" related so aptly to Tanner's 1893 *The Banjo Lesson* — was highly appropriate.

On December 26, 1921, Tanner was proposed for the prestigious Cross of the Legion of Honor,[26] the highest recognition that the French government bestowed upon nonmilitary personnel, and in April 1923 the award was confirmed, in recognition of the fact that Tanner had "exhibited his works and received numerous awards in French Salons since 1894.... [He] is recommended for this distinction by Léon Bénédite, curator of the Luxembourg Museum, and Mr. Ernest T. Rosen, secretary general of the committee for the exhibition of American Painters and Sculptors at Luxembourg."[27]

In December 1923 Tanner boarded a ship for New York to participate in his important one-man exhibition of religious paintings at Grand Central Art Galleries.[28] This exhibition, which proved to be his last major show during his lifetime, opened on January 21, 1924, and included nineteen familiar religious titles. A reviewer for the *New York Times* stated:

> Though there is no tremendous emotional or spiritual inspiration in the painting of H. O. Tanner, there is at least a dignified hint that we may, after all, be the sons of God, or that humanity is not only a thing of the flesh. It is when the artist is doing a direct piece of unself-conscious painting that he is aesthetically, and therefore emotionally, more successful.[29]

Another article revealed that Tanner's philosophy of art had remained constant since the first decade of the century and suggests that he had not lost interest in racial issues:

"My effort has been not only to put the Biblical incident in the original setting," said Mr. Tanner, "but at the same time to give the human touch which makes the whole world kin and which ever remains the same. While giving truth of detail not to lose sight of more important matters — by this I mean that of color and design should be as carefully thought out as if the subject had only these qualities. To me it seems no handicap to have a subject of nobility worthy of one's best continued effort. There is but one thing more important than these qualities, and that is to try to convey to the public the reverence and elevation these subjects impart to you, which is the primary cause of their choice."[30]

With the success that came to Tanner during the mid-1920s were tragedies in his personal life. Bishop Benjamin Tucker Tanner died on January 15, 1923, and Henry must have been distressed that his distance in France kept him from the funeral. His old artist friends Henry Boddington and Paul Bartlett both died two years later. But the most damaging blow was the fatal illness that had afflicted his wife since 1924. Jessie Tanner died on September 25, 1925, leaving a tremendous void in the artist's life. Married for nearly twenty-six years, their happiness had defied the stern advice given in the Book of Daniel (2:43): "And whereas thou sawest iron mixed with miry clay, they shall mingle themselves with the seed of men: but they shall not cleave one to another, even as iron is not mixed with clay." Tanner was sixty-six years old when he lost his "iron," and his active career was essentially over.

During the period of Tanner's greatest recognition, a succession of movements swept the art world. Modernism experienced a general détente after the First World War,[31] and the tempo of innovation slackened somewhat.[32] In the mid-1920s the Neo-Romantics emerged, inspired in part by the disturbing images of Picasso. Tanner, in earlier years, had borrowed ideas from the circle of Gauguin and was affected by the surface emphasis of Cubism. But his late works display little interest in current developments. Tanner's conservatism was already recognized in 1924 by a critic for *New York World*, who reviewed the primarily recent works in Tanner's last major New York City showing:

> The artist's work seems to have changed hardly at all since his last appearance here [in 1919]. He still sticks to the cool color arrangements, in which blue predominates, and within its limited range plays slight variations in closely related tone and color.
>
> In the oriental scenes and the heavily swathed figures, bathed in an unearthly light, he expresses the mood of brooding, mysticism that has always been the keynote of his work.[33]

Tanner was facing problems other than critical dissatisfaction. His son was ill, and between 1926 and 1929, he was preoccupied by a lawsuit against the Bethel African American Episcopal Church in Philadelphia. The elders of the church had commissioned a bronze plaque of the denomination's founder, Bishop Richard Allen, but then attempted to cancel the order.[34] Tanner was represented in the lawsuit by Raymond Pace Alexander, the husband of his niece, Sadie Tanner Mossell Alexander. As a result, they became good friends, and the Alexanders' visits to France and faithful correspondence over the last decade of Tanner's life were a source of comfort and joy. Mrs. Alexander acquired a number of his paintings during his lifetime.[35]

Tanner wrote to the Alexanders with good news on May 30, 1927: "I have sent the picture ordered by Cheyney and hope it will be liked. The N.Y. Art Club [sic] awarded me a money prize and medal this last winter, and the National Academy of Design (N.Y.) has elected me an Academician which though late is better than never."[36] The painting commissioned by the Cheyney Training School for Teachers in Pennsylvania has been identified by Marcia Mathews as *Nicodemus Coming to Christ*, a painting still preserved at the school.[37] This was a reprise of Tanner's 1907 version (see cat. no. 47), and its completion caused him much difficulty in the painful years after the war.

The prize from the National Arts Club was for a painting entitled *At the Gates*. Atlanta collector J. J. Haverty owned a version of the work, but Tanner himself could not precisely identify which one. He wrote to Haverty on October 29, 1929: "I did not answer your kind note as soon as I wished, on account of the picture *At the Gates*. I painted two pictures of this same subject — of course from different points of view and different effects. I have been unable to find out definitely, which one you acquired."[38]

Haverty was one of the artist's keenest supporters. In addition to *At the Gates*, he already owned a picture called *Road to Emmaus* (location unknown), and he took an option to purchase *Supper at Emmaus* (location unknown), which Tanner had on his easel in 1929. He also bought in 1929 *The Destruction of Sodom and Gomorrah* (cat. no. 98) and two other lost works — a good shepherd and a sketch.[39]

Despite the demand for his work in America, Tanner's production decreased considerably during the late 1920s. Before the war he could be found working on up to twenty pictures at a time, but his health now precluded bringing so many works to satisfactory completion. After 1925 he often sent older paintings to exhibitions. His energy seems to have improved around 1930 but by no means to its previous level. In the spring of that year, Tanner wrote to J. S. Carpenter, his representative in Des Moines (who worked closely with Grand Central Galleries in New York):

> I have 5 or 6 pictures underway — all unfinished — but I hope soon to remedy this state of affairs. I have not changed my principle at this date — unless I believe in a canvas I do not send it out — However, things are beginning to change and I have two which I hope to finish within the month . . . I have been working on a tempera mixture for the last 5 or 6 years and have finally a wonderful binder. I am now using it exclusively and I am sure you will find no loss of quality in my painting.[40]

Tanner's determination to break new ground through experimentation with painting media and methods had begun as early as 1910. His continued preoccupation with technique during the next decade is clear from an inscription dated January 28, 1920, on the back of *Head of a Jew in Palestine* (cat. no. 48). The work was painted in oil, and after drying for two or three years, Tanner rubbed back the background with an emulsion and then painted in tempera. Tanner's 1930 statement that he was using a "wonderful binder" indeed points to a new approach, although his search for the ideal mixture, which combined parchment glue, varnish, linseed oil and alchohol, had lasted for decades.[41] The effect of this complicated medium can be seen in a number of paintings, such as *Head of a Disciple* (fig. 88). This work has a thick enamellike surface with patterned brushstrokes in the background which call to mind thirteenth-

Fig. 88 Henry O. Tanner, *Head of a Disciple*, n.d., oil and tempera on panel, 13 × 9 ¼", Merton Simpson, New York.

Fig. 89 Georges Rouault, *Christ*, c. 1935– 38, 19 ³/₈ × 15 ¹/₈", oil on canvas, Philadelphia Museum of Art, The Samuel S. White, 3rd, and Vera White Collection.

century Limoges enamels and parallel the encrusted surfaces of religious subjects (fig. 89) by the younger French artist Georges Rouault (1871–1958). Atherton Curtis attempted to connect Tanner's mixing methods with the practices of fourteenth-century Flemish artists.[42] The Orientalist painter Decamps had experimented with surface buildup through manipulation of pigments in the 1830s and 1840s. Tanner's crusty accumulation of pigments just might be seen as his echo of the use of collage in the early phases of Cubism. Although not a modernist by generation or by temperament, Tanner's quiet persistence with his media and techniques and his profoundly individual vision gave his late work a direct beauty that cannot be called *retardataire*.

The final years of Tanner's life coincided with the Great Depression, which confronted the United States with its worst crisis since the Civil War. The economic situation affected many of Tanner's patrons, virtually all of whom were Americans. When the stock market crashed in 1929, Tanner had orders on hand worth 80,000 francs, nearly all of which were lost to him.[43] His dealer J. S. Carpenter wrote in September 1931 that the prospect for sales was bleak:

> The times in this country are very strenuous . . . In fact, we are in the worst depression this country has known for many years, and it has almost reached the stage of a panic. . . . Our Art Association has suspended activities for the year. That is, we are not going to ask our members for any membership dues, and will simply fill our gallery with a loan collection of pictures, and let it hang through the year.[44]

The situation was particularly grave for many African-Americans who learned the cruel truth of the saying "last hired, first fired."[45] In 1933 Tanner was unhappy to find that one of his African-American patrons and acquaintances, John Nail, had been adversely affected: "I was so very sorry to hear about Nail. I was so very sorry to hear that Nail was the only man of 'our group' who ever bought one of my pictures to be forced to sell. It is too bad but I do not suppose if he had not bought them he would have had the $1200—(or more) stored away when he could have called upon it!"[46]

During these troubled times Tanner found himself increasingly unable to work. He wrote to his favorite sister, Mary Tanner Mossell, in December 1931: "I have been having some trouble with my eyes, and I am only within the last weeks or so been using them. So it is small doses of writing and reading. . . . Have orders ahead for two or three pictures of good size, but the trouble is to get them done."[47]

In a letter to Sadie Alexander in June 1932, Tanner seemed hesitant to undertake a new painting but still confident of his abilities:

> Of course I am glad to make a picture for you and should be very glad to do it—if you really wanted the picture. . . .
>
> I do not have on hand anything of subject you should prefer nor any other picture of this size. I am glad that you want it because I know that my work is better than it has ever been—the question of time does not figure in it—it does take longer, but that does not—as you know—make it worth any more.[48]

In the spring of 1933 the artist fell into a hole in a sidewalk while walking the streets of Paris at night and had to be hospitalized.[49] Although he had several orders for paintings, he did not sell a single work in 1933, most probably because he did not finish any.[50] During this period, Tanner was again distracted by a lawsuit to recover a cash loan he had made to Clarence Cameron White, a black composer and professor of music at Hampton University.[51] Further bad news came early in 1934: J. J. Haverty canceled his option on *Supper at Emmaus* because "it is now three years since this picture was ordered . . . and the Depression has made us all poor."[52] Haverty also complained about the condition of *Road to Emmaus*, already in his collection, asking Tanner to repair it. The artist ended up exchanging the award-winning *Etaples Fisher Folk* (cat. no. 90) for *Emmaus*, a transaction that again left him less well off.[53]

Tanner's public career fell into relative obscurity. In the mid-1930s, the black printmaker Albert Smith (1896–1940), who had lived in France since 1933, wrote to the African-American collector Arthur Schomburg: "Sometime ago, you remember, you asked me to see about a Tanner,—well he is a mystery painter to me—his works are not on display in Paris dealers, and there are but one or two in the museums, where they go to I don't know and would like to know."[54] Smith wrote again to Schomburg on May 17, 1936, about an exhibition of the League of Professional American Artists held at Gallérie Ecalle in Paris:

> Tanner is hanging opposite me with two of his blue-colored subjects. And I always feel that when you have seen one Tanner you have seen them all. For one Tanner seems but a continuation of other Tanners. Nevertheless I feel a deep respect for his work that is really a series of formulas that never vary and make him the artist he is.
>
> Personally I remember seeing him but once since I have been in France. I understand through the chatty American secretary of the organization that he has a farm somewhere down the line and that with the communion that the earth gives you he finds solitude that gives birth to his paintings. I must say that the American white artists hold him in deep respect.[55]

Tanner described the conditions of his life in a letter of March 22, 1936, to his dealer Edwin S. Barrie, director of the Grand Central Art Galleries:

> My health is quite a little better so that nearly everyday I work on small pictures and with some success but I am not able yet to commence new pictures of any importance, and do not see myself doing so this summer. . . .
>
> I have given up my studio in Paris, which I have had for 30 years and it is only in the summer I could work on a [large] picture. . . . I am then in the country [at Trépied] and have more rooms. This does not mean that the quality of the work has lost but that I am not so energetic and can do less — and also that I have financial worries along with it. The exchange value of the $ being only 60 cents has very much upset me financially. The money I had been able to save I had put into property and now my property is mostly rented to work people who cannot find work and those houses which formerly made a good income now bring only enough to pay taxes and not always enough. . . .
>
> Please excuse this wandering letter, what I mean to say is that though I am better than last summer I still have to avoid any strain that would overdo myself.[56]

The fact that Tanner had given up his boulevard Saint-Jacques studio on the edge of the Latin Quarter suggests his virtual retirement. A measure of his obscurity at this point is recalled by Jean Hélion (1904–87), the French painter who took over Tanner's studio: "My only recollection of [the studio] is that it was occupied by a colored painter from, I think, Virginia, whom I only met once, and cannot remember his name."[57]

But Tanner did not cease making art altogether. Among the few attempts of his last years were images of the good shepherd (cat. nos. 100–102), a favorite theme representing his steadfast concern for the shared needs and hopes of people of all races. He must still have been at work in 1936 on *Return from the Crucifixion* (cat. no. 105), which was purchased by Howard University in March 1937. James Porter eloquently described Tanner's power: "The old sincerity persisted, as did his ability to suggest infinite meaning with a reduced palette — a certain indication of the mastery of his art."[58]

A letter from Tanner to Margaret Bryant, the daughter of an early Atlanta supporter, Wesley Clifford, gives a vivid sense of Tanner's mood and artistic production shortly before his death. He wrote to her on May 3, 1937: "You know I am getting to be quite an old man and cannot hop about so lively. I still work each day — but not so many hours as formerly — but I am happy to say that I have a good many friends who think my work has not dropped off. It is only within the last year that we sold the place at Trépied."[59]

The last work on Tanner's mind was a portrait of Raymond Pace Alexander. The artist referred to his careful working methods, which had persisted over the decades, on February 2, 1937: "I should be able to make the studies and drawings necessary to make a portrait in about 10 days or 2 weeks and I should finish the portrait within 2 or three months at most."[60] This proposed portrait of his niece's husband was never realized. Henry Ossawa Tanner died in his sleep on May 25, 1937. Two weeks before his death, he said to his good friends and patrons Atherton and Ingeborg Curtis: "How beautiful spring time is in Paris! The earth is awakening once more."[61] His biographer Marcia M. Mathews observed most eloquently:

No death could have been more peaceful or less free of suffering. When his friends read in the newspapers that he was gone they were shocked by the suddenness of it. They knew Tanner was old and not very strong, but death seemed far away. Yet they knew it was the way he would have wanted to go, with the paint still fresh on his last canvas. . . . Tanner was buried on May 27 in the cemetery at Sceaux next to his beloved Jessie.[62]

Artist's careers do not necessarily end with their deaths. Scholars make painstaking investigations of their lives and works in the hope of broadening knowledge not only of their artistic development but of the periods in which they lived. Museums extend artists' reputations and influence through acquisition and exhibition. The great nineteenth-century French critic Charles Baudelaire remarked: "A simple method of learning an artist's range is to examine his public."[63] The most significant way in which artists perpetuate their vision is through making works of art that have an impact on their peers or followers, who might be inspired by an idea or adapt a manner of execution.[64] Thus artists affect future developments long after their own deaths.

Tanner's influence on other artists had less to do with the impact of individual works than of his career as a whole. The generation of African-American artists who contributed to the Harlem Renaissance,[65] born some forty years after the Emancipation Proclamation, would be difficult to imagine without the example of Tanner's single-minded pursuit of artistic success and his subsequent international recognition. The impact of Tanner's career was by no means race-bound. The life of Henry Ossawa Tanner — namesake of the abolitionist John Brown of Osawatomie; student of Thomas Eakins and Thomas Hovenden in America; élève of the Académie Julian in Paris; Franco-American master of biblical and Oriental themes; contributor to the First World War effort; and African-American artist par excellence — was an inspiration and a challenge to aspiring painters, and his work is a monument of sturdy endeavor and exalted achievement.   DFM

81

WAR SCENE, ETAPLES, FRANCE
c. 1914
Oil on cardboard
14 3/4 × 18″ (37.47 × 45.72 cm)
Clark Atlanta University Collection of Afro-American Art,
Atlanta

82

STUDY FOR AMERICAN RED
CROSS CANTEEN
1918
Charcoal and white chalk on buff laid paper
14 3/16 × 16 5/16″ (36.04 × 41.43 cm)
Merton Simpson, New York

83

AMERICAN RED CROSS
CANTEEN, WORLD WAR I
1918
Charcoal on paper
17 1/2 × 22 3/4″ (44.45 × 57.79 cm)
National Museum of American Art, Smithsonian Institution,
Washington, D.C., gift of Mr. and Mrs. Norman B. Robbins

84

AMERICAN RED CROSS
CANTEEN, TOUL, FRANCE,
WORLD WAR I
1918
Oil on canvas
14 3/16 × 16 5/16″ (36.04 × 41.43 cm)
Signed, inscribed, and dated lower right: *H. O. Tanner/Toul/1918*
American Red Cross, Washington, D.C.

85

INTERSECTION OF ROADS,
NEUFCHATEAU, WORLD WAR I
1918
Oil on canvas
25 5/8 × 31 7/8″ (65.09 × 80.96 cm)
Signed and dated lower left: *H O Tanner/1918*
American Red Cross, Washington, D.C.

Fig. 90 Henry O. Tanner, *American Red Cross Canteen at the Front*, 1918, oil on canvas, 48 × 61″, American Red Cross, Washington, D.C.

The Tanners were residing in Trépied near Etaples, at the outbreak of World War I. They were evacuated on August 25; Henry recorded, "We heard [the] grumbling of cannon firing all day."[1] On August 28 they departed France for Rye, in southern England.

Unlike Tanner's other paintings of war subjects, which were made during the last months of the conflict in 1918, *War Scene, Etaples, France* (cat. no. 81) might have been made before the Tanners left France, or at least early in the war. Jesse Tanner inscribed the title and date of the painting on its back. The site and subject and the colorful depiction of the scene do not relate to Tanner's later paintings of Red Cross themes, and this small panel with bits of debris brushed into the paint is obviously a quick sketch made on the spot.

The Tanners were back in France by October 1914 and lived in Paris or in Trépied, depending upon conditions of the war. But Tanner was unable to paint during this time; he felt profoundly discouraged and questioned the significance of his work and his life. In the draft of a letter of September 14, 1914, probably addressed to Atherton Curtis, he said:

81 WAR SCENE, ETAPLES, FRANCE

Soon you can work say some of my friends — but how can I? What right have I to do that which I like to do, what right to be comfortable? In London I saw some of the Canadian contingent and many volunteers, fine, handsome, intelligent men going out to fight, to suffer and die for principles which I believe in as strongly as they and sit down to paint a little picture, and thus make myself happy — No it cannot be done.[2]

A commissioned portrait of Booker T. Washington (cat. no. 86) is one of the few works that can definitely be attributed to these years. Tanner had joined the Red Cross in December 1917, and not until the last months of the war, after his plans to grow vegetables at Red Cross field hospitals had been a success, did he apply to make sketches for paintings in the Neufchâteau region where he was stationed.

Three large paintings remain the property of the Red Cross — *American Red Cross Canteen, Toul, France, World War I* (cat. no. 84), *Intersection of Roads, Neufchâteau, World War I* (cat. no. 85), and *American Red Cross Canteen at the Front* (fig. 90). None appears to have been painted at the site, and the two large related drawings have more the appearance of composition studies than direct, annotative sketches. Perhaps Tanner worked up his paint-

82 STUDY FOR AMERICAN RED CROSS CANTEEN

83 AMERICAN RED CROSS CANTEEN, WORLD WAR I

ings from small painted sketches, such as a study for the architectural setting of the Toul scene (Montgomery, Alabama State University), or he might have used other smaller drawings, photographs, or even postcards; views of the exterior and interior of Red Cross canteens were circulated during the war.

Tanner's permit to sketch specifically limited him to Red Cross activities, and all his work was reviewed by censors. He probably did not feel constrained by these restrictions, since in keeping with his aesthetic sensibilities, he did not try to convey the emotions of his writings in paint. Tanner limited himself to figures and light effects, such as those in the lively interior of the canteen, or in the two exterior scenes whose bluish tonalities relate to his earlier work. The still figures of soldiers in their olive-drab battle dress standing in front of the canteen at Toul form a subdued but powerful image based on the warm colors of the uniforms in contrast to the cool black of the buildings against the twilight sky. In *Intersection of Roads, Neufchâteau, World War I*, figures are silhouetted against and illuminated by a strong, single source of artificial light, a device Tanner would explore numerous times in his work of the 1920s.

Tanner also found time to study one subject not related to the war in a painting entitled *Old House, Neufchâteau, Vosges* (location unknown), which was shown at the Carnegie International in 1921.   DS

84 AMERICAN RED CROSS CANTEEN, TOUL, FRANCE, WORLD WAR I

85 INTERSECTION OF ROADS, NEUFCHATEAU, WORLD WAR I

86

PORTRAIT OF BOOKER T.
WASHINGTON
1917
Oil on canvas
31 ³/₄ × 25 ⁵/₈″ (80.65 × 65.09 cm)
Signed, inscribed, and dated lower left: *H. O. Tanner/Paris/1917*
State Historical Society of Iowa, Museum Bureau, Des Moines

Booker T. Washington (1856-1915), the famous African-American educator and spokesman, was a good friend of the Tanner family. He hired Halle Tanner Dillon, Henry's sister, to be resident physician at the Tuskegee Institute, which he had headed since 1881, and he followed Henry's career with interest, writing about him and encouraging the purchase of his work. The Washingtons visited Tanner in Paris in 1899, and Washington wrote a long account of that visit for the *Washington Colored American*.[1] Two years later in *Up from Slavery*, Washington referred to this visit again, describing Tanner as the embodiment of the principle of success in which he believed:

> My acquaintance with Mr. Tanner reinforced in my mind the truth which I am constantly trying to impress upon our students at Tuskegee — and on our people throughout the country, as far as I can reach them with my voice — that any man, regardless of colour, will be recognized and rewarded just in proportion as he learns to do something well — learns to do it better than some one else — however humble the thing may be.[2]

The commission for the Washington portrait (cat. no. 86), which came from the Iowa Federation of Colored Women's Clubs, most likely resulted from Tanner's friendship with J. S. Carpenter. The president of a bridge-building company in Des Moines, Carpenter collected the artist's work and served informally as his agent in the Midwest. By the time of the commission, Carpenter owned four paintings by Tanner.[3] As president of the Des Moines Association of Fine Arts, he would have been a logical consultant in choosing an appropriate artist for the portrait.

Tanner's picture is a memorial to Washington, who had died in November 1915. It is probably based on a photograph, as well as Tanner's memories, and in contrast to the formality and symbolism of Tanner's portrait of Bishop Hartzell (cat. no. 42), Washington is shown simply, against a plain background in a relaxed half-length pose, with the lapels of his unbuttoned, light-colored jacket falling in rhythmic soft folds to the bottom edge of the canvas.

Tanner painted very little during the war years, so few contemporaneous works can be compared with this portrait. But its color scheme and technique would be distinctive at any point in his career. The black, white, and gray values of the photograph may have inspired Tanner to use colors — greens, browns, pinks — that are varied in hue but similar in value, so that the effect of the painting, keyed to the medium value of Washington's coat, is nearly monochromatic, unlike the dramatic contrasts of Bishop Hartzell's portrait. This color scheme foreshadows the tonalities of Tanner's paintings in the

86 PORTRAIT OF BOOKER T. WASHINGTON

1930s. The image appears to have been quickly and economically painted with thin washes; sure strokes of very liquid paint build up form. Informal but arresting, the portrait captures a strong likeness and emphasizes the unusual luminosity of Washington's eyes, in a technique that is daring in its depiction of skin tones and as innovative as *Fishermen at Sea* (cat. no. 78) and *Christ Learning to Read* (cat. no. 70) had been a few years earlier.　DS

8 7

DANIEL IN THE LIONS' DEN
c. 1914–17
Oil on paper mounted on canvas
41¹/₈ × 49⁷/₈″ (104.46 × 126.68 cm)
Signed and inscribed lower left: *H. O. Tanner/Paris*
Los Angeles County Museum of Art, Mr. and Mrs. William
Preston Harrison Collection

Daniel in the Lions' Den is a reinterpretation and modernization of an 1895 picture for which Tanner received an honorable mention from the Salon jury of 1896 (see fig. 16). He rendered the subject again in quite a different composition around 1900 (location unknown). The story is of the Old Testament prophet who was enslaved, elevated in rank, falsely accused, sentenced to death in a den of lions, and then reprieved by religious faith (Dan. 6:16–23).

The basic components of the 1895 painting and this one are essentially the same; however, the horizontal format of the Los Angeles version allows the right side of the picture to move off into infinite space, hinting at the presence of more lions. The intense square of light in the lower half of the composition, contrasted with the upper torso and face of Daniel, obscured by deep shadow, echoes the earlier picture, but the source of the light is not visible. Small grills at the top of the doors could not provide such bursts of daylight, but they suggest larger openings in the ceiling similar to the trap door depicted in the 1895 version. This inference of a hidden light source is typical of Tanner's pictures after 1908. The blue-green palette, accented with yellows, greens, and lavender, is also characteristic of the artist's production in mid-career. Aided by geometric elements and directional brushstrokes, the palette supports the sober mood and movement in the painting.

Daniel in the Lions' Den has been criticized for a certain passivity,[1] but given Tanner's state of mind during World War I, its message becomes clearer. The depression that he felt is expressed in its subdued feeling, Daniel's general sense of hopelessness, and the less-than-fiery attitude of the lions, who pace to and fro, paying little heed to their fellow captive.

The canvas support of the Los Angeles *Daniel* was found to be stretched over a painting of *Job and His Three Friends* (cat. no. 57); Tanner was most likely reusing his stretchers, which were expensive, as he did with *Fishermen at Sea* (cat. no. 78). There is no evidence (nor does it accord with his character) to suggest that Tanner was attempting to avoid French customs duty by shipping two works for the price of one. The underlying pictures could not have been intended for secondary buyers because they were discovered only during the past two decades.

The extensive exhibition history of the picture and plentiful references to it clearly reflect recent social and political interests in the United States. The painting was frequently cited between the late 1960s and 1970s, a period during which Tanner and his work received renewed attention as a result of the civil rights movement.   DFM

87 DANIEL IN THE LIONS' DEN

88

THE GOOD SHEPHERD

c. 1917

Oil on canvas

29 1/4 × 33 1/4" (74.3 × 84.46 cm)

Signed lower right: *H. O. Tanner*

New Orleans Museum of Art

89

THE GOOD SHEPHERD

(*Lost Sheep*)

1922

Oil on canvas

32 × 24" (81.28 × 60.96 cm)

Signed and dated lower left: *H. O. Tanner/1922*

The Newark Museum, New Jersey, gift of Mr. and

Mrs. Henry H. Wehrhane, 1929

These two superb paintings justify the rhetorical question raised by Evelyn Marie Stuart: "Who cannot recognize a Genth or a Melchers, a Tanner, a Hawthorne, or a Garber by sight?"[1] Indeed the pictures reveal Tanner's individuality in choice of subject, palette, and technique.

Tanner turned to the theme of the good shepherd, with substantial variations, throughout his career. The images are based generally on the Gospel of John (10:14–16). Tanner's preference for the subject was also rooted in African Methodist Episcopal liturgy, in which the Twenty-third Psalm is an important element: "The Lord is my Shepherd; I shall not want." During World War I and its aftermath, Tanner began again to ponder broad concerns of human suffering and injustice. John's Gospel describes Jesus as the good shepherd with his entire flock, as seen in the New Orleans painting (cat. no. 88). The Newark picture (cat. no. 89) depicts the shepherd's care for the lost sheep, a theme based on Matthew's account (18:12–14): "How think ye? if a man have an hundred sheep, and one of them be gone astray, doth he not leave the ninety and nine, and goeth into the mountains, and seeketh that which is gone astray? And if so be that he find it, verily I say unto you, he rejoiceth more of that sheep, than of the ninety and nine which went not astray."

For the scene with the flock, Tanner chose a horizontal format, spreading the sheep out in the basically flat landscape, while he gave the shepherd carrying the lost sheep a vertical format. The greenish mountain slopes on the right, albeit quite different in emphasis, provide major diagonal elements in both paintings and call attention to the principal vertical action in their foregrounds. In the background of the New Orleans picture, clouds move in various directions, further enlivening its panoramic format, while the horizontal brushstrokes of the hazy sky of the Newark *Good Shepherd* provide relief for the steep diagonal of the mountains. A thickly painted celestial disc, rising in the flock picture and setting in the other, pulls the background forward in a manner consistent with modernist works by other artists of the time. Contrasting areas of thick impasto and dry, pulled passages of the brush underline the two-dimensional nature of the canvas surfaces.

The two versions of *The Good Shepherd* seem at first monochromatic, but their distinctive palettes and light effects deserve individual attention. The horizontal picture is composed primarily of beautiful green shades and tints. The liquid, seemingly tangible light invokes numerous other colors. Mauve, blue, and lavender strokes run throughout the terrain on the right and in the sky, creating an almost physical sense of warmth. The pale, whitish-yellow horizontal band of sky behind the lonely shepherd is interrupted by a

88 THE GOOD SHEPHERD

ring of thicker brushstrokes around him, calling attention to the sacred subject of the painting.

The vertical picture has a blue-green appearance, and it too contains myriad colors, ranging from subdued yellows in the foreground to the deep purple of the cursory trees in the middle ground to the light mauves of the delicate sky. The unexpected green tint of the shepherd's beard and the shadow at his feet are Tanner's abstractions of the real world and add to the melancholy of the twilight scene. In spite of the lengthening rays cast by the setting sun or rising moon, the light pervading the composition seems to emanate from the mountaintops as a separate, spiritual source. An aureole of dry brush highlights around the rim of the man's cape and cloak, in the manner of the New Orleans picture, emphasizes that this is no ordinary shepherd.

When Tanner first turned to this theme early in the twentieth century, there were ample precedents for scenes of shepherds and shepherdesses with their flocks in French paintings of the Barbizon School.[2] Tanner's individual approach took the subject from the realm of genre painting into the sphere of religious and history painting without loss of simple directness. The two *Good Shepherds* reflect the balance Tanner sought to achieve with his biblical works. He wrote as a warning to any painter of religious pictures: "For him to suppose that his having such a subject can by any manner of means be construed as an excuse for making a picture in which the literary side shall be its only quality, or in which a so-called religious sentiment will take the place of the qualities loved by artists, thus furnishing an excuse for giving to the world an uninteresting canvas, is equally false."[3]

Tanner reiterated these ideas in the catalogue for his retrospective exhibition at the Grand Central Art Galleries at New York City in 1924. Writing about the Newark picture, a critic for the *New York Times* used the artist's views to launch his own praise, which could be applied to both versions of *The Good Shepherd*: "One of the most interesting of the group—there are nineteen in all—is 'The Lost Sheep.' It gives a vivid picture of desolation, with the rugged hills in the background, and all about the struggling vegetation, barren and hopeless."[4]   DFM

89 THE GOOD SHEPHERD

ETAPLES FISHER FOLK
1923
Tempera and oil on canvas
47 $^{5}/_{16}$ × 38 $^{5}/_{16}$" (120.17 × 97.31 cm)
Signed and dated lower right: *H. O. Tanner/1923*
High Museum of Art, Atlanta, J. J. Haverty Collection, 36.16

Tanner's reputation as an artist was well established by the end of the first decade of the twentieth century, and growing public awareness of his work led to more exhibition opportunities including one-man shows — at the American Art Galleries in New York in December 1908, at Thurber Art Galleries in Chicago in February 1911 and again in February 1913, and at Knoedler's Gallery in New York in April 1913. For the most part he continued to select biblical or Near Eastern subjects when only one or two works were required for a juried exhibition. But perhaps with the idea of varying the work that he had to show and sell, Tanner began to paint landscapes and genre subjects based on scenes around his home in the small village of Trépied. He showed *Dunes near Etaples* at the 1911 Thurber Art Galleries exhibition, and a picture titled *Etaples Fisher Folk* at both the Art Institute of Chicago and the Corcoran Gallery in Washington in 1912. Six paintings of Etaples subjects, including *Hayrick at Trépied, Moonlight — Road to Etaples*, and *Windy Day at Trépied*, were shown in exhibitions at Thurber Art Galleries and at Knoedler's Gallery in 1913.

This *Etaples Fisher Folk* (cat. no. 90) is not the one shown in Chicago in 1912. Not only is the painting dated 1923, but the technique of building up the surface into a thick layer of paint and the device of a lantern as the major source of light are consistent with other works of the 1920s. In fact, this dated painting, along with *Flight into Egypt* of 1923 (cat. no. 92) and *The Good Shepherd* of 1922 (cat. no. 89), has been used to define the characteristics of Tanner's style during this decade, when both his production and exhibition record were erratic due to the death of his wife, his son's nervous breakdown, and his own depression and ill health.

A comparison of *Etaples Fisher Folk* with genre scenes Tanner painted thirty years earlier is revealing. Clearly Tanner had moved away from the conventions of academic painting to a much more individual and personal style. Instead of a detailed, specific narrative acted out by the figures in the painting, Tanner has created an atmosphere of ambiguous action and emotion in which the only activity is the fisherman's leaning form and hands at work in an indistinct task. The motivation for the work appears to be a demonstration of a richly colored, heavily worked painted surface. The figures are flat and thickly outlined, emphasizing patterns and shapes. Even the shadows cast by the ribs of the lantern make a sharply defined pattern on the floor. Space is defined not by perspective but by recession from the bright light of the lantern in the foreground, and the weightiness of the figures comes not from carefully delineated volumes but from the tactile substance of the paint.

Even before the war Tanner was experimenting with new techniques and innovative materials, and his continuing investigations after the war are evident in the unusual combination of oil paints and water-based tempera in

Etaples Fisher Folk. In fact, these experiments are indirectly responsible for the painting's presence in the collection of the High Museum of Art. J. J. Haverty, a prominent Atlanta art collector who eventually owned five of Tanner's paintings, was originally drawn to the artist's biblical subject matter. When *Road to Emmaus*, which Haverty had purchased in the late 1920s, began to flake badly due to unstable materials, the collector requested a replacement. By this time, Tanner's age and ill health prevented him from undertaking a major biblical subject, and in September 1936, *Etaples Fisher Folk*, which was in stock at Tanner's dealer, Grand Central Art Galleries, was exchanged for the deteriorating painting.   DS

9 1

VIRGIN AND CHILD
(*Mary*)
c. 1922
Oil on canvas
32 × 25″ (81.28 × 63.5 cm)
Signed lower right: *H. O. Tanner*
Wadsworth Atheneum, Hartford, Connecticut, Ella Gallup
Sumner and Mary Catlin Sumner Collection

The image of the Virgin Mary pondering the enormous responsibility entrusted to her appears often in Tanner's oeuvre. The text offering a basis for this picture is the Gospel of Luke (1:26–29). As in *Mary* (cat. no. 50), Tanner depicted the Christ Child swaddled in a bundle of cloth over which a halo hovers, emphasizing the spirituality rather than the humanness of the newborn. The model for Mary could very well have been Tanner's wife, Jessie Olssen.

The basic compositional idea of a single figure as the vertical axis, played off against a horizontal or even vertical format in an interior setting, is consistent with Tanner's previous works. Accents on linear details — the semicircle of the Virgin's yellow belt, the red border of her slippers, the child's light green halo — encourage the viewer's eye to move about the composition but are not new. The juicy paint handling of the face contrasted with thick drybrush passages in the mauve, pink, lavender, and green fabrics is characteristic of Tanner's late manner, as are the bright outline of the mantle and the de-emphasized interior architecture.

Tanner explored several innovative devices in this picture. He gave a new role to the light, which seems to emanate from the painting itself, as if it were backlighted. In a masterful touch, Tanner allowed Mary's large figure to dominate the shallow space, catching the viewer in a conflict between fascination with such details as her belt and the halo, and the inclination to follow her gaze into infinity. The viewer's interest is continually drawn back to the face of the Virgin, which does not carry the puzzled and awed expression of Tanner's previous depictions of Mary. In the present picture, painted after the tragedies of World War I, the artist portrayed a mature woman whose demeanor manifests a profound understanding of the message of the annunciatory angel.

Virgin and Child was not mentioned by name in reviews when it was exhibited in New York in 1924. The deliberateness with which Tanner forced the viewer to contend with Mary and her thoughts, rather than observe a biblical scene, went unrecognized by a critic for the *New York Times*, who said: "The many religious titles are religious only in the title and are not human. The artist repeats the same color scheme and veils his picture with a blue haze too difficult to penetrate."[1] The celebrated artist, then over sixty years old, no doubt responded with a regretful shrug to this review, which so completely missed the human content of his work.   DFM

91 VIRGIN AND CHILD

FLIGHT INTO EGYPT

(*The Futile Guard*)

(*Mary and Joseph*)

1923

Oil on canvas

29 × 26″ (73.66 × 66.04 cm)

Signed and dated lower left: *H. O. Tanner/1923*

Estate of Sadie T. M. Alexander

THE SLEEPING DISCIPLES

(*Christ in the Garden of Gethsemane*)

c. 1923

Oil on canvas

28 × 23″ (71.12 × 58.42 cm)

Signed lower left: *H. O. Tanner*

Estate of Sadie T. M. Alexander

Flight into Egypt, which has borne the titles *The Futile Guard* and *Mary and Joseph*, is a late variant of one of Tanner's favorite subjects — the Holy Family's clandestine flight to escape King Herod's assassins (Matt. 2:12–14). Mary rides a donkey, clasping the child, with Joseph on foot behind her, both moving quietly in back of the lantern-carrying guard. *The Sleeping Disciples* (cat. no. 93), another painting very close in date and facture, depicts a traditional biblical image rarely painted by Tanner in which Jesus goes to Gethsemane with his disciples to pray (Matt. 26:36). Tanner portrayed the praying Jesus in the background, with two apostles slouched in sleep against a tree in the right foreground.

In both paintings Tanner returned to compositional ideas that came out of his trip to Morocco in 1912. He reworked *Street in Tangier* (cat. no. 74) for the setting of *Flight into Egypt*, and any number of seated or crouching Moroccan figures in earlier pictures served as prototypes for the sleeping disciples. The lantern motif harks back to *Night* of around 1905 (cat. no. 61), but these lanterns are more than bursts of light in dark compositions; their cast light leads the eye toward and accentuates the meaning of the principal figures. The glow from the lamps allowed the artist to use multiple colors to define these nighttime scenes. Always aware of "the qualities loved by artists" with which he wanted to convey religious content,[1] Tanner used lush paint and brushstrokes in the areas nearest the lanterns, played off against drier, scumbled touches farther from the source of illumination. Geometric elements create visual emphasis; the tree branch on the left of the massive trunk in *The Sleeping Disciples* draws the viewer to the faint figure of Jesus at prayer.

Both paintings were shown in Tanner's solo exhibition of religious subjects at New York's Grand Central Art Galleries in 1924, but neither seems to have attracted special attention from the press, although the sale of *Flight into Egypt* was briefly noted, with an illustration, in *Art News*.[2] The artist's aspirations for his religious paintings were reported by a critic for the *New York Times*:

> "My effort has been not only to put the Biblical incident in the original setting," said Mr. Tanner, "but at the same time to give the human touch which makes the whole world kin and which ever remains the same. While giving truth of detail

92 FLIGHT INTO EGYPT

93 THE SLEEPING DISCIPLES

not to lose sight of more important matters — by this I mean that of color and design should be as carefully thought out as if the subject had only these qualities. To me it seems no handicap to have a subject of nobility worthy of one's best continued effort. There is but one thing more important than these qualities, and that is to try to convey to the public the reverence and elevation these subjects impart to you, which is the primary cause of their choice."[3]

DFM

9 4

STUDY FOR THE HEAD OF THE
KNEELING DISCIPLE

c. 1924
Charcoal on tan laid paper
14 1/8 × 13 1/4" (35.88 × 33.66 cm)
Merton Simpson, New York

9 5

STUDY FOR THE KNEELING
DISCIPLE

c. 1924
Charcoal and vine charcoal on paper
13 9/16 × 9 3/4" (34.45 × 24.77 cm) sheet
Inscribed upper left: 6 [illegible]
National Museum of American Art, Smithsonian Institution,
Washington, D.C., gift of Mr. and Mrs. Norman B. Robbins

9 6

TWO DISCIPLES AT THE TOMB

(*The Kneeling Disciple*)
c. 1924
Oil on board
51 1/2 × 43 1/4" (130.81 × 109.86 cm)
Signed lower left: *H. O. Tanner*
Merton Simpson, New York

Two Disciples at the Tomb revisits the subject of Tanner's famous picture in the Art Institute of Chicago (cat. no. 59), but in a subtler interpretation. Here the youthful John kneels at the entrance to Jesus' tomb and Peter is seen only dimly in the background. John recorded (20:4–6): "So they ran both together: and the other disciple did outrun Peter, and came first to the sepulchre. And he stooping down, and looking in, saw the linen clothes lying; yet went he not in. Then cometh Simon Peter following him, and went into the sepulchre, and seeth the linen clothes lie."

Tanner apparently devoted a great deal of time to this new rendition; three charcoal studies from a model for the kneeling disciple are known. In one of them (cat. no. 95) Tanner worked on the pose of the principal figure in a manner consistent with the study used over two decades earlier for *The Resurrection of Lazarus* (cat. no. 39). In another sheet (cat. no. 94), he more closely observed light effects on the apostle's face. These two drawings show Tanner's accomplished loose handling and a tighter, more finished technique, with an economy of line suggesting posture and facial expression; the quickest lines and more deliberate rubbings are beautiful passages unto themselves. The drawings have sometimes been confused with studies for the Chicago picture in spite of the fact that John's pose is reversed here.[1]

Tanner carried over these studies of pose, expression, and light into the finished painting (cat. no. 96). The large figure of the kneeling John dominates. His posture and the vertical fluted folds of his garment underscore the importance of his figure, which is illuminated by the supernatural light from within the sepulcher. The thickly textured paint, blue-green palette, and striated

94 STUDY FOR THE HEAD OF THE KNEELING DISCIPLE

95 STUDY FOR THE KNEELING DISCIPLE

brushstrokes, which emphasize the canvas surface, are characteristic of Tanner's style during the early 1920s and of his continued experiments with pigments. Also typical is the manner in which color and light define the time of day—in this scene, night, as dawn approaches.

When shown at the Annual American Art Exhibition at the Art Institute of Chicago in 1926, the picture attracted the favorable attention of Karen Fish, a critic for *American Magazine of Art*: "As for Henry O. Tanner's 'Two Disciples at the Tomb,' little relates this remote blue-green scene to the yellow-lighted painting of the same name in the Institute's permanent collection, except the reverence, the mystery, the faith which breathes in all of Mr. Tanner's works."[2]

DFM

96 TWO DISCIPLES AT THE TOMB

97

THE THREE WISE MEN
(The Wise Men)
1925
Oil on canvas
25 × 35″ (63.5 × 88.9 cm)
Signed lower left: *H. O. Tanner*
Peter Michael Frank, Alexandria, Virginia

Fig. 91 James Tissot, *The Journey of the Magi*, c. 1894, oil on canvas, 27 7/8 × 40″, The Minneapolis Institute of Arts, The William Hood Dunwoody Fund.

Tanner showed a painting entitled *The Wise Men* in his first major solo exhibition at the American Art Galleries, New York, in 1908, but it probably was not this picture. A photograph of an unlocated work in the Tanner papers at the Archives of American Art records a painting with the same general composition, but rendered in greater detail with the flat-roofed buildings of a Near Eastern town rising up the hillside on the right. The lost painting seems to be more consistent stylistically with others that can be firmly dated to around 1908. Unless Tanner made the present work as a large composition sketch for the more detailed painting, on the basis of style *The Three Wise Men* (cat. no. 97) would appear to date from the mid-1920s, when Tanner was reworking some of his earlier subjects in a looser technique using a palette dominated by blues and greens.

On May 21, 1925, J. S. Carpenter, the artist's patron and friend who acted informally as his midwestern agent after the war, wrote from Des Moines, ''I feel very sure I can place the 'Wise men' in the near future.''[1] Since Carpenter was president of the Des Moines Association of Fine Arts, and M. H. Cohen, the eventual purchaser of the painting, was a member of the association's board, it seems very likely that *The Three Wise Men* is the version Carpenter was attempting to sell.

The story of the wise men who searched for the newborn Christ is told in the Gospel of Matthew (2:1–12). They were the subject of one of James Tissot's few large-scale paintings of a biblical theme, *The Journey of the Magi*, around 1894 (fig. 91). He meticulously depicted every detail of costume, trappings, physical characteristics of men and beasts, topography, and light. Comparison of Tissot's treatment with the simplification of color and form to the barest essentials in *The Three Wise Men* demonstrates Tanner's preoccupation with the evocative power of biblical stories rather than their literal illustration.

DS

97 THE THREE WISE MEN

9 8

THE DESTRUCTION OF SODOM
AND GOMORRAH

(*The Burning of Sodom and Gomorrah*)
c. 1928
Oil on cardboard panel
20 3/8 × 36" (51.75 × 91.44 cm)
Signed lower right: *H. O. Tanner*
Inscribed on verso: illegible notes on technique
for application of paint
High Museum of Art, Atlanta, J. J. Haverty Collection, 49.32

The Destruction of Sodom and Gomorrah is one of the handful of biblical pictures that Tanner did not cull from the Gospels of the Four Evangelists. He based it on the account in Genesis (19:12–26) of the escape of Lot and his family from the fire and brimstone that destroyed the wicked cities:

> And the men said unto Lot . . . bring them out of this place: . . . the Lord hath sent us to destroy it. . . . Escape for thy life; look not behind thee, neither stay thou in all the plain. . . . The sun was risen upon the earth when Lot entered into Zoar. Then the Lord rained upon Sodom and upon Gomorrah brimstone and fire from the Lord out of heaven; And he overthrew those cities, and all the plain, and all the inhabitants of the cities, and that which grew upon the ground. But his wife looked back from behind him, and she became a pillar of salt.

Tanner played down the figures, who are barely visible in the right foreground. Instead he emphasized the holocaust in arching movements of green, blue, and mauve. These arcs counterpose the predominantly brown diagonals of the terrain, which flows like lava from an erupting volcano. Tanner unified these elements with his blend of tempera and oil, which emphasizes the picture's surface and adds an almost unearthly luminosity to the scene.

In a similar painting made a few years earlier (location unknown), the small figures are clearer, and light comes from the characteristic moon in the background. When the legendary black scholar W. E. B. Du Bois saw this earlier work in 1926 at the Metropolitan Museum of Art in New York, he was highly impressed. He certainly would have had a similar reaction to the Atlanta version of *The Destruction of Sodom and Gomorrah*. Du Bois put forth an interesting idea about the origin of Tanner's vision: "The artist's motive, one ventures to say, has been mainly the delineation of this seething, convoluted mass of smoke. Probably his inspiration came at the sight of some such terrific scene during the war. Nothing in natural events, indeed, could be imagined to typify more fittingly the wrath of God in the biblical story than the aspect of the sky after a great explosion."[1] DFM

98 THE DESTRUCTION OF SODOM AND GOMORRAH

9 9

DISCIPLES HEALING THE SICK
c. 1930
Oil on cardboard
36 × 48″ (91.44 × 121.92 cm)
Clark Atlanta University Collection of
Afro-American Art, Atlanta

Although the Acts of the Apostles describe numerous miraculous healings effected by Christ's disciples, none seems to fit the event depicted in *Disciples Healing the Sick*. Its narrative is difficult to interpret: two elderly men, a boy, and a kneeling woman, her arms extended, attend a youthful person lying on a stretcher. They are placed in the shadow of a massive tree, possibly the determining landmark of the locale, the bark of which is rendered with such rugged texture and whose limbs extend across the surface of the picture in such extravagant linear patterns that it dominates the composition. Between this and another tree stand a group of hooded figures who might be bearded men; separated from them, to the far right, are a bare-headed figure in white and a woman. At the left, set off from the others by branches and foliage, are two walking figures silhouetted against the sunlit landscape. Their attitude suggests a guide leading a blind follower, and their movement counterposes the stillness of the other inhabitants of the scene.

Neither *Disciples Healing the Sick* nor any other possibly related title appears in the exhibition records of the late 1920s or 1930s, and the painting remained in Tanner's studio until it was sold by the artist's son at Grand Central Art Galleries. Yet Tanner obviously considered the painting important: it is the largest work he painted after the second version of *Two Disciples at the Tomb* (cat. no. 96), its subject is new and not a reinterpretation of a theme he had treated before, and it contains more figures than Tanner had incorporated in a composition since *The Wise and Foolish Virgins* of 1906–1907. The ambition of this picture suggests that Tanner began it during a period of optimism and renewed strength in the late 1920s and early 1930s when he felt that interest in his art would endure. Perhaps, too, the subject was relevant at the time to Tanner's own recovery from illness and his son's regained health and growing prosperity in business.

Precise dating of *Disciples Healing the Sick* is difficult because it has no exhibition history, and its technique relates to only one other painting, the relatively large-scale *Good Shepherd* in the National Museum of American Art, which is also undated (cat. no. 102). The scumbled texture of the trunk and branches of the foreground tree recalls the surface treatment of the 1924 *Two Disciples at the Tomb*, but other segments of the panel are built up in a much more complicated and meticulous way—a technique Tanner used in small areas of other late paintings, such as the foreground of *Flight into Egypt* (cat. no. 103), completed no later than 1935. These meager clues support the dating of *Disciples Healing the Sick* to around 1930.

In a remarkably fresh and independent direction for Tanner, the painting is composed of layers of colors familiar from his work in the 1920s, but

intricately overlaid with brush and palette knife to achieve a nearly mono-chromatic tonality. The compellingly tactile surface of the painting calls attention to its flatness, and the cool shadow beneath the trees counter-balances the bright, hilly landscape beyond, recalling light effects Tanner studied in the Near East twenty years before, and creates a strong spatial tension in the work.

Although size is not the only gauge of the significance of a work in every artist's mind, for someone like Tanner, who for many years based his notion of success on the notice his paintings received in the annual Salon, size and the importance of the artistic effort were closely related. His climactic Salon success, *The Wise and Foolish Virgins*, was the largest canvas he ever attempted. By this standard, *Disciples Healing the Sick* was a major undertaking and, as a completely realized work of art, the most distinctive and conse-quential of Tanner's late career. DS

1 0 0

THE LOST SHEEP

(*The Good Shepherd*)
c. 1930
Oil and tempera on paperboard
10 5/8 × 8 1/8" (26.99 × 20.64 cm)
Inscribed on verso: illegible notes on technique
for application of paint
The Menil Collection, Houston

1 0 1

THE GOOD SHEPHERD IN THE
ATLAS MOUNTAINS

(*The Good Shepherd*)
c. 1936
Oil and tempera on board
9 1/4 × 13" (23.5 × 33.02 cm)
Inscribed on verso: *2 coats blanc d'Espagne/1 of colle, rather*
thick/color in tempera/Varnished in glue 10 per cent solu-
tion/with lanoline/2 weeks after washed color with alcohol.
Merton Simpson, New York

1 0 2

THE GOOD SHEPHERD (ATLAS
MOUNTAINS, MOROCCO)

c. 1936
Oil on fiberboard
29 7/8 × 36" (75.88 × 91.44 cm)
Signed lower right: *H. O. Tanner*
Signed and inscribed on verso: *H. O. Tanner, Etaples, Paris,*
43 Rue de Fleurus, 6
National Museum of American Art, Smithsonian Institution,
Washington, D.C., gift of Mr. and Mrs. Norman B. Robbins

Fig. 92 Henry O. Tanner, *The Good
Shepherd*, 1922, oil on burlap, 36 1/4 ×
28 3/4", Hampton University Museum,
Virginia.

These three interpretations of the good shepherd theme delineate the manner
in which Tanner could create great variety within the same subject. In *The
Lost Sheep* (cat. no. 100), the shepherd nestles the animal on his shoulder, in
keeping with the gospel parable about the delight of finding a stray sheep
(Matt. 18:12–13). The small picture of *The Good Shepherd in the Atlas Mountains* (cat. no. 101) depicts an isolated herder without his flock in the rugged
Atlas Mountains of Morocco. Perhaps the most subtle rendition of the parable
is the large painting of the shepherd with his flock (cat. no. 102), a scene set in
the same Moroccan mountains, in which a lamb strays from the group in the
right foreground.

In the Menil picture, in which the shepherd clings tenderly to the lamb,
the figure stands out in the craggy landscape as if to underscore the herder's
care and kindness. A well-defined celestial body, a source of heavenly light,
looms in the background. In the Simpson painting, the Atlas Mountains loom
above and dominate the lonely shepherd, who is precariously posed at the edge
of a seemingly bottomless ravine. The shepherd in the National Museum's
picture, unaware of his straying sheep, is equally minuscule in relation to his
vast surroundings. Tanner's approach to the theme of the good shepherd was
explained by the black artist Romare Bearden: "In his religious painting,
especially the last works, Tanner tells us much of what he thinks about the
world and of man's place in it. This kind of self-exploration when integrated by
a personality of real proportion can be both vital and transcendent."[1]

100 THE LOST SHEEP

The image of the shepherd in these three pictures evolved stylistically out of the 1922 *Good Shepherd* in the collection of Hampton University (fig. 92). The figure wears a clearly defined burnoose, or North African headdress, and carries a lamb, characteristics that are particularly noticeable in the Menil painting.

The compositions of the paintings deal with the same basic elements: landscape on the left, figure on the right, and contrasts of diagonal, horizontal, and vertical lines and shapes. These components had long enhanced visual movement in Tanner's works, but they are now superseded by an extremely thick buildup of paint and almost chiseled brushstrokes. After years of experimentation Tanner had finally found a proper binder for an oil and tempera mixture, creating such highly raised surfaces that they call to mind sculpture in low relief.

These works are especially difficult to date. Tanner pointed out time and again in his correspondence of the 1930s that he had several works underway at once, and it is often impossible to determine when a picture was completed. The Menil *Lost Sheep* and *Fishermen Returning at Night* (see fig. 72) seem to

Fig. 93 Henry O. Tanner, *The Good Shepherd*, c. 1930, oil and tempera on board, 29 1/4 × 36″, Merton Simpson, New York.

101 THE GOOD SHEPHERD IN THE ATLAS MOUNTAINS

be among his first successes with the new binder in 1930; another, larger *Good Shepherd* (closely related to the Menil picture) in the Simpson collection (fig. 93) might be an unresolved use of the technique. The brushstrokes of the two Atlas Mountain scenes are not so pronounced; perhaps the artist did not apply the binder. An inscription on the verso of the National Museum of American Art *Good Shepherd* gives Tanner's address as 43 rue de Fleurus, where he moved permanently in 1934, circumstantially supports a mid-1930s date. We know that during the last years of his life Tanner returned to his memories of the Moroccan landscape. In June of 1936 he wrote to a cousin in Chicago: "You should enjoy a trip to the Orient [Far East] very much I am sure. I have never been there but I enjoyed my stay in North Africa, Egypt and Palestine very much and I am sure that if you would add these you would be pleased."[2]

Tanner showed an unidentified *Good Shepherd* in 1933 in Paris at the Simonson Galleries, where it seems not to have attracted the attention of contemporary critics. His exhibition of this subject toward the end of his life underscores his respect for the messages he believed to be inherent in it. His son wrote: "Though my father felt that the presence of God stretches out through the cosmos and his love extends to other worlds than our own, he also felt that man has an active role to play and should not submit passively to his fate. Christ watches over his flock ('The Good Shepherd' was a favorite subject of his)."[3]   DFM

102 THE GOOD SHEPHERD (ATLAS MOUNTAINS, MOROCCO)

103

FLIGHT INTO EGYPT
by 1935
Oil on panel
24 × 28" (60.96 × 71.12 cm)
Signed lower left: *H O. Tanner*
Private collection

In the late 1920s and early 1930s Tanner's depression over the death of his wife, worry about his son, who had suffered a mental breakdown, and his own ill health curtailed his artistic production, and a worsening international economy and the declining popularity of his painting style reduced opportunities for him to exhibit. During these years he dated his work even less frequently than he had previously, and in many ways, a chronology for Tanner's last decade is as difficult to establish as for his early career, before his first trip to France. The correspondence surrounding this *Flight into Egypt* (cat. no. 103) is especially useful for the light it sheds on the artist in 1935.

On January 12 of that year, Maudelle Brown Bousfield wrote to Tanner from her home in Chicago, introducing herself as the daughter of his cousin, Menie Tanner Brown, who was the child of George Tanner, a brother of Bishop Tanner. As Mrs. Bousfield explained with justifiable pride in a subsequent letter, she was the principal of the Stephen A. Douglas school, "one of the largest schools in Chicago, and the first and only colored principal in the system, a position obtained through competition. I have been in the principality seven years now."[1] Inspired by a visit to Tanner's niece in Philadelphia, Sadie T. M. Alexander, who owned a number of his works, and by her admiration for *Two Disciples at the Tomb* (cat. no. 59) in the Art Institute of Chicago, Mrs. Bousfield inquired about the possibility of buying one of the artist's paintings. Tanner promptly replied that he had two small works available, *Hiding of Moses* and *Flight into Egypt*, and that he would charge $200 for either of them — a reduction of his usual price of $350 to $400 for a painting of this size — due to hard times and his wish that he "should like some of my family to have some of my works."[2] *Flight into Egypt* was selected, and on April 9, Mrs. Bousfield informed Tanner that she was "thrilled" with the painting, which had arrived the day before.[3]

This correspondence does not provide an exact date for *Flight into Egypt*, but it does place it in time, and the style of the work suggests that it was painted in the late 1920s or early 1930s. As such, it is the last datable treatment by Tanner of one of his favorite themes, although in a letter of April 14, 1936, a little more than a year before his death, the artist announced to the director of the Grand Central Art Galleries that he had three pictures on hand — finished versions of works called *The Good Shepherd* and *Flight into Egypt*, and a half-finished *Return from the Crucifixion*.[4]

A comparison of this picture with the earliest version of the theme, inscribed "Jerusalem, 1899" (cat. no. 49), indicates the changes of artistic intent in Tanner's approach to the subject over the approximately thirty-five years that separate the two. Considering the numerous and varied depictions of the theme that Tanner made in the interim, the basic conception of the

103 FLIGHT INTO EGYPT

scene is remarkably similar. In both pictures the figures are placed to the right and move toward the left, Mary rides one donkey while Joseph walks at her side leading a second. The vestige of hilly terrain with ruins and low walls in the background of the later work recalls Tanner's impressions of his first trips to the Holy Land.

Instead of a continuous, deep, receding space, however, in the Bousfield picture, Tanner limited the field to three clearly defined planes. The realistically depicted tree on the right in the earlier work is replaced by the attenuated abstract forms that represent trees in many paintings of his last decade. Tanner here combined two light sources, a technique he employed extensively in the 1920s—a half-visible full moon, and a hidden lantern carried by Joseph which illuminates and silhouettes the figures. Neither light source controls the space or the tonality of the work as does the moonlight in the 1899 painting, which washes over the scene and unifies the range of its colors.

But most noticeable is the difference between the technique of the two works. The earlier *Flight into Egypt* is traditionally painted, with colors chosen and brushstrokes placed to create an effect of deep space and solid form as revealed in light. In the later version, space, solidity, and light are indicated, but subordinated to the rich colors and thickly textured surfaces of discrete areas. A thick glaze covers the entire surface of the painting, announcing the work as a highly finished object admirable in itself, quite apart from its illusionistic or narrative aspects.

Tanner experimented with painting materials and techniques to achieve the thick, smooth, shiny and clear surface varnish seen on this late *Flight into Egypt*. Rarely is it found in such an excellent state of preservation: in some cases the varnish has darkened or deteriorated due to Tanner's variations in formula or application; in others it has been erroneously removed during restoration or covered over with another coat of varnish. Concerned about the grime produced by the coal-burning furnaces used in Chicago, Mrs. Bousfield wrote to Tanner about a year after the painting arrived, asking if she should wash it with soap and water and cover it with glass to preserve its appearance.[5] Tanner cautioned against the soap, but suggested she wash it quickly and lightly with water, dry it immediately, and glaze it to protect it from a harmful atmosphere.[6] According to family history, this is the only treatment the painting has ever received.   DS

104

STUDY FOR MARY

1933

Pencil and conte crayon on paper

15 1/16 × 14 3/16" (38.26 × 36.04 cm)

Inscribed, signed, and dated lower left: *Study for/Return from the Crucifixion/H. O. Tanner/1933*

National Museum of American Art, Smithsonian Institution, Washington, D.C., gift of Mr. and Mrs. Norman B. Robbins

105

RETURN FROM THE CRUCIFIXION

1936

Oil and tempera on plywood

20 × 23 1/2" (50.8 × 59.69 cm)

Signed and dated lower right: *H. O. Tanner/1936*

Permanent collection, Howard University Gallery of Art, Washington, D.C.

Tanner's letters during the 1930s are filled with signs of ample confidence in his artistic abilities during his final years. He wrote to his niece Sadie Alexander on December 27, 1936: "Also I am getting older but I believe and friends believe my work is still up to its average — and I hope beyond."[1] The handsome drawing (cat. no. 104) for the head of Mary, identified by the inscription as a study for *Return from the Crucifixion*, is proof of his continued prowess as a draughtsman. The flowing lines of the model's headdress and arm are things of beauty in themselves. The darks and lights achieved with the edge of the crayon, using a minimum of rubbing, provide details that animate the composition, giving it a portraitlike quality. The face is one of the most expressive of Tanner's production. The mature artist, surely as a result of tragedies in his own life as well as his response to the devastation of war, truly understood sadness and presented it here almost as if it were palpable.

The sheet seems also to have served as a study for a painting called *Return from the Cross* in the Simpson collection (fig. 94), in which John accompanies Mary in compliance with the edict of Jesus (John 19:26–27): "When Jesus therefore saw his mother, and the disciple standing by, whom he loved, he saith unto his mother, Woman, behold thy son! Then saith he to the disciple, Behold thy mother! And from that hour that disciple took her unto his own home."

Tanner rendered the theme again a few years later in *Return from the Crucifixion* (cat. no. 105). John and Mary are in the foreground, followed by other mourners; three empty crosses stand on Golgotha in the background. Tanner's basic conception of the subject goes back to his 1904 *Return of the Holy Women* (cat. no. 56); Mary wears the same headdress.

Although the idea for the present *Return from the Crucifixion* reflects its antecedent (and its landscape setting recalls *A View in Palestine*, cat. no. 46), Tanner once again found a fresh interpretation for a revisited subject. The horizontal format is defied by a diagonal upward thrust of the foreground, which is interrupted by the verticality of the mourners, but taken up again behind them, leading to the three crosses in the right background. The cross on the far right bends away from the picture, but the dash of bright light above it — perhaps a subtle allegory for the place occupied by the repentant criminal crucified alongside Jesus (Luke 23:39–43) — leads the eye back to the left and on to the horizon. A dark brown diagonal stroke just below the horizon draws

Fig. 94 Henry O. Tanner, *Return from the Cross*, c. 1930, oil and tempera on canvas mounted on Masonite, 10 1/8 × 16", Merton Simpson, New York.

104 STUDY FOR MARY

the focus back to Mary and John. The blend of oil and tempera gives an overall luminosity to the picture, even in its shadows.

The aged artist, as always concerned with profound issues of human freedom, was undoubtedly expressing his hopes and fears for humankind through this picture. He wrote from Paris to his niece and her husband, Sadie and Raymond Pace Alexander, on November 16, 1933: "Things are very disturbed over here. No one knows what may come or what Hitler may decide to do, as no one dares to oppose him in Germany. Those who do not believe in his plans seem thoroughly cowed."[2]

Return from the Crucifixion, Tanner's last signed and dated work, was purchased through public subscription by Howard University in March of 1937, just two months before the artist's death. It was altogether fitting that Tanner should be so honored and that his last work should be acquired by an African-American institution on whose board his father had served.

DFM

105 RETURN FROM THE CRUCIFIXION

The following abbreviations are used throughout the notes for frequently cited books, articles, newspapers, and archives.

AN: Archives Nationales, Paris

AP: Alexander Papers, FF32, Archives, University of Pennsylvania, Philadelphia.

B. T. Tanner 1894: Tanner, Benjamin T. *Theological Lectures*. Nashville, 1894.

Cole 1900: Cole, Helen. "Henry O. Tanner, Painter." *Brush and Pencil*, vol. 6, no. 3 (June 1900), pp. 97–107.

CR: *Christian Recorder*

DET: *Daily Evening Telegraph*, Philadelphia

Harlan 1977: Harlan, L. R., ed. *The Booker T. Washington Papers*. Vols. 1–14. Urbana, Ill., 1972–89.

Hartigan 1985: Hartigan, Lynda Roscoe. *Sharing Traditions: Five Black Artists in Nineteenth-Century America*. Washington, D.C., 1985.

IS: *International Studio*

MacChesney 1913: MacChesney, Clara T. "A Poet-Painter of Palestine." *International Studio*, vol. 50, no. 197 (July 1913), pp. 11–15.

Mathews 1969: Mathews, Marcia M. *Henry Ossawa Tanner, American Artist*. Chicago, 1969.

Milner 1988: Milner, John. *The Studios of Paris: The Capital of Art in the late Nineteenth Century*. New Haven, 1988.

NYT: *New York Times*

PAFA: Archives, Pennsylvania Academy of the Fine Arts, Philadelphia.

Scarborough 1902: Scarborough, W. S. "Henry Ossian [sic] Tanner." *Southern Workman*, vol. 31, no. 12 (Dec. 1902), pp. 661–70.

Simmons 1887: Simmons, William J. *Men of Mark: Eminent, Progressive and Rising*. Cleveland, 1887; reprint, New York, 1968.

Tanner 1909: Tanner, Henry O. "The Story of an Artist's Life, Parts I and II." *The World's Work*, vol. 18, nos. 2 and 3 (June and July 1909), pp. 11661–66, 11769–75.

TCF: Tanner clipping file, Archives of American Art, Smithsonian Institution

TP: Tanner papers, Archives of American Art, Smithsonian Institution

Woods 1987: Woods, Naurice Frank, Jr. "The Life and Work of Henry O. Tanner." Ph.D. diss., Columbia Pacific University, 1987.

Woods 1989: Woods, Naurice Frank, Jr. "The Hidden Origins of Henry O. Tanner's African-American Genre Paintings." Unpublished ms., 1989.

PAGES 11–21

Race, Public Reception, and Critical Response in Tanner's Career

1. F. J. Campbell, "Henry O. Tanner's Biblical Pictures," *Fine Arts Journal*, vol. 25, no. 3 (March 1911), p. 166.
2. L. M. Igoe, *250 Years of Afro-American Art: An Annotated Bibliography* (New York, 1981).
3. "Afro-American Painter Who Has Been Famous in Paris," *Current Literature*, vol. 45 (Oct. 1908), p. 405.
4. B. T. Tanner, *The Negro's Origins and Is the Negro Cursed* (Philadelphia, 1869), p. 22.
5. P. Revell, *Paul Laurence Dunbar* (Boston, 1979), p. 17.
6. Simmons 1887.
7. Harlan, vol. 1, p. 550.
8. Booker T. Washington, *Up from Slavery* (1901; reprint, New York, 1963), p. 202.
9. Quoted in Harlan, vol. 6, pp. 177–78.
10. "Afro-American Painter," p. 406.
11. Ibid.
12. For an understanding of such assumptions see N. J. Payne, "Hidden Messages in the Pursuit of Equality," *Academe: Bulletin of the American Association of University Professors*, vol. 75, no. 5 (Sept.–Oct. 1989), pp. 19–22.
13. "Tanner Exhibits Paintings," *NYT*, Jan. 29, 1924, p. 9.
14. Quoted in Mathews 1969, pp. 142–43. The present writer has not had access to the original document, but one must wonder if the percentages of racial blood mentioned were reversed in the editorial process.
15. Quoted in Mathews 1969, pp. 196–97.
16. Smith to Schomburg, May 17, 1936, Albert Smith papers, Schomburg Center for Research in Black Culture, New York Public Library.
17. Cedric Dover, *American Negro Art* (Greenwich, Conn., 1960), p. 29.
18. Tanner to Sadie Alexander, May 23, 1936, AP.
19. Tanner to Sadie Alexander, Jan. 22, 1937, AP.
20. Francis B. Shaefer, *Brush and Pencil*, vol. 5, no. 3 (Dec. 1899), p. 136.
21. Vance Thompson, "American Artists in Paris," *Cosmopolitan*, vol. 29 (May 1900), p. 20.
22. Arthur Hoeber, *Commercial Advertiser*, Jan. 14, 1901, TCF.
23. J. W. Cromwell, *The Negro in American History* (Washington, D.C., 1914), pp. 219–27.
24. R. E. Jackman, *American Arts* (Chicago, 1928), pp. 208–11.
25. A. Locke, *The Negro in Art* (Washington, D.C., 1940), pp. 135–36.
26. James A. Porter, *Modern Negro Art* (New York, 1943), pp. 64–70.
27. A. Locke, "Henry Ossawa Tanner, 1859–1937," in *Memorial Exhibition of Paintings by Henry O. Tanner* (Philadelphia, 1945), n.p.
28. See, for example, H. Bhalla and E. B. Gaither, *Henry O. Tanner: An Afro-American Romantic Realist (1859–1937)* (Atlanta, 1969), n.p.
29. M. M. James, "Henry O. Tanner," *Negro History Bulletin*, Feb. 1957, p. 116.
30. Walter A. Simon, "Henry O. Tanner—A Study of the Development of an American Negro Artist: 1859–1937" (Ph.D. diss., New York University, 1960).
31. Woods 1987.
32. For a review of Mathews's book, see Robert Pincus-Witten, "Marcia M. Mathews, Henry Ossawa Tanner, American Artist," *Art Bulletin*, vol. 53, no. 3 (Sept. 1970), p. 337.
33. B. Novak, *American Painting of the Nineteenth Century: Realism, Idealism, and the American Experience* (New York, 1969).
34. Ibid., p. 261.
35. Lois M. Fink, *American Art at the Nineteenth-Century Salons* (Cambridge, Eng., 1990), pp. 173–75.
36. *Memorial Exhibition of Paintings by Henry O. Tanner* (Philadelphia, 1945).
37. Spelman College, *Henry O. Tanner, An Afro-American Romantic Realist (1859–1937)* (Atlanta, 1969).
38. The Hyde Collection, *The Art of Henry Ossawa Tanner (1859–1937) from the Collection of The Museum of African Art/Frederick Douglass Institute*, Washington, D.C. (Glens Falls, N.Y., 1972).
39. Frederick Douglass Institute and National Collection of Fine Arts, *The Art of Henry O. Tanner (1859–1937)* (Washington, D.C., 1969).
40. Patricia Hills, *Turn of the Century America: Paintings, Graphics, Photographs, 1890–1910* (New York, 1977).
41. J. Gray Sweeney, *Themes in American Painting* (Grand Rapids, Mich., 1977).
42. Charles C. Eldridge, *American Imagination and Symbolist Paintings* (New York, 1979).
43. Cedar Rapids Arts Center, *Three Nineteenth-Century Afro-American Artists: Joshua Johnston (c. 1765–1830), Robert S. Duncanson (1821–1872) and Henry O. Tanner (1859–1937)* (Cedar Rapids, Iowa, 1980).
44. David Sellin and James K. Ballinger, *Americans in Brittany and Normandy 1860–1910* (Phoenix, 1982).
45. *Le Petit Journal des Grandes Expositions: La Peinture Américaine des Collections du Louvre* (Paris, 1984).
46. Hartigan 1985.
47. T. E. Stebbins, Jr., et al., *A New World: Masterpieces of American Painting 1760–1910* (Boston, 1983).

48. MacChesney 1913, pp. 11–15.
49. M. A. Stevens, ed., *The Orientalists: Delacroix to Matisse: The Allure of North Africa and the Near East* (Washington, D.C., 1984).
50. *The Quest for Unity: American Art Between World's Fairs 1876–1893* (Detroit, 1983).
51. Hartigan 1985, p. 69.
52. For the history of France's museum for living artists, see G. Lacambre, *Le Musée du Luxembourg en 1874* (Paris, 1974), pp. 7–11.
53. Curtis authored, among other titles, *Auguste Raffet* (New York, 1903) and *Bellows Lithographs* (New York, 1928).
54. Quoted in Woods 1987, p. 125.
55. W. E. B. Du Bois, "Tanner," *Crisis*, vol. 27, no. 7 (May 1924), p. 12.
56. Ibid. Both Du Bois and Tanner had forgotten the patronage of Bishop Daniel A. Payne.
57. Ibid.
58. May 20, 1897, "M. Tanguy," F21 2151, AN.
59. The original customs invoices for these transactions are in the possession of Dr. Walter O. Evans, Detroit.
60. These exchange rates are based on contemporary issues of the *World Almanac*.
61. Tanner to Coates, Feb. 10, 1909, PAFA.
62. Mathews 1969, p. 178.
63. Ibid., p. 202.
64. Quoted in Mathews, pp. 231–32.
65. L. Goodrich, *Thomas Eakins*, vol. 2 (Washington, D.C., 1982), p. 160.
66. Tanner to Sadie Alexander, June 19, 1932, AP.
67. Goodrich, *Thomas Eakins*, p. 270.
68. Ibid.
69. As in the case of many artists the question of money was one of the least glamorous sides of Tanner's personality and career, and, in spite of certain successes, he often sounded plaintive in this regard. The artist's continuous concern for money seems to have been somewhat of a source of embarrassment for Dr. Booker T. Washington and strained Tanner's friendship with Harrison S. Morris (see Harlan, vol. 7, pp. 497 and 517; March 4, 1904, MLB; March 6, 1904, GOF; and March 8, 1904, MLB, PAFA). In later years, he complained about the patronage of African-Americans in general and the city of Philadelphia in particular (AP, passim).
70. Tanner 1909, p. 11772.
71. Mathews 1969, p. 123.
72. Ibid., p. 181.
73. Florence L. Bentley, "Henry O. Tanner," *Voice of the Negro*, vol. 3, no. 11 (Nov. 1906), p. 480.
74. Minister of Foreign Affairs to Minister of Fine Arts, Feb. 20, 1922, "M. Tanner," F21 4342, AN.

75. *The Remarkable Morgan State Collection* (Baltimore, n.d.), n.p.
76. J. R. Mellow, *Charmed Circle: Gertrude Stein and Company* (New York, 1974), p. 8.
77. Lois M. Fink, "Elizabeth Nourse: Painting the Motif of Humanity," in *Elizabeth Nourse, 1859–1938, A Salon Career*, ed. Mary Alice Heeken Burke (Washington, D.C., 1983), passim.
78. P. Beecher, *A Pastoral Legacy: Paintings and Drawings by the American Artists Ridgway Knight and Aston Knight* (Ithaca, N.Y., 1989).
79. Scarborough 1902, p. 664. ("A mon élève Tanner son maître et ami, toujours confiant dans le succès de son fini.")
80. Benjamin-Constant to Tanner, Jan. 21, 1894, AP.
81. Morris to Tanner, April 16, 1897, MLB, PAFA.
82. Morris to Tanner, May 16, 1898, MLB, PAFA.
83. Morris to Tanner, June 13, 1898, MLB, PAFA.
84. Quoted in Mathews 1969, p. 216.
85. Quoted in Mathews 1969, pp. 213–14.
86. Coates to Tanner, Oct. 24, 1912, MLB, PAFA.
87. Clara T. MacChesney, "American Artists in Paris," *IS*, vol. 54 (Nov. 1914), p. 27.
88. Hale Woodruff, "My Meeting with Henry O. Tanner," *Crisis*, vol. 77 (Jan. 1970), pp. 8–9.
89. Ibid., p. 7.
90. Quoted in Mathews 1969, pp. 251–52.

PAGES 23–33

The Tanner Family:

A Grandniece's Chronicle

1. "Put Him Out," *Pittsburgh Gazette*, March 18, 1859, p. 1.
2. Ibid.
3. Eighteenth- and nineteenth-century census records housed in the Carnegie Library, Pittsburgh, contain references to the Tanner family; more particular information on the Tanner family may be found in Rollow Turner, *Black Pittsburgh: A Census Compilation, 1790–1840*, unpublished manuscript, University of Pittsburgh.
4. Carter G. Woodson, *The Negro History Bulletin* (April 1947), p. 147, and Rayford W. Logan and Michael R. Winston, *The Dictionary of American Negro Biography* (New York, 1982), p. 577.
5. Mathews 1969, p. 6.
6. The story of Sarah Miller's slave origins, told to me by my mother, is one I have known since childhood. My mother related this story again in 1975 at the

200th Anniversary of the Pennsylvania Abolitionists Society held at the Historical Society of Pennsylvania. Marcia Mathews, whose book *Henry Ossawa Tanner* was published in 1969, talked only briefly with my mother and never on this issue. Mathews gained much of her information from Henry Tanner's son, Jesse, who had lived his entire life in Europe, coming to America only for a short time as a boy. He had a skewed view of America and particularly of race relations in this country. Certainly the story as told by Mathews is more comforting than the one told by my mother, which shows how slavery tore at the fabric of the black family.
7. Personal papers of the author.
8. W. E. B. Du Bois, *The Souls of Black Folk* (Chicago, 1931), p. 197.
9. B. T. Tanner papers, Manuscript Division, Library of Congress. Benjamin Tucker Tanner kept daybooks in which he recorded his feelings and reflections on a number of subjects. The daybooks were given to the Library of Congress by my grandmother.
10. Ibid.
11. Ibid.
12. Ibid.
13. In the neighborhood of Third and Pine, in which the Tanners first lived, was the studio of the artist Robert M. Douglass, Jr., who was considered one of the early "Negro Pioneers." Henry Tanner wrote about Douglass in a letter to Professor James A. Porter, the art historian who created the Department of Art at Howard University: "I used to pass and always stopped to look at his pictures in the window. I must have been very young. . . . I believe that Robert Douglass's subjects were highly classical and somewhat in the style of Benjamin West." (Dr. Dorothy Porter Wesley, Washington, D.C.)
14. *CR*, c. 1874–75.
15. Henry McNeal Turner was an eloquent but often vituperative orator and writer who advocated that black Americans return to Africa because he believed they had no future in America. Turner's advocacy began in 1874 and continued for almost ten years, during which time he was named a bishop of the A.M.E. Church in Georgia. Benjamin Tanner used his position as editor of the *Christian Recorder* to denounce Turner during much of 1874 and 1875. In 1883, Turner used the pages of the *Christian Recorder* to criticize Tanner's position.
16. Dr. Carter G. Woodson, the founder of the Association for the Study of Negro Life and History, was a good and close friend of my parents. In fact, the Philadelphia Chapter of ASNLH was founded in our home at 1708 West Jefferson

Street in November 1929. The phrase which I attributed to Dr. Woodson was told to me by my parents.

17. Letter from Sadie T. M. Alexander to Mrs. Howard Thurman, Oct. 24, 1958. Personal papers of the author.

18. Oct. 17, 1882, personal papers of the author.

19. *CR*, vol. 19, no. 38 (Oct. 13, 1881), p. 1.

20. Simmons 1887, p. 987.

21. *CR*, vol. 24, no. 23 (June 24, 1886), p. 1.

22. Harlan, vol. 3, p. 137.

23. Ibid.

24. Louis R. Harlan, Booker T. Washington's biographer, referred to Dr. Cornelius Nathaniel Dorsette as Washington's "close friend and confidant." Washington, in his papers located in the Library of Congress, calls Dr. Dorsette, "perhaps the most successful colored physician in the Gulf States."

25. Harlan, vol. 3, p. 166.

26. Archives and Special Collections on Women in Medicine, Medical College of Pennsylvania, Philadelphia.

27. A white woman, Annie M. Longshore, failed the medical boards but was admitted to practice medicine in Alabama before Dr. Dillon.

28. Private papers of the author.

29. Private papers of the author.

30. Quoted in Mathews 1969, p. 97.

31. Quoted in Mathews 1969, pp. 251–52.

32. Mathews 1969, pp. xii–xiii.

33. Quoted in Mathews 1969, p. xiii.

PAGES 56–85

Student Years and Early Career

1873–1890

1. Tanner 1909, p. 11662.

2. Ibid.

3. Darrel Sewell, *Thomas Eakins: Artist of Philadelphia* (Philadelphia, 1982), p. x.

4. Joseph Pennell, *The Adventures of an Illustrator: Mostly in Following His Authors in America and Europe* (Boston, 1925), pp. 10, 26, 29–30.

5. L. F. Orr, "Walter Gay 1856–1937," in *The Preston Morton Collection of American Art*, ed. K. H. Mead (Santa Barbara, Calif., 1981), p. 176.

6. Tanner 1909, p. 11662.

7. Ibid.

8. Ibid.

9. Mathews 1969, chap. 1, passim.

10. Tanner 1909, p. 11663.

11. Ibid.

12. W. E. B. Du Bois, *The Philadelphia Negro*, p. 174. Some twenty years later a family of four adults and two children could eat for one week for $2.16, slightly more than one lesson with Mr. Williams.

13. Tanner 1909, p. 11663.

14. M. Teski, R. Helsabeck, F. Smith, and C. Yeager, *A City Revitalized* (Lanham, Md., 1983), pp. 66–67.

15. Tanner 1909, p. 11663.

16. Ibid., p. 11664.

17. Ibid.

18. Tanner, "Compulsory Education and Valedictory Address," *CR*, vol. 15, no. 28 (July 12, 1877), p. 2.

19. Tanner 1909, p. 11664.

20. Ibid.

21. B. T. Tanner, *Hints to Ministers* (Philadelphia, 1902), p. 10.

22. G. Collins, *The Brighton Story: Being the History of Paul Smiths, Gabriels, and Rainbow Lake* (Lakemont, N.Y., 1977), pp. 1, 62, 90, 121–32.

23. W. E. B. Du Bois, *John Brown* (1909; reprint, New York, 1962), p. 110.

24. For a discussion of the famous abolitionist's time in the Adirondack region, although one tinged by racism, see R. P. Warren, *John Brown: The Making of a Martyr* (New York, 1929), pp. 57–86.

25. B. Quarles, *Blacks on John Brown* (Urbana, Ill., 1972), pp. 23–24.

26. Tait's influence on Tanner is evident in comparison of works such as Tait's *Maternal Solicitude* (1873, Cleveland Museum of Art) and Tanner's *Ewe with Dead Lamb and Crows* (Rae Alexander-Minter). For Tait, see W. H. Cadbury and H. F. Marsh, *Arthur Fitzwilliam Tait: Artist in the Adirondacks* (Newark, Del., 1986), pp. 40–97. See also "C. A. Wardner, 'Sunset on Adirondack Trails,'" Ms., Microfilm 4.31, Adirondack Museum, Blue Mountain Lake, New York. (I am grateful to Craig A. Gilborn and Jerold Pepper of The Adirondack Museum for providing this information.)

27. Tanner 1909, p. 11664.

28. Ibid.

29. Ibid., p. 11663.

30. W. C. Brownell, "The Art Schools of Philadelphia," *Scribner's Monthly*, vol. 28 (1879), pp. 737–50.

31. PAFA.

32. Rogers to Corliss, Sept. 30, 1878, PAFA.

33. Pennell, *The Adventures of an Illustrator*, p. 53.

34. Ibid., pp. 53–54.

35. Ibid., p. 54.

36. For a discussion of the master as teacher, see L. Goodrich, *Thomas Eakins*, vol. 1 (Cambridge, Mass., 1982), pp. 172–89.

37. Pennell, *The Adventures of an Illustrator*, p. 50.

38. Ibid., pp. 49–50.

39. Tanner 1909, p. 11665.

40. "The 'Century's' American Artists Series: Henry O. Tanner," *Century Magazine*, n.s. 37 (Nov. 1899–April 1900), p. 962. A brief biography of the black artist, which appeared in the 1899–1900 volume of *Century Magazine*, went so far as to state: "He studied at the Pennsylvania Academy of Fine Arts in Philadelphia, mainly under the late Thomas Hovenden," although Academy records show that Hovenden did not begin to teach there until the fall of 1886.

41. Scarborough 1902, p. 662.

42. J. Fauset, "Henry Ossawa Tanner," *Crisis*, vol. 27 (April 1924), p. 258.

43. *CR*, vol. 18, no. 18 (April 29, 1880), p. 2.

44. *CR*, vol. 19, no. 47 (Nov. 24, 1881), p. 3.

45. For an indication of his views on race, see Pennell, *The Adventures of an Illustrator*, pp. 2, 23, 54.

46. Ibid., p. 54.

47. Tanner 1909, pp. 11664–65.

48. *CR*, vol. 20, no. 13 (March 30, 1882), p. 2.

49. Tanner 1909, p. 11665.

50. *CR*, vol. 22, no. 12 (March 20, 1884), p. 2, quoting from the *Philadelphia Press*.

51. Ibid.

52. Ibid.

53. Tanner 1909, p. 11663.

54. Goodrich, *Thomas Eakins*, vol. 2, pp. 11–12.

55. Simmons 1887, p. 185.

56. Tanner 1909, p. 11665.

57. Ibid., p. 11663.

58. Woods 1987, p. 68.

59. Scarborough 1902, p. 664.

60. Tanner 1909, p. 11665.

61. Mathews 1969, pp. 33–34.

62. Tanner 1909, p. 11666.

63. For an intelligent, general discussion of this period, see Carlyn G. C. Romeyn, "Henry O. Tanner: Atlanta Interlude," *Atlanta Historical Society Journal*, vol. 27, no. 4 (Winter 1983–84), pp. 27–40.

64. Mathews 1969, p. 36.

65. Tanner 1909, p. 11666.

66. Mementos of this friendship are housed at Trevor Arnett Library, Atlanta University.

67. Romeyn, "Henry O. Tanner," p. 37. Tanner added to this confusion by mentioning at the 1893 World's Columbian Exposition that he was a professor at Clark University.

68. W. A. Simon, "Henry O. Tanner—A Study of the Development of an American Negro Artist: 1859–1937" (Ph.D. diss., New York University, 1961), p. 99.

69. Carlyn G. Crannell [Romeyn], "In Pursuit of Culture: A History of Art Activity in Atlanta 1847–1926" (Ph.D. diss., Emory University, 1981), p. 196.

70. Romeyn, "Henry O. Tanner," p. 37.

71. Mathews 1969, p. 40.

72. Woods 1987, pp. 74–75.

73. Tanner 1909, p. 11666.

74. Ibid.

75. Goodrich, *Thomas Eakins*, vol. 1, p. 296.

76. Jacob C. White papers, Leon Gardiner Collection, Library Company of Philadelphia.

77. Tanner 1909, p. 11666.

Cat. nos. 1–4

1. Tanner 1909, p. 11663.
2. Ibid.
3. Ibid.
4. Scarborough 1902, p. 663.
5. Ibid.

Cat. no. 5

1. Tanner 1909, p. 11663.
2. Ibid.
3. Woods 1987, p. 75.
4. *CR*, vol. 22, no. 12 (March 20, 1884), p. 2.
5. Ibid.
6. Simmons 1887, p. 183.
7. Ibid., p. 181.

Cat. nos. 6, 7

1. TP, frame 323.
2. Tanner 1909, p. 11665.
3. Simmons 1887, pp. 183–84.

Cat. no. 8

1. Note attached to the verso of the painting, signed by Scull's son, Edward Marshall Scull.
2. Tanner 1909, p. 11665.

Cat. nos. 9–11

1. Tanner 1909, p. 11665.
2. Kate Upson Clark, "Old Win-ne-wan's Star," *Harper's Young People*, vol. 9, no. 428 (Jan. 10, 1888), pp. 186–87.
3. Louise Stockton, "In the Days of Witchcraft," *Our Continent*, vol. 2, no. 8 (Aug. 30, 1882), p. 235.
4. *CR*, vol. 20, no. 30 (July 27, 1882), p. 2.
5. *CR*, vol. 20, no. 35 (Aug. 31, 1882), p. 2.
6. Simmons 1887, p. 182.

Cat. no. 12

1. B. T. Tanner, *Hints to Ministers* (Nashville, 1894), p. 22.
2. Natalie Spassky, *American Paintings in the Metropolitan Museum of Art*, vol. 2 (New York, 1985), pp. 541–42.
3. Tanner 1909, p. 11665.
4. Leonfranc Holford-Strevens, *Aulus Gellius* (Chapel Hill, N.C., 1989), pp. 11–12.

Cat. nos. 13–15

1. Tanner 1909, p. 11666.
2. *CR*, vol. 26, no. 24 (Aug. 9, 1888), p. 1.

PAGES 86–145

Paris, Racial Awareness, and Success 1891–1897

1. Tanner 1909, p. 11770.
2. Milner 1988, pp. 11–12.
3. Ibid., p. 12.
4. A. Boime, *The Academy and French Painting in the Nineteenth Century* (London, 1971), pp. 48–49.
5. Ibid.; and Milner 1988, p. 12.
6. Milner 1988, p. 12.
7. Ibid.
8. Tanner 1909, p. 11771.
9. Ibid.
10. Cole 1900, p. 107.
11. Milner 1988, p. 13.
12. C. Fehrer, "New Light on the Académie Julian," *Gazette des Beaux-Arts*, May–June 1894, p. 208.
13. For a discussion of Tanner's personal relationships with his teachers, see Walter A. Simon, "Henry O. Tanner – A Study of the Development of an American Negro Artist: 1859–1937" (Ph.D. diss., New York University, 1961), pp. 127–30, 134–35, 137; and Scarborough 1902, p. 664. Scarborough gave Tanner's middle name as "Ossian," probably confusing "Ossawa" with Henry Ossian Flipper (1856–1940), a former slave who graduated from West Point in 1877; see Harlan, vol. 4, p. 498.
14. M. A. Stevens, ed., *The Orientalists: Delacroix to Matisse – The Allure of North Africa and the Near East* (Washington, D.C., 1984), pp. 116–17.
15. "Autorisations Données à des Copistes" (for Ecoles Flamande et Hollandaise, Allemande, Suisse, Italienne, Anglaise, Espanole, Française), 1882–1920, LL 23, 24, 27, and 31, Archives des Musées Nationaux, Musée du Louvre, Paris.
16. Ibid., LL 31, p. 123; also see Pierre Rosenberg, *Chardin 1699–1779* (Paris, 1979), p. 116.
17. J. Manet, *Journal (1893–1899): Sa jeunesse parmi les peintres impressionistes et les hommes de lettres* (Paris, 1979), pp. 140–41.
18. Tanner 1909, p. 11771.
19. Ibid.
20. Quimper, Musée des Beaux-Arts, *L'Ecole de Pont-Aven dans les Collections Publiques et Privées de Bretagne* (Quimper, France, 1978–79), following cat. no. 75, and "Chronologie."
21. J. Rewald, *The History of Impressionism* (New York, 1961), p. 554.
22. Tanner 1909, p. 11771.
23. Ibid.
24. *L'Ecole de Pont-Aven* 1978–79, following cat. no. 75.
25. Phoenix Art Museum, *Americans in Brittany and Normandy 1860–1910* (Phoenix, 1982), p. 56; and Woods 1987.
26. Henry Bataille, *Théâtre Complet*, vol. 1 (Paris, n.d. [by 1918]), p. 11.
27. Mathews 1969, pp. 62, 76.
28. Simon, *Tanner*, pp. 147–48. For information on Rodman Wanamaker in this context, see Harlan, vol. 8, pp. 342–43, nn. 2–3.
29. James A. Porter, *Modern Negro Art* (1943; reprint, New York, 1969), p. 68.
30. Tanner made light of his illness in an amusing account of his stay at the hospital, Tanner 1909, p. 11772.
31. Ibid.
32. F. P. Noble, "The Chicago Congress on Africa," *Our Day*, vol. 12, no. 70 (Oct. 1983), p. 299.
33. Ibid., p. 285.
34. Statement in Tanner's hand in the files of the Pennsylvania School for the Deaf, Philadelphia. The statement accompanied the painting *The Thankful Poor* (cat. no. 28) and is signed "H. O. Tanner, 2908 Diamond Street," which was the family residence.
35. P. Revell, *Paul Laurence Dunbar* (Boston, 1979), chronology.
36. Ibid., pp. 44, 80.
37. B. T. Tanner 1894, p. 65.
38. Statement in Tanner's hand in the files of the Pennsylvania School for the Deaf, Philadelphia.
39. Tanner 1909, p. 11772.
40. Statement in Tanner's hand.
41. Harlan, vol. 8, p. 43, n. 13.
42. "Art Notes," *DET*, April 28, 1894, p. 11.
43. Scarborough 1902, p. 664.
44. "Art Notes," p. 11.
45. Tanner 1909, p. 11772.
46. "Art Notes," p. 11.
47. Milner 1988, pp. 52–53; and for an excellent discussion on all segments of the Salon, see G. M. Ackerman's introduction, "The Glory and Decline of a Great Institution," in E. M. Zafran, *French Salon Paintings from Southern Collections* (Atlanta, 1982), pp. 8–23.
48. Quoted in Milner 1988, p. 52.
49. Tanner 1909, pp. 11771–72.
50. Judy Le Paul, *Gauguin and the Impressionists at Pont-Aven* (New York, 1987), p. 98.
51. Ibid., p. 99, n. 33.
52. This work has blue to blue-green color samples, in the artist's hand, on the verso, a Grand Central Art Galleries label (#126 *Aix-en-Provence*), and the authentication stamp of the artist's son, Jesse Ossawa Tanner. These factors suggest that the work remained in Henry O. Tanner's possession over several decades.
53. Le Paul, *Gauguin and the Impressionists at Pont-Aven*, p. 99.
54. N. C. Cooper-Lewter and H. H. Mitchell, *South Theology: The Heart of American Black Culture* (San Francisco, 1986), p. 96.
55. Ibid., p. 99.
56. Scarborough 1902, p. 666.
57. B. T. Tanner 1894, pp. 60–61.
58. G. Chapman, *The Dreyfus Case: A Reassessment* (New York, 1955). Julie Manet reported anti-Semitic or racist feelings among the aging Impressionists during Dreyfus's retrial in 1899. Manet, *Journal*, p. 211ff.
59. Harlan, vol. 4, p. 3.
60. Carlyn G. C. Romeyn, "Henry O. Tanner: Atlanta Interlude," *Atlanta Historical Society Journal*, vol. 27, no. 4 (Winter 1983–84), p. 38.

61. Ibid.
62. Harlan, vol. 4, p. 58.
63. Salon awards customarily included first, second, and third class medals, a few honorable mentions, and the medal of honor.
64. Ackerman, *French Salon Paintings from Southern Collections*, p. 17.
65. "Salons de 1894–1897," F21 4090B, dossier 1, AN.
66. Tanner 1909, p. 11772.
67. Ibid.
68. Ibid.
69. Quoted in Mathews 1969, p. 80. The Société des Peintres Orientalistes Français, founded in Paris in 1894, regularly exhibited "Oriental" works and could have been one source of Wanamaker's interest.
70. Tanner 1909, p. 11773.
71. As far as can be determined, no sketchbooks belonging to Tanner survive, if indeed he made use of them.
72. Morris to Tanner, April 16, 1897, MLB, PAFA.
73. Tanner to Dept. of Fine Arts, June 14, 1897, "M. Tanner," F21 2151, AN.
74. Tanner to Morris, June 23, 1897, TF, PAFA.
75. M. D. Sheriff, "Invention, Resemblance, and Fragonard's Portraits de Fantaisie," *Art Bulletin*, vol. 69, no. 1 (March 1987), p. 83.
76. Tanner to Morris, May 22, 1898, TF, PAFA.
77. Dewey F. Mosby, *Alexandre-Gabriel Decamps 1803–1860*, vol. 1 (New York, 1977), pp. 59–62.
78. Albert Maignon, "Le Salon de 1897," *Gazette des Beaux-Arts*, vol. 18, no. 481 (May 1897), p. 53.
79. Mathews 1969, p. 90.
80. Morris to Tanner, Nov. 29, 1897, MLB, PAFA.

Cat. nos. 16–18

1. Cole 1900, p. 107.
2. Milner 1988, p. 13.

Cat. no. 19

1. L. Goodrich, *Thomas Eakins*, vol. 1 (Cambridge, Mass., 1982), p. 181.
2. G. P. Weisberg, *The Realist Tradition: French Paintings and Drawings 1830–1900* (Cleveland, 1980), pp. 42–44.
3. Dewey F. Mosby, *Alexandre-Gabriel Decamps 1803–1860*, vol. 1 (New York, 1977), pp. 84–85.
4. Scarborough 1902, p. 664.

Cat. nos. 20, 21

1. Tanner 1909, p. 11771.
2. "Art Notes," *DET*, April 28, 1894, p. 11.
3. Scarborough 1902, p. 664.

Cat. nos. 24, 25

1. Tanner 1909, p. 11771.
2. Henry Bataille, *Théatre Complet*, vol. 1 (Paris, n.d. [by 1918]), pp. 11, 15.
3. It is not known if Tanner had personal contact with the Knights. For a recent discussion of them, see Pamela Beecher's thoughtful work in *A Pastoral Legacy—Paintings and Drawings by the American Artists Ridgway Knight and Aston Knight* (Ithaca, N.Y., 1989).
4. Tanner 1909, p. 11771.
5. Scarborough 1902, p. 664.
6. "Art Notes," *DET*, April 28, 1894, p. 11.
7. Harlan, vol. 4, pp. 58–59.
8. Tanner 1909, p. 11772.

Cat. no. 26

1. Characteristic ceremonial Breton dress included a decorative vest, full canvas trousers (*bragou braz*), and a leather belt with a large buckle of decorated copper.
2. Statement in Tanner's hand in the files of the Pennsylvania School for the Deaf, Philadelphia.

Cat. nos. 27–29

1. Mathews 1969, p. 70.
2. Statement in Tanner's hand in the files of the Pennsylvania School for the Deaf, Philadelphia. Information about the World's Congress on Africa, and Tanner's participation in it, can be found in Frederick Perry Noble, "Africa at the Columbian Exposition," *Our Day*, vol. 9, no. 59 (Nov. 1892), pp. 773–89; "The World's Congresses of 1893," *The Review of Reviews* (American ed.), vol. 6, no. 33 (Oct. 1892), pp. 322–26; Frederick Perry Noble, "The Chicago Congress on Africa," *Our Day*, vol. 12, no. 70 (Oct. 1893), pp. 278–300; David Burg, "The World's Congress Auxiliary," *Chicago's White City of 1893* (Lexington, Ky., 1976), pp. 235–85.
3. Noble, "The Chicago Congress on Africa," p. 285.
4. *CR*, vol. 22, no. 12 (March 20, 1884), p. 2.
5. Statement in Tanner's hand in the files of the Pennsylvania School for the Deaf, Philadelphia.
6. *CR*, vol. 31, no. 41 (Oct. 5, 1893), p. 2.
7. *DET*, Oct. 7, 1893.
8. Ibid.
9. Ibid.
10. Mathews 1969, p. 37.
11. Quoted in Woods 1987, p. 74.
12. Guy C. McElroy et al., *Facing History: The Black Image in American Art, 1710–1940* (Washington, D.C., 1990), p. 102.
13. Lois Marie Fink, "Elizabeth Nourse: Painting the Motif of Humanity," in *Elizabeth Nourse, 1859–1938: A Salon Career*, ed. Mary Alice Heeken Burke (Washington, D.C., 1983), p. 105.

14. Quoted in Woods 1989, p. 19.
15. Ibid., p. 2.
16. The depiction of African-Americans in American art has been discussed in the following works: E. C. Parry III, *The Image of the Indian and the Black Man in American Art, 1500–1900* (New York, 1974); Peter H. Wood and Karen C. C. Dalton, *Winslow Homer's Images of Blacks: The Civil War and Reconstruction Years* (Austin, Tex., 1989); Hugh Honour, *The Image of the Black in Western Art* (Cambridge, Mass., 1989); and McElroy, *Facing History*.
17. McElroy, *Facing History*, pp. 64, 85.
18. Statement in Tanner's hand in the files of the Pennsylvania School for the Deaf, Philadelphia.
19. Woods 1989, p. 12.
20. McElroy, *Facing History*, p. 102.
21. Scrapbook of Thomas Hovenden 1840–1895, roll 13, frame 0262, Archives of American Art, Smithsonian Institution.
22. Woods 1989, p. 15.
23. *Southern Workman*, vol. 22, no. 11 (Nov. 1894), p. 187.
24. *CR*, Aug. 23, 1894, p. 2.
25. Fink, "Elizabeth Nourse," pp. 108–109.
26. Woods 1989, p. 16.
27. *DET*, Sept. 17, 1894.
28. Tanner 1909, p. 11772.
29. Scarborough 1902, pp. 665–66.
30. Ibid., p. 666.

Cat. no. 30

1. *CR*, vol. 31, no. 16 (April 19, 1894), p. 8.
2. Scarborough 1902, p. 664.

Cat. nos. 31–34

1. Tanner to Durham, May 23, 1895, William Randolf Dorsey collection.
2. Tanner 1909, p. 11661.

Cat. no. 37

1. Scarborough 1902, p. 669.

Cat. nos. 38, 39

1. Tanner 1909, p. 11775.
2. Andor Pigler does not even index the subject of Lazarus in his *Barockthemen*, vol. 2 (Budapest, 1974), p. 644.
3. W. H. Burgess III, *The Hyde Collection* (Glens Falls, N.Y., 1972), p. 7.
4. Henry H. Mitchell, *Black Preaching* (Philadelphia, 1970), p. 98.
5. Quoted in Mathews 1969, p. 80.
6. Ibid.
7. Albert Maignon, "Le Salon de 1897," *Gazette des Beaux-Arts*, vol. 18, no. 481 (May 1897), p. 53. ("Un mot seulement sur la *Résurrection de Lazare*, par Tanner, oeuvre remarquable d'un jeune Américain, dont la portée dépasse grandement ce que le peintre nous avait montre aux précédents Salons. Le

ressouvenir de Rembrandt, qui se devine dans la compréhension de la scène, n'est pas fait pour nous déplaire, car il n'absorbe pas le sentiment personnel de l'artiste. Le tableau garde une impression véritablement biblique; nous retiendrons le nom de l'auteur, comme un de ceux qui, demain, deviendront célèbres.")

8. *Harper's Weekly*, vol. 41 (Aug. 7, 1897), p. 780.
9. Tanner 1909, p. 11773.
10. Tanner to Roujon, May 3, 1897, and May 7, 1897, "M. Tanner," F21 2151 and letter 3936, AN.
11. Ibid., Morris to Roujon, letter 6095.
12. Ibid., no number.
13. Ibid., F21 4275, dossier 37.
14. H. O. Tanner, "A Visit to the Tomb of Lazarus," *A.M.E. Church Review*, Jan. 1898, pp. 359–61.

Cat. no. 40

1. MacChesney 1913, pp. 11–12.

Cat. no. 42

1. Hartzell to Tanner, TP, frame 487.

PAGES 146–199
Celebrated Salon Artist and Religious
Painter 1897–1907

1. B. T. Tanner 1894, p. 65.
2. Quoted in Scarborough 1902, pp. 665–66.
3. Jessie Fauset, "Henry Ossawa Tanner," *Crisis*, vol. 27, no. 6 (April 1924), p. 258.
4. Ibid.
5. See Tanner 1909, p. 11663.
6. Ibid.
7. Statement in Tanner's hand in the files of the Pennsylvania School for the Deaf, Philadelphia.
8. M. Wentworth, *James Tissot* (Oxford, 1984), p. 175.
9. For a discussion of the history of this project see P. Vaisse, "La Peinture Monumentale au Panthéon sous la IIIe République," in *Le Panthéon Symbole des Révolutions: De l'Eglise de la Nation au Temple des Grands Hommes* (Montreal, 1989), pp. 252–58.
10. Scarborough 1902, p. 669.
11. V. Thompson, "American Artists in Paris," *Cosmopolitan*, vol. 29 (May 1900), p. 18.
12. Ernest Renan, *Vie de Jésus* (Paris, 1863). Several English translations existed in Tanner's day, including one by C. E. Wilber (New York, 1886).
13. B. T. Tanner 1894, p. 51 and passim.
14. Wentworth, *James Tissot*, pp. 175, 181–82.
15. Cole 1900, p. 105.
16. G. P. Weisberg, *The Realist Tradition: French Paintings and Drawings 1830–1900* (Cleveland, 1980), pp. 231, 284.

17. F. J. Campbell, "Henry O. Tanner's Biblical Pictures," *Fine Arts Journal*, vol. 25, no. 3 (March 1911), p. 165.
18. A. Blaugrund, *Paris 1889: American Artists at the Universal Exposition* (Philadelphia, 1989), p. 159.
19. M. Quick, *American Expatriate Painters of the Late Nineteenth Century* (Dayton, 1976), p. 102.
20. Morris to Tanner, May 16, 1898, MLB, PAFA.
21. Ibid. Tanner's notes were made directly into the official Salon catalogues, which are unlocated. He provided this service through 1905 (Trask to Tanner, June 30, 1905, PAFA).
22. Gabriel Paulin, "Exhibition of the American Art Association of Paris," *Brush and Pencil*, vol. 4, no. 2 (May 1899), p. 106.
23. N. C. Cooper-Lewter and H. H. Mitchell, *Soul Theology: The Heart of American Black Culture* (San Francisco, 1986), p. 96.
24. Jesse Tanner quoted in Mathews 1969, p. xiii.
25. Tanner 1909, p. 11774.
26. Tanner 1909, p. 11773.
27. Ibid.
28. S. Shaw, *William of Germany* (London, 1913), p. 176.
29. Tanner 1909, p. 11773.
30. Ibid., p. 11774.
31. Cole 1900, pp. 102–103.
32. Francis J. Ziegler, *Philadelphia Record*, Jan. 12, 1901, TCF.
33. "Twentieth Annual Salon at the Academy of Fine Arts," Jan. 13, 1901, TCF.
34. Arthur Hoeber, *Commercial Advertiser*, Jan. 14, 1901, TCF.
35. Mathews 1969, p. 97.
36. Cole 1900, p. 104.
37. Scarborough 1902, p. 669.
38. Cole 1900, p. 104.
39. Quoted in Mathews 1969, p. 100.
40. Tanner to Morris, May 1, 1899, TF, PAFA.
41. Morris to Tanner, June 12, 1899, MLB, PAFA.
42. Mathews 1969, p. 105, is vague about the date of this transaction. She erred in saying that Bok acknowledged the receipt of the first three paintings on July 23, 1901 (p. 106), because only one picture was sent on Sept. 25, 1901 (unpublished letter in Tanner's hand written from Etaples, Dr. Walter O. Evans collection, Detroit).
43. Morris to Tanner, April 14, 1902, MLB, PAFA; and Mathews 1969, p. 106.
44. Tanner 1909, p. 11774.
45. Mathews 1969, pp. 110–11; and Harlan, vol. 3, pp. 33–34.
46. Scarborough 1902, p. 669.
47. J. Brown, *Velásquez, Painter and Courtier* (New Haven, 1982).
48. L. Goodrich, *Thomas Eakins*, vol. 1 (Cambridge, Mass., 1982), pp. 59–60, 106.

49. Ibid., pp. 201–202. For a discussion of Juan de Pareja, see E. J. Sullivan and N. A. Mallory, *Painting in Spain 1650–1700 from North America Collections* (Princeton, 1982), p. 99.
50. Mathews 1969, p. 128.
51. Quoted in Mathews 1969, p. 128.
52. Mathews 1969, p. 109.
53. Ann J. Lane, *The Brownsville Affair* (Port Washington, N.Y., 1971), p. 6.
54. Mathews 1969, p. 112, stated that the Tanners arrived on June 23, 1902. However, Tanner wrote to Beatty from Etaples on July 25, Archives, Carnegie Institute, Pittsburgh.
55. MacChesney 1913, p. 12.
56. Tanner to Alexander (of the *Ladies Home Journal*), Dec. 10, 1902, Dr. Walter O. Evans collection, Detroit.
57. Mathews 1969, p. 112.
58. Morris to Tanner, March 21, 1903, MLB, PAFA.
59. Mathews 1969, pp. 112–13.
60. Harlan, vol. 7, pp. 442–43.
61. Ibid., p. 458.
62. Tanner to Morris, March 2, 1904, TF, PAFA.
63. Morris to Tanner, March 4, 1904, MLB, PAFA.
64. Arthur Z. Bateman, *Brush and Pencil*, Feb. 1904, TCF.
65. Jessie Tanner to Trask, March 6, 1904, PAFA.
66. See Mathews 1969, pp. 115–20.
67. Harlan, vol. 7, p. 517.
68. Ibid., p. 497.
69. "M. Tanner," F21 4275, dossier 37, AN. The purchase order was dated May 19, 1906, and payment was made June 27, 1906.
70. "Afro-American Painter Who Has Been Famous in Paris," *Current Literature*, vol. 45 (Oct. 1908), p. 408.
71. *Philadelphia Inquirer*, June 3, 1906, TCF.
72. Tanner to Beatty, May 16, 1907, Archives, Carnegie Institute, Pittsburgh.
73. "The American Negro Who Leads France in Art," *North American* (Philadelphia), June 10, 1906, n.p.
74. "Pennsylvania Academy," *Globe* (New York), Jan. 21, 1907, TCF.
75. Campbell, "Tanner's Biblical Pictures," p. 164.
76. "Negro's Paintings a Paris Sensation," *Times* (Scranton), May 22, 1908. This article appeared in the Scranton, Pennsylvania, newspaper because "the distinguished artist is a brother of Mrs. N. D. Temple, the wife of Dr. Temple, pastor of the Howard Place African Methodist Episcopal Church."
77. Ibid.
78. Georges Bal, "M. Tanner a terminé son envoi au Salon," *New York Herald* (Paris), March 28, 1908.
79. Campbell, "Tanner's Biblical Pictures," p. 164.
80. Ibid.

81. "Negro's Paintings a Paris Sensation."
82. Bal, "M. Tanner a terminé son envoi au Salon."
83. See Andor Pigler, *Barockthemen*, vol. 2 (Budapest, 1974), pp. 554ff.
84. *Revue des Beaux-Arts*, May 3, 1908, TCF.
85. Tanner 1909, p. 11774.

Cat. no. 43

1. Tanner 1909, p. 11774.

Cat. no. 44

1. Tanner 1909, p. 11772.
2. Ibid.; Tanner identified the *animalier* as "Fremiel." For Frémiet, see H. W. Janson, "Emmanuel Frémiet," in P. Fusco and H. W. Janson, *The Romantics to Rodin* (Los Angeles, 1980), pp. 272–80.
3. B. T. Tanner, *The Negro's Origin and Is the Negro Cursed* (Philadelphia, 1869).
4. Tanner 1909, p. 11773.
5. Hartigan 1985, p. 108.
6. Cole 1900, p. 99.

Cat. no. 45

1. Tanner 1909, p. 11773.
2. Quoted in Mathews 1969, p. 80.
3. Elbert Francis Baldwin, "A Negro Artist of Unique Power," *Outlook*, vol. 64 (April 7, 1900), p. 793.
4. Cole 1900, p. 101.
5. Mathews 1969, p. 94.
6. Cole 1900, p. 100.
7. Morris to Tanner, May 16, 1898, MLB, PAFA.
8. Ibid., Jan. 13, 1898.
9. Ibid., May 16, 1898.
10. Ibid., Dec. 17, 1898.
11. Ibid., Ogden to Morris, Sept. 21, 1898.
12. Ibid., Morris to Tanner, Nov. 22, 1898.
13. "The Academy's Annual Show," *Philadelphia Inquirer*, Jan. 15, 1899, p. 6.
14. Commissioners of Fairmount Park, *W. P. Wilstach Collection* (Philadelphia, 1913), unpaged, #45.

Cat. no. 46

1. Tanner 1909, p. 11773.
2. Ibid., p. 11774.
3. B. T. Tanner 1894, p. 51.

Cat. nos. 47, 48

1. Francis J. Ziegler, *Philadelphia Record*, Jan. 12, 1901, TCF.
2. Quoted in Mathews 1969, p. 76.
3. B. T. Tanner 1894, p. 126.
4. N. C. Cooper-Lewter and H. H. Mitchell, *Soul Theology: The Heart of American Black Culture* (San Francisco, 1986), p. 99.
5. Tanner 1909, p. 11774.
6. E. C. Parry III, in *Three Nineteenth-Century Afro-American Artists* (Cedar Rapids, Iowa, 1980), n.p.
7. Helen Cole, "American Artists in Paris," *Brush and Pencil*, vol. 4, no. 4 (July 1899), p. 201.

Cat. no. 49

1. Tanner 1909, p. 11774.
2. Ibid.
3. Helen Cole, "American Artists in Paris," *Brush and Pencil*, vol. 4, no. 4 (July 1899), p. 201.
4. Francis B. Shaefer, "The Pittsburgh Exhibit," *Brush and Pencil*, vol. 5, no. 3 (Dec. 1899), p. 136.
5. *Philadelphia Inquirer*, Jan. 13, 1901, TCF.

Cat. no. 50

1. Daniel Burke, "Henry Ossawa Tanner's *La Sainte-Marie*," *Smithsonian Studies in American Art*, vol. 2, no. 2 (Spring 1988), p. 66.
2. Ibid., pp. 66–67.
3. Ibid., p. 69.
4. Cole 1900, p. 105.
5. Francis J. Ziegler, *Philadelphia Record*, Jan. 12, 1901, TCF.
6. Melville E. Wright, "Philadelphia Art Exhibit," *Brush and Pencil*, vol. 20, no. 5 (Feb. 20, 1901), p. 270.

Cat. nos. 51–53

1. Henry O. Tanner, "The Mothers of the Bible: Sarah, Hagar, Rachel, and Mary," *Ladies Home Journal*, vol. 19, no. 10 (Sept. 1902), p. 9.
2. Ibid., vol. 19, no. 11 (Oct. 1902), p. 13.
3. Ibid., vol. 20, no. 2 (Jan. 1903), p. 13.

Cat. no. 54

1. Mathews 1969, p. iii.
2. Ibid.
3. "Religious Works in Tanner Exhibit," *NYT*, Dec. 19, 1908, p. 7.

Cat. no. 55

1. B. T. Tanner 1894, pp. 139–40.
2. Tanner 1909, p. 11774.
3. "Religious Works in Tanner Exhibit," *NYT*, Dec. 19, 1908, p. 7.

Cat. no. 56

1. Tanner 1909, p. 11774.
2. "The Pennsylvania Academy of the Fine Arts Annual Exhibit," *Public Ledger*, Jan. 20, 1907, TCF.
3. David Lloyd, "The Exhibition of the Pennsylvania Academy of the Fine Arts," *IS*, vol. 31, no. 121 (March 1906), pp. 22–23.

Cat. no. 57

1. Arthur Hoeber, "The International Exhibition in Pittsburgh," *IS*, vol. 27, no. 105 (Nov. 1905), p. 40.
2. For references to *Judas*, see letter of Jan. 11, 1906, from John W. Beatty to Tanner, and letter of May 16, 1907, from Tanner to Beatty, Archives, Carnegie Institute, Pittsburgh.

Cat. no. 58

1. Tanner 1909, p. 11774.
2. Ibid., p. 11775.

Cat. nos. 59, 60

1. Florence L. Bentley, "Henry O. Tanner," *Voice of the Negro*, vol. 3, no. 11 (Nov. 1906), p. 480.
2. Ibid.
3. James A. Porter, *Modern Negro Art* (1943; reprint, New York, 1969), pp. 74–75.

Cat. no. 61

1. Tanner to Purves, May 3, 1920, Archives, Herbert F. Johnson Museum of Art, Cornell University, Ithaca, N.Y.
2. Tanner to Morris, Nov. 19, 1900, GOF, PAFA.
3. Arthur Hoeber, *Commercial Advertiser*, Jan. 14, 1901, TCF.
4. Tanner 1909, p. 11774.
5. Ibid.
6. *NYT*, Jan. 12, 1901, TCF.
7. *Philadelphia Inquirer*, Jan. 13, 1901, TCF.
8. *Philadelphia Ledger*, Jan. 14, 1901, TCF.
9. Hoeber, *Commercial Advertiser*.
10. Charles H. Caffin, "American Studio Notes," *IS*, vol. 16 (July 1901), p. 47.

Cat. no. 62

1. William R. Lester, "Henry O. Tanner, Exile for Art's Sake," *Alexander's Magazine*, vol. 7, no. 5 (Dec. 15, 1908), p. 71.

PAGES 200–241

North Africa and Orientalism 1908–1914

1. J. W. Cromwell, *The Negro in American History*, (Washington, D.C., 1914), p. 226.
2. M. Stevens, "Western Art and Its Encounter with the Islamic World 1798–1914," in *The Orientalists: Delacroix to Matisse—The Allure of North Africa and the Near East* (Washington, D.C., 1984), p. 23, n. 84.
3. For notices on this figure see C. Saunier, "Un Artiste Romantique Oublié—Monsieur Auguste," *Gazette des Beaux-Arts*, (2 parts) June–July 1910, pp. 441–60, 51–59; and D. Rosenthal, "Jules-Robert Auguste and the Early Romantic Circle" (Ph.D. diss., Columbia University, 1978).
4. Dewey F. Mosby, *Alexandre-Gabriel Decamps 1803–1860* (New York, 1977).
5. A. Joubin, *Lettres de Eugène Delacroix écrites du Maroc, en 1832* (Paris, 1930), letter no. 9, Feb. 27, 1832 (author's translation).

6. J. W. Cromwell, *The Negro*, p. 226.
7. Mathews 1969, p. 145.
8. Georges Bal, "M. Tanner a terminé son envoi au Salon," *New York Herald* (Paris), March 28, 1908.
9. "Studio Note," *IS*, vol. 37, no. 147 (May 1909), p. 244.
10. William R. Lester, "104th Annual Exhibition of the Academy of Fine Arts Is Ready," Jan. 1909, TCF.
11. Johnson to Trask, Oct. 21, 1908, GOF, PAFA.
12. "Religious Works in Tanner Exhibit," *NYT*, Dec. 19, 1908, p. 7.
13. Ibid.
14. "Exhibitions of the Month," *Independent*, vol. 65 (Dec. 31, 1908), p. 1600.
15. "N.Y. American Art News," Jan. 16, 1908, TCF.
16. Mathews 1969, p. 133.
17. "Reception to Artist: H. O. Tanner One of Greatest Painters His Race Has Ever Produced," *Boston Herald*, Dec. 30, 1908.
18. "Afro-American Painter Who Has Become Famous in Paris," *Current Literature*, vol. 45 (Oct. 1908), pp. 404–408.
19. Tanner 1909, p. 11775.
20. *Globe* (New York), April 17, 1909.
21. Ann J. Lane, *The Brownsville Affair* (Port Washington, N.Y., 1971), p. 113.
22. Ibid., pp. 70, 111, and 138–39.
23. Quoted in Mathews 1969, pp. 142–43.
24. Quoted in "Afro-American Painter Who Has Become Famous in Paris," p. 407.
25. Madame Tanner, Jan. 25, 1911, "M. Tanner," F21 4275, dossier 37, AN.
26. Quoted in Mathews 1969, pp. 146–47. Monroe erred in her claim that only one of the works had not been shown previously: *Hills Near Jerusalem* and *Hebron* were older works (see Exhibition Chronology). But in general Monroe's descriptions help to determine more accurate dating for the paintings she mentioned.
27. H. H. Arnason, *History of Modern Art* (Englewood Cliffs, N.J., 1968), p. 84.
28. An excellent synopsis of these events, for the general reader, may be found in the chronology of S. Hunter, *Modern French Painting 1855–1956* (New York, 1956), pp. 237–39.
29. MacChesney 1913, p. 12.
30. E. A. Taylor, "The American Colony of Artists in Paris," *IS*, vol. 46, no. 184, (June 1912), p. 288, pointed out that Tanner was traveling in Morocco in 1912. Mathews 1969, p. 145, said the trip took place in 1910.
31. MacChesney 1913, p. 14.
32. G. Diehl, *Henri Matisse* (Paris, 1954), p. 62.
33. M. Ward in *Adventure and Inspiration: American Artists in Other Lands* (New York, 1988), p. 81.
34. MacChesney 1913, p. 11.

35. There seems no reason to believe that Tanner's new method was inspired by the work of American painter Albert Pinkham Ryder (1847–1917), as some writers have claimed. See for example Mathews 1969, p. 127.
36. Coates to Tanner, Oct. 24, 1912, PAFA.
37. MacChesney 1913, p. 14.
38. Ibid.
39. "Paintings by Henry O. Tanner," *NYT*, April 12, 1913, TCF.
40. Quoted in Mathews 1969, p. 147.
41. Ibid., p. 148.
42. Ibid., p. 149. This society of artists, rarely mentioned in the annals of art history, deserves special study.
43. Woods 1987, p. 125. Tanner's print production merits further examination.
44. Clara T. MacChesney, "American Artists in Paris," *IS*, vol. 54 (Nov. 1914), p. 27.
45. Ibid.

Cat. no. 63

1. Kathleen James, research assistant for this exhibition, made this astute observation.

Cat. no. 64

1. Hartigan 1985, p. 111.
2. Mathews 1969, p. 147.

Cat. no. 66

1. F. J. Campbell, "Henry O. Tanner's Biblical Pictures," *Fine Arts Journal*, vol. 24, no. 3 (March 1911), pp. 163–66.
2. James William Pattison, "Opening of the Hackley Art Galleries," *Fine Arts Journal*, vol. 27, no. 8 (Aug. 1914), p. 530.

Cat. no. 67

1. Clement-Janin, *Action*, April 30, 1910, TCF.
2. Charles Louis Borgmeyer, "The Luxembourg Museum and Its Treasures," *Fine Arts Journal*, vol. 25, no. 5 (May 1912), p. 303.

Cat. nos. 69, 70

1. Harriet Monroe, "Artist Shows His Pictures," *Chicago Daily Tribune*, Feb. 2, 1911, p. 5.
2. "Paintings by Henry O. Tanner," *NYT*, April 13, 1913, TCF.
3. Raymond Wyer, "Art Collecting and Psychology," *IS*, vol. 58, no. 232 (June 1916), pp. 121–26.

Cat. no. 71

1. Hartigan 1985, p. 111.

Cat. no. 72

1. "Paintings by Henry O. Tanner," *NYT*, April 12, 1913, TCF.

Cat. nos. 75–77

1. MacChesney 1913, p. 11.
2. Ibid., pp. 12, 14.
3. A. Joubin, *Lettres de Eugène Delacroix écrites du Maroc, en 1832* (Paris, 1930), letter no. 9, Feb. 27 (author's translation).
4. James William Pattison, "Loan Exhibition," *Fine Arts Journal*, vol. 27, no. 2 (Feb. 1914), p. 89.
5. W. J. Peckham, "American Art at Shepherd's Bush," *IS*, vol. 53 (Sept. 1914), p. 58.
6. Clara T. MacChesney, "American Artists in Paris," *IS*, vol. 54, no. 213 (Nov. 1914), p. 27.

Cat. no. 78

1. Hartigan 1985, p. 116, n. 30.
2. Ibid.
3. Ibid., p. 110.

PAGES 242–289

The War Years and Late Work 1914–1937

1. S. E. Morrison, H. S. Commager, and W. E. Leuchtenburg, *A Concise History of the American Republic*, vol. 2 (New York, 1977) pp. 541–42.
2. Mathews 1969, pp. 153–54.
3. East Sussex was the home of Henry James (1843–1916), whom Tanner met at least once; ibid., p. 154.
4. Quoted in Mathews 1969, pp. 156–57.
5. Mathews 1969, p. 159.
6. Tanner to Wyer, April 18, 1915, Museum of Art, Muskegon, Michigan.
7. Quoted in Mathews 1969, p. 156.
8. Morrison, *American Republic*, vol. 2, p. 545.
9. Mathews 1969, p. 160.
10. M. Williams, "A Pageant of American Art," *Art and Progress*, vol. 6 (Aug. 1915), p. 347.
11. Morrison, *American Republic*, vol. 2, p. 547.
12. Quoted in Mathews 1969, p. 159.
13. Raymond Wyer, "Art Collecting and Psychology," *IS*, vol. 58, no. 232 (June 1916), p. 126.
14. Mathews 1969, p. 161.
15. Booker T. Washington, *Working with the Hands* (New York, 1904), passim.
16. J. M. Cooper, Jr., *Walter Hines Page: The Southerner as American 1855–1918*, (Chapel Hill, N.C., 1977), p. 25.
17. Mathews 1969, p. 161.
18. Ibid., p. 162.
19. C. H. Harrison, *With the American Red Cross in France 1918–1919* (Chicago, 1947). Harrison actually knew Tanner and wanted to buy one of his works; see Mathews 1969, p. 174.
20. Quoted in Mathews 1969, pp. 162–73.
21. Ibid., p. 173.
22. Ibid., pp. 179–80.
23. See P. Redd, "The Carnegie Interna-

tional Exhibition," *American Magazine of Art* (June 1923), p. 320.

24. Karen Fish, "The Annual American Exhibition at the Art Institute of Chicago," *American Magazine of Art*, vol. 17 (Dec. 1926), pp. 622–25.

25. Mathews 1969, p. 180.

26. Minister of Foreign Affairs to Minister of Fine Arts, Feb. 20, 1922, "M. Tanner," F21 4342, AN. ("Par lettre du 26 décembre 1921, mon prédécesseur a eu l'honneur de vous consulter sur l'attribution éventuelle de la croix de Chevalier de la Légion d'Honneur à M. Henry O. Tanner, citoyen américain, artiste peintre, demeurant à Paris . . .")

27. Ibid. (" . . . exposé ses oeuvres et reçu de nombreuses récompenses dans les salons français depuis 1894 et qui est recommandé pour cette distinction par M. Bénédite, Conservateur du Musée du Luxembourg, et M. Ernest T. Rosen, secrétaire général du 'comité pour l'exposition des Peintres et Sculpteurs Américains au Luxembourg.' ") Tanner apparently did not receive news of the award until 1923; see Mathews 1969, p. 182. The Legion of Honor Archives were not fully available at the time of the author's research in France.

28. Mathews 1969, pp. 183–86.

29. "Art Exhibitions of the Week," *NYT*, Jan. 27, 1924, p. 12.

30. "Tanner Exhibits Paintings," *NYT*, Jan. 29, 1924, p. 9.

31. S. Hunter, *Modern French Painting* (New York, 1956), p. 206.

32. Ibid., pp. 206–207.

33. *New York World*, Jan. 27, 1924, quoted in Mathews 1969, p. 201.

34. The plaster model for the plaque is unlocated. AP, passim.

35. AP, passim.

36. Tanner to Sadie and Raymond Pace Alexander, May 30, 1927, AP.

37. Mathews 1969, p. 202.

38. Tanner to Haverty, Oct. 29, 1929, collection of Betty Haverty Smith, Atlanta.

39. Ibid.

40. Quoted in Mathews 1969, p. 219.

41. Tanner's papers at the Archives of American Art, Smithsonian Institution, preserve his recipe, set down by the artist in November of 1935; quoted in Mathews 1969, p. 236:

   150 grs. of the water or syrup from 1/4 lb. of best linseed, soaked for 24 hrs., slightly cooked or raw.

   300 grs. of newly made glue from parchment (sheep skin) soaked 24 hrs., heated slightly 2 or 3 hrs., simmered for 1/2 hr. but not boiled hard.

   200 grs. of mastic varnish into which shall be added 25% of linseed oil of best quality or 10% poppy oil. The last is added to slow up boiling. This 200 grs. is to be 75% of mastic varnish and 25% of oil as directed. 15 grs. lanoline dissolved in essence mineral.

   Add to above mixture 15 or 20 grs. of alcohol 90%. This is added to make a better emulsion, too much will injure the glue but it also adds to keeping quality of the mixture as will a little essence mineral.

   Mix in the above order or glue can be added if the mixture in cooking is not like soft butter. Mixture to be used warm [with] equal parts of color.

42. Mathews 1969, p. 236.

43. Tanner to Sadie Alexander, Dec. 27, 1936, AP.

44. Quoted in Mathews 1969, p. 220.

45. Morrison, *American Republic*, p. 595.

46. Tanner to Sadie Alexander, Aug. 30, 1933, AP.

47. Tanner to Mossell, Dec. 16, 1931, AP.

48. Tanner to Sadie Alexander, June 19, 1932, AP.

49. Mathews 1969, p. 220.

50. Tanner to Sadie and Raymond Pace Alexander, Nov. 16, 1933, AP.

51. White to Tanner, July 5, 1932; and Howe to Tanner, May 31, 1935, AP.

52. Quoted in Mathews 1969, p. 226.

53. Ibid., pp. 240–41; also see Tanner to Haverty, Oct. 29, 1929, collection of Betty Haverty Smith, Atlanta.

54. Smith to Schomburg, Feb. 15, 1935[?], Albert Smith Letters, Schomburg Center for Research in Black Culture, New York Public Library.

55. Ibid., May 17, 1936.

56. Quoted in Mathews 1969, p. 241.

57. Hélion to Mosby, March 2, 1987.

58. James A. Porter, *Modern Negro Art* (1943; reprint, New York, 1969), pp. 75–76.

59. Quoted in Mathews 1969, p. 246.

60. Tanner to Sadie Alexander, Feb. 2, 1937, AP.

61. Quoted in Mathews 1969, pp. 247–48.

62. Ibid.

63. Charles Baudelaire, *Art in Paris 1845–1862*, trans. and ed. J. Mayne (London, 1965), p. 99.

64. For a discussion of the ways in which an artist can exercise influence see I. Sandler, "Hans Hofmann: The Pedagogical Master," *Art in America*, vol. 61, no. 3 (May–June 1973), pp. 48–55.

65. See Mary Campbell et al., "New York, The Studio Museum in Harlem," in *Harlem Renaissance: Art of Black Americans* (New York, 1987), passim.

Cat. nos. 81–85

1. Quoted in Mathews 1969, p. 154.
2. Ibid., p. 156.

Cat. no. 86

1. Harlan, vol. 5, pp. 142–44.
2. Booker T. Washington, *Up from Slavery* (1901; reprint, New York, 1963), p. 202.
3. Raymond Wyer, "Art Collecting and Psychology," *IS*, vol. 58, no. 232 (June 1916), p. 121–26.

Cat. no. 87

1. Mathews 1969, pp. 74–75.

Cat. nos. 88, 89

1. Evelyn Marie Stuart, "Contemporary Art as an Investment," *Fine Arts Journal*, vol. 35, no. 4 (April 1917), p. 257.
2. Dewey F. Mosby, in *Second Empire* (Philadelphia, 1978), p. 335.
3. Tanner 1909, p. 11775.
4. "Tanner Exhibits Paintings," *NYT*, Jan. 29, 1924, p. 9.

Cat. no. 91

1. "Art Exhibitions of the Week," *NYT*, Jan. 27, 1924, p. 12.

Cat. nos. 92, 93

1. Tanner 1909, p. 11775.
2. "Collector Acquires a Tanner Painting," *Art News*, vol. 22, no. 18 (Feb. 9, 1924), p. 2.
3. "Tanner Exhibits Paintings," *NYT*, Jan. 29, 1924, p. 9.

Cat. nos. 94–96

1. The Frederick Douglass Institute and the National Collection of Fine Art, *The Art of Henry O. Tanner (1859–1937)* (Washington, D.C., 1969), nos. 33, 34.
2. Karen Fish, "The Annual American Exhibition at the Art Institute of Chicago," *American Magazine of Art*, vol. 17 (Dec. 1926), pp. 624–25.

Cat. no. 97

1. Carpenter to Tanner, TP, frame 343.

Cat. no. 98

1. W. E. B. Du Bois, "The Looking Glass: Tanner," *Crisis*, vol. 31 (Jan. 1926), p. 146.

Cat. nos. 100–102

1. Quoted in Mathews 1969, p. 251.
2. Tanner to Maudelle Bousfield, June 18, 1936, Archives, Art Institute of Chicago.
3. Quoted in Mathews 1969, p. xiii.

Cat. no. 103

1. Bousfield to Tanner, TP, frame 938.
2. Tanner to Bousfield, TP, frame 908.
3. Bousfield to Tanner, TP, frame 934.
4. Tanner to director, Grand Central Art Galleries, TP, frame 1080.
5. Bousfield to Tanner, TP, frame 1069.
6. Tanner to Bousfield, TP, frame 1087.

Cat. nos. 104, 105

1. Tanner to Sadie Alexander, Dec. 27, 1936, AP.
2. Tanner to Sadie and Raymond Pace Alexander, Nov. 16, 1933, AP.

Cat. no. 1 *Harbor Scene*
PROVENANCE: Gift from the artist to his sister Halle Tanner Dillon Johnson; by descent in her family to present owner.

Cat. no. 2 *Seascape—Jetty*
PROVENANCE: Purchased by Sadie T.M. Alexander through Freeman's Auction House, Philadelphia, 1937.

Cat. no. 3 *Seascape*
PROVENANCE: Gift from the artist to his sister Sarah Elizabeth Tanner Moore; by descent in her family to present owner.

Cat. no. 4 *Ship in a Storm*
PROVENANCE: Estate of Maxwell Robinson, Chicago; purchased by present owner from Barnett-Adan Gallery, Washington, D.C., 1985.

Cat. no. 5 *Fauna*
PROVENANCE: Unknown.
EXHIBITIONS: Possibly Cincinnati, Board of Education, Methodist Episcopal Church, solo exhibition, 1890.

Cat. no. 6 *"Pomp" at the Zoo*
PROVENANCE: Gift from the artist to his sister Sarah Elizabeth Tanner Moore; by descent in her family to present owner.

Cat. no. 7 *Lion Licking Its Paw*
PROVENANCE: Mr. and Mrs. Philip Berman; gift to present owner, 1962.

Cat. no. 8 *Boy and Sheep Lying under a Tree*
PROVENANCE: Purchased by Edward Lawrence Scull, by 1884; by descent in his family to present owner.

Cat. no. 9 *It Must Be My Very Star, Come Down to Brooklyn, After All*
PROVENANCE: Commissioned from the artist by *Harper's Young People*, 1887.

Cat. no. 10 *The Witch Hunt*
PROVENANCE: Purchased by present owner at auction, Christie's, New York, 1987.

Cat. no. 11 *Waiting for the Lord*
PROVENANCE: Commissioned from the artist by *Our Continent*, 1882.

Cat. no. 12 *Study for Androcles*
PROVENANCE: By descent in the artist's family to Sadie T.M. Alexander.

Cat. no. 13 *Mountain Landscape, Highlands, North Carolina*
PROVENANCE: Guy Ward Mallon, possibly by 1896; presented by Mrs. Guy Ward Mallon to present owner, by 1934.

Cat. no. 14 *Georgia Landscape*
PROVENANCE: Sammy J. Hardiman; Dr. Robert P. Coggins, Atlanta; purchased by present owner, 1990.
EXHIBITIONS: Possibly Philadelphia, Pennsylvania Academy of the Fine Arts, 1889 [as *Early November*].

Cat. no. 15 *Sand Dunes at Sunset, Atlantic City*
PROVENANCE: By descent in the artist's family to Sadie T.M. Alexander.

EXHIBITIONS: Possibly Philadelphia, Pennsylvania Academy of the Fine Arts, 1885 [as *Back from the Beach*]; possibly New York, National Academy of Design, 1886.

Cat. no. 16 *Half-Length Study of a Negro Man*
PROVENANCE: Collection of the artist; by descent to Jesse O. Tanner; purchased by present owner through Grand Central Art Galleries, New York, 1969.

Cat. no. 17 *Half-Length Study of a Bearded Man with Long Hair*
PROVENANCE: Collection of the artist; by descent to Jesse O. Tanner; purchased by present owner through Grand Central Art Galleries, New York, 1967–68.

Cat. no. 18 *Bust-Length Study of a Bearded Man with Short Hair*
PROVENANCE: Collection of the artist; by descent to Jesse O. Tanner; purchased by present owner through Grand Central Art Galleries, New York, 1967–68.

Cat. no. 19 *Horse and Two Dogs in a Landscape*
PROVENANCE: Unknown

Cat. no. 20 *Bois d'Amour*
PROVENANCE: Collection of the artist, 1894; by descent in the artist's family to present owner.
EXHIBITIONS: Possibly Philadelphia, Earle's Galleries, with Thomas Hovenden, 1894.

Cat. no. 21 *Concarneau*
PROVENANCE: Gift from the artist to Mary Francisca Durham-Randolph, c. 1900; by descent in her family to present owner.

Cat. no. 22 *Edge of the Forest*
PROVENANCE: Purchased by present owner, 1984.
EXHIBITIONS: Possibly Philadelphia, Earle's Galleries, with Thomas Hovenden, 1894.

Cat. no. 23 *Studio Interior*
PROVENANCE: Collection of the artist; by descent to Jesse O. Tanner; gift to present owner, 1971.

Cat. no. 24 *Study for the Bagpipe Lesson*
PROVENANCE: Collection of the artist; by descent to Jesse O. Tanner; sold through Grand Central Art Galleries, New York, to Mr. and Mrs. Norman B. Robbins, 1967–68; presented to Frederick Douglass Institute of Negro Arts and History/Museum of African Art, Washington, D.C. [hereafter FDI/MAfA], 1972; transferred from National Museum of African Art [hereafter NMAfA] to present owner, 1983.

Cat. no. 25 *The Bagpipe Lesson*
PROVENANCE: Collection of the artist; Robert C. Ogden, by September 1895; gift to present owner, 1905.
EXHIBITIONS: Chicago, World's Columbian Exposition, *Special Exhibition of One Hundred American Art Students*, 1893; Philadelphia, Pennsylvania Academy of the Fine Arts, 1893–94; Philadelphia, Earle's Galler-

ies, with Thomas Hovenden, 1894; Atlanta, Cotton States and International Exposition, 1895.

Cat. no. 26 *The Bagpipe Player*
PROVENANCE: By descent in the artist's family to present owner.

Cat. no. 27 *The Banjo Lesson*
PROVENANCE: Robert C. Ogden; gift to Hampton Institute, 1894.
EXHIBITIONS: Philadelphia, Earle's Galleries, October 1893 [as *The First Lesson*]; Paris, Salon, 1894 [as *La Leçon de Musique*].

Cat. no. 28 *The Thankful Poor*
PROVENANCE: John T. Morris; bequeathed to Pennsylvania School for the Deaf, Philadelphia, 1915; purchased by present owner, 1971.
EXHIBITIONS: Philadelphia, Pennsylvania School for the Deaf, 1894.

Cat. no. 29 *Spinning by Firelight—The Boyhood of George Washington Gray*
PROVENANCE: Possibly commissioned by George Washington Gray, 1894; by descent in his family; purchased by present owner, 1989.

Cat. no. 30 *Florida*
PROVENANCE: From the artist to his brother, Carlton M. Tanner; from the estate of his widow, Frances Stanford Tanner to Dr. Jones, c. 1950–60; gift to Dr. Margaret Taylor Goss Burroughs, c. 1976–78; purchased by present owner, 1988.
EXHIBITIONS: Possibly Philadelphia, Earle's Galleries, with Thomas Hovenden, 1894 [as *Orange Grove*].

Cat. no. 31 *Study for the Young Sabot Maker*
PROVENANCE: Collection of the artist; gift to H. Dudley Murphy, by 1895; Raydon Gallery, New York, 1973; H. Alan and Melvin Frank; gift to present owner, 1983.

Cat. no. 32 *Study for the Young Sabot Maker*
PROVENANCE: Art market, New York; purchased by present owner through the Erving Wolf Foundation Gift and Hanson K. Corning Gift, by exchange, 1975.

Cat. no. 33 *Study for the Young Sabot Maker*
PROVENANCE: Collection of the artist; by descent to Jesse O. Tanner; sold through Grand Central Art Galleries, New York, to Mr. and Mrs. Norman B. Robbins, 1967–68; presented to FDI/MAfA, 1972; transferred from NMAfA to present owner, 1983.

Cat. no. 34 *The Young Sabot Maker*
PROVENANCE: Gift of the artist to his parents, Bishop and Mrs. Benjamin Tucker Tanner, perhaps as a fortieth wedding anniversary present, 1898; by descent in the artist's family to Sadie T.M. Alexander.
EXHIBITIONS: Paris, Salon, 1895; Philadelphia, Earle's Galleries, 1895; Philadelphia, Pennsylvania Academy of the Fine Arts, 1895–96; Philadelphia, Earle's Galleries, 1897.

Cat. no. 35 *Les Invalides*
PROVENANCE: Private collection; Hirschl and

Adler Galleries, New York, by 1968; possibly Mrs. Diana Bonnor Davis, by 1969; purchased by present owner through Hirschl and Adler Galleries, New York, 1983.

Cat. no. 36 *The Man Who Rented Boats*
PROVENANCE: Collection of the artist; by descent to Jesse O. Tanner; sold through Grand Central Art Galleries, New York, to Mr. and Mrs. Norman B. Robbins, 1967–68; presented to FDI/MAfA, 1972; transferred from NMAfA to present owner, 1983.

Cat. no. 37 *The Seine*
PROVENANCE: Gift of the Avalon Foundation to present owner, 1971.

Cat. no. 38 *The Resurrection of Lazarus*
PROVENANCE: Purchased from the artist at the Paris Salon by the French government for Musée du Luxembourg, 1897; transferred from Musée National d'Art Moderne to Musée du Louvre, 1980; transferred to present owner, 1986.
EXHIBITIONS: Paris, Salon, 1897.

Cat. no. 39 *Study of a Man for the Resurrection of Lazarus*
PROVENANCE: By descent in the artist's family to Sadie T.M. Alexander.

Cat. no. 40 *Bishop Benjamin Tucker Tanner*
PROVENANCE: By descent in the artist's family to present owner.

Cat. no. 41 *Portrait of the Artist's Mother*
PROVENANCE: By descent in the artist's family to Sadie T.M. Alexander.

Cat. no. 42 *Portrait of Bishop Joseph Crane Hartzell*
PROVENANCE: Gift of the artist to Bishop and Mrs. Joseph Crane Hartzell, 1902.

Cat. no. 43 *Study for the Jews' Wailing Place*
PROVENANCE: Vose Galleries, Boston, 1976; art market, Providence, 1976; Mr. and Mrs. Leonard Granoff, 1976; gift to present owner, 1984.

Cat. no. 44 *Lions in the Desert*
PROVENANCE: Collection of the artist; by descent to Jesse O. Tanner; sold through Grand Central Art Galleries, New York, to Mr. and Mrs. Norman B. Robbins, 1967–68; presented to FDI/MAfA, 1972; transferred from NMAfA to present owner, 1983.
EXHIBITIONS: Chicago, Art Institute, 1898 [as *Lions*]; Philadelphia, Pennsylvania Academy of the Fine Arts, 1899 [as *Lions*].

Cat. no. 45 *The Annunciation*
PROVENANCE: Rodman Wanamaker, 1898; purchased for the W. P. Wilstach Collection, Philadelphia, 1899.
EXHIBITIONS: Paris, Salon, 1898; Chicago, Art Institute, 1898; Philadelphia, Pennsylvania Academy of the Fine Arts, 1899; New York, The Century Club, 1899; Philadelphia, Pennsylvania Museum and School of Art, Wilstach Gallery, Memorial Hall, 1899.

Cat. no. 46 *A View in Palestine*
PROVENANCE: Bancroft Hill, by descent to Weyerhaeuser family; gift to present owner, 1946.

Cat. no. 47 *Nicodemus Visiting Jesus*
PROVENANCE: Purchased from the artist by Rodman Wanamaker, by January 1900; purchased by present owner for the Temple Collection, by March 1900.
EXHIBITIONS: Paris, Salon, 1899; Philadelphia, Pennsylvania Academy of the Fine Arts, 1900; Philadelphia, Pennsylvania Academy of the Fine Arts, 1908; Seattle, Alaska-Yukon Pacific Exposition, 1909; Boston, Vose Galleries, solo exhibition, 1921; St. Louis, City Art Museum, 1922; Richmond, Ind., Public Art Gallery, 1922; Columbus, Ohio, Gallery of Fine Arts, 1922; Chicago, Art Institute, 1923; New York, Grand Central Art Galleries, solo exhibition, 1924.

Cat. no. 48 *Head of a Jew in Palestine*
PROVENANCE: Collection of the artist; by descent to Jesse O. Tanner; sold through Grand Central Art Galleries, New York, to Mr. and Mrs. Norman B. Robbins, 1967–68; presented to FDI/MAfA, 1972; transferred from NMAfA to present owner, 1983.

Cat. no. 49 *Flight into Egypt*
PROVENANCE: Purchased from the artist by Daniel O'Day, December 1899; still in his collection, 1908; to Thomas Logudice, New York, by 1967; purchased by present owner, Founders Society Purchase, African Art Gallery Committee, 1969.
EXHIBITIONS: Possibly Pittsburgh, Carnegie Institute, 1899; possibly Pittsburgh, Carnegie Institute, 1900 [as *Departure into Egypt*]; Philadelphia, Pennsylvania Academy of the Fine Arts, 1901.

Cat. no. 50 *Mary*
PROVENANCE: Purchased from the artist by Rodman Wanamaker, 1901; purchased by William Cushing Loring, 1920; by descent to Stanton Loring; purchased by present owner, 1983.
EXHIBITIONS: Paris, Salon, 1900; Philadelphia, Pennsylvania Academy of the Fine Arts, 1901; Minneapolis, Society of Fine Arts, 1902; Portland, Oreg., Lewis and Clark Exposition, 1905; New York, American Art Galleries, solo exhibition, 1908.

Cat. no. 51 *Study for Isaac from the "Mothers of the Bible"*
PROVENANCE: Collection of the artist; by descent to Jesse O. Tanner; purchased by present owner, 1938.

Cat. no. 52 *Study for Rachel from the "Mothers of the Bible"*
PROVENANCE: Collection of the artist; by descent to Jesse O. Tanner; sold through Grand Central Art Galleries, New York, to Mr. and Mrs. Norman B. Robbins, 1967–68; presented to FDI/MAfA, 1972; transferred from NMAfA to present owner, 1983.

Cat. no. 53 *Study for Mary from the "Mothers of the Bible"*
PROVENANCE: Collection of the artist; by descent to Jesse O. Tanner; purchased by present owner, 1938.

Cat. no. 54 *The Good Shepherd*
PROVENANCE: Arthur Somers; George Edwin

Wibecan; by descent in his family; private collection, through Sotheby's, New York, December 2, 1982; purchased for present owner with funds from the Class of 1954 through Christie's, New York, 1988.
EXHIBITIONS: New York, American Art Galleries, solo exhibition, 1908.

Cat. no. 55 *Christ and His Disciples on the Road to Bethany*
PROVENANCE: Given by the artist in return for an annual stipend to Atherton Curtis, by 1904; gift to Musée National d'Art Moderne, Paris, by 1938; transferred to Musée du Louvre, Paris, 1980; transferred to present owner, 1986.
EXHIBITIONS: Paris, Society of American Artists, 1904; Liège, Belgium, Exposition Universelle, 1905; New York, American Art Galleries, solo exhibition, 1908.

Cat. no. 56 *Return of the Holy Women*
PROVENANCE: Collection of the artist; possibly sold illegally from Art Packing Company, New York, 1917; possibly purchased by Henry Schulteis, by 1919; recovered by J. S. Carpenter and held on consignment, 1919; purchased by present owner, Club of Forty Purchase, 1923.
EXHIBITIONS: Paris, Salon, 1906; Philadelphia, Pennsylvania Academy of the Fine Arts, 1907; New York, American Art Galleries, solo exhibition, 1908; Buffalo, Albright Art Gallery, 1910; St. Louis, City Art Museum, 1910; Pittsburgh, Carnegie Institute, 1911; Chicago, Art Institute, 1916; Boston, Vose Gallery, solo exhibition, 1921; Detroit, Institute of Arts, 1921.

Cat. no. 57 *Job and His Three Friends*
PROVENANCE: Collection of the artist; mounted beneath *Daniel in the Lions' Den* (Los Angeles County Museum of Art), unknowingly purchased from the artist by Mr. and Mrs. William Preston Harrison, 1918; gift to the Los Angeles County Museum of History, Science, and Art, 1922; purchased by present owner from the Los Angeles County Museum of Art through Sotheby's, New York, 1985.
EXHIBITIONS: Philadelphia, Pennsylvania Academy of the Fine Arts, 1905; New York, Society of American Artists, 1905.

Cat. no. 58 *Christ at the Home of Mary and Martha*
PROVENANCE: Purchased from the artist by present owner, June 1907.
EXHIBITIONS: Paris, Société Internationale de Peinture et Sculpture, 1907; Pittsburgh, Carnegie Institute, 1907; New York, American Art Galleries, solo exhibition, 1908.

Cat. no. 59 *Two Disciples at the Tomb*
PROVENANCE: Purchased from the artist by present owner through Robert Waller Fund, 1906.
EXHIBITIONS: Paris, American Art Students Club, 1906; Chicago, Art Institute, 1906; Philadelphia, Pennsylvania Academy of the Fine Arts, 1907; Kansas City, Mo., Fine Arts Institute, 1908; New York, American Art Galleries, solo exhibition, 1908; St. Louis,

City Art Museum, 1909; Buffalo, Fine Arts Academy, 1909; Berlin, Akademie der Künste, 1910; Pittsburgh, Carnegie Institute, 1925; Buffalo, Albright Art Gallery, 1926; Chicago, Art Institute, *A Century of Progress*, 1933; Rockford, Ill., Art Museum, 1936.

Cat. no. 60 *Study for the Disciple Peter*
PROVENANCE: Collection of the artist; by descent to Jesse O. Tanner; sold through Grand Central Art Galleries, New York, to Mr. and Mrs. Norman B. Robbins, 1967–68; presented to FDI/MAfA, 1972; transferred from NMAfA to present owner, 1983.

Cat. no. 61 *Night*
PROVENANCE: Mr. and Mrs. Atherton Curtis, 1905; possibly Robert C. Ogden, after 1905; to his daughter Mrs. Alexander Purves, by 1920; by descent in her family; gift to present owner, 1979.

Cat. no. 62 *The Disciples See Christ Walking on the Water*
PROVENANCE: Purchased from the artist, possibly through J. S. Carpenter, by present owner, 1921.
EXHIBITIONS: Paris, Société Internationale de Peinture et Sculpture, 1907; St. Louis, City Art Museum, *Special Exhibition of Paintings and Sculpture by Six American Artists Resident in Paris*, 1907; Chicago, Art Institute, 1908; New York, American Art Galleries, solo exhibition, 1908; Chicago, Thurber Art Galleries, solo exhibition, 1911.

Cat. no. 63 *In Constantine*
PROVENANCE: Purchased by present owner, 1981.

Cat. no. 64 *Flight into Egypt: Palais de Justice, Tangier*
PROVENANCE: William Scott Bond, 1914; by descent to Mr. and Mrs. John Baxter, 1952; gift to present owner, 1970.
EXHIBITIONS: Possibly New York, American Art Galleries, solo exhibition, 1908.

Cat. no. 65 *Christ with the Canaanite Woman and Her Daughter*
PROVENANCE: Purchased by present owner, 1967.
EXHIBITIONS: Possibly St. Louis, City Art Museum, 1911 [as *Christ and the Disciples*].

Cat. no. 66 *The Holy Family*
PROVENANCE: Purchased by present owner through Thurber Art Galleries, Chicago, February 10, 1911.
EXHIBITIONS: Chicago, Thurber Art Galleries, solo exhibition, 1911; Muskegon, Mich., Hackley Art Gallery, 1914; New York, Grand Central Art Galleries, solo exhibition, 1924; San Francisco, California Palace of the Legion of Honor, *First Exhibit of Selected Paintings by American Artists*, 1926.

Cat. no. 67 *The Three Marys*
PROVENANCE: Art Institute of Chicago, 1913; gift to the Carl Van Vechten Art Gallery, Fisk University, Nashville, 1950.
EXHIBITIONS: Paris, Salon, 1910; Chicago, Art Institute, 1910; Washington, D.C., Corcoran Gallery of Art, 1910; Chicago, Thurber Art Galleries, solo exhibition, 1911; Pittsburgh, Carnegie Institute, 1911; New York, Grand Central Art Galleries, opening exhibition of Cooperative Gallery of Painters and Sculptors Association, 1923.

Cat. no. 68 *Christ and His Disciples on the Sea of Galilee*
PROVENANCE: Purchased by a Mrs. Hodge from the J. W. Young Gallery, Chicago; A. W. Schmidt, 1950s; by descent in his family; purchased by present owner, 1980.
EXHIBITIONS: Pittsburgh, Carnegie Institute, 1910 [as *The Disciples See Christ Walking on Water*]; Chicago, Thurber Art Galleries, solo exhibition, 1911 [as *Disciples on the Sea of Galilee*]; Chicago, Thurber Art Galleries, solo exhibition, 1913 [as *Disciples on the Sea*].

Cat. no. 69 *Christ and His Mother Studying the Scriptures*
PROVENANCE: Edgar J. Kaufman; by descent in his family; purchased by present owner, 1986.
EXHIBITIONS: Chicago, Thurber Art Galleries, solo exhibition, 1911; possibly Washington, D.C., Corcoran Gallery of Art, 1912; possibly Chicago, Thurber Art Galleries, solo exhibition, 1913; possibly New York, Knoedler's Gallery, solo exhibition, 1913; possibly Chicago, Art Institute, 1913 [as *Jesus Learning to Read*].

Cat. no. 70 *Christ Learning to Read*
PROVENANCE: Purchased by J. S. Carpenter; gift from his wife, Mrs. Florence Carpenter, to present owner, 1941.
EXHIBITIONS: Possibly Washington, D.C., Corcoran Gallery of Art, 1912; possibly Chicago, Thurber Art Galleries, solo exhibition, 1913; possibly New York, Knoedler's Gallery, solo exhibition, 1913; possibly Chicago, Art Institute, 1913 [as *Jesus Learning to Read*]; Des Moines, Association of Fine Arts, 1922; Pittsburgh, Carnegie Institute, 1923; New York, Grand Central Art Galleries, solo exhibition, 1924.

Cat. no. 71 *Angels Appearing before the Shepherds*
PROVENANCE: Collection of the artist; by descent to Jesse O. Tanner; sold through Grand Central Art Galleries, New York, to Mr. and Mrs. Norman B. Robbins, 1967–68; presented to FDI/MAfA, 1972; transferred from NMAfA to present owner, 1983.

Cat. no. 72 *Entrance to the Casbah*
PROVENANCE: Purchased from the artist by present owner through Thurber Art Galleries, 1914.
EXHIBITIONS: Chicago, Thurber Art Galleries, solo exhibition, 1913; New York, Knoedler's Gallery, solo exhibition, 1913; Indianapolis, Herron School of Art, 1914.

Cat. no. 73 *Man Leading a Donkey in front of the Palais de Justice, Tangier*
PROVENANCE: Collection of the artist; by descent to Jesse O. Tanner; sold through Grand Central Art Galleries, New York, to Mr. and Mrs. Norman B. Robbins, 1967–68; presented to FDI/MAfA, 1972; transferred from NMAfA to present owner, 1983.
EXHIBITIONS: Chicago, Thurber Art Galleries, solo exhibition, 1913 [as *Moonlight—Palace of the Governor of Tangier*]; possibly New York, Knoedler's Gallery, solo exhibition, 1913.

Cat. no. 74 *Street in Tangier*
PROVENANCE: James and Shirley Gordon, by 1977; gift to FDI/MAfA, 1977; transferred from NMAfA to present owner, 1983.

Cat. no. 75 *Near East Scene*
PROVENANCE: William and Edith King Pearson; bequest to present owner, 1964.

Cat. no. 76 *Sunlight, Tangier*
PROVENANCE: Mr. and Mrs. Walter I. Frank; gift to present owner, 1924.

Cat. no. 77 *Gate to the Casbah*
PROVENANCE: Vose Galleries, Boston, by 1983; purchased by present owner, 1984.

Cat. no. 78 *Fishermen at Sea*
PROVENANCE: Collection of the artist; by descent to Jesse O. Tanner; sold through Grand Central Art Galleries, New York, to Mr. and Mrs. Norman B. Robbins, 1967–68; presented to FDI/MAfA, 1972; transferred from NMAfA to present owner, 1983.

Cat. no. 79 *Miraculous Haul of Fishes*
PROVENANCE: Possibly sold illegally from Art Packing Company, New York, 1917; possibly purchased by Henry Schulteis, still by 1919; recovered or bought back by J. S. Carpenter, after 1919; collection of the artist; gift to present owner, as reception piece, 1927.
EXHIBITIONS: Pittsburgh, Carnegie Institute, 1914; St. Louis, City Art Museum, 1923; New York, Grand Central Art Galleries, solo exhibition, 1924; Chicago, Art Institute, 1924; Philadelphia, Sesquicentennial Exhibition, 1926; New York, National Academy of Design, 1927.

Cat. no. 80 *Landscape*
PROVENANCE: Purchased by present owner through Sotheby's, New York, January 30, 1987.

Cat. no. 81 *War Scene, Etaples, France*
PROVENANCE: Collection of the artist; by descent to Jesse O. Tanner; purchased by present owner through Grand Central Art Galleries, New York, 1967.

Cat. no. 82 *Study for American Red Cross Canteen*
PROVENANCE: Collection of the artist; by descent to Jesse O. Tanner; purchased by present owner through Grand Central Art Galleries, New York, 1967.

Cat. no. 83 *American Red Cross Canteen, World War I*
PROVENANCE: Collection of the artist; by descent to Jesse O. Tanner; sold through Grand Central Art Galleries, New York, to Mr. and Mrs. Norman B. Robbins, 1967–68; presented to FDI/MAfA, 1972; transferred from NMAfA to present owner, 1983.

Cat. no. 84 *American Red Cross Canteen, Toul, France, World War I*
PROVENANCE: Presented by the artist to present owner, 1919.

Cat. no. 85 *Intersection of Roads, Neufchâteau, World War I*
PROVENANCE: Presented by the artist to present owner, 1919.

Cat. no. 86 *Portrait of Booker T. Washington*
PROVENANCE: Commissioned from the artist by the Iowa Association of Colored Women's Clubs, 1916; gift to present owner, 1917.

Cat. no. 87 *Daniel in the Lions' Den*
PROVENANCE: Collection of the artist to 1918; Mr. and Mrs. William Preston Harrison, 1918; gift to the Los Angeles County Museum of History, Science, and Art, 1922.
EXHIBITIONS: Possibly London, *Anglo-American Art Exhibition*, 1914; Los Angeles, County Museum of History, Science, and Art, *Summer Exhibition*, 1920; Los Angeles, County Museum of History, Science, and Art, 1921; Los Angeles, County Museum of History, Science, and Art, *Paintings by Contemporary American Artists Donated by Mr. and Mrs. Preston Harrison*, 1924; Los Angeles, County Museum of History, Science, and Art, *Mr. and Mrs. William Preston Harrison Galleries of Modern Art*, 1934.

Cat. no. 88 *The Good Shepherd*
PROVENANCE: Possibly on consignment from the artist to the Artists' Guild, Chicago, by February 1918; purchased by Dr. I. M. Cline, February 1918; purchased by the Isaac Delgado Museum of Art, 1930.

Cat. no. 89 *The Good Shepherd*
PROVENANCE: Purchased from the artist by Mr. and Mrs. Henry H. Werhane through Grand Central Art Galleries, New York, 1929; gift to present owner, 1929.
EXHIBITIONS: New York, Grand Central Art Galleries, solo exhibition, 1924.

Cat. no. 90 *Etaples Fisher Folk*
PROVENANCE: J. J. Haverty by exchange through Grand Central Art Galleries, New York, 1936; gift to present owner, 1949.

Cat. no. 91 *Virgin and Child*
PROVENANCE: Purchased from the artist by Mr. and Mrs. Paul Beer through Grand Central Art Galleries, New York, and J. S. Carpenter, 1927; Professor and Mrs. Holcombe M. Austin, 1973; purchased by present owner, 1973.
EXHIBITIONS: Possibly New York, Grand Central Art Galleries, solo exhibition, 1924 [as *Mary*].

Cat. no. 92 *Flight into Egypt*
PROVENANCE: Purchased from the artist by Mr. and Mrs. John E. Nail through Grand Central Art Galleries, New York, 1924; purchased by Sadie T.M. Alexander, 1933.
EXHIBITIONS: New York, Grand Central Art Galleries, solo exhibition, 1924 [as *The Flight*].

Cat. no. 93 *The Sleeping Disciples*
PROVENANCE: Purchased from the artist by Mr. and Mrs. John E. Nail through Grand Central Art Galleries, New York, 1924; purchased by Sadie T.M. Alexander, 1933.
EXHIBITIONS: New York, Grand Central Art Galleries, solo exhibition, 1924.

Cat. no. 94 *Study for the Head of the Kneeling Disciple*
PROVENANCE: Collection of the artist; by descent to Jesse O. Tanner; purchased by present owner through Grand Central Art Galleries, New York, 1967–68.

Cat. no. 95 *Study for the Kneeling Disciple*
PROVENANCE: Collection of the artist; by descent to Jesse O. Tanner; sold through Grand Central Art Galleries, New York, to Mr. and Mrs. Norman B. Robbins, 1967–68; presented to FDI/MAfA, 1972; transferred from NMAfA to present owner, 1983.

Cat. no. 96 *Two Disciples at the Tomb*
PROVENANCE: Collection of the artist; by descent to Jesse O. Tanner; purchased by present owner through Grand Central Art Galleries, New York, 1967–68.
EXHIBITIONS: Pittsburgh, Carnegie Institute, 1925; Buffalo, Albright Art Gallery, 1926; Chicago, Art Institute, 1926.

Cat. no. 97 *The Three Wise Men*
PROVENANCE: Purchased by M. H. Cohen, 1927; by descent in his family to present owner.

Cat. no. 98 *The Destruction of Sodom and Gomorrah*
PROVENANCE: Purchased from the artist by J. J. Haverty, 1929; gift to present owner, 1949.

Cat. no. 99 *Disciples Healing the Sick*
PROVENANCE: Collection of the artist; by descent to Jesse O. Tanner; purchased by present owner through Grand Central Art Galleries, New York, 1967.

Cat. no. 100 *The Lost Sheep*
PROVENANCE: Collection of the artist; by descent to Jesse O. Tanner; purchased by Merton Simpson through Grand Central Art Galleries, New York, 1967–68; purchased by present owner, 1972.

Cat. no. 101 *The Good Shepherd in the Atlas Mountains*
PROVENANCE: Collection of the artist; by descent to Jesse O. Tanner; purchased by present owner through Grand Central Art Galleries, New York, 1967–68.

Cat. no. 102 *The Good Shepherd (Atlas Mountains, Morocco)*
PROVENANCE: Collection of the artist; by descent to Jesse O. Tanner; sold through Grand Central Art Galleries, New York, to Mr. and Mrs. Norman B. Robbins, 1967–68; presented to FDI/MAfA, 1972; transferred from NMAfA to present owner, 1983.

Cat. no. 103 *Flight into Egypt*
PROVENANCE: Purchased from the artist by his cousin, Maudelle Bousfield, 1935; by

descent in her family; purchased by private collector, 1985; gift to present owner, 1990.

Cat. no. 104 *Study for Mary*
PROVENANCE: Collection of the artist; by descent to Jesse O. Tanner; sold through Grand Central Art Galleries, New York, to Mr. and Mrs. Norman B. Robbins, 1967–68; presented to FDI/MAfA, 1972; transferred from NMAfA to present owner, 1983.

Cat. no. 105 *Return from the Crucifixion*
PROVENANCE: Purchased from the artist by present owner through public subscription, March 1937.

ACKNOWLEDGMENTS

First of all, the authors would like to thank the lenders whose generous co-operation has made possible this exhibition and its catalogue. They freely provided information and photographs — or allowed their homes to be invaded by photographers — and in some instances permitted their cherished paintings or drawings to be brought to the museum for study and conservation. We are especially indebted to Merton Simpson, whose comprehensive collection of the artist's work served as a starting point for our study of Tanner's development and technique. Demands were exceptionally great upon the National Museum of American Art, Smithsonian Institution, which holds the largest collection of Tanner's paintings, drawings, and prints. Richard Murray, Abby Torrones, Ann Creiger, and Mark Palumbo arranged study visits, expedited photography orders, and supplied documentary materials with alacrity.

In addition to the lenders, we thank the following individuals and public institutions who have contributed much useful information about works in their collections: John Biggers; Constance Brown; Mrs. Ross M. Dalby; Leon Fouks, M.D.; Mr. and Mrs. John H. Hewitt; Noah G. Hoffman; Mrs. M. A. Hopkins; Joseph Johnson; Mrs. Harmon W. Kelley; Dr. Richard Long; Mr. and Mrs. D. Scott Mahoney; Richard B. Moore; Betty Haverty Smith; Thurlow Tibbs; Mr. and Mrs. Robert Trescher; Dr. Joan Walker; Brooklyn Museum of Art; Central State University, Wilberforce, Ohio; DuSable Museum of African-American History, Inc., Chicago; Mabee-Gerrer Museum of Art, Shawnee, Oklahoma; Museum of Fine Arts, Houston; North Carolina Central University Museum, Durham; North Carolina Museum of Art; University of Nebraska Art Galleries, Lincoln; Whitney Museum of American Art, New York; and Wilkie House, Inc., Des Moines.

Our research was to a large extent made possible by the following individuals who pioneered the field of Tanner studies: Warren N. Robbins, who as founder and director of the Frederick Douglass Institute of Negro Arts and History/Museum of African Art, secured for the museum the collection of Tanner's work that is now in the National Museum of American Art, and, with Carroll Greene, Jr., and Robert Hilton Simmons, organized in 1969 the first major retrospective of the artist's career; Marcia M. Mathews, who utilized archival materials provided by the artist's son to write the first and only book-length biography of Henry O. Tanner, published in 1969; and Lynn Moody Igoe, whose *250 Years of Afro-American Art: An Annotated Bibliography*, published in 1981, is the standard work on the subject. Mrs. Igoe kindly sent us an updated bibliography for Tanner when we began this project. Dr. Naurice Frank Woods, Jr., generously allowed us to consult his 1987 dissertation on Henry O. Tanner and an unpublished article on the artist's African-American genre paintings, both of which provided valuable new insights into the artist's life and career.

For their assistance with her research, Dr. Alexander-Minter would like to thank: Adele Logan Alexander; the late Romare Bearden; Office of the President and Art Department, Berea College; Charles L. Blockson, Blockson Collection, Temple University; Herb Boyd and Eliza Dinwiddie-Boyd; Marie Dutton Brown; Dr. Mary Schmidt Campbell, New York Department of Cultural Affairs; Richard V. Clarke; Dr. Johnetta B. Cole, Spelman College;

Kinshasha Holman Conwill, Studio Museum of Harlem; Rachel Dach, Historical Society of Pennsylvania; Dr. Helen O. Dickens, University of Pennsylvania; Cleveland H. Dodge Foundation, Inc.; Dr. Jualynne E. Dodson; Drew Theological Seminary Library; Laurel T. Duplessis, Hampton University; Samuel S. Fels Fund; Prof. John Hope Franklin, Duke University; Dr. Janessa Northington Gamble, University of Wisconsin Medical School, Madkow; Mrs. Johnson Garrett; Jacqueline A. Goggin, Library of Congress, Manuscript Division; Leroy Graham; Dr. and Mrs. Sheldon Hackney, University of Pennsylvania; Lynda Roscoe Hartigan, National Museum of American Art; Mrs. Margaret Jerrido, Medical College of Pennsylvania Archives; Benjamin Tanner Johnson; John Quincy Johnson; Diana Lachatanere, Schomburg Center for Research in Black Culture, New York Public Library; Prof. C. Eric Lincoln, Duke University; Mark Frazier Lloyd, University of Pennsylvania Archives; Marcia M. Mathews; Madeline W. Murphy; Dovie Touchstone Patrick, Robert W. Woodruff Library, Atlanta University Center; Pennsylvania Council on the Arts; Laura Rheinstein, New York; Prof. William Seraile, Lehman College, City University of New York; Tanya Serdiuk, Burke Library, Union Theological Seminary; Dr. Elinor DesVersey Sinnette, Moorland-Spingarn Research Center, Howard University; Edward D. Smith, Anacostia Museum; Chantal and Jacques Tanner; the late Jesse Ossawa Tanner; Rollo Turner, University of Pittsburgh; Dr. Nancy Duckney, Washington, D.C.; Dr. Dorothy Porter Wesley; Prof. David W. Wills, Amherst College; and Murray N. Wortzel, Lehman College Library, City University of New York.

Dr. Mosby would like to thank: Prof. Gerald Ackerman, Pomona College; Joan Wardner Allen; Nancy E. Allyn, Herbert F. Johnson Museum of Art, Cornell University; Mary Curtis Bok; Yveline Cantarel-Besson, Archives des Musées Nationaux, Paris; the reference staff of the Everett Needham Case Library of Colgate University; Philippe Fleury, Archives des Musées Nationaux; Sally Gibson, Sterling and Francine Clark Art Institute; Christophe D. and Véronique J. Mosby; Dr. M. Lee Pelton, Dean of the College, Colgate University; Jerold Pepper, Adirondack Museum; Sally Wardner Richards; Joseph P. Rishel; Dr. Merle Schipper, Professor of Art History, California State University at Northridge; Malcolm Sweet, Schomburg Center for Research in Black Culture, New York Public Library; Charles H. Trout, President of Washington College and former Dean of the Faculty and Provost of Colgate University; and Carol Wünderlich. Dr. Mosby especially would like to express his gratitude to Jeanie Newlun, Secretary to the Director, The Picker Art Gallery, Colgate University, for her unstinting dedication to this project.

I would like to express my gratitude to: Derrick Beard; Tritobia Benjamin, Howard University Art Museum; Dr. Caroline Boyle-Turner; Jacqueline Brown, Wilberforce University; Mary Alice Heekin Burke; Judy Carson, High Museum of Art; Theresa R. Christopher, DuSable Museum of African-American History, Inc.; Dr. Gloria Chisum; Donald Collier; Dr. Guy C. Craft, Robert W. Woodruff Library, Atlanta University Center; Pearl Cresswell, Fisk University; Amenia Dickerson, DuSable Museum of African-American History, Inc.; Mary Doehring, American Red Cross; Dr. David Driskell; Tina

Dunkely, Waddell Gallery, Clark Atlanta University; Elaine Estes, Public Library of Des Moines; Lois Fink, National Museum of American Art; Paul Forlot, Director of Research, Laboratoires Pharmaceutiques, Bergaderm S.A., Paris; Christopher Fulton, Allentown Art Museum; Charles Gelbert, Harmon Foundation; Susan Glasheen, Museum of Art, Rhode Island School of Design; Mary Lou Hultgren, Hampton University; Lynda Roscoe Hartigan, National Museum of American Art; Steve Harvey; Mrs. Jenelsie Walden Holloway, Spelman College; Dr. Arlene B. Holtz, Wilson Middle School, Philadelphia; Walter Hyleck, Berea College; Lynn Moody Igoe; Clifton Johnson, Amistad Research Center; Mr. Samuel Josefowitz; June Kelly, June Kelly Gallery; Lou Kontos, Greater Lafayette Museum of Art; Judy Lakson, High Museum of Art; Mrs. Bette A. D. Lawrence; Alden Lawson, Howard University; James Lewis, Morgan State University; Cheryl Leibold, Pennsylvania Academy of the Fine Arts; Jack Lufkin, State Historical Society of Iowa; Mr. Mills, Spelman College; Elsie S. Oliver, Vose Galleries; Belinda Peters, Clark Atlanta University; Norman Prendergast; Michael Quick, Los Angeles County Museum of Art; Dr. Konrad Reuger; Edith Roach, Grand Central Art Galleries; J. Gray Sweeney; Rick Stewart, Dallas Museum of Art; Diana Strazdas, Carnegie Museum of Art; Dr. Anne Terhune; Richard W. Thompson; Judy Throm, Archives of American Art; Thurlow Tibbs, Evans-Tibbs Collection; Jeannette Touhy; Reino Tuomola, Cedar Rapids Museum of Art; Jill Waltrous Walsh, Des Moines Art Center; Jerry C. Waters, Fisk University; and Caroline Wistar, LaSalle University.

In Philadelphia the staffs of the Free Library of Philadelphia, Historical Society of Pennsylvania, Library Company of Philadelphia, and Pennsylvania Academy of the Fine Arts have been most helpful, as always. At the Pedagogical Library of the Philadelphia Public Schools, Doreen Velnich and her staff provided enlightening information about the schools Tanner attended.

At the Philadelphia Museum of Art, initial research for this project was carried out with thoroughness and ingenuity by Kathleen James; the infinite questions that arose during the last year of work on the catalogue were deftly fielded by Sylvia Yount, who combined her research with that of Ms. James to produce the chronology. Robert Wolterstorff and Courtney Ganz also participated in research for the exhibition. Holly Trostle Brigham served as coordinator during the first six months of implementation of the exhibition schedule, and as exhibition coordinator for the five months before the opening, Mark Dallas Butler coped resourcefully with myriad urgent details relating to both the exhibition and the catalogue. Ellen Doney cheerfully coordinated the paperwork for the exhibition from its early stages.

Carol Abercauph examined and carried out conservation treatment on numerous paintings by Tanner, and John Grauer attended to many details of framing, guided by Marigene Butler and Mark Tucker. Faith Zieske examined and arranged for the conservation of works on paper, and was assisted in matters of framing by Phoebe Toland and Robert Barfield.

Martha Small has been in charge of all the registraral arrangements for the exhibition at the Philadelphia Museum of Art and its subsequent tour to

Detroit, San Francisco, and Atlanta; as they travel, many of the objects will be well protected by crates constructed by Michael MacFeat, David Goerk, and Michael Gibbons. David Wolfe designed the exhibition space assisted by Matthew Jacks, and it was installed with spirit and care by Gary Hiatt, Donald Hiatt, Donald Kaiser, Martha Masiello, and Linda Stoudt.

Programs to accompany the exhibition were developed by Elizabeth Anderson, Marla Shoemaker, Glenn Tomlinson, and Jean Woodley. Danielle Rice oversaw their work and collaborated with William C. King, who made the introductory film.

Suzanne Wells has administered the Tanner special exhibition project in all of its aspects from its inception, and Cathy Shomstein has prepared the grant requests which now support it. To these members of the museum staff, and to the many more who have contributed to the realization of this exhibition and its catalogue, we offer our sincerest thanks for their interest and support.

Although Suzanne Kotz and the production team at Marquand Books have been saluted by the Director, we would like to add our thanks for meeting an extraordinary challenge with unflagging skill.

Finally, we offer our deepest gratitude to Anne d'Harnoncourt, whose intellect, diplomacy, determination, and energy have brought this exhibition into being.

DARREL SEWELL

PHILADELPHIA MUSEUM OF ART

Cover: *The Banjo Lesson*, 1893 (p. 117)

Produced by Marquand Books, Inc., Seattle
Edited by Suzanne Kotz
Designed by Scott Hudson
Composition by The Type Gallery, Seattle
Printed in Japan by Nissha Printing Co., Ltd.

Library of Congress Cataloging-in-Publication Data
Mosby, Dewey F., 1942–
    Henry Ossawa Tanner : catalogue / by Dewey F. Mosby and Darrel Sewell ; introductory essay by Dewey F. Mosby ; biographical essay by Rae Alexander-Minter. — 1st trade ed.
        p.   cm.
    Includes bibliographical references and index.
    ISBN 0-8478-1346-0 (cloth) — ISBN 0-87633-086-3 (paper)
    1. Tanner, Henry Ossawa, 1859–1937 — Exhibitions. I. Tanner, Henry Ossawa, 1859–1937. II. Sewell, Darrel, 1939–
III. Alexander-Minter, Rae, 1937–   . IV. Philadelphia Museum of Art. V. Title.
N6537.T35A4   1991
759.13 — dc20   90-24849